The Latin American
Ecocultural Reader

The Latin American
Ecocultural Reader

EDITED BY
Jennifer French and Gisela Heffes

NORTHWESTERN UNIVERSITY PRESS
EVANSTON, ILLINOIS

Northwestern University Press
www.nupress.northwestern.edu

Printed in the United States of America

10   9   8   7   6   5   4   3   2   1

Library of Congress Cataloging-in-Publication Data

Names: French, Jennifer, editor. | Heffes, Gisela, editor.
Title: The Latin American ecocultural reader / edited by Jennifer French and Gisela
   Heffes.
Description: Evanston, Illinois : Northwestern University Press, 2021. | Includes
   bibliographical references.
Identifiers: LCCN 2020028025 | ISBN 9780810142633 (paperback) | ISBN
   9780810142640 (cloth) | ISBN 9780810142657 (ebook)
Subjects: LCSH: Latin America—Literary collections. | Latin America—
   Environmental conditions—History.
Classification: LCC PN849.L292 L38 2021 | DDC 808.803272—dc23
LC record available at https://lccn.loc.gov/2020028025

To Henry
To Sarah and Nathaniel

CONTENTS

ACKNOWLEDGMENTS

We are enormously grateful to the individuals and institutions that have supported our work on this book. Williams College and Rice University have generously provided us with much-needed time away from the classroom and administrative service and contributed to the very substantial costs of producing and publishing a book of this kind. At Rice, the Department of Spanish and Portuguese, the Humanities Research Center, and the School of Humanities have generously contributed to defray the costs of the book. At Williams we are thankful for support from the Office of the Dean of Faculty and the Class of 1963 Sustainability Development Fund. We also appreciate the grant we received from the Association for the Study of Literature and the Environment, which helped to cover the cost of translating a number of the selections.

Among the many individuals to whom we are indebted, first and foremost is Jane Canova of the Center for Foreign Languages, Literatures, and Cultures at Williams College. Jane took on the vastly laborious task of managing the permissions for all the sixty-four selections that appear in the reader. It is not an exaggeration to say that the book would never have been completed without Jane's extraordinary level of organization, persistence, and resourcefulness.

The writers and translators whose work appears in these pages have been an inspiration to us. We are deeply grateful for their contributions to Latin American ecoculture, and for allowing us to reproduce their work here. Among the writers, special thanks are due to Homero Aridjis, Esthela Calderón, Fernando Contreras Castro, Juan Carlos Galeano, and Samanta Schweblin. We are indebted to Jannine Montauban, as we are honored to include here Eduardo Chirinos's poems, in memoriam. The translators who kindly worked with us include Leslie Bary, Arthur Dixon, Steven Dolph, Patricia González, Paul J. Kaveney, Elizabeth Kieffer, George McWhirter, Charles A. Perrone, G. J. Racz, Rose Schreiber-Stainthorp, and Grady C. Wray.

A number of students (some of them now alumni) of our institutions contributed to the project by researching the authors represented here and writing drafts of the one-paragraph introductions that precede each selection: Adam Calogeras, Madeline Walsh, Nicholas Wallach, Mariana Nájera, and Abigail González.

The project has also been enriched over the years by dialogue with numerous colleagues in the fields of ecocriticism and Latin American literary and cultural studies. Their advice and generous suggestions enabled us to fill in important gaps and identify sources beyond the limits of our own specialized expertise: Rolena Adorno, Jens Andermann, Mark Anderson, Laura Barbas-Rhoden, Esthela Calderón, Agnes Lugo-Ortiz, Jorge Marcone, Malcolm McNee, Rob Nixon, Elizabeth Paravisini-Gebert, Mary Louise Pratt, and Steven F. White.

At Northwestern University Press, we have been privileged to work with editors who understood and appreciated the significance of the project: Gianna Francesca Mosser (now at Vanderbilt University Press), Anne Gendler, Patrick Samuel, and Trevor Perri. Liz Hamilton provided invaluable help with permissions.

The support, encouragement, and patience of colleagues and staff in our home institutions is deeply valued. At Rice, Lora Wildenthal, Luis Duno-Gottberg, Denise Rosse Michalak, and Paula Platt. We are also very thankful to Matthias Henze and the Program in Jewish Studies. At Williams, Nicholas Howe, Henry Art, Leyla Rouhi, and Gail Newman.

And, finally, at home in Vermont: Paul Fischer and Barbara French. At home in Texas: Kenneth Loiselle. In Argentina, Perla Heffes. Somewhere, close to the dying of the light, our late fathers, George French and Marcos Oscar Guerenstein.

The general organization of this book is chronological. Where the dates of the creation and initial publication of a given work are known to diverge substantially, our chronology is based on the date of the work's creation. Otherwise we have favored the date of initial publication over the date of the first published English translation.

Throughout *The Latin American Ecocultural Reader*, works previously published in English appear under the title of the English translation. In cases where this title is significantly at variance with the original, the original title is often included in the brief essay that precedes the selection in order to assist the reader in identifying the work. With the exception of periodical titles, we have also translated titles of other works originally published in languages other than English when they appear in the general introduction, the historical overviews that open each section of the book, and the one-paragraph essays preceding each individual selection. In the "Suggestions for Further Reading" following the introductions to each part of the book, we have provided bibliographic information for works translated into English and for editions of as-yet untranslated works in Spanish and Portuguese.

Unless otherwise indicated, notes to the selections are based on notes prepared by the translator or (in the case of previously-published translations) by the original editor of that translation. Such notes have been revised for style and length.

The Latin American
Ecocultural Reader

Genealogies of Latin American Environmental Culture

The Latin American Ecocultural Reader responds to the realities of our time. As we write these words, the news reports are filled each week with stories of floods, droughts, hurricanes, pandemic, and wildfires, all triggered or exacerbated by the effects of anthropogenic climate change. Sea levels rise, oceans acidify, glaciers disappear, corals bleach to white, and atmospheric carbon levels continue to surpass one alarming threshold after another. We find ourselves in the midst of a massive extinction event representing the disappearance of roughly half of all species over the course of the next century, while the agricultural and other systems that support the earth's human populations are dangerously close to collapse. As Idelber Avelar (2014, 111) writes, citing Walter Benjamin's famous "Theses on the Philosophy of History," the ecological crisis of the present constitutes a "moment of danger," an instant in which an image of the past "flashes up" unexpectedly, compelling us to take hold of it before it disappears forever. Ours is a Benjaminian undertaking in that we endeavor to seize hold of the images of the region's environmental and (un)natural history before they are lost in the rapidly accelerating processes of environmental degradation, so many victims of what Peter Kahn (2002, 93) calls "environmental generational amnesia." At the same time, the project is also a genealogical one in that we take the contemporary exhaustion or discrediting of dominant Western epistemologies and ontologies as an opportunity to survey the alternatives, some of which have been here, in one form or another, all along.

The Latin American Ecocultural Reader responds to the precariousness of the contemporary moment by reconfiguring the Latin American canon from a pre-Columbian past to the present, creating a history that sifts through layers of accumulated environmental catastrophes as well as ecological awareness and appreciation. This methodological approach reveals striations in complex patterns of sameness and difference that stretch through decades and centuries. The various strains of Latin American environmental thought in evidence today—Amerindian ontologies, ecofeminism, popular-national telluric imaginings, syncretic Afro-Latin cultural practices, even the pope's 2015 encyclical on the environment—all have genealogies that can be traced in tandem (there is mutual contamination as well as competition) through continuities and ruptures as political and economic forms and technologies change, becoming increasingly complex. The survival and (re)emergence of these various strains of Latin American environmental thought are inversely related to the operations of power that shape dominant ideologies and epistemologies while eclipsing others.

As Michel Foucault (2003, 9) writes, scholarship is genealogical when it puts local knowledges that are discontinuous, marginalized, and delegitimized into play against the "unitary theoretical instance that claims to be able to filter them, organize them into a hierarchy, organize them in the name of a true body of knowledge, in the name of the rights of a science that is in the hands of the few." A genealogy is an antiscience—not the vindication of ignorance, which gets plenty of support these days from the fossil fuel industry, or the romantic return to intuition and unmediated experience, but rather "an insurrection of knowledge . . . against the centralizing power-effects that are bound up with the institutionalization and workings of any scientific discourse organized in a society such as ours" (9). This insurgency has been led in recent years by Amerindian intellectuals and activists, many of them situated in the Andean region, where Indigenous environmental thought has recently acquired new political force and visibility, as well as in the Amazon basin, Mexico, and Central America. For this and other reasons, *The Latin American Ecocultural Reader* prioritizes Amerindian environmental knowledge thematically and theoretically, but we also draw attention to what might be thought of as "creole ecologies," where "creole"—a word inextricably implicated in colonial circuits of power—is used in Eduard Glissant's sense of processes of adaptation and hybridization on the part of humans and other species transported, often against their will, from Europe and Africa to the Americas, where they enter into complex and dynamic relations with local cultures and ecosystems (Bongie 1998, 7).

This introduction is organized according to three main sections. The first provides a brief overview of the field of ecocriticism as it has emerged since the 1990s, when it first appeared on the scene in college and university departments of English and other Anglophone contexts; we highlight in particular the debates and divisions that have moved the field forward to its present engagement with the environmental justice movement and the ecocultural production of the Global South. The second section turns more specifically to Latin America and lays out, historically and theoretically, one major strand of the overarching narrative that runs through the eight chronological parts that follow: how nature has been (and continues to be) implicated in structures of colonial and neocolonial domination and exploitation, beginning with the European colonizers' insistence that the millions of people they encountered in the Americas, many of whom inhabited highly complex societies and urban built environments, were living in a so-called state of nature. In the third section, we discuss the survival and continuity of alternative intellectual traditions, including the recent reemergence of long-suppressed Amerindian ontologies and epistemologies into the political domain, along with some of their implications for the work that we do as scholars of Latin American cultural production.

Ecocriticism: Definitions and Debates

Ecocriticism is an emerging discipline that has developed in recent decades in the United States and Great Britain and examines the relationship between literature, culture, and the environment.[1] While the field has gained prominence and visibility, ecocriticism, by definition, inhabits a space on the periphery of the more traditional disciplines within the humanities, drawing on the work of colleagues in the natural and social sciences; it is (also by definition) an activist approach to the study of literature and culture. In her influential introduction to *The Ecocriticism Reader: Landmarks in Literary Ecology*, Cheryl Glotfelty (1996) argued that the concepts of space and place should become categories of literary and cultural analysis, much as gender, social class, race, and colonialism had earlier. In considering the future of the field, Glotfelty identified three primary areas of concern: (1) the assessment and critique of the ways that nature, broadly understood, is represented in works of popular and canonical literature; (2) the recuperation and reconsideration of the marginalized tradition of literature that focuses on nature and place, including particular places; and (3) the theoretical exploration of the symbolic construction of species (including the human) and their relation to the environment, and the articulation of alternatives not based on the dualisms that have conventionally structured Western thought (xxiv).

Much has been accomplished since Glotfelty and Fromm published *The Ecocriticism Reader*, and the field of ecocriticism has grown and diversified in important ways.[2] Greg Garrard's *Ecocriticism*, published in Routledge's popular New Critical Idiom series in 2004, identifies a wide range of positions taken by writers, activists, and others; the debates among them have served to move the field forward. These positions include the "cornucopian" claim—most typically espoused by industrial antienvironmentalist groups—that the threats and dangers to the environment presented by modern civilization are mere illusions and exaggerations. "Environmental activism," in Garrard's reckoning, is an improvement but still a tepid response to the current state of ecological crisis, failing to challenge either the systemic basis of the problem or its deep cultural roots. A more radical critique is offered by the deep ecology movement, which is based on the proposals of poet Gary Snyder and philosopher Arne Næss. Making its initial appearance in the early 1970s, deep ecology is today best known for the movement's commitment to the intrinsic value of all life-forms, human and nonhuman, and insistence on the real danger of the earth's rapidly expanding human population. For Snyder and Næss, the flourishing of the nonhuman is incompatible with a human population that exceeds the carrying capacity of the earth (Garrard 2004, 21).

Ecofeminism is another position that makes a significant contribution to literary and cultural studies linked to the environment. Much as deep ecologists identify the anthropocentric dualism that pits humanity against nature as the definitive source of antiecological beliefs and practices, ecofeminism holds androcentrism responsible for setting men and women against each other and the planet. Whereas anthropocentrism claims humans' superiority with respect to nature—be it in the possession of an immortal soul or the ability to reason—androcentrism, consciously or unconsciously, views man as superior to woman. As a position, therefore, ecofeminism contests the "logic of domination" according to which "women have been associated with nature, the material, the emotional, and the particular while men have been associated with culture, the non-material, the rational, and the abstract" (Garrard 2004, 23). While ecofeminism and deep ecology clearly share a commitment to the defense of the nonhuman, ecofeminism is much more explicit about its pledge to undermining a logic of domination that extends to oppression on the basis of race, sexual orientation, class, species, and gender. (Some ecofeminists, in fact, have specifically pointed out what they see as gender bias in the conceptualization of deep ecology.)[3] In her classic book *Feminism and the Mastery of Nature*, Val Plumwood (1993) articulates a sweeping critique of the "logic of dualism" in the Western intellectual tradition. In response to those who depict "criticism of the dominant forms of reason as the rejection of all reason and the embrace of irrationality," Plumwood asserts that ecofeminism does not require the abandonment of "all forms of reason, science and individuality" so much as "their redefinition or reconstruction in less oppositional and hierarchical ways" (4).

Ecofeminism has expanded and diversified over the years, often in dialogue with environmental justice, queer ecology, and other movements. While there are different trends within ecofeminism, this field of inquiry remains a critical examination of hegemonic Western thought and practices. As Carolyn Merchant (2008, 28) puts it, "ecofeminists seek to overcome both the domination of women and the domination of nature." They also recognize, as Plumwood notes, that the category of "nature" is "a field of multiple exclusions and control, not only of non-humans, but of various groups of humans and aspects of human life which are cast as nature" (28). Therefore, "racism, colonialism and sexism have drawn their conceptual strength from casting sexual, racial and ethnic difference as closer to the animal and the body construed as a sphere of inferiority, as a lesser form of humanity lacking the full measure of rationality or culture" (28).

Social ecology and eco-Marxism draw on a rich tradition that includes such figures as Murray Bookchin, Raymond Williams, and the Frankfurt School and that has emphasized the economic roots of environmental degradation and the link between the domination of nature and the domination of other people. These green Marxists point to the ways that the historical spread of capitalism has disrupted traditional subsistence economies and degraded ecosystems around the world by seeking ever-increasing quantities of raw materials to feed distant markets. Green Marxists reject the capitalist ethos of endless growth and expose ideological structures that legitimate and naturalize systems that dominate and exploit both human laborers and nonhuman nature. They argue that shortage is not simply a natural or objective fact with respect to the natural world but a function of desire and the flow of capital, including the intentions that guide production and the technologies that facilitate it. According to this logic, if the political structures of society were changed (and production satisfied real needs instead of the accumulation of capital), the ecological problem of limits would substantially diminish, if not disappear.

In its early stages ecocriticism was, as Glotfelty (1996, xxv) pointed out, "predominantly a white movement" within literary and cultural studies. It has become more racially and geographically diverse over time and now has important links to the global environmental justice movement, which affirms the right of all persons to share equally the benefits of a healthy environment (defined as the spaces in which people live, work, play, and develop spiritually) and works to rectify the disproportionate incidence of environmental contamination in communities inhabited by minorities (whether defined by class, ethnicity, or race) (Sze 2002). Ramachandra Guha and Joan Martínez-Alier laid much of the theoretical groundwork for the convergence of the rural third-world notion of "environmentalism of the poor" and the urban notion of environmental justice as it is used in the United States in their 1997 collaboration *Varieties of Environmentalism: Essays North and South*. Their ideas have been echoed more recently by Rob Nixon's pathbreaking work of postcolonial ecocriticism *Slow Violence and the Environmentalism of the Poor*, which examines some of the strategies writers have developed to overcome the temporal and geographic displacements that obfuscate the often catastrophic effects of environmental and biological hazards created in the Global North and deployed, overwhelmingly, in the South. In the same vein, George Handley and Elizabeth DeLoughrey's *Postcolonial Ecologies* (2011) demonstrates that the "global south has contributed to an ecological imaginary and discourse of activism and sovereignty that is not derivative of the Euro-American environmentalism of the 1960s and '70s" (8). They propose a methodology that engages nonhuman agency by considering the ways in which ecology works outside "the frames of human time and political interest," and they call for an epistemology that recovers the "alterity of both history and nature, without reducing either to the other" (3). Drawing from the work of Donna Haraway, *Postcolonial Ecologies* suggests that the "central common ground between ecocritical and postcolonial critique" should be based on the appeal to an "imagination of a totality and an otherness that nevertheless cannot be possessed" (8).

The commonality that runs across the various positions that activist scholars have taken in the field of ecocriticism is a shared dissatisfaction with the notion, which became increasingly commonplace in the humanities disciplines of the late twentieth century, that "there is no nature" outside the symbolic constructions of human beings. From the beginning, ecocriticism has pushed back against both the industrialist faith in technological progress and, simultaneously, academic orthodoxies associated with poststructuralism and the so-called linguistic turn in the humanities and social sciences, which hold to the notion that reality as we know it is a cultural and specifically linguistic construct, if more often than not an intensely ideological one. *What Is Nature? Culture, Politics, and the Non-Human*, published in 1995 by philosopher Kate Soper, has been an important touchstone for ecocritics seeking to chart a careful course through the difficult channels of biocentric and anthropocentric approaches to environmental ethics and politics. As Soper (1995, 150) argues, the fact that ecocritics identify the specificity of the ecocritical project in its insistence on the critic's responsibility to an irreducibly material reality does not exempt anyone from attending to "the multiple dimensions and repercussions of its own social impact" given how frequently the concept of "nature" has been invoked to justify and legitimate hierarchical social arrangements that systematically disadvantage women and sexual minorities and people of color.[4]

The Coloniality of Nature

Latin American ecocriticism owes to its Anglophone counterpart the development of a particular mode of engagement in cultural texts, one that stems from a practical concern for the health of regional and global environmental systems and develops hybrid methodologies that respond to that concern without (re)imposing hegemonic or metaphysical determinations of nature and the natural. As Avelar (2014, 117) suggests, however, "when it comes to this renewed imbrication between cultural and ecological questions, Latin America is not a terrain among others." Latin America is the locus of important ecological contests in the present, including the political battles over the conservation of tropical rain forest in Amazonia and Central America, the Nicaraguan government's plans for a second interoceanic canal, controversies surrounding the allocation of water resources in the Andes (often related to glacier melt and the long history of mining in the region), not to mention widespread popular protests against the effects of monocrop agriculture, soil and water system toxification, oil spills, air pollution, and the abandonment of regional food sheds, to name only the most frequent headlines. The "abundance" of natural resources the European colonizers encountered in the New World created the conditions of possibility for an economy based on the exploitation of human beings and nonhuman nature through the extraction of mineral wealth, monoculture, Black slavery, and the encomienda system. This economy endures to the present day, despite technological, economic, and political transformations at the local, regional, and geopolitical levels. In this sense, the unlimited exploitation of natural resources has been a constant in the economic history of Latin America.

The "coloniality of nature" is a concept put forth by Walter Mignolo to convey the enduring effects of the mutual complicity among economic interests, symbolic constructions of difference, and the development of scientific methodologies in the centuries following Europeans' arrival in the Americas. Latin America is also, as Avelar points out, the place where Western modernity first conceived itself as such, in contrast to the Amerindian Other confined by the imperial gaze to a so-called state of nature.[5] According to the thesis established decades ago by the Mexican philosopher Edmundo O'Gorman (2006, 192), America was not so much "discovered" by Europeans as invented by them, and invented in the unmistakable image of "nature"—a repository of natural commodities and a tabula rasa literally awaiting the arrival of Christian missionaries to inscribe the foundational tenets of human society on *homo naturalis*, or "natural man."[6] This discourse of nature—to borrow Fernando Mires's term[7]—was from the beginning an ambivalent one, signifying at once the prelapsarian earthly paradise of the Garden of Eden and the terrifying wilderness that haunts the Mediterranean imagination from earliest antiquity as the locus of a "fundamental hostility" to human civilization (Harrison 1992, 13). These discursive formations extend back well before the Europeans' arrival in the New World, and they have produced reactions across a wide range of genres and media, geographies and temporalities, including the symbolic or spiritual appreciation of nature and the nonhuman that manifests itself historically in the form of nineteenth-century Romanticism, for example, or in the telluric nationalisms of the early twentieth century, as well as the more utilitarian ethos that sees the natural world primarily as resources to be exploited for human benefit. The weaving of these positive and negative connotations makes up the complex and highly contested European/Western concept of "nature" that informs relations between the natural or nonhuman world and the human.

The production of European modernity took place at the material and discursive levels simultaneously, accelerating, symbolizing, and intensifying a transformation that may have already been implicit in the ancient ontological distinction at the heart of Mediterranean and Judeo-Christian cultures, which recognize a special distinction and unique destiny for the human person as the most godlike of all the species and—for Christians—the only one capable of achieving salvation.[8] As Gabriela Nouzeilles (2002, 19) writes, perhaps with Jan van der Straet's famous engraving of Amerigo Vespucci standing before a nude Amerindian woman in mind, "The natural space and the body of the colonized other are the mirror on the surface of which the modern imperial subject contemplates himself and produces by inversion his own image. All the representations that result from this schema are based on a chain of mutually reinforcing oppositions, according to which the West always occupies the place of spirit, reason, and order against the bodies and disordered passions of beings that are confused with a subhuman nature." As invisible infectious microbes touched off the collapse of Amerindian populations from one end of the continent to another, and in turn prompted the regrowth of forests in landscapes that had previously been carefully managed to support large populations, local histories were erased from the landscape and "America" became the perfect foil against which the (white, masculine) Western imperial subject constituted himself as the only agent of history, the subject of modernity.

The sixteenth and seventeenth centuries were, not coincidentally, a crucial period in the development of Western philosophy and science. The epistemological shifts that took place at this time bear emphasis; they were perhaps anticipated in the astrolabe and sextant displayed by Vespucci in his mythic encounter with the inviting Amazon. A scant one hundred fifty years would transpire between Columbus's landing at Hispaniola and the publication of René Descartes's famous *Discourse on Method*, the seminal text of philosophical and scientific modernity in the West and one of the most decisive articulations of the disembodied, ahistorical subject and his claims to mastery of nature. Rooted in ancient Mediterranean philosophy and the distinction between body and soul, matter and spirit that Christian theology inherited from the philosophy of the Greeks, Descartes's famous *cogito* nevertheless represented a distinct break with that tradition in the degree of autonomy granted to the subject. "I knew," writes Descartes (1999, 25), "that I was a substance, the whole essence or nature of which was to think and which, in order to exist, has no need of any place and does not depend on anything material." Echoing his English contemporary Francis Bacon, Descartes simultaneously declared that the new science would enable those who wielded its knowledge "thereby [to] make ourselves, as it were, the lords and masters of nature" (44). The new rationality exemplified by Descartes and Bacon—constructed, as scholars have recently shown, on modes of empirical inquiry that were developed, if not widely publicized, by agents of Spain and Portugal[9]—would evolve in tandem with consumer capitalism and the autonomous individual of liberal political philosophy.

The Latin American Ecocultural Reader tracks this shift in the production of scientific knowledge in the early modern/colonial Atlantic world while also seeking alternative epistemologies that, as María Iñigo Clavo (2016, 7) puts it, "will help us to break the duality of the human and natural sciences (subject/object)." We are interested in the ways of knowing that were left behind by the dubious progress of Western scientific modernity, including the work of recognized Renaissance intellectuals like José de Acosta, but also captured in the writings dedicated to the lives of religious women and men who practiced what historian Jorge Cañizares-Esguerra (2006b, 178) refers to as "colonization as spiritual gardening." According to Cañizares-Esguerra, in the seventeenth-century Americas the moral and spiritual "improvement" of the human person was often undertaken through the cultivation of particular plant species, be it in the convent gardens and mission fields of the Iberian territories or the Protestant farmsteads to the north. This conflation of self and soil continued well into the eighteenth century, when Spain and Portugal were perceived to have sunk decisively below the horizon of European modernity. Count Buffon and other Enlightenment intellectuals touched off the polemic that would become known as the Dispute of the New World with their disparaging appraisals of American flora and fauna, prompting creole writers from Chile to Mexico to take up their pens in defense of *la patria*. (A number of Jesuit priests, bearing up after the order's expulsion from Iberian territories, also wrote nostalgic treatises from exile in Italy and France.) As Santa Arias (2009, 332) explains, these writings were "rooted" in the geographic space of the Americas, dominating the areas of history and literature "with texts that exalt the land and evoke the landscape, [including] the human and natural diversity of the regions." These eighteenth-century evocations prefigure the conflation of nature and the nation-state typical of Romantic nationalisms.

But as Mires warns, we also observe throughout many decades of Ibero-American cultural production the notion that nature is not a repository of spiritual values—as in the North American "wilderness ethic"—so much as a danger to be overcome in the interest of establishing a modern and civilized nation. This concept is brought into the national (only nominally postcolonial) period with the 1845 publication of Domingo F. Sarmiento's *Facundo: Civilization and Barbarism*, which famously represents the pampas that extend south of the Argentine capital with an image of "the desert as a void whose obliterating power resists human imagination" (Nouzeilles 2007, 253). The conflation of wild, unsettled spaces with violence and political unrest—often implicitly or explicitly tied to indigeneity—is an inescapable element of Latin American political thought from Sarmiento's time to our own; as in *Facundo* itself, the menace of the wilderness is often intertwined with more positive, even sublime evocations of the unsettled landscape. Sarmiento's ambivalent conceptualization of wilderness largely complemented economic developments of the late nineteenth century, when the massive influx of British (and later U.S.) capital created new infrastructure aimed at getting primary products—wood, bananas, beef, and so on—to distant markets. The frontier, liminal space between the settled coast and the wild hinterland of the interior became a site of intense economic activity and extraordinary environmental degradation, at the very same time that the products themselves became the new key to national identities, be they, as Fernando Coronil (1997, 37) puts it, "oil nations, banana republics, or plantation societies, for example, or broadly as underdeveloped or backward nations."

Given that history, the body of regionalist literature that developed in the early twentieth century has been of particular interest to the first generation of Latin American ecocritics.[10] Known traditionally as the *novela de la tierra*—literally, the "novel of the earth"—regionalism played a central role in articulating a conservative telluric nationalism in countries that traditional elites perceived as besieged with city-dwelling immigrants. More recently, scholars have productively reread regionalism as an important counterpoint to the cosmopolitan and urbane poetics associated with the bourgeoning and rapidly modernizing capitals, drawing attention to the ways that Uruguay's Horacio Quiroga (1878–1937), Colombia's José Eustasio Rivera (1888–1928), and a number of other writers documented the ecological ravages the export boom created for the interior, which included deforestation, drought, and soil erosion. These realist strains are often juxtaposed with ironic invocations of the Janus-faced mythology of wilderness the regionalists inherited from Sarmiento and other nineteenth-century intellectuals.

The mercantilization of daily life, the predominance of the culture industry, and the conversion of social life into a society of spectacle are the defining characteristics of the logic of consumer capitalism, which expands to nearly fill the totality of the social sphere in the twentieth century. In this context, conceptualizations of nature have also changed. Nouzeilles identifies two moments of quasi-exception. The first is that of modernism and the vanguards, when nature and the primitive "operate as a critical 'remainder' or outside from which to question capitalism," and the second is postmodernism, which, according to Jameson (1991), develops when the separation between culture and nature falls along with other modern dichotomies (Nouzeilles 2002, 27). It is in this last stage that ecological or environmentalist tropes are inscribed as representative; but as Nouzeilles suggests, the version that is imposed in art as in public discourse is that of an alternative space, a repository of aesthetic and political values, the most visible specificity of which is a celebration of the natural that has become, finally, one of the most valuable goods on the postmodern market.

An Insurrection of Knowledges

The other side of this process is the systematic suppression of forms of knowledge that do not abide by the modern/Western epistemology that divides subject from object and places them in opposition to each other. As Merchant (1989, 149–63) argues, the emergence and consolidation of mechanistic conceptualizations of the cosmos, which replaced earlier tropes of an actively nurturing Mother Earth, coincided with the practical marginalization of women's knowledge, paradigmatically represented by the figures of the midwife and the witch. Scholars in the fields of Black studies and Native American studies have abundantly demonstrated the ways in which the construction of Euromodernity elided and obscured the intellectual traditions and contributions of non-European peoples. In Latin America, the intellectual cultures of enslaved Africans and those of the western hemisphere's originary peoples were demonized, occluded, and repressed from the earliest stages of colonization (Mignolo 2011, 10–14). As the Europeans' desire to codify, describe, and assign value to the previously unknown varieties of flora and fauna they discovered in the New World sent their own well-established system of scientific knowledge production into overload, forcing the emergence of new, increasingly modern methods of classification (Rodríguez 2004, viii), the evangelizing arm of the imperial machinery was actively engaged in the eradication of African and Amerindian knowledge. The devil, it was understood, "had control over the weather, plants, animals, and landscapes in the New World" (Cañizares-Esguerra 2006b, 121), and he held Amerindian populations in thrall through the activities of local shamans, healers, and other bearers of specialized knowledge. As Western knowledge of the natural world, the body, and the physical properties of both became recognizably modern, empirical, and technological, Black and Amerindian intellectuals developed what Mignolo (2002, 471) has described, using W. E. B. Du Bois's notion of "double consciousness," as the ability to maintain subalternized epistemic paradigms that interacted with Spanish and Western epistemologies without being assimilated by them.

Amerindian knowledge in particular is often dramatically different from Western knowledge—many would say they are diametrically opposed—because many Amerindian ontologies are not anthropocentric.[11] Whereas Western cultures, theistic or otherwise, have tended to understand humankind as occupying a special place in the universe and pursuing a special destiny outside the potential of nonhuman animals, Amerindian cultures do not differentiate hierarchically between human and nonhuman species or, for that matter, between nature and culture. Anthropologist Philippe Descola (2013, 17) writes, "From the luxuriant forests of Amazonia to the glacial spaces of the Canadian Arctic, certain peoples envisage their insertion into the environment in a manner altogether different from our own. They regard themselves, not as social collectives managing their relations with the ecosystem, but rather as simple components of a vaster whole within which no real discrimination is really established between humans and nonhumans." Descola's work is closely related to that of Eduardo Viveiros de Castro (1998, 472), whose writings on the shamanistic cultures of the Amazonian basin emphasize the "perspectival" quality of their cosmologies, which hold that many species share a common internal form—"spirit" or "soul"—that is "formally identical to human consciousness" regardless of the external bodily form in which it is concealed. Unlike Western cultures, which understand the physical body/matter to be what human and nonhuman animals hold in common, with the human distinguished by its singular possession of rationality and consciousness, Amerindian cultures, particularly those organized economically and ecologically around the hunt, instead see rationality and consciousness as common to a multitude of species, despite the bodily differences that divide them. The work of the shaman is to mediate between human beings and other inhabitants of a universe that is "populated by extra-human intentionalities endowed with their own perspectives" (Viveiros de Castro, 472). As the Brazilian anthropologist (472) writes, "it is shamans who administer the relations between humans and the spiritual component of the extra-humans, since they alone are capable of assuming the point of view of such beings and, in particular, are capable of returning to tell the tale. If Western multiculturalism is relativism as public policy, then Amerindian perspectivist shamanism is multinaturalism as cosmic politics."

The reemergence of long-suppressed Amerindian and border epistemologies is one of the most vital developments of the late twentieth century and one with profound implications for politics and intellectual life in the Americas, including ecocriticism and the environmental humanities more broadly. Drawing inspiration from recent political events in Peru, Ecuador, and Bolivia, where the Indigenous-popular movement has conjured sentient entities such as mountains, water, and soil—what the West calls nature—into the public arena, anthropologist Marisol de la Cadena argues that Indigeneity, as a historical formation, exceeds the Western understanding of politics as usual—that is, of politics as a field in which rational human beings dispute the power to represent themselves and others vis-à-vis the state. According to de la Cadena, Indigeneity's current political emergence challenges the separation of nature and culture that underpins the prevalent notion of politics and the social contract on which it is predicated; thus the politics proposed by contemporary Indigenous movements is pluralistic not because of its enactment by bodies marked by gender, race, ethnicity, or sexuality (as multicultural theory would have it) but because it conjures nonhuman actors to the political arena.

Indigenous environmental politics is closely tied to Indigenous claims to land and the vindication of Indigenous intellectual traditions and cultural forms. In the context of the current attack against Indigenous communities and the territories they occupy throughout the Americas, these claims could not be more urgent. But we also caution against the reification of cultural difference, including through a false politics of authenticity and essentialized identities. For Eduardo Gudynas and others, Indigenous and non-Indigenous intellectuals alike, the enshrining of the rights of nature within the Ecuadoran constitution has prompted a wider reflection on the idea of nature having intrinsic value—value, in other words, not assigned by humans—which would be a passage toward broader recognition of Nature as a bearer of rights; that is, a subject of rights.[12]

By the same token, recent years have demonstrated the fecundity at the edges of cultural fields, as witnessed in the flourishing of innovative aesthetic forms that draw on multiple artistic and cultural traditions, media, and genres. *The Latin American Ecocultural Reader* features hybrid or creolizing works that destabilize boundaries, categories, and identities. These works have proliferated in recent years as artists and intellectuals are spurred by the crisis of climate change and environmental degradation to experiment with innovative artistic expression. In some cases, non-Indigenous artists and intellectuals are deeply engaged with non-Western traditions. In other cases, they are breaking boundaries within what remains a recognizably Western heritage, blurring the borders between science and art, or human and animal.

The logic of political ontologies associated with popular environmentalism in Latin America is legible and accessible when those ontologies are situated in multiple contexts: the collective and pandisciplinary project of articulating ways of knowing that do not rely on the epistemological separation of subject and object, and the long struggle, by Latin American intellectuals, toward the decolonization of knowledge, which we understand as the extrication of knowledge production from a state rationality that directs itself toward the consolidation of resources in the hands of the privileged few. By building critical frameworks based on these contexts we may be able to extend to Latin American environmental thought the same "cognitive advantage" Sylvia Wynter (1997, 148) claims for Black studies—that it "was and is compelled to challenge what Michel Foucault calls the 'ground' of our present epistemological order." The task is more necessary now than ever.

Notes

1. The origins of the term "ecocriticism" are somewhat uncertain. It has been suggested that William Rueckert may have coined the term in his 1978 essay "Literature and Ecology: An Experiment in Ecocriticism," but there is little agreement as to who first used the term. Carmen Flys Junquera, José Manuel Marrero Henríquez, and Julia Barella Vigal (2010, 17) maintain that William Howarth invented it in his essay "Some Principles of Ecocriticism" in the 1970s. Other terms that have circulated are "ecopoetics," "environmental literary criticism," and "green cultural studies." Some critics favor the prefix "eco-" over "enviro-" because while "environmental" connotes, in English, an anthropocentric and dualistic perspective, "eco-" implies "interdependent communities, integrated systems, and strong connections among constituent parts" (Glotfelty 1996, xx).

2. For a broad overview of the emergence of ecocriticism in both North America and Latin America, see Heffes (2013).

3. See, for example, Salleh (1984) and Merchant (2008).

4. See also the introduction in Coupe (2000).

5. This is also the central argument of Elliott (1970).

6. See also Jáuregui (2008), Quijano (2008), and Pagden (1987).

7. See Mires (1990).

8. See McGregor (2015).

9. See, for example, Cañizares-Esguerra (2006a), Barrera-Osorio (2006), and Pimentel (2003).

10. See Marcone (1998a, 1998b, 2000) and French (2005).

11. For an outstanding study of environmental culture among Black communities on Colombia's Pacific coast, see Escobar (2008, 111–55).

12. See Gudynas (2015).

ONE
New World Natures

The year 1492 is a world-historical turning point like no other. Columbus's arrival at the islands of Guanahani, Cuba, and Ayti, which he would promptly rename as San Salvador, Juana, and Hispaniola, touched off an ecological revolution the effects of which are still unfolding today. What happened and how is far from straightforward, however. As the environmental historian Shawn William Miller writes, one of the most transcendent facts in the history of the conquest and colonization of the Americas is the almost inconceivably high mortality rates among Native American populations. Today the scholarly consensus holds that the Indigenous population of the Americas declined by approximately 95 percent during the first century after Columbus's arrival (Crosby, 1972; Mann, 2005; and Miller, 2007). The primary cause was infectious disease: the nefarious biological agents that the recent arrivals deployed in most cases without the slightest degree of intentionality or awareness. Epidemics—particularly smallpox, but also typhus, measles, influenza, bubonic plague, cholera, malaria, tuberculosis, mumps, yellow fever, and pertussis—had already taken a toll on the inhabitants of North America well before the arrival of the first English colonists. The same illnesses had afflicted European populations for hundreds of years, enabling them to develop inherited biological immunities; the Europeans' tendency to live in close proximity to livestock and other animals also helped. In the Americas, where local populations had no such antibodies, diseases spread quickly and with devastating lethalness: everywhere, but especially in densely populated areas, entire communities would be wiped out. The original Arawak, Carib, and Taíno populations of the Caribbean islands were almost entirely gone within some fifty years of Columbus's arrival. The European diseases that ravaged them were quickly transmitted to the Mesoamerican mainland and Central and South America.

The earliest Spanish accounts tend to emphasize the (to European eyes) astonishing ways that local populations produced food to sustain themselves: with terraced gardens, in the Andes, for example, or with aquatic turtle farms in the Amazon River and its tributaries. In many places the land supported remarkably large populations, using agricultural and other techniques developed over hundreds if not thousands of years. For recipients of the cultural tradition set off by Christopher Columbus, accustomed to thinking of the Americas as a "new," "virgin," and "unspoiled" territory, the thought of intensive food production is surprising. But as Charles Mann (2005, 312–26) points out in his classic book *1491*, the lush, verdant landscapes that greeted those Europeans who arrived beginning in about 1550 were a relative novelty, themselves the product of the catastrophic decline of native populations. Previously, Native American societies had very high populations with relatively few sources of protein: as a result they had to manage their protein sources very carefully.

At the time of Columbus's voyages, the Europeans' world was theocentric and anthropocentric: they believed that the cosmos was created by an omnipotent God whose ultimate design was to bring about the salvation of human beings, who resembled God in having an immortal soul but who also resembled the other animals in that their souls were contained in fleshy, earthbound bodies. For Christians like

Columbus and his patrons, the king and queen of Spain, life on earth was of little importance in comparison with the afterlife. What is more, Columbus and his contemporaries fervently believed that the Second Coming of Jesus Christ was close at hand, and that they themselves could help to bring it about by leading the Christians in the conquest of the holy city of Jerusalem. Their victory against the Moors, it was believed, would bring about the apocalypse and God's kingdom would be once and forever established.

Columbus's mind-set closely resembled the Renaissance episteme that Foucault describes in *The Order of Things*. Columbus saw the universe as an infinite set of resemblances or similitudes in which the material world was the reflection of God's divine plan; he also believed in the Garden of Eden as a real place on earth. He struggled, as men of his time struggled, to assimilate his own observations and findings to the teachings of Christian tradition and to the documents of Mediterranean antiquity, which Europeans had begun to rediscover relatively recently. But as Ileana Rodríguez (2004, xiii) writes in *Transatlantic Topographies*, Columbus's discovery of the so-called New World and all the people, plants, animals, and things in it pushed the episteme of the Renaissance into overdrive, since Europeans suddenly had to account for a multitude of things of which the ancients had no knowledge. The scientific endeavor known as natural history expanded greatly as a result, with dozens of volumes produced in an attempt to gather and distribute knowledge about the fantastic resources Spain had recently acquired. New and more empirical ways of understanding and describing the world began to develop, as, for example, in Gonzalo Fernández de Oviedo y Valdés's *General and Natural History of the Indies'* vast illustrated catalog of newly discovered things, including many "natural wonders" like the flora and fauna of the Caribbean. Soon science and technology expanded beyond the bonds that had previously restrained them: rather than studying nature in order to understand the mind of the Creator, men now began to study nature in order to manipulate and exploit it. Some felt this change was right and necessary if the Catholic monarchs were to realize the full potential of the marvelous gift that had been bestowed upon them. Others, including the Jesuit provincial José de Acosta, heartily disagreed and felt that more restraint and reverence should be shown in Christians' interactions with nonhuman nature (Barrera-Osorio 2006, 120).

The European "discovery" of the Americas, especially the vast deposits of gold and silver found in Mexico and the Andes, changed their understanding of the world, human society, and an individual's relationship to both. Unprecedented economic opportunity lent fuel to the fire that Renaissance scholar Stephen Greenblatt (2005) calls "self-fashioning." Suddenly it was possible, in one man's lifetime, to dramatically change the status and destiny of his family on the basis of wealth acquired in the Indies. Nothing of the sort had ever happened before. As Miller (2007, 81) notes, a major factor in the changing environmental conditions in colonial Latin America was the simple fact that the Europeans rarely planned on staying there. Unlike Amerindians and their cultures, which had developed over millennia, the Europeans were newcomers to the scene, and many of them felt that the things that matter most—family, culture, "good" society—remained in Europe. And so their attitude toward the land was largely instrumental. Not only did they come to the Americas purely to make money, but most were planning to leave as soon as they had accumulated enough capital to significantly improve their standing at home. Rather than plan ahead for the longevity of their soil or other resources, many practiced a kind of scorched-earth economics with the aim of raising a quick profit and then heading home.

In contrast to the Puritans of New England, the early colonizers of the Caribbean and Central and South America were almost exclusively male. As the chronicles of the conquest suggest, they were sometimes given groups of Indigenous women to perform acts of domestic and sexual labor; more often they captured native women by force. These dynamics exacerbated the explorers' tendency to describe the land itself as "virgin" territory, a welcoming, tantalizing female body. As Margarita Zamora (1990–91, 134) writes of Columbus's Letter of Discovery, "The text creates in the reader a longing for the land. It employs a rhetoric of desire that inscribes 'the Indies' in a psychosexual discourse of the feminine whose principal coordinates are beauty and fertility and, ultimately, possession and domination." While that longing and will to power reverberated far and wide, the masculine colonial subject's repressed anxiety regarding the agency of the subordinated female emerges powerfully in Father Carvajal's account of the first European voyage down South America's mightiest river, significantly named the Amazon.

The cosmologies and ontologies that pertained among the Americas' originary peoples were dramatically different from Europeans'. Among Amerindian societies, as discussed in the introduction, humankind is more or less considered as one species among many, not particularly privileged or favored by divine beings. This part features a miraculous survival of the early colonial period: the *Popol Vuh*, sacred book of the Maya K'iche' of Guatemala. (We have used the contemporary spelling, K'iche', in our introductions and the earlier spelling, Quiché, when it appears in previously published texts.) In the creation story presented here, the gods fashion the first human beings out of maize; an earlier race of humans, made of wood, was turned into monkeys after being tormented by, among other beings, their own rebellious cooking implements. The text helps us to understand how fully the Indigenous people of Central America see themselves embedded in a larger biotic community.

This section also includes a number of texts that highlight the contrast between Amerindian and European methods of managing local environmental resources, especially *Royal Commentaries of the Incas*, by the Andean author known as Garcilaso de la Vega, El Inca. Son of an Inca princess and a Spanish conquistador, Garcilaso was critical of the Spaniards' short-term thinking with regard to environmental resources: Incan agricultural practices, in contrast, were designed to maintain soil fertility and biodiversity over the long term. Another key selection in this regard is "Plague of Ants," by the Dominican friar Bartolomé de las Casas. As Las Casas writes, the colonizers' effort to provide an income for themselves after the decline of the Indigenous population made mining unprofitable backfires horrendously as the cassia trees they plant en masse first crowd out endemic vegetation and subsequently cause the ant population to explode. Recognizable today as an ecological collapse triggered by the arrival of an invasive species, the episode calls to mind the many unforeseeable consequences of what environmental historian Alfred W. Crosby famously dubbed the Columbian exchange.

Suggestions for Further Reading

Ignatius of Loyola. 1522. "Spiritual Exercises." In *Personal Writings*, edited and translated by Joseph A. Munitiz and Philip Endean, 281–358. London and New York: Penguin, 1997.

Álvaro Núñez Cabeza de Vaca. 1542. *The Shipwrecked Men*, translated by Hugo Augenbraum. London and New York: Penguin, 2002.

Bernardino de Sahagún. 1545–1590. *Florentine Codex: General History of the Things of New Spain. Book 11: Earthly Things*, edited by Charles E. Dibble and Arthur J. O. Anderson. Salt Lake City: University of Utah, 1963.

Alonso Ercilla y Zúñiga. 1569. *The Araucana*, edited by Isaías Lerner. Madrid: Cátedra, 2005.

Felipe Guaman Poma de Ayala. 1615. *The First New Chronicle and Good Government*, translated and edited by Roland Hamilton. Austin: University of Texas, 2009.

Christopher Columbus

When Christopher Columbus (1451–1506) returned from the first of four journeys to the Indies in 1493, his letter to King Ferdinand and Queen Isabella included revelations that would alter the course of the coming centuries. Not only was there earth beyond Europe, Asia, and Africa, but this earth was vast, populated, and fertile. Before Columbus became an icon of conquest—sometimes a hero and sometimes a villain in global historical imaginations—he was the son of a wool merchant, born in Genoa. During his teenage years, he worked on a merchant ship, until an attack by French privateers in 1470 left him drifting toward the Portuguese shore on a wooden raft. Columbus studied navigation and mathematics in Lisbon. There he began to conceive of his fateful journey. Severely underestimating the distance between the Canary Islands and Japan, Columbus believed the shortest route to Asia lay west across the Atlantic rather than south and east. In 1491 Columbus found benefactors in Ferdinand and Isabella, who were intrigued by the prospect of discovery and desirous of expanding their Catholic empire. Columbus embarked in 1492 and landed on an island in the Bahamas, interpreting the wildly new sights there according to European intellectual frameworks of the time. His first account of the Indies describes the New World as if it might be the biblical Eden. The earth is laden with fruit and gold, and the native people are simple, humble, innocent. But Paradise had already seen a glimpse of horrors to come. Columbus kidnapped between ten and thirty Indians, many of whom subsequently died, to present at the court at Barcelona along with other "wonders" of the New World.

***

"Letter to Various Persons Describing the Results of His First Voyage and Written on the Return Journey" (1493)

TRANSLATED BY J. M. COHEN

Since I know that you will be pleased at the great success with which the Lord has crowned my voyage, I write to inform you how in thirty-three days I crossed from the Canary Islands to the Indies, with the fleet which our most illustrious sovereigns gave me. I found very many islands with large populations and took possession of them all for their Highnesses; this I did by proclamation and unfurled the royal standard. No opposition was offered . . .

When I reached Cuba, I followed its north coast westwards, and found it so extensive that I thought this must be the mainland, the province of Cathay.[1] Since there were no towns or villages on the coast, but only small groups of houses whose inhabitants fled as soon as we approached, I continued on my course, thinking that I should undoubtedly come to some great towns or cities. We continued for many leagues but found no change, except that the coast was bearing me northwards. This I wished to avoid, since winter was approaching and my plan was to journey south. As the wind was carrying me on I decided not to wait for a change of weather but to turn back to a remarkable harbor which I had observed. From here I sent two men inland to discover whether there was a king or any great cities. They travelled for three days, finding only a large number of small villages and great numbers of people, but nothing more substantial. Therefore they returned.

I understood from some Indians whom I had captured elsewhere that this was an island, and so I followed its coast for 107 leagues to its eastward point. From there I saw another island eighteen leagues eastwards which I then named "Hispaniola."[2] I crossed to this island and followed its northern coast eastwards for 188 leagues continuously, as I had followed the coast of Cuba. All these islands are extremely fertile and this one is particularly so. It has many large harbours finer than any I know in Christian lands, and many large rivers. All this is marvelous. The land is high and has many ranges of hills, and mountains incomparably finer than Tenerife. All are most beautiful and various in shape, and all are accessible. They are covered with tall trees of different kinds which seem to reach the sky. I have heard that they never lose their leaves, which I can well believe, for I saw them as green and lovely as they are in Spain in May; some were flowering, some bore fruit and others were at different stages according to their nature. It was November but everywhere I went the nightingale[3] and many other birds were singing. There are palms of six or eight different kinds—a marvelous sight because of their great variety—and the other trees, fruit and plants are equally marvelous. There are splendid pine woods and broad fertile plains, and there is honey. There are many kinds of birds and varieties of fruit. In the interior are mines and a very large population.

Hispaniola is a wonder. The mountains and hills, the plains and meadow lands are both fertile and beautiful. They are most suitable for planting crops and for raising cattle of all kinds, and there are good sites for building towns and villages. The harbors are incredibly fine and there are many great rivers with broad channels and the majority contain gold.[4] The trees, fruits and plants are very different from those of Cuba. In Hispaniola there are many spices and large mines of gold and other metals . . . [5]

The inhabitants of this island, and all the rest that I discovered or heard of, go naked, as their mothers bore them, men and women alike. A few of the women, however, cover a single place with a leaf of a plant or piece of cotton which they weave for the purpose. They have no iron or steel or arms and are not capable of using them, not because they are not strong and well built but because they are amazingly timid. All the weapons they have are canes cut at seeding time, at the end of which they fix a sharpened stick, but they have not the courage to make use of these, for very often when I have sent two or three men to a village to have conversation with them a great number of them have come out. But as soon as they saw my men all fled immediately, a father not even waiting for his son. And this is not because we have harmed any of them; on the contrary, wherever I have gone and been able to have conversation with them, I have given them some of the various things I had, a cloth and other articles, and received nothing in exchange. But they have still remained incurably timid. True, when they have been reassured and lost their fear, they are so ingenuous and so liberal with all their possessions that no one who has not seen them would believe it. If one asks for anything they have they never say no. On the contrary, they offer a share to anyone with demonstrations of heartfelt affection, and they are immediately content with any small thing, valuable or valueless, that is given them. I forbade the men to give them bits of broken crockery, fragments of glass or tags of laces, though if they could get them they fancied them the finest jewels in the world. One sailor was known to have received gold to the weight of two and a half *castellanos* for the tag of a breeches lace, and others received much more for things of even less value. For newly minted *blancas* they would give everything they possessed, even two or three *castellanos* of gold or an *arroba* or two of spun cotton. They even took bits of broken hoops from the wine barrels and, as simple as animals, gave what they had. This seemed to me to be wrong and I forbade it.

15 February 1493

At your orders
THE ADMIRAL

Notes

1. In the logbook and later in this letter Columbus accepts the native story that Cuba is an island that they can circumnavigate in roughly twenty-one days, yet he insists here and later, during the second voyage, that it is in fact part of the Asiatic mainland.

2. This is referred to in the logbook as Bohio or Bofio.

3. Columbus was mistaken; he probably heard the mockingbird.

4. This did not prove to be true.

5. These statements are also inaccurate.

Gonzalo Fernández de Oviedo y Valdés

In his *General and Natural History of the Indies*, Gonzalo Fernández de Oviedo y Valdés (1478–1577) chronicles the spectacles of the colonial Caribbean through the eyes of the Spanish elite. Oviedo spent his early life at the epicenter of Spain's nascent New World aspirations. He was born in Madrid and educated in Ferdinand and Isabella's court, where he served as page to the prince of Asturias until the prince's death in 1497. Oviedo was present at the court at Granada when Columbus received permission to embark on his first voyage, and he was also present at the court in Barcelona when Columbus returned with accounts of the wonders of the Americas. In 1514, Oviedo traveled to the island of Hispaniola as the newly appointed inspector of gold foundries in Santo Domingo. He became official historiographer of the Indies and returned to the Americas five times. In the fifty books of the *General and Natural History of the Indies*, Oviedo extensively details the geography of the coasts, capes, and isles of the Americas and the flora and fauna that thrive there. In the sheer breadth of his project, Oviedo models Pliny the Elder's *Natural History*. But unlike the Roman geographer, who separates his books by theme, Oviedo often intersperses descriptions of the natural world with native practices and cultures; in this and other ways he takes a geographic view of history (Ferrando 1957). Writing at the very beginnings of the exchange of natural products across the Atlantic, Oviedo also attempts to characterize similarities and differences in plants and animals from the New and Old Worlds, offering, for example, the first European description of a pineapple.

***

From *General and Natural History of the Indies* (1535–1557)

TRANSLATED BY NINA M. SCOTT

Concerning pinecones [pineapples], which is what Christians call them, because they look like them; this fruit the Indians call yayama, *and a certain type of the same fruit they call* boniama, *and another kind they call* yayagua, *as shall be explained in this chapter, although in other places it has other names.*

On this island of Hispaniola there are some thistles, each of which produces a pineapple (or, better said, an artichoke), because it looks like what Spaniards call a pinecone, yet without being one. This is one of the most beautiful fruits I have seen in all the world in which I have travelled . . . None of [the European estates and gardens] I have seen, had fruits like this pineapple or artichoke, nor do I think that anywhere in the world there is one to equal it in the things I shall now recount. These are: beauty of aspect; sweetness of scent; an excellent taste. So, among the five bodily senses, three of which can be applied to fruits, and even a fourth, which is touch, [this fruit] partakes most excellently of these four things or senses, above all the fruits or delicacies which man's diligence in the exercise of agriculture produces. It has yet another great advantage, which is that it is maintained and grown without any trouble to the farmer. [With respect to] the fifth sense, that of hearing, the fruit can neither hear nor listen, but in its stead, the reader can listen attentively to what I write about this fruit, and can be certain that I am neither mistaken nor prolix in what I might say thereof. For, given that the fruit cannot possess the other four senses which above I wished to attribute to it, it must be understood that it is the person who eats it who exercises these senses, and not the fruit itself (which has no spirit but vegetative and sensitive drives, as it lacks reason, which man, along with all the others, possesses). The vegetative drive is the one by means of which plants and all similar creatures grow; the sensitive drive receives impulses of benefit or harm, just as when one waters, cleans or digs around trees and plants they feel this cultivation and attention by thriving and growing; but when one neglects, singes or cuts them, they dry up and are ruined. Let us leave these matters to the experts and return to what I wanted to relate.

Contemplating the beauty of this fruit, man takes pleasure in seeing the composition and adornment with which Nature has endowed it and made it so pleasurable to his sight, for the delight of this sense. Smelling it, the other sense enjoys a mixed scent of quince, peaches, very fine melons and other delightful sensations which all these fruits, together or alone, with no unpleasantness, possess; not only the table onto which they are put, but a large part of the house in which a pineapple is found, if it is ripe and in perfect condition, smells very good and, above all other fruits, comforts the sense of smell in a marvelous and surpassing manner. To taste it is something so appetizing and sweet that in this case words fail me properly to praise the object itself, for none of the other fruits which I have named can in any conceivable way compare to this one. To touch it, if truth be told, is not all that soft or gentle, for it seems that the fruit itself wants to be picked up respectfully, with a towel or handkerchief, but once in your hand, no other gives such contentment. And, weighing all these attributes and individual features, there is no [person of] middling judgment who would not give these pineapples or artichokes preeminence over all fruits. Neither the illustration of my pen nor my words can bestow on the original the accurate description or the glory of this fruit in a manner so wholly satisfactory as to be able to explain the matter without a brush or a drawing, and even with these it would be necessary to use colors to make it more like (if not entirely, at least in part), to make it easier to understand than by what I do and say, because in some manner the reader's sight would be able to share in this truth. All this notwithstanding, I will include it the best way I know, as badly drawn as described; yet, for those who may have seen this fruit, that will suffice, and they will fill in the rest. And for those who never have seen it but here, the picture cannot displease them if they listen to the reading, with such emendation and declaration that I assure them that if ever they do see it they will pardon me if I did not know or was unable justly to praise this fruit. In truth, he who might wish to fault me must respect and take note of the fact that this fruit has different types and goodness of taste (one is better than another), and even [differs] in other ways. And he who would judge must take into consideration what has been said, and what more I shall say in the process or extensive commentary on the differences among these pineapples. And if, because of a deficiency in the colors and in the drawing, I am unable to make people understand what I would like to say, blame my opinion, in which, to my eyes, it is the loveliest of all the fruits I have seen, the one which smells and tastes the best. With respect to its size and color, which is green, it is lit up and nuanced with a strong yellow color; as it ripens it loses the green and becomes more a deep gold, and simultaneously its scent, like that of the most perfect peaches with a good dose of quince, gets stronger. This is the scent which comes closest to that of this fruit; [but] its taste is better than peaches, and juicier.

One peels around the outside and makes round cuts or slices, as the cutter wishes, for in each part, lengthwise or crosswise, it has little hairs and is easy to cut. On all these islands this fruit is as I have described, and very common, for it can be found on all of them and in Tierra Firme as well; as the Indians have many and diverse tongues, they call it by different names. At least in Tierra Firme, in an area of twenty or thirty leagues, one can encounter four or five languages; this fruit is one of the principal reasons why the few Christians who live in these lands can survive among these barbarous peoples.

Gaspar de Carvajal

Dominican friar Gaspar de Carvajal (1500–1584) was one of only a handful of survivors of Francisco de Orellana's 1542 expedition down the Napo and Amazon Rivers to the Amazon delta. In 1533 Carvajal left his native Spain for Peru, where he worked as a missionary. Almost a decade later, the friar joined Gonzalo Pizarro's expedition in search of La Canela—the Country of Cinnamon—east of Quito along the Coca and Napo Rivers. Much like El Dorado, La Canela emerged from mythologies of abundance in the New World rather than sound geographical information. These unstable foundations did not slow Pizarro, who recruited two hundred twenty Spaniards and more than four thousand natives for his expedition. Disaster soon struck: having crossed the Andes and entered the Amazon jungle, the explorers had no knowledge of local flora and fauna and no way to find food. Nearly half died of hunger. Pizarro thus sent Orellana ahead to search for food, with the chaplain among the fifty men who accompanied him. A fortunate few of them would be the first Europeans to reach the Amazon delta, but only because they were unable to turn around and head upstream to reconnect with Pizarro. As Carvajal characterizes the unfamiliar natural and cultural systems of the rain forest, the jungle is a monotonous green wasteland until they stumble upon the complex networks of resources harnessed by Indigenous communities. Toward the end of his narrative, Carvajal describes a military encounter with Tapuyas, an Indigenous group whose women traditionally fight alongside the men. The Spaniards take these female soldiers for the woman warriors of Mediterranean legend, and the region has been known as Amazonas ever since.

***

From *The Discovery of the Amazon* (ca. 1542)

TRANSLATED BY BERTRAM T. LEE

Seeing that we had come far away from where our companions had stopped and that we had used up what little food we had brought along, [too little] for so uncertain a journey as the one that we were pursuing, the Captain and the companions conferred about the difficulty [we were in], and the [question of] turning back, and the lack of food, for, as we had expected to return quickly, we had not laid in a supply of food; but, confident that we could not be far off [from some settlement], we decided to go ahead. This [was done] at the cost of no little hardship for all, and, as neither on the next day nor on the following one was any food found nor any sign of a settlement, in accordance with the view of the Captain I said mass, as it is said at sea, commending to Our Lord our persons and our lives, beseeching Him to deliver us from such manifest hardship and [eventual] destruction, for that's what it was coming to look like to us now, since, although we did wish to go back up the river, that was not possible on account of the heavy current, [and there was no alternative], for to attempt to go by land was out of the question so that we were in great danger of death because of the great hunger we endured.

And so, after taking counsel as to what should be done, talking over our affliction and hardships, it was decided that we should choose of two evils the one which to the Captain and to all should appear to be the lesser, which was to go forward and follow the river, [and thus] either die or see what there was along it, trusting in Our Lord that He would see fit to preserve our lives until we should see our way out. In the meantime, lacking other victuals, we reached a [state of] privation so great that we were eating nothing but leather, belts and soles of shoes, cooked with certain herbs, with the result that so great was our weakness that we could not remain standing, for some on all fours and others with staffs went into the woods to search for a few roots to eat and some there were who ate certain herbs with which they were not familiar, and they were at the point of death, because they were like mad men and did not possess sense; but, as Our Lord was pleased that we should continue on our journey, no one died . . .

Battle and Theft of Food from an Amazonian Village

Here we engaged in a perilous battle, because there were many Indians on the water and on land and from all sides they gave us a hard fight; and so, of necessity, although seemingly at the risk of the lives of all of us, we attacked and captured the first spot [we could], where the Indians did not cease to leap out on land at [i.e., to attack] our companions, because they continued to defend it [i.e., the land] courageously; and had it not been for the crossbows, which effected some remarkable shots here . . . , the landing would not have been won; and so . . . the brigantines were beached and one half of our companions jumped into the water and fell upon the Indians in such a manner that they made them flee, and the other half stayed on the brigantines defending them from the other warriors who were out on the water, for they did not cease, even though the land was won, to fight on, and although damage was being done to them by the crossbows, they nevertheless did not give up [their attempt] to carry out their evil design. The beginning of the settlement being won, the Captain ordered the Lieutenant with twenty-five men to run through the settlement and drive the Indians out of it and look to see if there was any food [there], because he intended to rest in the said village five or six days in order to let us recover from the hardships which we had endured; and so the Lieutenant went and made a foray for a distance of half a league out through the village, and this [he did] not without difficulty, for, although the Indians were in retreat, they kept up a defensive fight like men whom it vexed to abandon their homes; and, as the Indians, when they do not meet with success in their intentions at the beginning, always run away until they feel the second impulse to return to a normal state of mind, they were, as

I say, still fleeing; and, when the aforesaid Lieutenant had perceived the great extent of the settlement and of its population, he decided not to go on farther but to turn back and tell the Captain what the situation was; and thus he did turn back before the Indians could do him any damage, and, having got back to the beginning of the settlement, he found that the Captain was lodged in the houses and that the Indians were still attacking him from the river, and he [i.e., the Lieutenant] told him exactly how things were and [informed him] that there was a great quantity of food, such as turtles in pens and pools of water, and a great deal of meat and fish and biscuit, and all this in such great abundance that there was enough to feed an expeditionary force of one thousand men for one year . . .

Encounter with the Amazons

More than an hour was taken up by this fight, for the Indians did not lose spirit, rather it seemed as if it was being doubled in them, although they saw many of their own number killed, and they passed over them [i.e., their bodies], and they merely kept retreating and coming back again. I want it to be known what the reason was why these Indians defended themselves in this manner. It must be explained that they are the subjects of, and tributaries to, the Amazons, and, our coming having been made known to them, they went to them to ask help, and there came as many as ten or twelve of them, for we ourselves saw these women who were there fighting in front of all the Indian men as women captains (22), and these latter fought so courageously that the Indian men did not dare to turn their backs, and anyone who did turn his back they killed with clubs right there before us, and this is the reason why the Indians kept up their defense for so long. These women are very white and tall, and have hair very long and braided and wound about the head, and they are very robust and go about naked, [but] with their privy parts covered, with their bows and arrows in their hands, doing as much fighting as ten Indian men, and indeed there was one woman among these who shot an arrow a span deep into one of the brigantines, and others less deep, so that our brigantines looked like porcupines.

Popol Vuh (anonymous)

The *Popol Vuh*, sometimes translated as "The Council Book," is a venerable Mayan text that includes accounts of the beginning of the world, the creation of humans from maize, and the adventures of hero twins who become the sun and the moon. Written in the K'iche' language between 1554 and 1558, it is one of only a handful of works that survived the Spanish authorities' efforts to eradicate Central America's Indigenous cultures in the name of Christianity. Most precolonial Mayan texts were destroyed in the century after the Spaniards' arrival, including some forty Yucatecan books that Bishop Diego de Landa burned on a single night in Maní in 1562. It was long held that the *Popol Vuh* had been preserved through oral transmission before it was transcribed as a single poem, but recent archaeological evidence suggests that there were much older written versions, and stucco panels in El Mirador, Guatemala, hint that some of these stories date back to roughly 300 B.C.E. Between 1701 and 1703, Friar Francisco Ximénez translated the only extant K'iche' manuscript of the *Popol Vuh* into Spanish. The text all but disappeared in the nineteenth century and was rediscovered in Chicago's Newberry Library by Guatemalan scholar Adrián Recinos in 1941. His classic Spanish rendition of the *Popol Vuh* is the basis of the English version presented here. In contrast to the Judeo-Christian creation story told in Genesis, the *Popol Vuh* represents humans as participants in the relations of the natural world rather than inherently dominant entities. Humans are crafted from corn and are subject to the rage of tortilla griddles and water jugs: ample warning of the need for humility.

***

From *Popol Vuh: The Sacred Book of the Ancient Quiché Maya* (ca. 1554–1558; 1701)

TRANSLATED BY DELIA GOETZ AND SYLVANUS G. MORLEY

Part I, Chapter 2

Of earth, of mud, they made [man's] flesh. But they saw that it was not good. It melted away, it was soft, did not move, had no strength, it fell down, it was limp, it could not move its head, its face fell to one side, its sight was blurred,[1] it could not look behind. At first it spoke, but had no mind. Quickly it soaked in the water and could not stand.

And the Creator and the Maker said:[2] "Let us try again because our creatures will not be able to walk nor multiply. Let us consider this," they said.

Then they broke up and destroyed their work and their creation: And they said: "What shall we do to perfect it, in order that our worshipers, our invokers, will be successful?"

Thus they spoke when they conferred again: "Let us say again to Xpiyacoc, Xmucané, Hunahpú-Vuch, Hunahpú-Utiú: 'Cast your lot again. Try to create again.'" In this manner the Creator and the Maker spoke to Xpiyacoc and Xmucané.

Then they spoke to those soothsayers, the Grandmother of the day, the Grandmother of the Dawn,[3] as they were called by the Creator and the Maker, and whose names were Xpiyacoc and Xmucané.

And said Huracán, Tepeu, and Gucumatz when they spoke to the soothsayer, to the Maker, who are the diviners: "You must work together and find the means so that man, whom we shall make, man, whom we are going to make, will nourish and sustain us, invoke and remember us."

"Enter, then, into council, grandmother, grandfather, our grandmother, our grandfather, Xpiyacoc, Xmucané, make light, make dawn, have us invoked, have us adored, have us remembered by created man, by made man, by mortal man. Thus be it done.

"Let your nature be known, Hunahpú-Vuch, Hunahpú-Utiú, twice mother, twice father, Nim-Ac, Nima-Tziís, the master of emeralds, the worker in jewels, the sculptor, the carver, the maker of beautiful places, the maker of green gourds, the master of resin, the master Toltecat, grandmother of the sun, grandmother of dawn, as you will be called by our works and our creatures.

"Cast the lot with your grains of corn and the *tzité*.[4] Do it thus, and we shall know if we are to make, or carve his mouth and eyes out of wood." Thus the diviners were told.

They went down at once to make their divination, and cast their lots with the corn and the *tzité*. "Fate! Creature!" said an old woman and an old man. And this old man was the one who cast the lots with Tzité, the one called Xpiyacoc. And the old woman was the diviner, the maker, called Chiracán Xmucané.

Beginning the divination, they said: "Get together, grasp each other! Speak, that we may hear." They said, "Say if it is well that the wood be got together and that it be carved by the Creator and the Maker, and if this [man of wood] is he who must nourish and sustain us when there is light when it is day!

"Thou, corn; thou, *tzité*; thou, fate; thou, creature; get together, take each other," they said to the corn, to the *tzité*, to fate, to the creature. "Come to sacrifice here, Heart of Heaven; do not punish Tepeu and Gucumatz!"

Then they talked and spoke the truth: "Your figures of wood shall come out well; they shall speak and talk on earth."

"So may it be," they answered when they spoke.

And instantly the figures were made of wood. They looked like men, talked like men, and populated the surface of the earth.

They existed and multiplied; they had daughters, they had sons, these wooden figures; but they did not have souls, nor minds, they did not remember their Creator, their Maker; they walked on all fours, aimlessly.

They no longer remembered the Heart of Heaven and therefore they fell out of favor. It was merely a trial, an attempt at man. At first they spoke, but their face was without expression; their feet and hands had no strength; they had no blood, nor substance, nor moisture, nor flesh; their cheeks were dry, their feet and hands were dry, and their flesh was yellow.

Therefore, they no longer thought of their Creator nor their Maker, nor of those who made them and cared for them.

These were the first men who existed in great numbers on the face of the earth.

Part I, Chapter 3

Immediately the wooden figures were annihilated, destroyed, broken up, and killed.

A flood was brought about by the Heart of Heaven; a great flood was formed which fell on the heads of the wooden creatures.

Of *tzité*, the flesh of man was made, but when woman was fashioned by the Creator and the Maker, her flesh was made of rushes. These were the materials the Creator and the Maker wanted to use in making them.

But those that they had made, that they had created, did not think, did not speak with their Creator, their Maker. And for this reason they were killed, they were deluged. A heavy resin fell from the sky. The one called Xecotcovach came and gouged out their eyes; Camalotz came and cut off their heads; Cotzbalam came and devoured their flesh. Tucumbalam came, too, and broke and mangled their bones and their nerves, and ground and crumbled their bones.

This was to punish them because they had not thought of their mother, nor their father, the Heart of Heaven, called Huracán. And for this reason the face of the earth was darkened and a black rain began to fall, by day and by night.

Then came the small animals and the large animals, and sticks and stones struck their faces. And all began to speak: their earthen jars, their griddles, their plates, their pots, their grinding stones, all rose up and struck their faces.

"You have done us much harm; you ate us, and now we shall kill you," said their dogs and birds of the barnyard.

And the grinding stones said: "We were tormented by you; every day, every day, at night, at dawn, all the time our faces went *holi, holi, huqui, huqui*, because of you. This was the tribute we paid you. But now that you are no longer men, you shall feel our strength. We shall grind and tear your flesh to pieces," said their grinding stones.

And then their dogs spoke and said: "Why did you give us nothing to eat? You scarcely looked at us, but you chased us and threw us out. You always had a stick ready to strike us while you were eating.

"Thus it was that you treated us. You did not speak to us. Perhaps we shall not kill you now; but why did you not look ahead, why did you not think about yourselves? Now we shall destroy you, now you shall feel the teeth of our mouths; we shall devour you," said the dogs, and then, they destroyed their faces.

And at the same time, their griddles and pots spoke: "Pain and suffering you have caused us. Our mouths and our faces were blackened with soot; we were always put on the fire and you burned us as though we felt no pain. Now you shall feel it, we shall burn you," said their pots, and they all destroyed their [the wooden men's] faces. The stones of the hearth, which were heaped together, hurled themselves straight from the fire against their heads causing them pain.

The desperate ones [the men of wood] ran as quickly as they could; they wanted to climb to the tops of the houses, and the houses fell down and threw them to the ground; they wanted to climb to the treetops, and the trees cast them far away; they wanted to enter the caverns, and the caverns repelled them.

So was the ruin of the men who had been created and formed, the men made to be destroyed and annihilated; the mouths and faces of all of them were mangled.

And it is said that their descendants are the monkeys which now live in the forests; these are all that remain of them because their flesh was made only of wood by the Creator and the Maker.

And therefore the monkey looks like man, and is an example of a generation of men which were created and made but were only wooden figures.

Part III, Chapter 1

Here, then, is the beginning of when it was decided to make man, and when what must enter into the flesh of man was sought.

And the Forefathers, the Creators and Makers, who were called Tepeu and Gucumatz said: "The time of dawn has come, let the work be finished, and let those who are to nourish and sustain us appear, the noble sons, the civilized vassals; let man appear, humanity, on the face of the earth." Thus they spoke.

They assembled, came together and held council in the darkness and in the night; then they sought and discussed, and here they reflected and thought. In this way their decisions came clearly to light and they found and discovered what must enter into the flesh of man.

It was just before the sun, the moon, and the stars appeared over the Creators and Makers.

From Paxil, from Cayalá,[5] as they were called, came the yellow ears of corn and the white ears of corn.

These are the names of the animals which brought the food: *yac* (the mountain cat), *utiú* (the coyote), *quel* (a small parrot), and *hoh* (the crow). These four animals gave tidings of the yellow ears of corn and the white ears of corn, they told them that they should go to Paxil and they showed them the road to Paxil.

And thus they found the food, and this was what went into the flesh of created man, the made man; this was his blood; of this the blood of man was made. So the corn entered [into the formation of man] by the work of the Forefathers.

And in this way they were filled with joy, because they had found a beautiful land, full of pleasures, abundant in ears of yellow corn and ears of white corn, and abundant also in *pataxte* and cacao, and in innumerable *zapotes, anonas, jocotes, nantzes, matasanos*, and honey. There was an abundance of delicious food in those villages called Paxil and Cayalá. There were foods of every kind, small and large foods, small plants and large plants.

The animals showed them the road. And then grinding the yellow corn and the white corn, Xmucané made nine drinks, and from this food came the strength and the flesh, and with it they created the muscles and the strength of man. This the Forefathers did, Tepeu and Gucumatz, as they were called.

After that they began to talk about the creation and the making of our first mother and father; of yellow corn and of white corn they made their flesh; of cornmeal dough they made the arms and the legs of man. Only dough of corn meal went into the flesh of our first fathers, the four men, who were created.

Notes

1. *Xa cul u vach.*
2. *Ahtzac, Ahbit*, variants of *Tzacol* and *Bitol.*
3. *R' atit quih, R'atit zac.* The word *atit* may be taken here in the collective sense, including the two grandparents Xpiyacoc and Xmucané, who are later called by their names in the text. The same expression is found farther on.
4. *Erythrina corallodendron*: *Tzité, árbol de pito* in Guatemala; *Tzompanquahuitl* in the Mexican language. It is used in both countries to make fences. Its fruit is a pod which contains red grains resembling a bean which the Indians used, as they still do, together with grains of corn, in their fortunetelling and witchcraft.
5. *Paxil* means separation, spreading of the waters, inundation. *Cayalá*, derived from *cay*, "rotten," may also be interpreted as putrid matter in the water. These legendary places which gave to the Middle American people the native fruits which are the base of their subsistence and economic development, were found, in the opinion of Brasseur de Bourbourg, in the region of Tabasco, where the Usumacinta River, after watering northern Guatemala, divides into various branches and overflows this entire region during the period when the rivers rise. This phenomenon is similar in its cause and effects to the inundations by the Nile that spread the fertile sediment which produces the rich harvests of Egypt. Bancroft believed that Paxil and Cayalá were in the region of Palenque and the Usumacinta. Both opinions would have some foundation if it were possible to establish the location of these mythological places, for that was, without doubt, the region which was inhabited for some time by the Guatemalan tribes in their wanderings toward the lands of the south.

Bartolomé de las Casas

Friar Bartolomé de las Casas (1484–1566) was among the earliest and most influential Spaniards to document and condemn European abuses against Indians. Throughout his long life, Las Casas produced books and letters exposing the horrific human cost of Spanish colonization. Son of a Spanish merchant, he traveled to the island of Hispaniola in 1502 with Governor Nicolás de Ovando and was rewarded with an encomienda, a royal grant of land and its native inhabitants. After his ordination as a Dominican friar in 1512, Las Casas worked to evangelize Indigenous populations, but he was disturbed by practices of quasi-enslavement permitted under the encomienda system and his own complicity in them. He returned the native serfs under his command to the governor in 1514. Las Casas left for Spain and served briefly as priest-procurator of the Indies, but his attempts to establish "towns of free Indians" and to promote farmer colonization proved ineffective. Back in Santo Domingo, he composed works like *A Short Account of the Destruction of the Indies* (1542), which argued that colonial abuses were sinful, that Indians were by nature dignified, innocent, and capable of conversion to Catholicism. These efforts prompted the "New Laws" of 1542, which largely dismantled the hereditary encomienda system. The selection presented here is from the much longer *History of the Indies*, published posthumously. Las Casas likens the plague of ants that overtakes the city of Santo Domingo on the island of Hispaniola to the biblical plagues by which God convinced the Egyptians to end the Israelites' enslavement. Today's readers will recognize an ecological collapse triggered by the colonizers' decision to import the invasive cassia tree for commercial cultivation after the Indigenous workforce had been wiped out by smallpox.

✳ ✳ ✳

"Plague of Ants" (ca. 1561)

TRANSLATED BY SANDRA FERDMAN

Around this time, in the year 1518 or 1519, something else happened on this island. By the will or consent of God, to relieve them of the anguished and tortured lives they endured toiling in all sorts of labor, but mostly in the mines, and to punish those who oppressed them by making them suffer their absence, there came a terrible plague in which nearly all the few Indians left perished, with only a small number surviving. The epidemic was smallpox, brought over by someone from Castile, and which attacked the poor Indians. The pox, which burns like fire, grew out of the earth's heat. The Indians, whose custom it was to wash themselves in the rivers at every opportunity, took to washing themselves even more in their anguish. As a result the smallpox was locked inside their bodies, and, as in a devastating pestilence, all died in a short time. Added to these causes were the thinness and meager substance of their bodies from lack of food, their nakedness, their sleeping on the ground, the excessive labor, and the little or no care for their health and preservation they received from those whom they served. Finally, seeing that the Indians were dying, the Spaniards began to understand the need they had and would continue to have of them, which moved them to make some effort to cure them, but this was of little help to most, for it ought to have begun many years earlier. I do not believe that 1,000 souls were left alive or escaped this misery, from the infinite number of people who had lived on this island and whom we saw with our own eyes . . .

And because they realized that the Indians were dying, they began to slacken off and leave the mines, for they had no one left to send there to die or even to kill, and so they looked instead for other profits and new ways to acquire wealth, one of which was to plant cassia trees, which grew so quickly and in such numbers that it seemed as if this soil had not been created for any other tree, nor these trees for any other soil but this one, so ordered by Divine Providence and nature. In a very few days, many great estates were established of these cassia trees, from which the entire populated world could have been supplied. Their stalks were very big and thick, full of pulp, very honey-sweet. Ask the doctors and pharmacists if their virtue is lesser or greater than that of Alexandria.

The citizens of this island, that is to say, the Spaniards, because there is nothing left to say about the Indians, were not just a little proud, promising themselves many riches by putting all their hopes in the cassia tree. It would be good to believe that they might have attributed to God a part of this prospect, but they were already beginning to enjoy the fruits of their labors and to fulfill their expectations when God sent over this whole island and over the island of Saint John, principally, a plague. One might have feared, if it continued to grow, that the plague would totally depopulate them.

This plague was an infinite number of ants that were on this island and on the other and that could not be stopped in any way nor by any human means because of the sheer number of them. The ants bred on this island had an advantage over the ones on Saint John in the amount of damage done to the trees they destroyed, and the ants of the other island had an advantage over these in their fierceness, as they bit and caused greater pain than wasps that bite and hurt men. They could not defend themselves from these ants at night in their beds, nor could they survive if the beds were not placed on four small troughs filled with water. The ants on this island began to eat the trees from the root up, and as though fire had fallen from the sky and burned them, they stood all scorched and dried out. They also attacked the orange and pomegranate trees, of which there were many groves, very pretty and full on this island, and they left none without burning them out completely. To see it was a great pity. Many groves were destroyed in the city of Santo Domingo, and among them a very important one belonging to the Dominicans' monastery, and in a place called La Vega another one, quite notable, belonging to the Franciscans.

These trees stood behind the cassia trees, and, as they were sweeter, they destroyed them even more quickly and burned them out. I believe that they devastated over one hundred million trees that were planted for profit. It was, certainly, a great shame to see so many properties, so rich, annihilated by such a relentless plague. The grove of Saint Francis in La Vega was full of orange trees that gave sweet, dry, and bitter fruit. There I saw very beautiful pomegranate trees and cassia trees, and great stalks of cassia, nearly four hands in length. And just a short time later I saw all of it charred out. I saw the same thing in many other cassia tree estates that were in that area. The spreads of cassia trees on that land, and those that could have been planted, would without doubt have been enough, alone, to provide for all of Europe and Asia, even if they had been eaten as one eats bread, because of the great fertility of that land and its size . . .

As the citizens of Santo Domingo saw the affliction of this plague grow, doing such damage to them, and as they could not end it by any human means, they agreed to ask for help from the Highest Tribunal. They made great processions begging Our Father to free them from such a plague so harmful to their worldly goods. In order to receive divine blessing more quickly, they thought of taking a saint as a lawyer, whichever one by chance Our Lord should declare best suited . . . Fortune fell on Saint Saturnin, and receiving him with happiness and joy as their patron, they celebrated him with a feast of great solemnity, as they have each year since then, by vow, as I believe . . . From that day on one saw by plain sight that the plague was diminishing, and if it did not end altogether, it was because of their sins. I now believe that it no longer exists, because they have again restored some of the cassia trees, and orange and pomegranate trees. I say restore referring not to what the ants burned out, but to the new trees that were planted.

Jean de Léry

Jean de Léry (1534–1611) offers an engaging account of his year among the Tupinamba Indians in his 1578 *History of a Voyage to the Land of Brazil, Otherwise Called America*. Born in Margelle, France, in the midst of the tumultuous Protestant Reformation, Léry trained as a Calvinist in Geneva. He traveled to Brazil in 1556, having been promised by Nicolas Durand, Chevalier de Villegagnon, that the religious freedom of the Calvinist participants would be protected in the French colony he was establishing on an island in the bay of Rio de Janeiro. The Catholic Chevalier's promises proved illusory, however, when he turned against the Calvinists. Léry and his coreligionists fled to a trading post on the mainland, where they lived in close proximity with the Tupinamba for roughly a year before returning to France. His account of the experience, published twenty years later, frequently compares the Tupinamba's practice of cannibalism with the brutality he observed during the religious wars between European Catholics and Protestants. Léry's *History*, not surprisingly, is a key source for Michel de Montaigne's well-known essay "Of Cannibals." He also offers extensive accounts of the exotic flora and fauna of tropical Brazil. In the excerpt presented here, Léry discusses a species of tree known locally as *araboutan*, which the Europeans refer to as brazilwood and harvest in enormous quantities for the purpose of making a red dye back in Europe. (Brazilwood eventually gave the country its name.) In the quoted dialogue with a Tupinamba man—which may or may not be the author's invention—Léry's interlocutor expresses his bafflement at the secular colonists' commitment to extracting surplus value from nature.

✳✳✳

"Of the Trees, Herbs, Roots, and Exquisite Fruits Produced by the Land of Brazil" (1578)

TRANSLATED BY JANET WHATLEY

Having already treated the four-footed animals as well as the birds, fish, reptiles, and things having life, movement, and feeling that are to be seen in America, before I speak of religion, war, civil order, and other customs of our savages that are still to be dealt with, I will continue by describing the trees, herbs, plants, fruits, roots—all the things commonly said to have a vegetative soul—which are to be found in that country.

First, since brazilwood (from which this land has taken the name that we use for it) is among the most famous trees, and now one of the best known to us and (because of the dye made from it) is the most valued, I will describe it here. This tree, which the savages call *araboutan*, ordinarily grows as high and branchy as the oaks in the forests of this country; some are so thick that three men could not embrace a single trunk . . .

It has a leaf like that of boxwood, but of a brighter green, and it bears no fruit. As for the manner of loading it on the ships, take note that both because of the hardness of this wood and the consequent difficulty of cutting it, and because, there being no horses, donkeys, or other beasts to carry, cart, or draw burdens in that country, it has to be men who do this work: if the foreigners who voyage over there were not helped by the savages, they could not load even a medium-sized ship in a year. In return for some frieze garments, linen shirts, hats, knives, and other merchandise that they are given, the savages not only cut, saw, split, quarter, and round off the brazilwood, with the hatchets, wedges, and other iron tools given to them by the French and by others from over here, but also carry it on their bare shoulders, often from a league or two away, over mountains and difficult places, clear down to the seashore by the vessels that lie at anchor, where the mariners receive it. I say expressly that it is only since the French and Portuguese have been frequenting their country that the savages have been cutting their brazilwood; for before that time, as I have heard from the old men, they had almost no other way of taking down a tree than by setting fire to the base of it . . .

During the time that we were in that country we made fine fires of this brazilwood; I have observed that since it is not at all damp, like most other wood, but rather is naturally dry, it gives off very little smoke as it burns. One day one of our company decided to bleach our shirts, and, without suspecting anything, put brazilwood ash in with the lye; instead of whitening them, he made them so red that although they were washed and soaped afterward, there was no means of getting rid of that tincture, so that we had to wear them that way.

If the gentlemen over here with their perfectly starched pleats—those who send to Flanders to have their shirts whitened—choose not to believe me, they have my permission to do the experiment for themselves, and, for quicker results, the more to brighten their great ruffs (or rather, those dribble-catchers more than half a foot wide that they are wearing these days), they can dye them green if they please.

Our Tupinamba are astonished to see the French and others from distant countries go to so much trouble to get their *araboutan*, or brazilwood. On one occasion one of their old men questioned me about it: "What does it mean that you *Mairs* and *Peros* (that is, French and Portuguese) come from so far for wood to warm yourselves? Is there none in your own country?" I answered him yes, and in great quantity, but not of the same kinds as theirs; nor any brazilwood, which we did not burn as he thought, but rather carried away to make dye, just as they themselves did to redden their cotton cord, feathers, and other articles. He immediately came back at me: "Very well, but do you need so much of it?" "Yes," I said (trying to make him see the good of it), "for there is a merchant in our country who has more frieze and red cloth, and even" (and here I was choosing things that were familiar to him) "more knives, scissors, mirrors, and other merchandise than you have ever seen over here; one such merchant alone will buy all the wood that several ships bring back from your country." "Ha, ha!" said my savage, "you are telling me of wonders." Then, having thought over what I had said to him, he questioned me further, and said, "But this man of whom you speak, who is so rich, does he never die?" "Certainly he does," I said, "just as others do." At that (since they are great discoursers, and pursue a subject out to the end) he asked me, "And when he is dead, to whom belong all the goods that he leaves behind?" "To his children, if he has any, and if there are none, to his brothers, sisters, or nearest kinsmen." "Truly," said my elder (who, as you will judge, was no dullard), "I see now that you *Mairs* (that is, Frenchmen) are great fools; must you labor so hard to cross the sea, on which (as you told us) you endured so many hardships, just to amass riches for your children or for those who will survive you? Will not the earth that nourishes you suffice to nourish them? We have kinsmen and children, whom, as you see, we love and cherish; but because we are certain that after our death the earth which has nourished us will nourish them, we rest easy and do not trouble ourselves further about it."

And there you have a brief and true summary of the discourse that I have heard from the very mouth of a poor savage American. This nation, which we consider so barbarous, charitably mocks those who cross the sea at the risk of their lives to go seek brazilwood in order to get rich; however blind this people may be in attributing more to nature and to the fertility of the earth than we do to the power and the providence of God, it will rise up in judgement against those despoilers who are as abundant over here, among those bearing the title of Christians, as they are scarce over there, among the native inhabitants. Therefore, to take up what I said elsewhere—that the Tupinamba mortally hate the avaricious—would to God that the latter might be imprisoned among them, so that they might even in this life serve as demons and furies to torment those whose maws are insatiable, who do nothing but suck the blood and marrow of others. To our great shame, and to justify our savages in the little care that they have for the things of this world, I had to make this digression in their favor.

José de Acosta

José de Acosta (1540–1600) was a Jesuit missionary who became one of the order's most influential members in South America. Acosta was born in Medina del Campo, Spain, to a family of probable *converso* (Jewish) origin, in the same year that Ignacio de Loyola established the Society of Jesus. He became a novitiate at age eleven; four of his brothers would also join. Acosta was active in the Jesuit organization in Peru for a decade and a half, beginning in 1572, then returned to Spain after a brief stay in Mexico. Acosta's first major publication, *De procuranda Indorum salute*, published in Latin, is a practical treatise on evangelization; among other things, it argues for the importance of catechizing Native Americans in their own languages. The selection presented here comes from *Natural and Moral History of the Indies* (1590), a sweeping account of both the vast and complex physical geography of the New World and the histories, politics, and cultures of the Indigenous peoples of Peru and Mexico. It represents Acosta's attempt to integrate information gathered on behalf of soldiers, merchants, and fellow missionaries in the Americas into the intellectual frameworks of Renaissance humanism, which were derived from biblical tradition and Mediterranean antiquity. In the excerpt presented here, Acosta recapitulates the hierarchy of being typical of Western cosmologies, in which species are ranked according to their proportion of "spirit" to "matter," so as to contrast the traditional Christian notion that the physical world should be studied only as a pathway to knowledge of its Creator with the use of science to exploit nature in the silver mines at nearby Potosí.

∗∗∗

"Of the Three Kinds of Mixtures That Will Be Dealt with in This History" (1590)

TRANSLATED BY FRANCES M. LÓPEZ-MORILLAS

Having dealt in the preceding book with matters concerning the elements and single entities in the Indies, in this book we shall deal with compounds and mixtures, insofar as they seem to conform to our aims. And, although there are many other kinds, we will reduce this subject to three, namely, metals, plants, and animals. Metals are like plants hidden in the bowels of the earth and have some resemblance to plants in the manner in which they are produced because the places from which their roots arise, and their trunk as it were, can be perceived; these are the large and small veins that are very well interlaced and organized among themselves. And in a way it seems that minerals grow in the same manner as plants, not because they have

41

real vegetable and inner life, for this is true only of real plants, but because they are produced in the bowels of the earth in such a way, by the virtue and efficacy of the sun and the other planets, that over a long period of time they gradually grow and almost, one might say, propagate. And, just as metals resemble the earth's hidden plants, we may also say that plants are like animals that remain in one place, whose life is ruled by the nourishment nature supplies them at their birth. But animals are greater than plants, for because they have a more perfect nature they also need more perfect nourishment; and Nature gave them movement to seek it and senses to find and recognize it. Hence, harsh and barren land serves as substance and nourishment for metals, and fertile and more amenable land is substance and nourishment for plants. Plants themselves are the food of animals, and both plants and animals are food for men, with the lower order of nature always serving the higher and the less perfect subordinated to the more perfect. This makes us understand how far are gold and silver, which greedy men in their covetousness hold so dear, from being a worthy object for man, for they are many degrees lower than man, and man is subject and subordinate only to the Creator and universal Maker of all things as his proper end and repose, and all other things are worthy only insofar as they guide him and help him to attain this goal. The man who contemplates created things from this viewpoint, and ponders them, can gain advantage from knowledge and consideration of them, using them to know and glorify the Author of them all. The man who goes no further than to understand their properties and uses, or who is merely curious as to knowledge of them or covetous in acquiring them, will find that in the end these creatures will be as the sage has said: "to the feet of the unwise and foolish they are a snare and a net into which they fall and are entangled."[1] Therefore, with the aim and intention I have expressed, to the end that the Creator may be glorified in his creatures, I mean to write something in this book of the many things worthy of mention in the Indies concerning the metals and plants and animals peculiar to those parts. And because to deal with them accurately would be a very large task, and one that requires greater knowledge than my own and more time than I have at my disposal, I will say that I intend to deal briefly with some things about these three groups that I have proposed and that I know from experience or by true accounts given me, leaving longer exposition of these matters to others more curious and diligent than myself.

Notes

1. Acosta was not the first historian of the Indies to discuss Potosí, a city known for its silver wealth throughout the sixteenth-century world, but given his two visits to the city, one in the company of Viceroy Toledo, he contributed a higher degree of familiarity with the town and its mining operations. The most comprehensive *historia* of Potosí, combining elements of history and story, was written in the late colonial period by its native son Bartolomé Arzáns de Orsúa y Vela. Arzáns relied on documents about Potosí's mining industry along with local lore to write the massive, three-volume *Historia de la villa imperial de Potosí*; modern edition edited by Lewis Hanke and Gunnar Mendoza (Providence, R.I.: Brown University Press, 1965).

Garcilaso de la Vega, El Inca

By the time he wrote *Royal Commentaries of the Incas*, Garcilaso de la Vega, El Inca (1539–1616), had solidified his position as a literary and scholarly voice uniquely positioned at the juncture of the Old World and the New. Garcilaso (not to be confused with the Golden Age Spanish poet of the same name) was born in Cuzco while the conquest was still under way. Son of an Inca princess and a Spanish conquistador, he spent portions of his childhood with each parent, living with his mother's family and speaking Quechua and subsequently working as a scribe for his father, who imposed an education emphasizing rhetoric and other classical disciplines. As a result, Garcilaso often uses a philosophical and literary terminology inherited from European tradition to conceptualize Andean religious beliefs. In 1560, Garcilaso moved to Spain, where he became a captain in the Spanish army and, briefly, a priest. His literary brilliance emerged first in his translations of the Italian León Hebreo's *Dialoghi di amore* (*Dialogues of Love*) and subsequently in his account of Hernando de Soto's exploration of Florida. In the *Royal Commentaries*, Garcilaso turned to his native Peru, writing about Incan culture, customs, and particularly governance based in part on the stories he had heard from his mother's family. While conceding the advantages of Christian salvation, Garcilaso nonetheless represents Incan civilization as fundamentally noble, analogous to the civilizations of Mediterranean antiquity. In the selection presented here, he implicitly shows that the agricultural systems of the Incas—including the partitioning and tilling of land according to precise rules—demonstrate strong cultural and economic systems deserving of Europeans' respect.

***

From *Royal Commentaries of the Incas and General History of Peru* (1609)

TRANSLATED BY HAROLD V. LIVERMORE

Book V, Chapter I

How They Increased the Agricultural Land and Divided It among Their Vassals

When the Inca had conquered any kingdom or province and established the form of government in its towns and the way of life of the inhabitants in accordance with their idolatrous religion and their laws, he ordered that the agricultural land should be extended. This implies, of course, the area under maize. For this purpose irrigation engineers were brought: some of these were extremely skilled, as is clearly demonstrated by their works, of which some survive today and others have been destroyed leaving only traces behind. These engineers made the necessary irrigation channels, according to the amount of land that could be turned to account: the greater part of Peru is poor in grain-bearing land, and the Incas therefore tried as far as possible to extend what there was. Because the country falls within the torrid zone, irrigation is necessary, and great attention was paid to this: not a grain of maize was sown unless channeled water was available. They also dug channels to water their pastures when the autumn rains were delayed: as they had an infinite quantity of flocks, they had to give their pastures the same attention as their grainlands. The channels for the pastures were destroyed when the Spaniards entered Peru, but traces of them are still to be found.

Having dug the channels, they levelled the fields and squared them so that the irrigation water could be adequately distributed. They built level terraces on the mountains and hillsides, wherever the soil was good; and these are to be seen today in Cuzco and in the whole of Peru. In order to make these terraces they would construct three walls of solid masonry, one in front and one at each end. These sloped back slightly (like all the Indian walls) so as to withstand the weight of earth with which they are filled to the level of the top of the walls. Above the first platform they built another smaller one, and above that another still smaller. In this way the whole hill was gradually brought under cultivation, the platforms being flattened out like stairs in a staircase, and all the cultivable and irrigable land being put to use. If there were rocky places, the rocks were removed and replaced by earth brought from elsewhere to form the terraces, so that the space should not be wasted. The first platforms were large, according to the configuration of the place: they might be one or two or three hundred measures broad and long. The second were smaller and they diminished progressively as they were higher up, until the last might contain only two or three rows of maize plants. This shows how industrious the Incas were in extending the area which could be planted with maize. A water channel was commonly brought fifteen or twenty leagues to water a few measures of soil, so that it should not be wasted.

Having thus extended the cultivable land, each settlement in each province measured all the land assigned to it and divided it into three parts, one for the Sun, one for the king, and one for the inhabitants. In the division care was taken that the inhabitants should have enough to sow for themselves, and rather too much than too little. When the population of a town or province increased, part of the area assigned to the Sun or the Inca was transferred to their subjects, so that the only lands reserved by the king for himself or for the Sun were those which would otherwise have remained ownerless and untilled. The terraces were usually assigned to the Sun and the Inca, since the latter had been responsible for constructing them. In addition to the irrigated maize fields, other land without a supply of water was divided among them for dry farming and sown with crops of great importance, such as three they call *papa*, *oca*, and *añus*. This land was also divided in due proportion between the Sun, the Inca, and a third part for their subjects, but as it was waterless and of low productivity, it was sown only for a year or two and then rested while another part was sown. In this way the poor soil was kept under control, and there was always an abundance of it for use.

The maize fields were sown every year, and as they were always supplied with water and manure like gardens, they always bore fruit. With the maize they planted a seed rather like rice which they call *quinua*, which also grows in a cold climate.

Book V, Chapter II

Their System of Agriculture; the Festival of Tilling the Land Assigned to the Inca and the Sun

They also had an established system in cultivating the soil. They first tilled the part assigned to the Sun and then that of the widows and orphans and those who were unable to work owing to age or ill health. The latter were regarded as the poor, and the Inca therefore bade that their land be tilled for them. In each village, or in each quarter, if it were a large village, there were men appointed exclusively to attend to the cultivation of what we shall call the poor. These men were called *llactacamayu*, "aldermen or councillors of a town." When the time came to plough, or sow, or bring in the harvest, it was their duty to go out at night and climb a sort of watch tower or beacon they had for the purpose and sound a trumpet or horn to attract attention, and then announce: "On such and such a day the lands of the disabled are to be tilled: let each attend to the task assigned him." The inhabitants of each quarter knew from traditional practice which land was assigned to them, since it was that of their relatives or nearest neighbors. Each was obliged to take his own food from his home so that the poor should not have the trouble of feeding them. They used to say that the aged, the sick, and widows and orphans had enough troubles of their own, without attending to others. If the poor had no seed, this was supplied from the storehouses, of which we shall speak later. Land belonging to soldiers on campaign was also tilled by the community, like that of the widows, orphans, and poor, for when their husbands were away on military service, wives were reckoned as widows, and received this service as being in need of charity. The children of those killed in war were very carefully brought up until they married.

After the cultivation of the land of the poor, they tilled their own, taking turn and turn about, as the saying is. They then tilled the *curaca*'s land, which was always the last to be attended to in each town or province. Hence in the time of Huaina Cápac, an Indian *regidor* in a village of the Chachapoyas was hanged for having the land belong[ing] to the *curaca*, who was a relative of his, tilled before that of a widow: this was because he had broken the order established by the Inca for tilling the soil, and the gallows were erected on the *curaca*'s own land. The Inca ordered that his subjects' land should be given priority over his own, because it was said that prosperity of the subjects redounded to the king's service: if there were poor and needy, they would be of little use in peace or war.

Book V, Chapter III

The Quantity of Soil Given to Each Indian, and How It Was Manured

Each Indian was given a *tupu*, which is a *fanega* [1.6 bushels —Eds.], of land for growing maize: however, this is a *fanega* and a half in Spain. *Tupu* is also applied to a league's distance, and as a verb it means "to measure." Any measure of water, wine, or other liquid is called *tupu*, and so are the long pins the women use to fasten their garments with. A measure of seed has another name, *poccha*, meaning "*fanega*."

A *tupu* of land was enough to maintain a peasant and his wife without family. As soon as they had children, each boy was given a *tupu* and each girl half a *tupu*. When the male children married, the father gave them the measure of land he had received for their support, and if he turned them out of his house, he could not keep the land.

The daughters did not receive their portions when they married, for their land was not regarded as a dowry, but as a means of support. As their husbands were given land for their maintenance, they themselves could not have any; women were not provided for after marriage, but only before marriage and if they became widows. Their fathers kept the land assigned to their daughters if they needed it; otherwise it was returned to the community for no one could buy it or sell it.

They dealt with the land for growing other crops without irrigation in the same way as the fields provided for maize growing.

Noblemen, such as the *curacas*, lords of vassals, were given land in proportion to the number of their wives and children, concubines, and servants. Similarly Incas, those of the royal blood, received the best of everything wherever they lived, apart from their common share in the property of the king and of the Sun which they all enjoyed as children of the latter and brothers of the former.

They fertilized the soil by manuring it, and in the valley of Cuzco and almost all the highland area they treated their maize fields with human manure, which they regarded as the best. They go to great trouble to obtain it, and dry it and pulverize it in time for the sowing season. In the whole of Collao, which is more than 150 leagues long, the climate is too cold for growing maize, and they sow potatoes and other vegetables for this they use the manure of the Peruvian sheep, which they regard as more beneficial than any other.

On the seacoast, from below Arequipa to Tarapacá, a distance of over 200 leagues along the coast, they use no other manure but the dung of sea birds, of which large and small varieties occur on the coast of Peru in such enormous flocks that they seem incredible to anyone who has not seen them. They breed on some uninhabited islands off the coast, where they deposit an amount of dung that is no less incredible. From a distance the heaps of it look like the snowy crests of a range of mountains. In the times of the Inca kings these birds were so carefully watched that no one was allowed to land on the islands during the breeding season under pain of death, so that they should not be disturbed or driven from their nests. It was also illegal to kill them at any season either on the islands or elsewhere, under pain of the same penalty.

TWO
Creole Landscapes

The period of Spain's and Portugal's economic and political rule over a vast swath of the western hemisphere extends from the early sixteenth century to the first decades of the nineteenth. At that time Spain's overseas possessions—with the important exceptions of Cuba, Puerto Rico, and the Philippines—gained their independence through a series of protracted and hard-fought wars, while the Brazilians negotiated a peaceful transition to independence under the continued rule of the Portuguese royal family, the Braganzas. The latter half of the period of official Iberian domination is the chronological span with which this section is concerned.

The seventeenth and eighteenth centuries saw important economic, ecological, cultural, and political changes in the Spanish and Portuguese realms alike. The extraction of precious metals had obsessed the Iberian colonizers since Columbus's first landing at Santo Domingo, and mining remained the most important economic activity throughout the colonial period. This was especially the case in Mexico and the Andes, where extremely large and lucrative deposits of silver (Mexico, Bolivia) and gold (Colombia) were found. In the mining regions, the system known as the *mita* forced groups of Native Americans to provide labor and often tribute to the Crown and local elites at regular intervals throughout the year. In other areas the hacienda gradually replaced the encomienda as the principal institution by which the descendants of the conquistadors controlled the labor of Indigenous Americans, whose numbers continued to plummet due to the uncontrolled spread of European diseases. Whereas their forebears had once received the right to Indigenous labor directly from the Spanish Crown in exchange for the nominal commitment to evangelize "their" Indians, the local elites of the seventeenth and eighteenth centuries instead lay claim to vast expanses of rural land. This move effectively forced many of the surviving Amerindians to either migrate toward the growing cities or else become landless agricultural workers, or campesinos.

In some areas, this shift prompted local elites to pursue economic activities that required large swaths of land and relatively little labor, such as cattle ranching and sheep grazing. Elsewhere the concentration of rural lands in the hands of a few individuals and families prompted a transition from diversified agricultural production intended to supply local needs to the large-scale production of one or two cash crops for sale on the international market. In this context, the author of the 1780 *Geographical Description of Mexico*, Francisco Javier de Clavijero, marvels at the survival of floating gardens and other pre-Columbian agricultural techniques capable of supporting a population density considered extremely high by contemporary European standards. As Ibero-American elites turned to monocrop agriculture, the most important cash crops were cacao, tobacco, and above all sugar, an exceptionally lucrative product that Europeans had craved since it was first introduced from Asia in the fifteenth century. It would be difficult to exaggerate sugar's significance for the long-term trajectory of Brazil and the Caribbean islands, where it was cultivated intensively. The development of sugar plantations in areas where the Native American population had already declined catastrophically prompted local elites to turn to the transatlantic slave trade for the labor required to cultivate, harvest, and process the cane. While Black slavery had existed in the Caribbean islands since the Europeans' first arrival there, the enslaved populations of Puerto Rico and especially Cuba increased exponentially as sugar became a significant part of the island's economy. José Martín Félix de Arrate y Acosta describes the early development of Cuba's sugar industry with pride in his 1761 book *Key to the New World*. The rapacity associated with sugar was not limited to the inhuman conditions in which enslaved Blacks were forced to work, both in the fields and the infamous boiling houses. As environmental historian Shawn William Miller (2007, 79) writes, "Sugar is one of agriculture's most ravenous activities, for in addition to burning forests for fields and depleting soils of their fertility, practices typical of many crops, it also destroys forests well beyond the plantation in gathering immense quantities of firewood." Having already resulted in the deforestation of Madeira—a Portuguese possession in the North Atlantic, once so thickly forested it was given a name meaning "wood"—the sugar industry would bring about devastating ecological changes throughout the Caribbean archipelago. In contrast, the seemingly limitless supply of firewood in the Brazilian rain forest would become a source of pride in André João Antonil's *Brazil at the Dawn of the Eighteenth Century*, another selection included in this part.

Arrate and Antonil provide important examples of the new cultural identities based on a sense of connection to the land that began to develop during the seventeenth and eighteenth centuries, particularly but not exclusively among the descendants of the Iberian conquistadors. In the Spanish-speaking areas of Latin America, the word "creole" is most commonly used to identify these lighter-skinned local elites, and it is to their writings that the title of this section most obviously applies. As José Antonio Mazzotti (2000, 11) notes in his authoritative study of creole identities in colonial Latin America, a sense of pride and attachment to the bounteous land of the Americas was central to notions of criollismo beginning in the sixteenth century. In its earliest usage, "criollo" applied to Afro-descended slaves who were born in the Americas; when applied to whites, the term was initially a demeaning one intended to convey the degeneration of European stock exposed to what early modern medical science considered the unfavorable conditions of the western hemisphere. Those who identified as creoles—some of whom, not coincidentally, controlled sizable landholdings—invoked the beauty and natural fecundity of the American landscape in self-defense.

A similar dynamic would resurface in the eighteenth-century Dispute of the New World, which began with the publication of *Natural History* (1749) by one of the leading figures of the French Enlightenment, Georges-Louis Leclerc, Count Buffon. Taking as his point of departure the apparent absence, in the Americas, of the elephants, lions, and other giant beasts that populated the wild spaces of Europe and Africa, Buffon developed an elaborate set of theories regarding the alleged inferiority of New World nature. Buffon argued that the humidity of the Americas had produced a race of humans who, unlike Europeans, were too indolent to work the land and make it productive. As Antonello Gerbi (1973, 8) summarizes in *The Dispute of the New World*, "Nature in America is weak because man has not tamed it, and man has not tamed it because he in his turn is cold in love and more similar to the cold-blooded animals, closer to the watery putrescent character of the continent." (In fact, paleontologists have since determined that mammoths, *Megatherium*, and other prehistoric megafauna were likely hunted to extinction soon after the first humans arrived in the Americas.) If Buffon's theorizing touched a nerve with many educated creoles, it was a special source of irritation for the dozens of Jesuit priests who found themselves exiled to Italy or France after the order of expulsion was pronounced in 1767. The copious writings they produced in the 1770s and '80s are often drenched in nostalgia for the American landscapes of their birth, whose majesty and unparalleled fertility are underscored at every turn (332). The examples provided here are from Francisco Javier de Clavijero's *Geographical Description of Mexico* (1780) and Juan Ignacio Molina's *Geographical, Natural, and Civil History of Chile* (1782).

As historian Jorge Cañizares-Esguerra (2006b, 178–214) explains, cultivation served a spiritual function as well as an economic one in the colonial Americas, where creoles, converts, and settlers practiced various forms of "colonization as spiritual gardening" in order to eradicate the devil and poisonous snakes, spiders, and other supposedly demonic creatures from the American wilderness. Father Antonio Ruiz de Montoya, one of the founders of the vast system of Guarani missions in lands now belonging to Paraguay, Argentina, and Brazil, describes the process of settling the seminomadic Guarani in Spanish-style towns surrounded by extensive fields. The towns, known as *reducciones*, served to separate the Guarani from their traditional sacred places, while agricultural labor provided the discipline necessary for moral and spiritual improvement. At the same time, cultivation had an important role in the spiritual life of religious women in colonial Latin America, including the creole saints Rosa of Lima and Mariana of Quito, the latter also known as the Lily of Quito. Like the portraits of Mexico's famous Crowned Nuns, the hagiographies of Rosa and Mariana invoke the *hortus conclusus*, or "enclosed garden," a traditional metaphor for the Virgin Mary as well as an actual landscape feature, based on verses from the biblical Song of Solomon (4:12): "A garden locked is my sister, my bride, a garden locked, a fountain sealed."

The ramifications of these two developments—specifically the shift from subsistence agriculture to large-scale monocrop production designed for sale on the international market and the simultaneous emergence of cultural identities based on a sense of belonging to a uniquely beautiful and fecund land—would be significant during the struggles for independence and the early national period, which form the context for the selections presented in part 3.

Suggestions for Further Reading

Cristóbal de Acuña. 1641. *Nuevo descubrimiento del Gran Río de las Amazonas*, edited by Ignacio Arellano, José María Díez Borque, and Gonzalo Santonja. Madrid/Frankfurt: Iberoamericana/Vervuert / Universidad de Navarra, 2009.

Joseph Gumilla. 1741. *El Orinoco ilustrado y defendido*. Caracas: Academia Nacional de la Historia, 1963.

Rafael Landívar. 1782. *Rusticatio mexicana*, edited and translated by Raydon W. Regenos. New Orleans: Middle American Research Institute, Tulane University, 1948.

André Pierre Ledru. 1797. *Viaje a la isla de Puerto Rico en el año 1797*. Río Piedras, Puerto Rico: Ediciones del Instituto de Literatura Puertorriqueña / Universidad de Puerto Rico, 1957.

Félix de Azara. 1809. *Viajes por la América Meridional*, translated by Francisco de las Barras de Aragón. Madrid: Calpe, 1923.

Antonio Ruiz de Montoya

Following Viceroy Francisco de Toledo's 1570 order that all nonsedentary Amerindian communities in the Viceroyalty of Peru be settled, or "reduced," in mission towns to facilitate their conversion to Christianity, the Society of Jesus established some thirty *reducciones* in the region extending from eastern Bolivia to the borderlands shared by modern-day Paraguay, Argentina, and Brazil. These economically self-sufficient *reducciones* sought to preserve aspects of Indigenous culture that did not conflict with Catholic teaching, notably the Guarani language. One of the principal architects of the mission system was the Peruvian-born Jesuit Antonio Ruiz de Montoya (1585–1652); his *Spiritual Conquest of Paraguay*, as it is commonly known, is among the most important historical sources. Montoya wrote his account in Spain in 1639, having traveled there to convince the king to arm the mission Guarani against the repeated incursions of the Portuguese-speaking slave hunters known as *bandeirantes*. The Crown's acquiescence undoubtedly had as much to do with the geopolitical desirability of establishing a sizable military force to guard the Brazilian border as it did with concern for the welfare of the Guarani. Nevertheless, Montoya's account is a fascinating document of the Jesuit mind-set and practices, particularly the use of agriculture as a means of disciplining Guarani bodies and minds. The selections presented here suggest that the Jesuits understood their mandate in terms of a fundamental reorganization of the Guaranis' relationship to the natural world: from a seminomadic lifestyle based on sustainable agroforestry practices, the Guarani were "reduced" to a settled agricultural system in which cattle ranches replaced the traditional hunt and the forest was off-limits, prohibited to the Guarani as the devil's dark abode.

✳✳✳

From *The Spiritual Conquest Accomplished by the Religious of the Society of Jesus in the Provinces of Paraguay, Paraná, Uruguay, and Tapé* (1639)

TRANSLATED BY GRADY C. WRAY

Introduction

My experience is like that of the great Desert Father Aphrahat, who, in his solitude and retreat, heard the sounds of the waves that tossed the ship of the Church and the fire with which the horrendous monster Julian the Apostate threatened to destroy it.[1] Aphrahat came out of the wilderness, leaving his beloved solitude, depriving himself of the vital and celestial airs with which spiritual seeds in the desert are sown, come to life, and grow, and he entered the ruckus, restlessness, and drudgery of the cities. Despite his crude and rustic manner of speaking, he did not hesitate to enter the lofty and cultivated spaces of the royal palaces to see if he could tame the winds, smooth the waters, and extinguish the flame with which the aforementioned apostate scorched the earth. Such was the manner in which I came to this court and to the feet of His Catholic Majesty, may heaven bless him with a long life. My intention is to make peace between the Spaniards and the Indians, a difficult order in that peace has not been achieved in the more than one hundred years since the Western Indies were discovered. Many things move me to ensure this peace: Christian charity, the state of total abandonment in which the Indians find themselves, the example of my predecessors who conquered them and left rare examples to emulate, and my almost thirty years of unswerving devotion to this work. My guiding principle has been to teach them and convert them to our Holy Faith, and my desire has been crowned by work and the daily exposure to the perils of death and of being eaten by barbarians.

All this time, I have lived in the province of Paraguay, as if in the desert. I have crossed fields and traversed mountains in search of those wild beasts, the barbarous Indians, so as to increase the fold of the Holy Church and the service of His Majesty; and with the aid of my companions, we zealously established thirteen reductions, or settlements, at the cost of hunger, lack of clothing, and the unimaginable and frequent dangers that made it seem even more as if I were in the desert. Due to our efforts, the Indians, who lived previously according to their customs in the hills, fields, and mountains, where five or six houses made up each village, have already been led to large settlements, and due to the continued preaching of the Gospel, they have changed from rustic beings into Christian subjects. Going without the ways and the language of the Spanish for many years and always obliged to use the Indian language, I have become almost a rustic myself, far removed from courtly language; and it is of little help that I have been forced to eat the common foods that the Indians eat, such as roots, squash, herbs, beans, and similar things.

And now, I have been forced to leave my desert solitude and turn to the Royal Court and the feet of His Majesty due to the hostile invasion, the burning of churches, the wounding and mistreatment of priests, sacrilege, the theft of ornaments from the churches and of the meager adornments of the religious men who were preaching in eleven towns; even the banishing of the most saintly and venerable Sacrament from the altars of four churches—all this by those dwelling in São Pablo, Santos, São Vicente, and other villages made up of men whose actions forced them to flee the light of justice.[2] I have traveled on foot some two thousand leagues, through the dangers and perils of the sea, rivers, and other enemies, which is no small feat, to request the immediate resolution for the harm that threatens to cause great hindrances in His Royal Service, or to put it another and better way, that threatens to cause damage to, and risks the loss of, the Royal Crown's most precious jewel.

General Observations

So as to explicate what has been said about the past reductions and about those that I will now describe, I will offer some general observations, which are common to all reductions and settlements. It is not my intention to describe the virtues and deeds of those who operate this vineyard: those who have left their homelands, families, and comforts and who have placed themselves in foreign lands, sacrificing themselves to hunger, nakedness, and even to the sword (as we will later see), renouncing any honors they might have received among our fellow Spaniards in the form of episcopal seats, pulpits, or illustrious occupations (the bait that the falcon that soars most high will sweep down upon and take). Nor do I wish to compare the spiritual conquest to other illustrious ones; because this one completely lacks any exterior luster, rather it bears the interior luster of infinite souls . . .

[In this region] nature has showed itself very miserly, not having supplied the precious metals that abound in other locations . . . However, nature has proved generous by not troubling the natives with idols and false devotion, thus allowing for the easy embrace of Catholic truth and constant firmness in retaining it. For the price of a *cuña*, we buy their goodwill.[3] A *cuña* is a wedge of iron that weighs a pound, and it is a tool with which they live. Previously, *cuñas* were made of stone, and they would use them to cut the brush from their fields. When presented with a *cuña* (which in Spain is worth four or six farthings) an Indian cacique will come down from the mountains, hills, and hidden areas where he lives, and he and his vassals, who number around one hundred to two hundred souls when all are counted, will become part of the settlement, and, if catechized correctly, they will be baptized. Their interest is piqued with mere hooks, needles and pins, beads and trinkets.

They work very hard, and each male has his individual plot of land from the time he is eleven years old. They willingly assist one another; there is no selling or buying, because they very generously help each other with whatever their needs may be, without self-interest. They afford others who pass through their land the same generosity; therefore, all theft ceases, and they live in peace, without dispute.

Every day of the year at sunrise they hear Mass, and afterward, they turn to their labors . . .

It would be to our dishonor if for a transitory interest we exposed ourselves to the frequent risk of death that one suffers in those parts; it would be even more foolish to leave the comfort of a religious college to work among nonbelievers if in the end it were to serve mere human interest. However, no Christian with good judgment will criticize us for instructing the Indians to dedicate themselves to farming, whereby they attain something with which to cover themselves (they aspire to no greater wealth) so that nakedness may not prevent them from entering the temples (as sometimes happens) to hear the Divine Word. As shepherds of such a flock, we must oblige them to do so.

I confess it is my intention that the Indians not be used in personal service, because I seek the common good for both the Indians and the Spaniards; His Majesty lays out these reasons in His Royal Ordinance, and I will include them at the end. Nor do I aspire for them to be idle, because it would be a culpable aspiration. My desire is for them to pay His Majesty the tribute that their poverty allows, [bearing in mind that] it is with great difficulty that they support themselves and their families. If His Majesty should desire to use these tributes to reward the services of Spaniards, it would be justly done, and no one would object. Indeed, this we request, for it is good for the Spaniards to be remunerated with these tributes; but to put the Indians in their hands for personal service would only serve the sword that slits the throats of Jesus's sheep like those who go to slaughter.[4]

Notes

1. Aphrahat or Aphraates (ca. 270–345), also known as the Persian Sage, was a Syriac Christian writer who practiced an early form of communal monasticism. Montoya's information was inaccurate. Aphrahat is not generally associated with the Desert Fathers, hermits who sought solitude in the Egyptian desert. He also died some fifteen years before Julian the Apostate became emperor of Rome.

2. Montoya is referring to the infamous *bandeirantes*, Portuguese subjects, many of mixed race, who invaded Spanish territory seeking Indians to kidnap and sell into slavery. Their base of operations was São Paulo, at the time a frontier settlement.

3. Montoya refers to a wedge-shaped tool used to clear ground and break up the soil for planting. Before the Jesuits' arrival, the Guarani used *cuñas* made of stone; the metal *cuñas* provided by the Jesuits made agricultural labor easier, thus, according to Montoya, the Jesuits found them useful for establishing relations with Guarani and ultimately recruiting them for the missions.

4. As an alternative to the encomienda, Montoya proposes that the Guarani be settled under Jesuit authority on missions, where their labor will generate profits that can subsequently be directed to the local Spaniards.

Saint Rosa of Lima

Saint Rosa of Lima (1586–1617) was the first Roman Catholic saint to have been born in the Americas. She was famous for her piety in her native city during her lifetime and acquired widespread veneration soon after her death. Like her role model, Saint Catherine of Siena, Rosa was a tertiary of the Dominican order, living at home as a mystical bride of Christ rather than entering a convent. But it is her resemblance to another famous Italian saint, Francis of Assisi, that primarily interests us here: like Saint Francis, Rosa had an extraordinary connection to nonhuman nature throughout her life. Baptized as Isabel Flores de Oliva, she loved to make puns with her surnames, Flores, or "flowers," and Oliva, "olive," and took the religious name of Rosa de María because one of the family's servants claimed to have seen the image of a rose imposed on baby Isabelita's face. Roses, long associated with the Virgin Mary, were transplanted from Europe to the Americas, and their appearance was often taken as a sign of God's favor to the hearty souls who embraced the faith in a wild and dangerous land. (In Mexico, the Virgin of Guadalupe instructed the Indian Juan Diego to gather *rosas de Castilla* in order to prove her favor to a skeptical Spanish bishop.) The excerpts presented here, from a nineteenth-century document based on the 1671 bull of canonization, show Rosa communing with God's creatures in the private hermitage she built in the family garden. Like Saint Francis, whose "Canticle of the Sun" exhorts "Brother Sun," "Sister Moon" and "all the creatures" to praise their creator (Santmire 1985, 106–120), Rosa sings praise-songs in concert with birds and even mosquitoes.

✳✳✳

From *The True Life of Saint Rosa of Lima, Patron Saint of America, the Philippines, and the Indies*

TRANSLATED BY PAUL J. KAVENEY

In order to imitate the contemplative withdrawal from the world of the holy Anchorites who dwelt with Our Lord Jesus Christ in the solitude of the desert, when she was a very young girl, Rosa fled from childish games and withdrew to the most secluded parts of the house to be all alone there, hidden with her God. When she was just a little bit older, she constructed for herself a small oratory and a little altar fashioned out of the shade-casting branches of the trees in her garden. No sooner would she rise from the table or her bed than she would run to the oratory as the place of her spiritual recollection and prayer. It was a common saying in her family that "If you're looking for Rosita, try out in the garden." She would pass the nights alone in her bedroom in prayer. She avoided leaving the house to pay visits, visits that so overly upset her that she would injure her foot with a stone or rub garlic into her eyes—how much better it seemed to her than to gaze upon the vanities of the world! Always desiring more solitude and seclusion, she struggled and worked hard to obtain it. Finally, after that wondrous revelation of the Mother of God and the baby Jesus in the Chapel of the Rosary, she obtained permission from her mother to construct in the most secluded part of the garden a small cell, five feet long by four feet wide, to be able to immerse herself in handiwork, but mostly in spiritual recollection and contemplation, rejoicing that there was no room for anyone other than herself and her Bridegroom. In that happy hermitage she would prepare still greater ascensions in her heart and, having risen above where she knelt, she seemed to live more outside her body than in it. (Around this time, a matron of well-known piety had a vision of Rosa, who appeared to her in the form of a star; this was indeed sensible and fitting that Lima, called the City of Three Kings, should have its own star to guide them to the King of Kings, Christ Our Lord.) By special divine dispensation, Rosa heard and saw many masses that were being celebrated far from her place of meditation, as if she were physically present. Many mosquitoes made their way into this small hermitage, but not one ever bit or even touched Rosa, even though they would furiously attack any other religious persons who went there. She taught these small creatures to sing divine praises in their own way and led them in song in such an admirable manner that it seemed Rosa had achieved a dominion reserved for an innocent and primitive state, living in that solitude as if it were Paradise. Whenever she was alone in this humble shack or believed no one to be listening, with a voice most sweet and strong she would break out in solemn praise of angelic love both in conversation and in song (sometimes in prose, sometimes in verse), with such fervor and zeal that, unbeknownst to her, it made the hearts of those listening ring with sentiments of love and repentance. She commissioned a series of short devotional prayers that, like so many other arrows taken from the same quiver of divine love, greatly pleased and were of benefit to those who read and used them. She lovingly importuned the true God, her soul's Bridegroom and her heart's joy, with these prayers; and to the most benevolent Jesus she wholeheartedly and fervently declared that, in her single person, she herself loved and venerated Him with a most perfect love with which all those blessed in Heaven loved Him . . .

On a certain day at nine o'clock in the morning, she was roused to divine contemplation by a little bird's song. She then fell into ecstasy from which she did not regain consciousness until afternoon. With much effort she managed to attract her fellow man to the exercise of prayer, principally mental in nature. She insistently begged her confessors to persuade the penitent to practice it in any form possible, even exhorting those same preachers to inflame their listeners' appreciation and esteem of this holy exercise as a great panacea for all sins, and to spread the practice of pious meditation throughout the town. She was particularly fond of reciting the Marian Rosary as established by Saint Dominic; that is, with consideration for the Mysteries every decade, for in the rosary are united the passion of mental and vocal prayer, petitions, praises, and thanksgiving. Indeed, Rosa's enthusiasm and advice were of great benefit to many souls.

Every afternoon during the Lenten season preceding her death, Rosa would sing canticles and praises to God for an entire hour, alternating with a certain little bird that admirably trilled while flying in circles in front of her hermitage until sunset. The two would do this with such order and in such concert that when the little bird trilled, the virgin became quiet; when she sang in turn, the little bird remained listening in such attentive silence that it did not even peep. In a wholly exceptional case, she even incited the very plants to pray and praise God, repeating the verse, "O all ye things that spring up in the Earth, bless the Lord . . ." At these words the trees visibly leaned down until they touched the ground with their canopies, as if adoring their Creator in a deeply reverential act. It is so true that one who lives intimately in union with the Lord is of the same spirit as He—all things will even obey that person! . . .

It was the constant opinion of all persons in Lima who at that time enjoyed a reputation of saintliness and perfection that all Rosa's actions and movements were impelled by the Holy Spirit like a true daughter of God. Everyone agreed that she was fully gifted with wisdom and governed by a knowledge instilled from Heaven. Indeed, when scholars of scripture posed the most difficult theological questions, she could expound with the most sublime judgment, profound declarations, and in precise terms upon the mystery of the Holy Trinity, the hypostatic union of the divine Word, the Holy Sacrament of the altar, the profound secret of predestination, the nature of grace, and other theological matters. With our divine Savior, everyone praised the Almighty Father, Lord of the heavens and of the earth, for revealing such grand things to the meekest, most innocent and humble while hiding them from wise and prudent men.

This virgin lived more in the heavens than on earth. Wherever she found the name "Jesus" written, she would stop for a moment, feeling her heart aflame with a fire of love. On many an occasion, Jesus himself, gazing upon her with gentle and affectionate eyes, would appear on the flat surface she had read as a Word or Verb, in which are enclosed all the treasures of God's wisdom and knowledge, utterly worthy of being read by a soul such as hers. While Rosa was engaged in doing her handiwork, Jesus would come to sit gently on the cushion of her workbox, and by means of signs spoke to this loved one's heart, professing His divine love in all His movements and actions. Frequently—almost daily—Rosa's saintly soul enjoyed these types of gifts, and whenever her Bridegroom delayed, she lamented in tender cries and groans until He arrived. In her games with that divine Child, whose throat possesses a sweetness impossible to describe, when she would win their game, she felt herself at that moment cured from the sore throat she suffered; but, whenever she lost, the soreness would return along with the patience to endure it. While obediently relating this wonder to her mother, rays of light would shoot from her face as if she were an angel. Once, finding herself near death, without strength, and bereft of all human aid, that same one who knows when to assist at the most opportune moment in times of tribulation appeared. Benevolently moving her closer to the fragrant flagon of his pierced side, He made her drink from the life-giving water from the fountains of the Savior, with which the infirm girl instantly regained her health. Certain innocent girls saw her accompanied by the boy Jesus, and that sometimes she would stroll with Him, conversing in the most secret of exchanges. Being that the boy's manner of walking was so grave and majestic, it was apparent who He was, and rays of light leapt from wherever He planted the soles of His feet. So that Rosa would not become too attached to any other plant, but rather to Him (who is the Flower of the Field and Lily of the Valley), it happened that a basil plant—also called the royal plant—which the virgin girl painstakingly cultivated in order to offer it to the King of the Ages upon her altar, was found dried out and uprooted one day. As she lamented over it with great distress and feeling, Jesus Christ Himself appeared to her and told her that He had uprooted and hurled aside that plant with His own hands, for He alone desired to be her true basil plant.

With these manifestations the Lord confirmed the truth of what He had told a certain person in a moment of ecstasy; that is, that He carried Rosa in the most intimate part of His divine heart because He knew that His love was requited. He alone possessed with complete tranquility the precious heart of the young virgin girl.

Saint Mariana of Quito

The Lily of Quito, Mariana de Jesús (1618–45) was the daughter of wealthy Spaniards settled in what is now the capital of Ecuador. They died young, and Mariana was subsequently raised in the home of her elder sister and brother-in-law. She lived as a *beata*, an uncloistered holy woman, under the spiritual guidance of a Jesuit confessor. Like Isabel Flores de Oliva, later Saint Rosa of Lima, Mariana practiced strict corporeal discipline: in addition to vows of perpetual chastity, she subjected herself to fasting, self-flagellation, and sleep deprivation. Also like Rosa, Mariana's close connection to nature was seen as a sign of God's favor, as when lilies sprang from the soil where a servant poured blood extracted from her veins in an act of penance. The selection presented here is from *The Life of Saint Mariana de Jesús*, written in 1697 by the Ecuadoran Jesuit Jacinto Morán de Butrón and published roughly thirty years later in Madrid. Butrón hoped that Mariana's canonization would add to Ecuador's spiritual luster, much as Rosa's had done for Lima and Peru; Mariana, however, would not be recognized as a saint until 1950. In the following fragment, a very young Mariana sets out with her nieces to begin life as hermits guarding the shrine of the Virgin Mary at Mount Pichincha, a volcano that perpetually threatened Quito. They are prevented by the arrival of a divine emissary. When the volcano's imminent eruption, together with the spread of cholera and diphtheria, threatened to destroy Quito a few years later, Mariana publicly offered her life in exchange for the city's deliverance. She fell ill that same day, as the telluric activity ceased and plagues lessened, and she died soon after.

***

"She Flees to the Desert and God Sends Her Back Home" (1697)

Father Jacinto Morán de Butrón

TRANSLATED BY PAUL J. KAVENEY

The populous city of Quito is founded on the slopes of the famous Mount Pichincha. Although it fertilizes the lushness of its fields and provides the necessary plentiful waters for its fountains, attentively serving the city in the care and cleanliness of its streets with the many streams that it pays as tribute, it is the bow that God fixed in His heavens in order to fling His arrows of justice . . .

This volcano erupted in the year 1580, causing general destruction throughout the whole province. Although it quieted its fury for eighty years, it erupted again on the 27th of October, 1660, a day that, as not passed and dead, shall live on perpetually in memory as long as this vile stepfather-like and perfidious mount lasts. It was a Wednesday between seven and eight o'clock in the morning when, declaring war on the city, this prideful monster shot off its artillery, vomiting stones, tar, and sulfur in such quantity that it would have been more than enough to ruin this province had divine mercy not tempered justice. Divine intervention spared the city by having the stones and infernal vomit fall in the direction of the sea, so that it served—like Jonah's admonitions to Nineveh—merely as a threat and not a punishment. The sky became dreadfully dark with night lasting nearly twenty-four hours. Small stones fell like bullets, and so much sand and ash fell like scattershot that, besides sermonizing to mortals about the dust from which they are formed, the sheer quantity of it shocked them into believing it could end up being their wretched tomb . . . The most indomitable beasts came down fleeing from the mountains to the plazas, and forgetting their brutal, ill tempers against men, sought their friendship as if they were tamed, giving an example to rational people to cast aside animosity and enmities . . .

The first eruption of this volcano, then—which was in 1580, as I said—left this city and its environs so fearful that, just as God placed an armed cherub in Paradise, the Most Illustrious Municipal Council determined to place on guard an image of Mary, supreme empress of the heavens, which exquisite artistry managed to extract from a composition of crude stone. They took the image to the deformed mouth of Pichincha, five leagues' distance removed from the city, and climbing a most rugged slope, there placed Mary's holy likeness and divine semblance, so that as master over Almighty God (in the form of the boy Jesus in her arms), she could guard against His wrath. An appropriate means, certainly, when it is this lady's office to bring the earth to order and its movements in just concert.

For some years the visits that the nearby residents paid were frequent. With time, however—that clothes moth that consumes even what is deemed inexhaustible—the ingrates forgot to venerate Mary's statue. They left their protector so without adornments, so without respects and reverence, that the only ones to visit her were those engaged in the hunt, giving chase to the deer of that mountain. A perpetual affront testifying to Quito's ingratitude! And perhaps they would have left her forgotten until now had the most devout Recollects of Saint James not taken this image of Mary and placed it in the best part of their temple like a precious relic, wherein they reverently keep her adorned in a clean tabernacle and very frequently celebrate the sacraments to her. Their chapel is embellished with ex-votos in which are expressed the miracles repeatedly worked by her patronage.

Before these most religious Recollects of Saint James took this rich treasure hidden in the countryside down to their church, the Venerable virgin Mariana heard tell of the supreme Mary's neglected state caused by culpable idleness and half-hearted devotion. She felt the insult to the utmost and slowly meditated on what she should do if she prided herself on being a true servant. It even seemed that the dispute was raised against her personally if she did not manage to remedy the offense with her efforts! And so she determined to set out in person to mend such an enormous failing. Although she initially resolved to leave alone and as a fugitive, she changed her mind and judged it more appropriate to communicate this decision to her nieces and friend Doña Escolástica Sarmiento to see if she found companions in her plan. She proposed to them her intent to go and serve most Holy Mary on Mount Pichincha and the aptness of the site as a place to submit to austerity and penitence, since its solitude enticed her to surrender wholly to contemplation. She explained that Mary was a magnet drawing her to choose that place as the center of her desires; besides fulfilling her duty as a slave, she would there enjoy the affections of her Bridegroom. This she told them more with the hope that they would offer to accompany her as companions than to inform or consult them. And although they all promised to follow her they did not fail to raise doubts about the soundness of her decision (all by then being of age and legal competence) . . . The plan seemed good to them all, and . . . they arranged to set out on their journey when the first opportunity presented itself.

Doña Jerónima de Paredes—who, being Mariana's eldest sister, presided over the house like a mother—stepped out on a necessary visit; the occasion struck Mariana as perfect. She called together her companions and, with the few valuables that her fervor deemed necessary for the desert, encouraged them to take flight. It was three o'clock in the afternoon and in the absence of their sister—for she alone could reprimand them—the four of them left. Disguised in their outfits, faces covered out of modesty and dissimulation, they quickened their step, having nothing more to orient them than the star of Mary, nor more course than what the Anchorites had in the deserts. They ascended through the city's quarry toward the place called La Chorrera and, leaving the populated area, went up more than half a league of most rugged incline, their feet serving as wings flying them to solitude. The Bridegroom from the Song of Songs could not have had a more delightful afternoon than to see his spouse ascend through the verdant lushness of Pichincha, since He saw in its hills his Lily: *Lilium convallium*! Overjoyed, they celebrated the success of their escape, but, in short, their joy was spoiled by an unexpected event, for there exist chance occurrences that sound like mysteries. Upon reaching a small meadow by means of a steep slope and having passed a ditch, a bull came out onto the path to meet them. Furious, it charged at them in such a fast sprint that they had to hurl themselves into the ditch to escape its wrath. The beast pawed at the earth as if to threaten them and stood there in their path, making further travel impossible. Hidden in the ditch, each time they tried to look for another path, the bull startled and followed them. The Venerable virgin Mariana was deeply afflicted and made the powerful sign of the cross repeatedly, fearing it to be the devil impeding their progress to prevent the triumphs she was to wage against him in the desert. But seeing that the bull would not stop threatening, she recollected herself inwardly to consult with her Bridegroom, whether this was divine mystery or chance. After a short time during which it is judged that God enlightened her understanding with supreme light, making clear by supernatural inspiration that it was not His will that she live a hermitic life in the desert, but rather that of a recollect virgin at home, she told her companions with unexpected resolve, "Sisters, my Bridegroom's bidding is not that we go to Pichincha, but rather that we return home at once. Our love of God and Mary brought us here; now let us be carried back by that same love." Lo, a remarkable occurrence! Upon the Venerable virgin Mariana saying these words, the bull, which shortly before followed their every movement furiously, went away so docile without a single beastly gesture, and they quickly lost sight of it. I do not know what can be said of that strange bull in that place, for it was so close to the city where such ferocity is unusual. I can only say that I have not known bulls knowing how to oversee judgment correctly fulfilled as this one did, knowing how to steer the steps of the path God intended for Mariana. The novitiate Anchorites returned but, as much as they hurried their steps, they could not conceal their departure. The Venerable virgin Mariana's sister and brother-in-law felt her decision to be dangerous to the utmost degree, much more so that their daughters were involved in Mariana's scheme. And although they could forgive the pious motive for fleeing, they reprimanded Mariana and her nieces with affected anger and severity, deciding to apply to Mariana, who was only twelve years old, as source of those pious and holy schemes, the final and efficient remedy.

André João Antonil

Brazil at the Dawn of the Eighteenth Century, written by the Italian Jesuit Giovanni Antonio Andreoni (1649–1716) under the Portuguese pseudonym André João Antonil, is an authoritative account of the economic underpinnings of colonial Brazilian society at the turn of the eighteenth century. Born in Tuscany, Antonil studied law before joining the Jesuit order in 1667. In 1681 he set out for Brazil in the company of Father António Vieira, who would become one of the most famous and influential Jesuit missionaries in South America. Antonil spent the rest of his life in Bahia; thus while his information on the sugar industry was gathered firsthand, the descriptions of recently discovered gold mines to the south came from informants. Antonil's discussion of the mines is so detailed that after initially allowing publication in 1711, Portuguese authorities quickly banned the book, originally titled *Cultura e Opulência do Brasil*, and confiscated existing copies to avoid compromising the security of a lucrative industry (Coates 2012, xiii). In Antonil's account, the "opulence" of the burgeoning mining industry threatens the "culture" of the established planter aristocracy that produced sugar, tobacco, and cattle; thus his conclusion asks the Crown to intervene by lowering the cost of food and slaves on behalf of the planters. The excerpts presented here describe the environmental requirements of the sugar industry, emphasizing the idea that Brazil's vast wooded interior will supply a limitless quantity of firewood for the mills' furnaces, in implicit contrast to the Caribbean islands, which were quickly stripped bare. At the same time, Antonil imposes a perverse moral economy according to which the slaves are punished for their supposed sins, while the long-suffering cane must be protected from its enemies.

$$* * *$$

From *Brazil at the Dawn of the Eighteenth Century* (1711)

TRANSLATED BY TIMOTHY COATES

Book Two

Chapter I. The Choice of Land on Which to Plant the Cane, and for Supplying Provisions Needed for the Mill

Whether the lands are good or bad determines if a royal mill will yield a profit or a loss. Those lands which are called *massapés*—black, thick earth—are the best for planting cane. Next come the *saloens*, red earth capable of only a few years of cuttings, for it is soon exhausted. The *areiscas*, which are a mixture of sand and *saloens*, are useful for growing cassava and vegetables, but not for cane. I would say the same about the white earth called Lands of Sand, like those of Camamú and of Saubâra.

The land chosen for pasture around the mill must have water and must be fenced, either with live plants, such as pines, or with stockades and rods cut from the bush. The best pasture has a lot of grass, partly on the high ground and partly on the low ground. In this way, at all times of the year, the oxen and the other beasts will find something to eat, either in the one part or in the other. The pasture must be kept clear of all the other plants that kill the grass. In the winter, the pigs must be kept out of it because otherwise they root it all up. There should be one or two stockyards in it where the oxen can be put to eat the sprouts of the cane, and to be on hand to use with the carts. Likewise the other beasts should be in their respective runs, so that it will not be necessary to search high and low for them.

Besides mares and oxen, the sheep and the goats should also be kept in the pastures. The smaller animals, such as turkeys, hens, and ducks, should be kept around the mill, as they are the easiest to slaughter for meals for unexpected guests. Since sheep and horses graze very close to the root of the grass, they are prejudicial to the pasture of the oxen. For this reason it would be better for them to be pastured separately, if possible.

The woods will supply the timber and the firewood for the ovens. The marshy ground in which mangrove trees grow will yield timbers for roofs and shellfish. The *apicus* will yield the clay to refine the sugar in the molds and for the pottery. In the opinion of some people, the manufacture of pottery cannot be omitted from the royal mills.

A royal mill needs all these different kinds of lands. Some serve for cane, others for growing food for the people, and others for the building and equipment of the mill, apart from the materials imported from the Kingdom of Portugal. However, not all the mills can enjoy such good fortune; on the contrary, there is not one lacking some of these things . . . All in all, it depends on whether the plantation owner has or lacks capital, people, faithful and experienced employees, oxen and animals, boats and carts, whether his plantation is well or poorly managed. If he does not have people to work and cultivate the lands at the proper time, then this will be the same as owning an uncleared forest with little or no profit. Just as in civilized life, it is not enough to have a good nature if one does not have a master who, with his instruction, helps one to improve.

Chapter III. Enemies of the Cane in the Field

Variations in the weather are the principal enemy of the cane, as is also the case with other fruits and crops of the earth. With much reason, God armed the elements against us in punishment for our sins. Perhaps it was so we would learn patience, or that we would remember that He is the author and the preserver of all things, and that we should have recourse to Him in such crises.

The fields on the hillsides are better able to resist successive rains, but they are the first to suffer from drought. On the other hand, the flat lands do not respond so quickly to the force of excessive heat, but they suffer sooner from excessive rains. The cane of Bahia requires rain in the months of October, November, and December, and for the new plants in February. It also later needs the sun, which usually does not fail, just as the rains do not fail in those months. However, the most dangerous, continual, and most familiar enemy of the cane is the wild grass. It persecutes the cane more or less throughout its life. While the cane must be planted and cut at certain seasons, weeding it is a continual necessity that obliges the planter's slaves to go about always with a hoe in hand. Whenever any other occupation outside the cane fields is finished, then time is never wasted in ordering them to weed. This is an exercise that should be a constant with those who bring up their children properly and take care to cultivate the soul. Even though this enemy, the wild grass, suffices for many, there is no lack of equally troublesome and dangerous others. As soon as the cane begins to sprout above the earth, the goats immediately try to attack it. The oxen and the horses begin by eating the shoots, and they afterward tear down and trample the cane. The rats and the pigs root it out. Thieves steal it in sheaves, and no lad or wayfarer passes by who does not want to eat and toy with it, at the cost of whoever planted it. Although the farmers resign themselves somehow to enduring the petty thefts of the fruits of their labor, they are sometimes compelled in a righteous anger to kill pigs, goats, and oxen that their owners did not trouble to keep in fenced pastures or more distant places. This was even when they have been begged to do so and warned to put a stop to this damage. This in turn gives way to complaints, enmities, and hatreds, which end in deaths or with bloody and insulting deeds of vengeance. For this reason, everyone should try to protect his own cane fields and avoid giving others any cause for making justifiable complaints against his own carelessness.

Chapter VIII. Furnaces, Their Equipment, the Required Firewood, and the Ash Used for Leaching

Next to the milling house, which is also called the building for the mill, is the building for the furnaces. These are actually consuming mouths that inhale wood from the countryside, black holes of perpetual fire and smoke giving lively images of the volcanoes of Mounts Vesuvius and Etna. One might almost say the furnace looks like Purgatory or Hell. Near the furnaces there are those condemned to work them, which are the slaves with yaws and those with an imbalance in their humors that ties them to this tiring work in order to purge themselves by their prodigious sweat of the acidic humors filling their bodies. Other slaves can be seen there, the wicked and perverse, locked in long and heavy iron chains in this demanding work. They pay for their wicked excesses with little or no hope of mending their ways.

On the royal mills, there are usually six furnaces and numerous additional assisting slaves called firewood stokers. The openings for the furnaces are ringed with iron. This is not only to give more support for the bricks but also to prevent the stokers from causing an accident when they feed the fire. At its mouth, each furnace has two holes that are vents allowing the fire to puff and blow. The pillars between them have to be very strong, made of brick and baked lime, but the body of the furnace is made from bricks with clay to better resist the intense heat of the fire. Neither baked lime nor hard stone will do this. The cauldrons are a bit larger than the kettles. The source for the fire is wood. Only Brazil, with its vast stretches of countryside, can supply the needs of so many furnaces. It has done this for many years and will do so for many more in the future. How many furnaces there are on the mills of Bahia, Pernambuco, and Rio de Janeiro that operate day and night, six, seven, eight, and nine months of the year! To understand how abundant this countryside is, just the region around Jaguaripe provides sufficient firewood for the many mills along the coast of the Recôncavo of Bahia. In reality, it supplies almost all those in that region. They begin to cut firewood in Jaguaripe in July because the mills in Bahia start milling in August.

Georges-Louis Leclerc, Count Buffon

Distinguished by graceful prose, detailed illustrations, and an observation-based mode of analysis, the 1749 *Natural History* produced by Georges-Louis Leclerc, Count Buffon (1707–88) was one of the most widely read texts in what would become an explosion of natural histories published in eighteenth-century Europe. Leclerc served as director of the Royal Botanical Gardens in Paris from 1739 until his death. There he assembled a large collection of preserved animal specimens that formed the basis for the observations in the *Natural History*. Collaborators around the world sent these specimens to Buffon along with descriptions of the animals' behavior and ethnographic details about how local Indigenous communities understood and interacted with them. Much of this would be incorporated into the *Natural History*. Buffon's discussions of the physiology and behavior of particular species are held together by his controversial theory of the inferiority of New World nature, which is based on the idea that the origin of natural diversity is the degradation of ideal types due to adverse environmental conditions. According to Aristotle's *History of Animals*, which ranks organisms according to their perceived proximity to the Greek ideal of the human male, large land mammals were thought to fall directly below humans. That hierarchy would be replicated in Buffon's *Natural History*, where the Americas' lack of megafauna like that of Eurasia and Africa—rhinoceroses, lions, elephants, and so forth—is taken as a symptom of New World nature's relative unsuitability to these "higher" life-forms. The selections presented here demonstrate some of the charm of Buffon's writing but also his alarming inclination to naturalize racist assumptions about the peoples and cultures of the New World.

***

From *Buffon's Natural History, Abridged* (1749–1788)

ANONYMOUS TRANSLATION

The Jaguar

The jaguar resembles the snow leopard in size, and for the most part in the form of the spots with which his skin is decorated. In disposition he also resembles him. He is less terrible, less ferocious, than the panther and the leopard. The ground of his color, like that of the latter, is a bright yellow, and not grey, like that of the snow leopard. His tail is shorter than that of either of those animals; his hair is longer than the panther's, but shorter than that of the snow leopard; it is frizzled while he is young, but smooth and straight when he attains his full growth.

The jaguar lives by prey like the tiger; but a lighted torch will put him to flight, will deprive him of all courage, all vivacity; and on such occasions, especially if already satiated, one dog alone is sufficient to give him chase. He seems in all respects to partake of the indolence arising from the nature of the climate; nor does he discover any activity or alertness, unless when pressed by hunger.

Almost all the authors who have written the history of the New World, have made mention of this animal; some under the name of *tiger*, or *leopard*, others under the names which it bears [in] Brazil, Mexico, and so forth. They also speak of another animal of the same genus, and perhaps indeed of the same species, under the name of *ocelot*.

The jaguar is found in Brazil, in Paraguay, in Tucuman, in Guiana, in the country of the Amazons, in Mexico, and in all parts of South America.

The Coati

The animal of which we are now about to treat, many authors have called *coatimondi* . . . It is of a smaller size than the raccoon; its body and neck, its head and nose are of a more lengthened form; its upper jaw is an inch, or an inch and a half, longer than the lower one; and its snout, which is moveable in every direction, turns up at the point. The eyes of the coati are also smaller than the eyes of the raccoon; its hair is longer and coarser, its legs are shorter, and its feet longer; but, like the raccoon, its tail is decorated with rings; and on each of its feet there are five claws.

This animal has a practice of eating its own tail, which when not mutilated, is longer than its body. The coati generally carries its tail aloft; it can be moved with ease in any direction. From this circumstance one general inference may be drawn; namely, that in those parts which are elongated to a great degree, and of which the extremities are consequently very remote from the seat of the senses and the center of feeling, that feeling must be weak, and the more so, the greater the distance, and the smaller the part.

In other respects, the coati is an animal of prey that subsists on flesh and blood. Like the fox, it destroys small animals and poultry, hunts for the nests of little birds, and devours their eggs. It is probably due to these similarities that some authors have considered the coati as a species of small fox. It inhabits Brazil and Guiana.

The Llama

The llama is about four feet high; its body, comprehending the neck and head, is five or six feet long; its neck alone is near three feet. The head is small and well proportioned, the eyes large, and nose somewhat long, the lips thick . . . The ears are four inches long, and move with great agility. The tail is seldom above eight inches long, small, straight, and a little turned up at the end. It is cloven-footed, like the ox; but the hoof has a kind of spear-like appendage behind, which assists the animal to move and support itself over precipices and rugged ways. The back is clothed with short wool, as is the crupper and tail; but it is very long on the belly and sides. These animals differ in color; some are white, others black, but most of them brown.

These useful, and even necessary animals, are kept at no expense to their masters; for, as they are cloven-footed, they do not require to be shod, nor do they require to be housed, as their wool supplies them with a warm covering. Satisfied with a small portion of vegetables and grass, they want neither corn nor hay for food; they are still more moderate in what they drink, as their mouths are continually moistened with saliva, which they have in a greater quantity than any other animals. The natives hunt the *guanaco*, or wild llama, for the sake of its fleece. The dogs have much trouble to follow them; and, if they do not come up with them before they gain the rocks, both hunters and dogs are obliged to desist in their pursuit.

The pacos are a subordinate kind to the llamas, much in the same proportion as the ass is to the horse: they are smaller, and not so serviceable; but their fleece is more useful: their wool is fine and long, and as merchandise is as valuable as silk. The natural colour of the pacos is that of a dried rose-leaf, which is so fixed, that it undergoes no alternation at the hands of the manufacturer. They not only make good gloves and stockings of this wool, but also form it into quilts and carpets, which bring a higher price than those of the Levant.

The pacos also resemble the llamas in their form, excepting that their legs are shorter, and their muzzles thicker and closer. They inhabit and climb over the highest parts of the mountains. The snow and ice seem rather agreeable than inconvenient to them. When wild, they keep together in flocks, and run very swiftly; and, so soon as they perceive a stranger, they take flight, driving their young before them. The ancient monarchs of Peru rigorously prohibited the hunting of them, as they multiply but slowly; but since the arrival of the Spaniards in these parts, their number is greatly decreased, so that at present there are very few remaining. The flesh of these animals is not so good as that of the *guanacos*; and they are only sought after for their fleece, and the bezoar they produce. The method of taking them, proves their extreme timidity, or rather their weakness. The hunters drive the flock into a narrow passage, across which they have stretched a rope about four feet from the ground, with a number of pieces of linen or cloth hanging on it. The animals are so intimidated by these rags agitated by the wind, that they stop, and, crowd together in a heap, which allows the hunters to kill great numbers of them with the greatest ease. If there are any *guanacos* among the flock, these less timid creatures, they leap over the rope with great agility. The example is immediately followed by the whole flock, and they escape the stratagem of their pursuers.

José Martín Félix de Arrate y Acosta

Born into one of Cuba's aristocratic creole families, José Martín Félix de Arrate y Acosta (1701–65) served for many years as Havana's regidor, the city councilman appointed by the king and entrusted with veto power that he could exercise in the sovereign's name. The historical record suggests that Arrate was a dedicated public servant, committed to ensuring the prosperity, cleanliness, and reputation of the city. This is nowhere more apparent than in the pages of *Key to the New World*, one of the earliest histories of Cuba. Although the book was not published until the nineteenth century, it circulated in manuscript copies and left a visible influence on subsequent writers. Like a number of other authors represented in this section, Arrate was moved to defend his home from European aspersions: in this case the offender was Manuel Martí, dean of Alicante, who criticized the cultural and intellectual achievements of Americans in a widely read letter to a student considering emigration. Arrate's response, all things considered, is relatively placid. Taking his title from a 1634 royal decree designating Havana "the Key to the New World," Arrate underscores the hospitality of his fellow creoles and the pulchritude of the island's racially diverse population, which he attributes to the salubrious climate and landscape. He extols the natural beauty and fecundity of the island, where the landscape is greatly improved by agriculture and the construction of country homes for the planter aristocracy. The leisurely lifestyle Arrate describes is made possible by the island's slave economy and the monocrop production of sugarcane, which produced roughly five million pounds of sugar annually in the mid-eighteenth century.

***

"On the Goodness and Excellence of the Open Spaces of This City and the Entertainment and Recreation Outings That One Enjoys" (1761)

TRANSLATION BY GRADY C. WRAY

Because the celebrity of distinguished cities is so enhanced by the beauty, fertility, and number of their open spaces, the descriptions of these areas are widely renowned. In the Kingdom of Spain, Valencia, Granada, and Murcia serve as examples of this truth, as their lovely orchards and delightful meadows are much celebrated. Therefore, I must believe that I am not at fault when I expound upon what the beauty and fecundity of this island have in common with them. Nor am I remiss in particularly describing this country's uncommon excellences. It is singularly praised by the many people with good sense and taste who pass through it; even more so when some serious and disinterested authors describe and celebrate its special ornateness and grandeur, the attractiveness of its groves, the agreeableness of its sites, the fertility of its fruit trees, and other good qualities of the surrounding lands. The authority of so many pens tells us that even in the past, when the farms and gardens were cultivated less efficiently than they are today, the countryside was nevertheless pleasing to see. Today they have improved incomparably due to the better care and disposition that the gardeners and hacienda owners have dedicated to this culture.

I am persuaded that some of the most truthful information on this matter will come across as poetic fiction because there are some so incredulous as to deny credence to anything they cannot see and credit only what appears to their own eyes. Although they may be skeptical of me I cannot avoid, not even at such a cost, expressing something about the beauty and fecundity of our fields.

Generally, these fields are spread among a variety of lively plains and beautiful hills that are not always prominent, but because they are constantly green and with such a perpetual pleasantness, one cannot differentiate summer from autumn or winter because summer's oppressive heat does not cause the fields to wither and wilt nor do winter's freezes make them sterile. To the contrary, winter makes flowers fall like snow instead of frost upon the fields, and summer enriches them with grains and fruits that produce such an abundance of everything that, even among the rustic trees and in the most uncultivated mountains, those who are lost or wandering in the forests cannot perish due to lack of sustenance, as Father Florencia wrote without exaggeration. He could add, with equal truthfulness, that they would not perish even due to lack of drink, because there are vines like Herrera mentions, which provide water not only to cool down but also to quench thirst.

It is rare for our lands to experience thirst because, with the exception of the Chorrera River, they do not have any other fast-flowing river in the vicinity that waters and fertilizes them. The abundance, frequency, and benefits of rainfall make up for what the lands lack and impart freshness and fecundity that they enjoy, regularly preserving many water sources in the streams and ravines that are formed in the crevices of the earth and provide nectar and moisture even in times of drought.

As to the natural elegance, beauty, and pomp of their appearance, many country homes adorn and grace this territory. They range from rustic constructions to fine civil architecture, and they are at well-proportioned distances, situated on the flatlands and on the riverbanks with a pleasing appearance that delights and amuses those who pass by on their way.

All the surrounding lands, whether from the eastern strip or the western and southern part, are so traveled today that even carts and buggies make their transit across them comfortably and easily. They go to the haciendas of the region and hardly ever find a forested hill or wild terrain for five or six leagues in every direction.

In neighboring districts, there are more than two thousand working estates and near eighty sugar mills. These mills annually produce more than fifty thousand quintals of sugar,[1] which is of much better quality than what foreigners are able to cut and purify through various refining processes. There are many others that make syrup at quite a considerable cost in this city, and there is no lack of places for the preparation of tobacco, tile factories, limekilns, and coal-burning ovens. In the most mountainous parts of the region, there are tanneries for tanning hides from which there is a great benefit. There are more than 2,000 head of large cattle divided among 216 herds, and 245 lesser lots that produce enough meat for the population. Breeding is very prolific, and the last herds have not been affected by the worm epidemic that spread over many areas and caused much damage. Had it not been for the epidemic, the expansion of these ranches would have been incomparable, but there has not been much damage, thanks to God's goodness . . .

All I have said about the productivity of our lands and the cultivation that they have today is confirmed by the growing amount of harvested fruits, which provide one-tenth of the income of the haciendas in this district. According to the sales made by the lessees in the last four-year period, they reached a sum of 63,698 pesetas and 2 reales annually, a quantity that is distributed in parts and portions to different destinations . . .

Though our city may not offer the celebrated outings available in the more opulent cities of other regions, with their ornate public spaces and beautiful tree-lined streets full of fountains and other artistic delights, I will nevertheless end this chapter by mentioning some of the outings that this city offers for the recreation of those who dwell herein as they take their ease and enjoy themselves . . . Even without including the bay area, which is not currently in use but would be extremely pleasant to visit, the opposite shore provides those interested in relaxation with an attractive sense of tranquility, as I have mentioned before. Leaving this one out, we have others to which many are accustomed already, for example the Port of Punta and the Camino de Caleta, which is a natural grove where one can enjoy the cool shade of the beach-grape plants and the clear smoothness of this most delectable trail. There is the sea view from the edge, and on the other side is the view of the orchards that are nestled in that expanse. Leaving through the Port of Tierra toward the road where today they are planting huge shade trees, one can head to Cocales and to the two neighborhoods surrounding Our Lady of Guadalupe and the Most Holy Christ of Health, or, one can choose another recreational option such as the Arsenal, where its machines and hustle and bustle can amuse and take up one's time and attention with much pleasure, not only for those interested in nautical outings but for those who are not.

Note

1. The quintal was a standard unit of measure in the eighteenth century, with one quintal weighing one hundred pounds.

Francisco Javier de Clavijero

Born in Veracruz, Mexico, to a creole mother and a Spanish father charged with the colonial administration of Teziutlán and Jicayán in Mixteca, two regions of majority Indigenous populations, the young Francisco Javier Clavijero (1731–87) developed an attachment to Mexico's Indigenous cultures that would later motivate him to enter the Dispute of the New World in their defense. After being ordained a priest in the Society of Jesus in 1754, Clavijero dedicated himself to the study of pre-Columbian and conquest-era Aztec codices, often to the detriment of his teaching duties. However, Clavijero didn't begin writing *Geographical Description of Mexico* (1780) until he and the rest of the order were expelled from Spain's New World empire in 1767. Exiled to Bologna in modern-day Italy, Clavijero found himself in the company of some four thousand other displaced Jesuits. A number of them, including Clavijero himself, made use of their famous erudition to contradict the assertions of New World inferiority made by European philosophers like DePauw and Buffon. The Jesuits levied their intimate knowledge of the land, people, and historical documents of their respective *patrias* against European scholarship they represented as overly abstract and theoretical. Clavijero bases his defense of Aztec culture on the rational organization of their society as evident in the efficiency and sustainability of their agriculture. In his description of survivals from pre-Columbian agricultural systems still visible in central Mexico at the time, Clavijero goes so far as to suggest that Mexico's colonial authorities should reinstate the use of floating gardens on Lake Texcoco to control flooding—a possibility that remained until the draining of the lake was completed in 1975.

✳✳✳

From *Geographical Description of Mexico* (1780)

TRANSLATED BY GRADY C. WRAY

Seedbeds and Floating Gardens in Lake Mexico

The way the Mexicans made seedbeds and floating gardens is very simple, and it continues to this day. They weave together a large base of wicker or cattail roots, called *tolin*, along with other marsh grasses or other light materials that hold the soil of the seedbed together. On top of this base they add some type of light turf that floats on the lake; more than anything, they use mud they collect from the bottom of the lake. Typically they have an oblong shape: the length and width vary and, from what

I can judge, they generally measure some twenty-five to thirty yards long and six to eight yards wide. They rise about a foot above the surface of the water. These were the first seedbeds the Mexicans built after the foundation of Mexico, and they continued to make many more that served to cultivate not only corn, chilis, peppers, and other seed and fruits that were necessary for nourishment but also flowers and fragrant plants that they used in the worship of their gods and the delight of their lords.

Presently, they sow vegetables and flowers in them. All these plants grow well because the mud from the lake is very fertile and does not need rainwater to replenish itself. Some of these beds have a small tree or two and even a hut on them where those who care for these plants can take refuge from the burning sun and the rain. When the owner of a seedbed, or *chinampa* as they call them, wants to change from one place to another to get away from a bad neighbor or to be close to his family, he sets out in his canoe and tows his bed or garden wherever he wants. One finds these floating gardens in one of the most beautiful areas of Lake Mexico, where one's senses can perceive the world's sweetest pleasures.

Method of Cultivating the Earth

For the lands that could be irrigated, the Mexicans drew water from the rivers and made dams and irrigation ditches. The steep lands were not planted every year, but rather they let them rest until they were overgrown with great amounts of brush that they would burn. With the ashes, they replenished the salts that the water had robbed. The Spaniards employ this operation even today in the highlands, either to plant or to produce an abundant amount of hay for livestock. They made fences to protect the seeded fields out of stones, thorny bushes, and maguey cactus, which are the best, and they usually repair them if necessary and make new boundary markers in the month of *panquetzaliztli* that corresponds to our December, as we mentioned above.

The way they planted corn in the past, which continues even today, is this: The sower makes a hole in the soil with a sharp-tipped pole hardened by fire, and he tosses one, two, or more grains into the hole from a basket that hangs from his left shoulder. With his foot he moves a small amount of soil toward the hole and covers the seed. Then, he steps ahead a certain distance, which varies depending on the quality of the soil, where he makes another hole and continues in a straight line until the end of the field, where he turns around and makes another row parallel to the first. The rows come out as straight as if they had been drawn with a cord, and the distance between each plant is as if it had been premeasured. This type of planting, which is not presently used except among the poor Indians, is, although slower,[1] more useful because it better proportions the quantity of seeds to the strength of the land, and almost none of the grains that are planted are lost. The harvest in fields planted in this way is much more abundant. When the stalks reach a certain height, they pile more dirt around the base so it gets more nutrients and is more wind resistant. The women helped their husbands as they worked in the fields. The men were in charge of breaking the soil, planting, piling the soil, cutting, and removing kernels from the cobs, and the women shucked the cob and cleaned the kernels; weeding was a shared task.

Orchards, Gardens, and Forests

Besides the seedbeds used for corn and other seeds, the Mexicans had exquisite taste in the cultivation of orchards and gardens, where they had planted fruit trees, medicinal plants, and flowers in a beautifully ordered way. They put these areas to great use because the Mexican people take maximum pleasure in them and they have the custom of presenting kings, leaders, ambassadors, and others with bouquets of flowers, apart from the excessive amounts they dedicate to the worship of their gods in temples as well as prayer rooms.

Among the many ancient orchards and gardens, which they still recall, the most celebrated royal gardens were those of Mexico and Texcoco, mentioned above. They were the orchards of the lords of Iztapalapa and Huaxtepec. Inside his vast palace, the leader of Iztapalapa had various gardens and a great orchard whose grandeur, design, and beauty amazed the Spanish conquerors, among whom were Hernán Cortés and Bernal Díaz. It was spread out over many different areas with different varieties of plants and flowers that pleased the senses of sight and smell. Some of its well-formed paths were lined with fruit trees and others with cane trellises covered with fragrant flowers and herbs. Certain water canals bathed this garden, and canoes could enter the lake through others. In the midst of the orchard was a square pond so large that it measured four hundred feet on each side. It was made of stone and mortar, and it had steps all around it that reached the bottom. On all sides of the pond was a well-constructed brick platform on which four men standing side by side could easily pass. In the pond, one could see countless wild ducks, teals, and other aquatic birds. This famous garden was either planted or at least perfected by Cuitláhuac, the brother and successor to Montezuma II. He had many exotic trees transplanted in the orchard.

The orchard of Huaxtepec was much larger and more well known than the orchards of Iztapalapa. It had walking paths of two leagues and a variety of country houses that were two shots of a crossbow away from one another, and it had the most delightful gardens. An incredibly beautiful river passed through this orchard and heightened not only its beauty but also its pleasantness. This garden had many species of foreign plants that were brought from distant countries and grown with the greatest of care. The Spaniards preserved it for many years after the conquest and raised medicinal herbs that grew well in this climate for the hospital they constructed at that site, where the admirable hermit Gregorio López lived for some time.

The Mexican people's care and preservation of the forests was no less important for supplying the wood used in construction of their buildings and their canoes and for the different types of firewood and charcoal consumed in the temples, royal palaces, and private homes. Would to God that presently there were not so much liberty to demolish forests and that those who farm that realm today did not put their private needs before the public good, destroying, without rhyme or reason, many groves of trees in order to make larger fields for planting.

Note

1. It is not as slow as it appears, because the Indians who are accustomed to this practice do it with great speed. [—Author's note.]

Juan Ignacio Molina

Like the Mexican Francisco Clavijero, Chile's Juan Ignacio Molina (1740–1829) was a Jesuit who threw himself into the Dispute of the New World after the order's expulsion from Spain's American territories in 1767. Educated at the Jesuit College in Talca, Molina distinguished himself as an outstanding student of Latin and the natural sciences. At the time of the expulsion he was living at Bucalemu, a vast Jesuit hacienda that would later become the personal retreat of dictator Augusto Pinochet. Like many of his fellow Jesuits, Molina settled in Bologna after the expulsion, eventually receiving a position teaching Greek at the university there. But it was Molina's work as a geographer and natural historian that would secure his enduring reputation, particularly *Geographical, Natural, and Civil History of Chile*. Molina's book, like Clavijero's, pushes back against the French philosophes' disdain for the flora and fauna of the New World. In the selection presented here, he argues for the salubrity of Chile's climate, the lack of endemic diseases, even the absence of ferocious beasts. In these and other ways, Molina's work expresses a strong sense of topophilia—love of place—that, as the critic Santa Arias (2009) writes, contributed to the emergence of a protonational identity in the years leading up to the struggle for Chilean independence. As the reader will notice, however, Molina's vindication of Chile's geography, climate, flora, and fauna emphasizes those aspects of Chilean nature that most resemble the temperate regions of Europe. This tendency anticipates the skeptical treatment of tropical ecosystems and the human societies they support in writings by José María Samper and others, seen in part 4.

***

From *The Geographical, Natural, and Civil History of Chile* (1782)

ANONYMOUS TRANSLATION

General Excellence of Chile

Chile is one of the best countries in America. The beauty of its sky, the constant mildness of its climate, and its abundant fertility, all render it extremely agreeable as a place of residence. With respect to its natural products, it may be said without exaggeration that Chile is not inferior to any portion of the globe. The seasons succeed each other regularly, and are sufficiently marked, although the transition from cold to heat is very moderate. The spring in Chile commences, as in all the countries of the southern hemisphere, on September 22nd, the summer in December, the autumn in March, and the winter in June.

Precipitation

From the beginning of spring until autumn, there is throughout Chile a constant succession of fine weather, particularly between the 24th and 36th degrees of latitude; but in the islands, which for the most part are wooded, the rains are very frequent even in summer. The rainy season on the continent usually commences in April, and continues until the last of August. In the northern provinces of Coquimbo and Copiapo it very rarely rains; in the central ones it usually rains three or four days in succession, and the pleasant weather continues fifteen or twenty days. In the south the rains are much more frequent, and often continue for nine or ten days without cessation. These rains are never accompanied by storms or hail; and thunder is scarcely known in the country, particularly in places at a distance from the Andes, where it is seldom heard even in summer. Among those mountains, and near the sea, storms occasionally arise and pass over, taking their course to north or south according to the direction of the wind.

In the maritime provinces snow is never seen. In those nearer the Andes it falls about once in five years; sometimes not so often, and the quantity is very trifling; it usually melts while falling, and it is very uncommon to have it remain on the ground for a day.

In the Andes, on the contrary, it falls in such quantities from April to November, that it not only lies there constantly during that time, but even renders them wholly impassable during the greater part of the year. The highest summits of these mountains, which are constantly covered with snow, are distinguishable at a great distance by their whiteness, and form a very singular and pleasing appearance. Those inhabitants who are not wealthy enough to have ice-houses, procure snow from the mountains, transporting it by mules. The consumption of ice is very considerable, as a general use is made of it in summer to cool their liquors.

Mildness of Earthquakes

At present they produce only horizontal or oscillatory motions. From a course of accurate observations it has been ascertained, that earthquakes never occur unexpectedly in this country, but are always announced by a hollow sound proceeding from a vibration of the air; and as the shocks do not succeed each other rapidly, the inhabitants have sufficient time to provide for their safety. They have, however, in order to secure themselves, at all events, built their cities in a very judicious manner; the streets are left so broad, that the inhabitants would be safe in the middle of them, should even the houses fall upon both sides.

In addition to this, all the houses have spacious courts and gardens, which would serve as places of refuge. Those who are wealthy have usually in their gardens several neat wooden barracks, where they pass the night whenever they are threatened with an earthquake. Under these circumstances, the Chileans live without apprehension, and consider themselves in perfect security; especially as the earthquakes have never caused much sinking of the earth or falling of buildings. This, in my opinion, is owing to subterranean passages communicating with the volcanoes of the Andes, which are so many vent-holes for the inflamed substances, and serve to counteract their effects. Were it not for the number of these volcanoes, Chile would probably be rendered uninhabitable.

Salubrity of Climate

The inhabitants of Chile, notwithstanding the frequent occurrence of earthquakes, are very well satisfied with their country and, I am convinced, would not readily be induced to quit it for any other exempt from this calamity.

This preference is not founded solely upon that natural attachment to country, which is common to all men, but is derived from some advantages peculiar to Chile. A soil naturally fertile, and well adapted to every useful and valuable production, a mild and almost equable temperature of climate, and a remarkable salubrity, are the blessings enjoyed by this delightful country. Before the arrival of the Spaniards, contagious disorders were unknown: the small pox, which occasionally makes its appearance in the northern provinces, and is known by the name of the plague, was first introduced by them. At such times, the inhabitants of the neighboring provinces oblige every person coming from the infected district to perform a rigorous quarantine, and by that means have preserved themselves from the ravages of the destructive malady.

Whenever the Indians suspect any one to be attacked by it, which sometimes happens from their intercourse with the Spaniards, they burn him in his own hut, by means of fiery arrows. By this method, which is truly a violent one, they have hitherto prevented its progress and been exempted from this disorder.

A physician of the country, Matthias Verdugo, a monk of the order of St. John, was the first who, in 1761, introduced inoculation, and since that period it has been practiced with great success. Tertian and quartan fevers are also unknown there; and the inhabitants of the neighboring provinces who are afflicted with them, are accustomed to come into Chile for the benefit of their health, which they very soon recover. A violent fever, accompanied with delirium, is sometimes prevalent among the country people, particularly in summer and in autumn. This complaint, which the Indians cure with certain herbs whose properties they have learnt by experience, bears the name of *chavo longo*, which signifies the disorder of the head. The venereal disease is but little known in the Spanish settlements, and still less among the Indians. As the last have no word in their language expressive of it, there is every reason to presume that this malady was not known among them until after the arrival of the Spaniards. Rickets, a disease which for three centuries has been a scourge to Europe, is as yet unknown in Chile, and lame or deformed persons are very rarely to be met with. To many of the maladies peculiar to hot countries, such as Siam fever, the black vomit, and leprosy, Chile's inhabitants are equally strangers. No instance of hydrophobia has ever occurred, and M. de la Condamine justly observes that in South America the dogs, cats, and other animals are never afflicted with madness.

THREE
Nature and the Foundation of the Nation-States

As the literary critic Raymond Williams wrote, "The idea of nature contains, though often unnoticed, an extraordinary amount of human history" (1980, 67). This section is about the ideas of nature that circulated throughout a remarkable time in human history, the nineteenth century, when the New World possessions of Spain and Portugal formally established their political and economic independence and began their existence as sovereign states. It is also about the complex feedback loops among aesthetics, politics, and environments, all of which have influenced the ways that Latin American societies conceptualize, evaluate, and make use of the territory within their boundaries and the life-forms it contains.

In the Spanish dominions, Napoléon's invasion of the Iberian Peninsula sparked a crisis of legitimacy that enflamed the desire for political and economic autonomy, particularly on the part of creole elites, who had long found themselves excluded from the upper echelons of colonial power structures. The Bourbon reforms of the late eighteenth century had considerably increased Spanish-American resentment of the Crown's taxation policies, not to mention the outsize profits that peninsular merchants obtained through Spain's official monopolization of the import-export trade (Halperín Donghi 1993, 42–46). With the new political ideologies associated with the European Enlightenment abuzz everywhere, Spain's political crisis, coupled with the disruption in transatlantic trade caused by the European wars, prompted outspoken creoles like Argentina's Mariano Moreno to call for free trade. Representing the landowners on both banks of the Río de la Plata, he wrote "an eloquent and powerful plea for opening the port to British trade, not as a temporary financial expedient but as a necessity to economic well-being and particularly to pastoral and agricultural progress, which demanded free export" (Kilpatrick 1931, 66–67). Signed by a guild representative, José de la Rosa, Moreno's document addressed the viceroy of Buenos Aires in 1809: "Is it just that the fruits of our agricultural labors should be lost, because the unfortunate provinces of Spain can no longer consume them?" (quoted in Ward 1829, 491).

The profits to which Moreno and his companions felt themselves entitled would be a long time coming. On the one hand, the fifteen-year struggle for Spanish-American independence (1810–25) disrupted the economic growth of the late eighteenth century. Lucrative mines in Mexico and the Andes fell into disrepair, requiring huge sums of capital to regenerate. Agriculture was widely suspended or scaled back in the social upheaval, and passing armies had often helped themselves to ranchers' sheep and cattle, diminishing the herds. After the war, the market demand creole elites had anticipated largely failed to materialize, and Spanish-American agriculture continued to languish while cheap British manufactures flooded the cities and towns, displacing the products of local weavers and other artisans. Making matters far worse, a decade and a half of armed conflict had produced a highly militarized population, which particularly in rural areas demonstrated more loyalty to local officers than to the republican ideals that had supposedly motivated the fight against Spain. With economies largely stagnant, racial and regional tensions ran high, creating the conditions for the bitter civil wars that consumed many of the Spanish-American republics during the first decades after independence.

Brazil's transition, meanwhile, was considerably smoother. At the time of the Napoleonic invasion, the Portuguese royal family had called on the British Navy to provide safe passage to Rio de Janeiro, where they established a court that in 1825 declared its independence from Lisbon. Brazil's export economy surged, particularly in the sugar-producing region of the northeast. Like that of Cuba—which remained a Spanish possession until the turn of the twentieth century—the Brazilian sugar industry took advantage of the upheaval created by the Haitian Revolution to expand production dramatically. Coffee plantations developed in the area around Rio de Janeiro, and as herds gradually recovered in the Spanish-speaking Río de la Plata, Brazilian landowners also took up ranching in the southern territories of Mato Grosso do Sul and Paraná. The expansion of Brazil's sugar industry inevitably led to conflict with Great Britain given the British opposition to the transatlantic slave trade and the Brazilian planters' desire to increase their labor force of enslaved Blacks. Nevertheless, Brazil—like Spanish America—became a privileged market for British manufactures. Thus with different degrees of intensity and effectiveness, Latin America's postcolonial economies quickly became oriented toward the intensive production of a small handful of primary products for sale on the international market (Halperín Donghi 1993, 87–88).

Paraguay represents the exception to the historical developments of the early national period. While most of the new Spanish-American republics were consumed in civil wars and Brazil consolidated its dependent trade relation with Great Britain, Dr. José Gaspar Rodríguez de Francia (1814–40) kept the peace by ruling his tiny, landlocked country with an iron fist. In an effort to curtail the political threat represented by the creole and Spanish *yerba mate* merchants, Dr. Francia imposed strict controls on the export of Paraguay's principal product. The harvesting of *yerba mate* passed to the army, and the quantity of Paraguayan *yerba* sent downriver to Argentina shrank dramatically. Paraguay's tiny merchant class was livid, but as the Swiss physician Johann Rudolph Rengger observed in the selection presented here, the disruption of Paraguay's extractive economy produced a flourishing of local agriculture, including the return of traditional Guarani agroforestry, the cultivation of new and hybrid vegetable species, and the development of a textile industry using local cotton (Whigham 2009).

The political and economic transformations described here unfolded within discursive frameworks partially provided by the European Enlightenment and literary Romanticism, both of which consistently refer to Nature as the source of uncorrupted goodness and reason in contrast to the antiquated institutions that the revolutionary politics of the time endeavored to overcome. Eighteenth- and nineteenth-century aesthetic treatises divide representations of nature between the beautiful or picturesque and the sublime, which refers to the sensation of being overwhelmed by the perception of something much larger and more powerful than oneself. These notions would be mobilized mightily by Latin American writers of the nineteenth century, among them the Cuban Romantic Gertrudis Gómez de Avellaneda, whose feminist-abolitionist novel *Sab* is excerpted here.

For some the Prussian geographer Alexander von Humboldt was a particular influence. From 1799 to 1804 Humboldt traveled throughout the Americas in the company of the French botanist Aimé Bonpland, visiting Venezuela, Colombia, Cuba, Peru, Bolivia, Mexico, and the United States. Throughout the voyage they measured, sketched, and described the flora, fauna, and topographical features they encountered, filling copious notebooks with material that Humboldt would mine for decades to come. In his thirty-volume *Travels to the Equinoctial Regions of the New Continent* and other works, Humboldt would provide a new and appropriately scientific interpretation of a very old idea: the New World is defined as Nature, not the Garden of Eden encountered by Columbus or Buffon's mammalian degenerates, but as Mary Louise Pratt (1992, 118) puts it, "a dramatic, extraordinary nature, a spectacle capable of overwhelming human knowledge and understanding."

Nature is nationalism's most enduring and powerful trope, invisibly wedding the affective experience of human communities to the physical features of the territories they occupy. The writers featured in this section appropriate the aesthetic and intellectual frameworks produced by Humboldt and other Europeans, molding them to their own interests and purposes. One such writer is El Libertador himself, Simón Bolívar, who made good on Humboldt's failed attempt to reach the summit of Mount Chimborazo and turned the experience into "an allegory for his own epic political mission as liberator of the Américas" (Pratt 1992, 178). For Bolívar and others, the natural world is a terrain of power, used to metaphorically justify and amplify the claims to political legitimacy of local and regional elites on the eve of, during, and after the struggle for national independence.

Nowhere is this more apparent than in Domingo F. Sarmiento's *Facundo: Civilization and Barbarism*, one of the most influential books in Latin American history. Written by an aspiring political figure to denigrate his rival, the dictator Juan Manuel de Rosas, *Facundo* attempts to explain the failures of Argentinean politics through an argument about geography: "The disease from which the Argentine Republic suffers is its own expanse: the desert wilderness surrounds it on all sides and insinuates into its bowels; solitude, a barren land with no human habitation, in general are the unquestionable borders between one province and another." Like many of his creole contemporaries in the United States, Sarmiento saw lands inhabited by Indigenous groups as fundamentally empty, an act of willful blindness that led governments in North and South America to undertake the military extermination of Native American populations by century's end.

Nature is nationalism's most powerful trope, but nature is of course much more than a trope. As these writers create representations of nature as the rhetorical ground on which to stake their claims to political legitimacy, we cannot fail to notice that the "natural order" they invoke is in reality anything but natural. Hierarchically structured societies lurk everywhere, from the picturesque pastorals of Avellaneda and Andrés Bello to José María Samper's diatribe about the lowland Indians' innate "antipathy" to civilization. Viewed in this light, the selections presented here help us to understand that despite their enlightened rhetoric, Latin America's independence era and early national period failed to bring about the decolonization of nature. Or to act on the realization that Bolívar's beloved tutor Simón Rodríguez set down in his

1830 "Observations on the Terrain of Vincocaya": "If Americans want the POLITICAL revolution that the weight of things has made and that circumstances have protected to bring true wealth, they must pursue an ECONOMIC revolution and begin it in the fields."

Suggestions for Further Reading

Alexander von Humboldt. 1808. *Views of Nature*, edited by Stephen T. Jackson and Laura Dassow Walls; translated by Mark W. Person. Chicago: University of Chicago Press, 2014.

Jorge Isaacs. 1867. *María: A South American Romance*, translated by Rollo Ogden. LaVergne, Tenn.: Wildside Press, 2010.

José Hernández. 1871–79. *The Gaucho Martín Fierro*, translated by Kate Kavanagh. Albany: State University of New York Press, 1967.

José Martiniano de Alencar. 1875. *O sertanejo*. São Paulo: Companhia Editora Nacional, 1928.

Juan León Mera. 1877. *Cumandá, o, Un drama entre salvajes*, edited by Ángel Esteban. Madrid: Cátedra, 1998.

Simón Bolívar

Known as El Libertador, Simón Bolívar (1783–1830) led the revolutions that freed six future nations from Spanish control: Venezuela, Colombia, Panama, Ecuador, Bolivia, and Peru. He was born into one of Caracas's old creole families, inheriting one of the largest fortunes in Venezuela and a considerable number of slaves when his parents died young. He was subsequently raised by tutors, including Andrés Bello and Simón Rodríguez. Bolívar traveled to Mexico and Europe, married at seventeen, and was a widower two years later. In 1804 Bolívar returned to Europe, where he immersed himself in writings by Voltaire and Locke and struck up a friendship with Alexander von Humboldt. When Napoléon successfully invaded Spain in 1808, the empire was unsettled enough to make it possible for the colonies to begin the fight for independence, and Bolívar threw himself into the fray. After nearly a decade of conflict, he crossed the Andes with a Haitian army and took control of Colombia in 1819. He became president-dictator of Gran Colombia and spent the next several years liberating Peru, Venezuela, Ecuador, and Bolivia. He ruled over Colombia until his death from tuberculosis in 1830. Besides being South America's most celebrated military figure, Bolívar is also admired for the elegance and insight of his writing. The essay included here, "My Delirium on Chimborazo" (1822), records a dream Bolívar experienced a few months after climbing the famous Andean peak in July 1822. In doing so, he had bested Humboldt (1769–1859) and Charles-Marie de La Condamine (1701–74), both of whom had tried and failed. The brief essay encompasses a defining idea of Latin American Romanticism: that the continent's sublime landscapes inspire equally grand political visions.

***

"My Delirium on Chimborazo" (1822)

TRANSLATED BY FREDERICK H. FORNOFF

I was coming along, cloaked in the mantle of Iris, from the place where the torrential Orinoco pays tribute to the God of waters. I had visited the enchanted springs of Amazonia, straining to climb up to the watchtower of the universe. I sought the tracks of La Condamine and Humboldt, following them boldly. Nothing could stop me. I reached the glacial heights, and the atmosphere took my breath away. No human foot had ever blemished the diamond crown placed by Eternity's hands on the sublime temples of this lofty Andean peak. I said to myself: Iris's rainbow cloak has served as my banner. I've carried it through the infernal regions. It has ploughed rivers and seas and risen to the gigantic shoulders of the Andes. The terrain had leveled off at the feet of Colombia, and not even time could hold back freedom's march. The war goddess Belona has been humbled by the brilliance of Iris. So why should I hesitate to tread on the ice-white hair of this giant of the earth? Indeed I shall! And caught up in a spiritual tremor I had never before experienced, and which seemed to me a kind of divine frenzy, I left Humboldt's tracks behind and began to leave my own marks on the eternal crystals girding Chimborazo. I climb as if driven by this frenzy, faltering only when my head grazes the summit of the firmament. At my feet the threshold of the abyss beckons.

A feverish delirium suspends my mental faculties. I feel as if I were aflame with a strange, higher fire. It was the God of Colombia taking possession of me.

Suddenly, Time appears to me as an ancient figure weighed down by the clutter of the ages: scowling, bent over, bald, his skin lined, scythe in hand . . .

"I am the father of the centuries, the arcanum of fame and secret knowledge. My mother was Eternity. Infinity sets the limits of my empire. There is no tomb for me, because I am more powerful than Death. I behold the past, I see the future, and the present passes through my hands. Oh, child, man, ancient, hero, why such vanity? Do you think your Universe matters? That you exalt yourself merely by scaling one of the atoms of creation? Do you imagine that the instants you call centuries are enough to fathom my mysteries? Do you believe you have seen the Holy Truth? Are you mad enough to presume that your actions have value in my eyes? Compared to my brother, Infinity, everything is less than the tiniest point."

Overcome by a sacred awe, I answered: "Oh, Time, how can a wretched mortal who has climbed so high not simply vanish in thin air? I have surpassed all men in fortune, because I have risen to be the head of them all. I stand high above the earth with my feet; I grasp the eternal with my hands; I feel the infernal prisons boiling beneath my footsteps; I stand gazing at the glittering stars beside me, the infinite suns; I measure without astonishment the space that encloses all matter, and in your face I read the History of the past and the thoughts of Destiny."

"Observe," he said to me, "learn, hold in your mind what you have seen. Draw for the eyes of those like you the image of the physical Universe, the moral Universe. Do not conceal the secrets heaven has revealed to you. Tell men the truth."

The apparition disappeared.

Absorbed, frozen in time, so to speak, I lay lifeless for a long time, stretched out on that immense diamond serving as my bed. Finally, the tremendous voice of Colombia cries out to me. I come back to life, sit up, open my heavy eyelids with my own hands. I become a man again, and write down my delirium.

José María Heredia y Heredia

As the son of a relatively high-ranking official of the Spanish empire, José María Heredia y Heredia (1803–39) spent a peripatetic childhood among Cuba, Santo Domingo, Venezuela, and Mexico, where his father was assassinated in 1820. The family subsequently returned to Cuba, but José María, still very young, soon found himself banished from the island because of his subversive, anticolonial activities, which included advocating for the abolition of slavery. Like his compatriot and fellow poet José Martí (1853–95), Heredia was thus destined to spend much of his short life in exile; also like Martí, Heredia found a temporary home among the community of Cuban exiles in New York City. He visited Niagara Falls, the subject of one of his most celebrated poems, but left the country because of his great distaste for the English language. Heredia eventually settled in Mexico, where he taught literature and history, held a number of government posts, and wrote prolifically. He died there of tuberculosis at age thirty-six. Today Heredia is recognized as a major nineteenth-century poet and one of the founders of Latin American Romanticism. Though steeped, like Andrés Bello, in the Greek and Latin classics, Heredia found that Romanticism's heightened emotionalism, intimate tone, and tendency to project human states of mind onto nonhuman nature made it a fine vehicle to convey the turbulence and intense longing of Latin American political life, particularly Cuba's ongoing struggle for independence and the poet's nostalgia for his island home. Featured here is "In a Storm" (1822), written while the precocious Heredia was still an adolescent in Cuba.

***

"In a Storm" (1822)

TRANSLATED BY G. J. RACZ

> Wild hurricane! I feel your gusts encroach
> and, as you blow your stormy fire,
> inhale to all my heart's desire
> the breath of heaven's lord's approach.

> Oh, watch it brewing in the open sky,
> suspended on the pinions of the wind,
> unwavering, quiet, and fearsome in a flight
> so swift the tranquil earth can only view

impassively this ominous,
mysterious, and terrifying sight.
What, can't you see this bull? Its wounded hoofs
kick up the dirt with ardor few can bear,
then, raising its strong forehead and its gaze,
with swelling nostrils breathing out the blaze,
it bellows forth the tempest in thin air.

   Mid clouds and rage the trembling sun arrays
its glorious face in some sad hazy fog!
This sombrous orb can only cast a pale,
funereal, and murky light,
denoting neither day nor night.
Oh, dreadful color rivaling death's own veil!
The little birds all shake with fear, then hide
when they first sense the hurricane's fierce roar.
The forests hear, but can't respond before
this echoes off the distant mountainside.

   It's coming, don't you see? The blasts spread wide
a cloak of stupefying majesty!
My being salutes you, giant of the skies!
Oh, how the driving winds blow to and fro
that trim upon their clothing's darkened edge!
Look there on the horizon till
you see its speedy arms enfold in space
near everything in its embrace,
all I contrive to see from hill to hill!

   What blackness drapes the globe! Its forceful gales
go sending up in swirls of dust
the soil of every field it's headed toward!
Out rumbling clouds the carriage of the Lord
now hurtles downward, shooting from its wheels
a wingèd lightning bolt that, in its rush
to wound the ground and cause it fright,
bathes all earth's atmosphere in bluish light.

   What sound is that? Is it the rain? It falls
unleashed in torrents, blotting out the world
in horror that's chaotically unfurled.
Sky, clouds, and hillocks, forest held most dear,
where are you? Oh, I seek in vain!
You've disappeared. The shadowy tempest high
up in the skies churns round an ocean there

that buries all within its path.
At last, harsh world, we set out on our own:
the hurricane and I are now alone.

      Sublime storm! In the bosom of your blight,
as solemn inspiration swells my mind,
I leave this lowly, wretched land behind
and raise my own brow, filled with sheer delight!
Now where's that coward soul that fears
your awesome growl? I elevate myself
through you to God's high throne and hear there mid
the clouds the echo of your voice. I sense
the earth pay heed, then quake. How fervently
tears flow down these pale cheeks as I adore,
still tremulous, your utmost majesty.

Andrés Bello

Prolific writer, influential educator, and statist, Andrés Bello (1781–1865) is one of Latin America's most renowned nineteenth-century intellectuals. He was born in Caracas and educated by Friar Cristóbal de Quesada, a classicist who instilled the enthusiasm for Latin and Greek poetry that manifests itself in Bello's best-known work. At the University of Caracas Bello also studied philosophy, law, and medicine. In 1810 Bello accompanied his former pupil, Simón Bolívar, to London on a diplomatic mission to support the revolutionary junta; he ended up living there for nineteen years after the Venezuelan Republic collapsed, leaving him stranded. To make ends meet, Bello taught, translated, and worked for the legations of Chile and Colombia. He collaborated with Jeremy Bentham and produced a new edition of the Spanish classic *Cantar de mio Cid* (*Poem of My Cid*), based on research at the British Museum. He also edited two magazines, *Biblioteca Americana* and *Repertorio Americano*. Bello never went back to Venezuela; instead he accepted an invitation from Chilean dictator Diego Portales to serve that country's government. Bello settled in Chile with his Irish wife and surviving children; he wrote the country's civil code and served as founding rector of the University of Chile. The poem featured here, "Ode to Tropical Agriculture" (1826), was written during Bello's London exile as part of his unfinished epic *América*. Inspired by Virgil's *Georgics*, Bello urges citizens of the newly liberated republics to cultivate the soil and make peace with one another. He extols the virtues of rural life over dissipated, unruly urban centers. But as Catherine Davies (2007) writes, Bello's citizens are implicitly gendered male, whereas the land, America, and nature are consistently feminized.

* * *

"Ode to Tropical Agriculture" (1826)

TRANSLATED BY FRANCES M. LÓPEZ-MORILLAS

> Hail, fertile zone, that circumscribes
> the errant course of your enamored sun,
> and, caressed by its light,
> brings forth all living things
> in each of your many climes!
> You weave the summer's wreath of golden grain,
> and offer grapes to the bubbling pail.

Your glorious groves lack no tone
of purple fruit, or red, or gold. In them the wind
imbibes a thousand odors, and innumerable flocks
crop your green meadow, from the plain
bordered by the horizon, to the mountain heights,
ever hoary with inaccessible snow.

      You give sweet sugarcane, whose pure sap
makes the world disdain the honeycomb.
In coral urns you prepare the beans
that overflow the foaming chocolate cup.
Living red teems on your cactus plants,
outdoing the purple of Tyre.
And the splendid dye of your indigo
imitates the sapphire's glow.
Wine is yours, which the pierced agave
pours out for Anahuac's happy brood.
Yours too is the leaf that solaces
the tedium of idle hours, when its soft smoke
rises in wandering spirals.
You clothe with jasmine the bush of Sheba,
and give it the perfume that cools
the wild fever of riotous excess.
For your children the lofty palm brings forth
its varied products, and the pineapple ripens
its ambrosia. The yucca[1] grows its snowy bread,
and the potato yields its fair fruit,
and cotton opens to the gentle breeze
its golden roses and its milk-white fleece.
For you the passion plant displays
its fresh green branches, and sweet globes
and dangling flowers hang from climbing branches.
For you maize, proud chief of the tribe of grains,
swells its ears; and for you the banana plant
sags under dulcet weight. Banana, first
of all the plants that Providence has offered
to happy tropic's folk with generous hand;
it asks no care by human arts, but freely yields
its fruit. It needs no pruning hook or plow.
No care does it require, only such heed
as a slave's hand can steal from daily toil.
It grows with swiftness, and when it is outworn
its full-grown children take its place.

But, fertile zone, though rich,
why did not Nature work with equal zeal
to make its indolent dwellers follow her?
Oh, would that they could recognize the joy
that beckons from the simple farmer's home,
and spurn vain luxury, false brilliance,
and the city's evil idleness!
What vain illusion has a grip on those
whom Fortune has made masters of this land,
so happy, rich and varied as it is,
to make them leave hereditary soil,
forsaking it to mercenary hands?
Shut in blind clamor of the wretched cities,
where sick ambition fans the flames
of civil strife, or indolence exhausts
the love of country. There it is
that luxury saps customs, and vices trap
unwary youth in ever stronger bonds.
There, youth does not tire from manly exercise,
but sickens in the arms of treacherous beauty
that sells its favors to the highest bidder;
whose pastime is to light the flame of outlaw love
in the chaste bosom of a youth.
Or dawn will find him drunk, perhaps,
at the base, sordid gaming table.

Meanwhile the wife lends an eager ear
to the ardent lover's seductive flattery.
The tender virgin grows in her mother's school
of dissipation and flirtation, and that example
spurs her to sin before she wishes to.
Is this the way to form the heroic spirits
that bravely found and undergird the state?
How will strong and modest youth emerge,
our country's hope and pride,
from the hubbub of foolish revels
or the choruses of lewd dances?
Can the man who even in the cradle
slept to the murmur of lascivious songs,
a man who curls his hair and scents himself,
and dresses with almost feminine care
and spends the day in idleness,
or worse, in criminal lust: can such a man
hold firmly to the reins of law,
or be serene in doubtful combat, or confront

the haughty spirit of a tyrannous leader?
Triumphant Rome did not thus view
the arts of peace and war; rather, she gave
the reins of state to the strong hand,
tanned by the sun and hardened by the plow,
who raised his sons under a smoky peasant roof,
and made the world submit to Latin valor.

　　　Oh, you who are the fortunate possessors,
born in this beautiful land,
where bountiful Nature parades her gifts
as if to win you and attract you!
Break the harsh enchantment
that holds you prisoner within walls.
The common man, working at crafts,
the merchant who loves luxury and must have it,
those who pant after high place and noisy honor,
the troop of parasitic flatterers,
live happily in that filthy chaos.
The land is your heritage; enjoy it.
Do you love freedom? Go then to the country,
not where the rich man lives
amid armed satellites, and where
Fashion, that universal dame,
drags reason tied to her triumphal car.
Go not where foolish common folk adore
Fortune, and nobles the adulation of the mob.
Or do you love virtue? then the best teacher
is the solitary calm where man's soul,
judge only of itself, displays its actions.
Do you seek lasting joys, and happiness,
as much as is given to man on earth?
Where laughter is close to tears, and always,
ah, always, among the flowers pricks the thorn?
Go and enjoy the farmer's life, his lovely peace,
untroubled by bitterness and envy.
His soft bed is prepared for him
by labor, purest air, and great content,
and the flavor of food easily won.
He is untouched by wasteful gluttony,
and in the safe haven of his loyal home
is host to health and happiness.
Go breathe the mountain air, that gives
lost vigor to the tired body, and retards
fretful old age, and tinges pink

the face of beauty. Is the flame of love,
tempered by modesty, less sweet, perchance?
Or is beauty less attractive
without false ornament and lying paint?
Does the heart hear unmoved
the innocent language that expresses love
openly, the intent equal to the promise?
No need to rehearse before the mirror
a laugh, a step, a gesture;
no lack there of an honest face
flushed with modesty and health, nor does
the sidelong glance cast by a timid lover
lose its way to the soul.
Could you expect a marriage bond to form,
arranged by an alien hand, tyrant of love,
swayed by base interests, for repute or fortune,
happier than one where taste and age agree,
and free choice reigns, and mutual ardor?

      There too are duties to perform: heal, oh heal
the bitter wounds of war; place the fertile soil,
now harsh and wild, under the unaccustomed yoke
of human skill, and conquer it.
Let pent-up pond and water mill
remember where their waters flowed,
let the axe break the matted trees
and fire burn the forest; in its barren splendor
let a long gash be cut.
Give shelter in the valleys
to thirsty sugarcane; in the cool mountains make
pear trees and apples forget their mother, Spain.
Make coffee trees adorn the slopes;
on river banks, let the maternal shade
of the bucare tree guard the tender cacao plants.
Let gardens flourish, orchards laugh with joy.
Is this blind error, foolish fantasy?
Oh agriculture, wetnurse of mankind,
heeding your voice, now comes the servile crowd
with curving sickles armed.
It bursts into the dark wood's tangled growth.
I hear voices and distant sounds, the axe's noise.
Far off, echo repeats its blows; the ancient tree
for long the challenge of the laboring crowd,
groans, and trembles from a hundred axes,
topples at last, and its tall summit falls.

The wild beast flees; the doleful bird
leaves its sweet nest, its fledgling brood,
seeking a wood unknown to humankind.
What do I see? a tall and crackling flame
spills over the dry ruins of the conquered forest.
The roaring fire is heard afar,
black smoke eddies upward, piling cloud on cloud.
And only dead trunks, only ashes remain
of what before was lovely green and freshness,
the tomb of mortal joy, plaything of the wind.
But the wild growth of savage, tangled plants
gives way to fruitful plantings, that display
their proud rows and orderly design.
Branch touches branch, and steals
the light of day from sturdy shoots.
Now the first flower displays its buds,
lovely to see and breathing joyful hope.
Hope, that laughing mops the tired farmer's brow,
Hope, that from afar
paints the rich fruit, the harvest's bounty
that carries off the tribute of the fields
in heaping baskets and in billowing skirts,
and under the weight of plenty, the farmer's due,
makes vast storehouses creak and groan.

      Dear God! let not the Equator's farming folk
sweat vainly; be moved to pity and compassion.
Let them return now from their sad despair
with renewed spirit, and after such alarms,
anxiety and turmoil, and so many years
of fierce destruction and of military crimes,
may beg your mercy more than in the past.
May rustic piety, but no less sincere
find favor in your eyes. Let them not weep
for a vanished golden dream, a lying vision,
a future without tears, a smiling future
that lightens all the troubles of today.
Let not unseasonable rains
ruin the tender crops; let not the pitiless tooth
of gnawing insects devour them.
Let not the savage storm destroy,
or the tree's maternal sap
dry up in summer's long and heated thirst.
For you, supreme arbiter of fate,
were pleased at long last to remove the yoke

of foreign rule, and with your blessing
to raise American man toward heaven,
to make his freedom root and thrive.
Bury accursed war in deep abyss,
and, for fear of vengeful sword,
let the distrustful farmer not desist
from noble toil, that nourishes
families and whole countries too.
May anxious worry leave their souls,
and plows no longer sadly rust.
We have atoned enough for the savage conquest
of our unhappy fathers.
No matter where we look, do we not see
a stubbled wilderness where once were fields,
and cities too? Who can sum up the dreadful count
of deaths, proscriptions, tortures,
and orphans left abandoned?
The ghosts of Montezuma, Atahualpa,
sleep now, glutted with Spanish blood.
Ah! from your lofty seat,
where choirs of winged angels veil their faces
in awe before the splendor of your face
(if luckless humankind deserves, perchance,
a single glance from you),
send down an angel, angel of peace, to make
the rude Spaniard forget his ancient tyranny,
and, reverent, hear the sacred vow,
the essential law you gave to men;
may he stretch out his unarmed hand,
(alas, too stained with blood!)
to his wronged brother.
And if innate gentleness should sleep
make it awake in the American breast.
The brave heart that scorns obscure content,
that beats more strongly in the bloody hap
of battle, and greedy for power or fame,
loves noble perils,
deems an insult, worthy of contempt,
and spurns the prize not given by his country.
May he find freedom sweeter far than power,
and olive branch more fair than laurel crown.
Let the soldier-citizen put off
the panoply of war; let the victory wreath
hang on his country's altar,
and glory be the only prize of merit.

Then may my country see the longed-for day
when peace will triumph:
peace, that fills the world
with joy, serenity, and happiness.
Man will return rejoicing to his task;
the ship lifts anchor, and entrusts herself
to friendly winds. Workshops swarm, farms teem,
the scythes to not suffice to cut the grain.

      Oh, youthful nations, with early laurels crowned,
who rise before the West's astonished gaze!
Honor the fields, honor the simple life,
and the farmer's frugal simplicity.
Thus freedom will dwell in you forever,
ambition be restrained, law have its temple.
Your people will set out bravely
on the hard, steep path of immortality,
always citing your example.
Those who come after you will imitate you eagerly,
adding new names to those whose fame
they now acclaim. For they will say, "Sons, sons
are these of men who won the Andes' heights;
those who in Boyacá, and on Maipo's sands,
and in Junín, and Apurima's glorious field,
humbled in victory the lion of Spain."

Note

1. In the original Spanish, Bello refers not to the spiky ornamental plant known as "yucca" but rather to "yuca," also known as "cassava," a starchy tubular root that can be prepared many different ways and is considered a staple food in many parts of Latin America. [—Eds.]

Simón Rodríguez

Best known as the tutor of El Libertador Simón Bolívar, Venezuela's Simón Rodríguez (1769–1854) was one of the most original intellectuals of nineteenth-century Latin America. While teaching at a primary school Rodríguez encountered the young Bolívar, an orphan like himself, albeit immensely rich. They met again in Paris in 1805, undertaking the tour that would culminate in Bolívar's legendary vow to liberate Spanish America. Rodríguez remained in Europe during the independence struggle. He returned to South America in 1823 to support educational reform in Peru, Colombia, and Bolivia. Soon after, Rodríguez published *American Societies in 1828*, which denounced the young republics' failure to satisfy the demand for economic and social change that had motivated the independence wars. Versed in science and engineering as well as philosophy, Rodríguez also wrote technical articles. The excerpt presented here is from his 1830 critique of a plan to build a dam and canals to divert water from Peru's Vincocaya region to irrigate new agricultural lands outside Arequipa. With the Upper Irrigation Canal near completion, Rodríguez proposed that the dam be abandoned in favor of a system of waterways, including the channel he discusses in our excerpt. As Ronald Briggs (2010, 74) writes, the choice reflects Rodríguez's "ecological sensibility," since he represents canals as working with the water's momentum rather than attempting to constrain it. Rodríguez also recommends sustainable forestry to maintain local microclimates and counterbalance the expansion of agriculture and ranching *Arequipeños* hoped would make their fortune. In distinctly ecological terms, Rodríguez argues for an "economic revolution" to complete the political revolution achieved by the independence wars. The innovative typography is a hallmark of his style.

***

"Observations on the Terrain of Vincocaya with regard to the Project of Redirecting the Natural Course of its Waters and Transporting them along the Zumbai River to the Fields of Arequipa" (1830)

TRANSLATED BY GRADY C. WRAY

REFLECTIONS

on the OVERALL STRUCTURE *of the Work*
and
on the Regulation of the DOWNWARD FLOW *of Water.*

To Follow the Example of the Upper Irrigation Canal can be Detrimental in Two Ways: First for the Channel Itself and also for the Lands it will Irrigate.

STRUCTURE *of the Work*

Following the example of the Upper Irrigation Canal would likely be detrimental to the channel if it were believed that the waters of Vincocaya did not need more of a structure than the one that irrigates the fields of Caima and Challapampa.

1st

The Upper Irrigation Canal runs for quite a distance along the course of the river; and the part that is elevated has the benefit of receiving moisture that the river brings to a certain height—its causeway does not touch the uneven ground of the gully—and from where it begins, the small farms that it irrigates benefit from its infiltrations.

However, the Charcani channel will pass through a parched terrain, high and far from the river. The capillary action of the soil will not be sufficient to carry the moisture to such a high level and over such a distance. Between the Upper Irrigation Canal and the channel there are no small farms, and if there ever were, it would be better to supply them with known water sources. There is no comparison between what the Vincocaya waters cost and what those of the Upper Irrigation Canal have cost.

The company must think about what to do with the steep terrain that will remain between the Upper Irrigation Canal and the channel, because there is water to irrigate it, and no matter how many precautions are taken against seepage, the land beneath the channel will get wet. In Arequipa the art of cultivating steep terrain is very well known: it can be cut into terraces.

2nd

The Upper Irrigation Canal carries one square yard of water, or 5/4 maximum; the Charcani channel will carry at least 5 yards, and if a channel is constructed in Vincocaya, instead of a dam, 8 or 10 yards will come through.

The Upper Irrigation Canal is properly called an Irrigation Canal—the Charcani channel will be more than half a river for Arequipa.

To contain the Upper Irrigation Canal a border of turf or grasses is all that is needed—the channel will need a wall.

When the Upper Irrigation Canal breaks, workers stop it by patching it with stones, leaves, and rags, and they send the water that keeps spilling out to the fields, or they let it fall to the river. The breaks in the channel will not be able to be remedied without fixing the opening or outlet; and in the meantime, the water will do much damage, especially if it spills out at night.

The Regulation of the DOWNWARD FLOW *of Water*

To follow the example of the Upper Irrigation Canal would be detrimental to the lands that the waters will irrigate if one believes that the channel must have the same downward flow as the Upper Irrigation Canal. Many who are interested in this effort want the flow to be greater, based on the idea that the force of the current will push the slime and sand, which could block the channel, to the lands below.

As to the DOWNWARD FLOW, observe that from the line of sight from the border of the watercourse where the work has stopped to the corresponding point in the gully the waters will come out (without descent and without apparent level correction) at 1,500 yards from the bridge of the Upper Irrigation Canal after running for 4,000 yards.

Suppose that the true point of departure is what the sight line indicates and that, in order to have a large downward flow of water, the bottom of the channel is lowered by one inch per yard. The loss of the level would be 111 yards—111 yards less in elevation. This will be a difference of more than a *topo*[1] and a half on the land. No matter how many *topos* the channel must run, by irrigating in each *topo*, the company will lose at least one *topo* in the front and a half *topo* in the back—and the newly irrigated lands will not have increased over the present ones more than 1,500 yards. *Please note that in this computation the type of curve of the gully's inclination is not figured.*

Has the pampa already been leveled? Does anyone know where the water will stop?

There is no lack of people who think that the leveling of the pampa should be the last step. Think about this a little more: it is merited.

As to the flow of mud and sand, observe that (1), thick sand will all settle in the outlet; (2), mud can be made up

> of very fine sand
> or of muddy clay
> or of sandy clay
> or of vegetable material.

The first three types make the land ready for fertilization, and the last type fertilizes it.

Sand, as fine as it may be, settles if the current is not strong.

The alumina of the muddy clay, the sandy clay, and the loam loosens and lasts much longer in suspension.

Light vegetable material, like leaves and flowers, fruits and small seeds, cover the surface of the water for a long time, and as they decompose, they loosen and mostly dissolve. On the banks of the rivers that flow into the Arequipa region, there are no trees, and the smaller plants that fall in the channel will always float. They will sink only when they have lost the air and the gasses that keep them on top of the water. There are not enough plants, nor is the channel long enough, to worry about deposits.

The mud composed of vegetation will fluctuate as it goes into the fields, and the silt that is made up of aquatic grasses and woody residue with the fine soils can be extracted by a very simple process:

An axle with two wheels on the end that are fitted with paddles a half yard apart go in the same direction of the radius.

The wheels are fixed to the axle and their diameter is proportionate to its depth, so they do not touch the bottom.

The axle is placed across the middle of a raft on top of two clamps that hold it together without keeping the wheels from turning.

One makes adjustments to this device by making two openings on the axle that fit into the clamps—therefore it stops the lateral escape. Each clamp has a movable wedge to calibrate the necessary distance between the wheels and the bottom.

This gear is like a waterwheel—each wheel is like a waterwheel without a rope— and each paddle a scoop for the water.

A horse, above the parapet of the channel, pulls the raft upward. A man on the raft corrects any change in course caused by the pulling of the device with the tip of a pole, and the wheels, moved by the current, agitate the water.

As it goes down, the wheels are tied in such a way as to serve as oars, and two others are attached, one on each end of the raft in the figure of a wheelbarrow—these two wheels will remove the accumulated materials in the center.

Four of these rafts going through once a month for the length of the channel will always keep it clean.

In case the channel is vaulted, the rafts will be taken up by hand with cranks.

ECONOMICS
Cleaning of the channel
and
irrigation of the land.

On the corresponding land, one saves in two ways: waste in caretaking and water distribution. Both a caretaker and a distributor are necessary, and they must either be on salary or paid either rent or an annual yield, the latter being preferable. For each one of these positions, give a land investment in perpetual, transferable property. Thus, the new establishments will have appropriate people who understand what is essential. Without water there will be no cultivation—neglect will increase costs—and inaccuracy of distribution will sow discord and, with time, increase the volume of disputes.

May the people of Arequipa open their eyes to this endeavor. Many useful projects are waiting to be carried out, and because of what is happening with the waters of Vincocaya and Tacna—in the region of Arequipa—and because of their soil and the temperament of their inhabitants, they are destined to be the Catalonia of Lower Peru.

NEW RURAL ESTABLISHMENTS
in Arequipa.

It would be only interjecting halfway if after having spoken about the material part of the enterprise, the formal part was not mentioned—Vincocaya and Charcani are the MEANS, cultivating new lands is the OBJECTIVE.

While the job is limited to *directing water*, the venture is paid by private funds—a private company can spend its money on whatever it wants (bearing in mind that the company can do something that has no effect now on any individual but could have an effect later).

As soon as *the preparation of the lands* begins, the business will belong to the public economic domain (unless it fails to assert the question, "How does this affect my neighbor?" A question for those who believe they are members of a society because they meet and greet one another on the streets, because they are seen, and because they seek each other out when necessary).

Rural establishments that will be built in the vicinity of Arequipa must be inclined to enrich the population and not impoverish it. The majority of those who make up the Vincocaya company are owners of the land that is presently being irrigated by the river—it is not normal for them to want to lessen or nullify their industry in one place merely for the pleasure of starting one in another. And it would be injurious to the members who *do not* have lands to think that because *they are landless*, they are indifferent to the well-being of their fellow citizens . . . Let's think on these things.

We must suppose two intentions of the Vincocaya company—it cannot avoid having these intentions, nor can it have others.

1. To take on new lands to produce new crops.
2. To initiate a new course of action in the rural economy.

As to the first intention, we must believe that the gentlemen of the company are aware that if they try to do on the new lands what they did on the old, they will encounter 4 obstacles:

> Lack of fertilizer
> Lack of laborers
> Lack of a population to stimulate consumption in the provinces,

[and] current price disproportion between local and remote sales, and transport.[2]

Second, they know that flax, hemp, forests, artificial meadows, and the offspring of lesser and greater livestock would make Arequipa prosper.

Besides maintaining moisture on the lands and fertilizing it with its waste residue (something that Peru very much needs!), the forests provide resins, tar, wood for construction, cork (cultivating the cork oak of that species), and firewood (taking advantage of pruning, trimming, and the natural life and death cycle of trees).

In the meadows, beehives can be maintained—the livestock would maintain the fields and supply the market. Need would indicate other branches of industry among the many that emerge from the immediate products of the animal material. It should be said that the temperature of the Arequipa valley is favorable to all that has been said and more.

As to the second intention, the gentlemen of the company know that the present countryside of Arequipa is the product of chance circumstances—water, which stimulates the fields, is subject to continuous, and at times bloody, disputes—the irrigation canals are poorly made; they waste much water and invite theft—the farmworkers attend only to the water that runs over the surface; they do not pay attention to seepage, although they see water break through and fall to the river from various points, especially around Tingo and in the Peña gully. They go there to swim and for recreation as well as to admire phenomena that some wells would make disappear.

CONCLUSION

In the antieconomic system [properly called *concurrence* or *opposition*],[3] the producer is the victim of the consumer, and both become the victim of the capitalist speculator: *"Each one for himself and God for everyone"* [is the maxim] without warning that the *social God for everyone* means:

> that each one thinks about the other
>
> as long as he thinks that everyone is thinking about him.

May the people of Arequipa be persuaded of a truth [unfortunately lesser known] that:

> the producers should consult one another
>
> so they do not produce more than is necessary.

Secrets, and misunderstood freedom, which imply that everyone may do what he wishes in his workshop or field, leave to chance what should be expected based on calculations—it makes the farmer who is educated an optimist, and the one who is uneducated a pessimist: the former attributes his losses to circumstances, and the latter to whatever he is told or whatever he feels like saying.

All misfortune is in superfluous production: it causes loss and poverty. Poverty puts people in difficult conditions—and destitution, in the end, sells them to capitalists who speculate on the whims or the condition of the producer . . . and do well for themselves.

How many descendants of rich property owners do we see today as brutes or beggars? This does not stop economists from extolling the virtues of agriculture or highly recommending the character and goods of the honorable farmer. Even the poets make us believe that people who live in the country are happy; especially shepherds because they spend almost all day sleeping.

Eclogues, idylls, and popular songs are in the libraries of certain masters—CRASS ignorance, hunger, and coarseness are in the shacks of their servants.

A POLITICAL revolution requires an ECONOMIC revolution.

Because of uneasiness over principles, and later, because of exaltation and delusions, the few men who felt a desire to be independent forced the masses to revolt first. They should calmly calculate and meditate much on the second revolution, because the joy of independence accentuates the need to be free.

> Mental impotence SUBDUES.
>
> Physical impotence ENSLAVES.

The ignorant man does not know how to govern himself, and the one who lives in misery cannot defend himself—one changes his status and the other only his master; but neither changes his condition: the happiness of both consists in believing that they are better off.

If Americans want true wealth from the POLITICAL revolution that the course of events has brought about and that circumstances have protected, they must pursue an ECONOMIC revolution and begin it in the fields—from there it will spread to the workshops of the few artisans they have—and daily they will notice improvements that they never would have achieved if it began in the cities.

Get involved, people of Arequipa, and DO SOMETHING, as Rodríguez has gotten involved, and SAY SOMETHING, and Arequipa will be the principal city of Peru. By overcoming two obstacles you will achieve it. One is *the aversion to getting together to take action*, and the other is *the fear of seeking advice about how to proceed*.

Form a plan of rural operations;
teach it so it can be executed;
and protect it so it can be preserved.

ECONOMIC SOCIETY
AGRICULTURAL SCHOOL
STUDENT ESTABLISHMENT

Look for streams of water,
they will give you what you need to mine
thick veins of precious metal.

—   .   .   .   .   —

—   .   .   .   .   —

—   .   .   .   .   —

Who would have thought that an IRRIGATION CHANNEL
        would motivate such writing?!
Either the writer is a *windbag*
        who took advantage of an IRRIGATION CHANNEL
or the *irrigation channel* was bursting to speak
        and took advantage of the WRITER.

Notes

1. A *topo* is a unit of measure equaling a league and a half—a little over five miles—used among the Indigenous people of South America.
2. As John Frederick Wibel (1975) explains, the landowning class of the Arequipa region, many of them wine producers, complained that the sale of *caña*, an inexpensive alcohol made from the distillation of sugarcane, drove down demand for wine in Peru. They also complained that the scarcity of human laborers and transport mules hampered their business in the years following the independence struggle (360–63).
3. In this passage and just below, square brackets are Rodríguez's. [—Eds.]

Johann Rudolf Rengger

Swiss naturalist Johann Rudolph Rengger (1795–1832) is best known for the book he wrote with Marcel Longchamp, *Historical Essay on the Revolution of Paraguay and the Dictatorial Government of Doctor Francia*, one of the key documentary sources on nineteenth-century Paraguay. Rengger and Longchamp arrived in Buenos Aires in 1818, seeking scientific and commercial opportunities in the former viceroyalty of the Río de la Plata. Alarmed at the political instability in Argentina, they traveled upriver to Asunción. Like Humboldt's friend Aimé Bonpland, who arrived a few years later, they soon found themselves prisoners of the autocratic Francia, who had closed Paraguay's borders to insulate his fledgling nation against aggression and interference from the south. Francia established a state monopoly on the sale of *yerba mate* and otherwise sharply curtailed international trade, further measures to increase stability by limiting the power of Paraguay's mercantile elite. Rengger and Longchamp's *Historical Essay* vents the authors' frustration with their irascible and idiosyncratic host, but the work presented here tells a somewhat different story. Rengger's *Journey to Paraguay in the Years 1818 to 1826*, published posthumously in a combination of Swiss German and French, is a scientist's wide-ranging account of the cultures and customs of Paraguay, along with detailed descriptions of topography, flora, and fauna. In the archive of nineteenth-century Latin America, it is a rare portrait of a country in which agricultural production is oriented toward a domestic rather than international market. In place of commercial monocropping, farmers practice sustainable agroforestry techniques developed during pre-Columbian times. And as Rengger grudgingly acknowledges, the inability to purchase imported clothes has forced Paraguayans to reinvigorate their domestic textile industry.

***

From *Journey to Paraguay in the Years 1818 to 1826* (1835)

TRANSLATED BY ELIZABETH KIEFFER

Agriculture

One of the primary occupations of the inhabitants of Paraguay is cultivation of the land.[1] While this is, to be sure, still in its nascent stages, the soil compensates with fertility for any lacking in industriousness, experience, and skill.

The plantings are located either in the forests or on the edges thereof and commonly on the slopes of hills. One rarely sees cultivation on the grass-covered plains.

The earth of the plains, composed of much sand and clay washed down from the heights, contains little humus. Furthermore, water there only slowly drains off following heavy rains. The plains are completely exposed to the strong winds as well. For these reasons, the inhabitants of Paraguay prefer to clear a piece of forestland, where the soil is always rich in humus, and to cultivate there under the protection of the trees. Or they lay out their plantings on the slope of a hill where the water cannot collect. The farmer must, of course, choose the plot according to what he intends to cultivate, or conversely, select the plantings in accordance with the type of soil.

In order to cultivate a new plot, the farmer clear-cuts a portion of woodland, making use of the large trunks to fence in the area and burning the remaining wood on-site. He then turns over or hoes the land, since due to the many stumps and roots a plow cannot be employed in the first year. The mixture of the rich forest loam with the ash from the burned trees renders now an extremely fertile soil. Such a *rozado*, as one calls a new plot, is usually planted with tobacco or corn, later with sugarcane or potatoes or watermelons, etc.

The care of the topsoil is extremely simple. Each year the land that is to be planted is either superficially hoed or plowed, or both, and then sown. Fertilization with manure is unknown in Paraguay, where they fertilize with the ash resulting from burning all the remaining roots, stems, and leaves of plants following the harvest. Similarly unknown is irrigation, which only rarely would be necessary. The tools of cultivation are likewise simple, limited to the plow, karst hoe, shovel, and rake. The Paraguayan farmer is unacquainted with the harrow; he gathers grass roots etc. by hand or with a simple rake. The shovel for digging is usually made from the shoulder blade of an ox bound onto a handle, although one does also find iron shovels. The karst hoe is iron. The plow is made up of a long wooden beam, one end of which is affixed to the yoke of the oxen; the other end is equipped with a guiding handle facing upward. At this end facing downward is a wooden plowshare directed forward, which is incapable of digging even a half foot deep into the ground.

Working the soil as it is done in Europe, moreover, is not at all necessary in Paraguay. The humus can be turned over easily. As this stratum is not very thick, with deep plowing the farmer would only churn up and bring to the surface the subsoil, those layers consisting of sand and clay. Furthermore, Paraguay's climate is both warm and humid. Prolonged droughts are rare, since abundant dew falls nearly every night. With such warmth and moisture, finally, all dead plant material easily decays and decomposes into the earth. These factors render fertilization and irrigation of the plots most unnecessary. When after several years, despite crop rotation, the productivity of the soil declines, a new *rozado* is created and the exhausted soil is left fallow until it regains its fertility.

Cotton

One branch of agriculture that has increased greatly in the last decade in Paraguay is the planting of cotton. Those Paraguayans who previously had been involved in shipping or in gathering Paraguay Herb (*yerba*), etc., and through such lines of business had acquired their clothing by means of trade with Buenos Aires, as a consequence of the trade prohibition, should they choose not to go around naked, now must cultivate and process cotton themselves. This was one of the few positive outcomes of Francia's dictatorship.

Cotton shrubs are planted, similar to sugarcane and manioc root, in long rows that are sufficiently widely spaced to allow the passage of a plow. Shrubs are spaced four to five feet apart in the rows. Cotton requires fairly rich soil. It is never planted in the *rozados* but rather in open areas exposed to the wind with adequate drainage of rainwater, since good air circulation is required for the fineness of the cotton and excess moisture is detrimental to growth . . .

Cotton provides the country dwellers of Paraguay nearly all their clothing. Azara unfairly disparages textiles produced here, for even in his time in this country cotton cloth was worked into shirts and hammocks, the beauty of which was admired even in Europe. It is true that the work proceeds only slowly, since cotton is spun from the spindle, only rarely on the most recently introduced wheel. Only the women know how to produce extremely fine, even, and strong strands. The weaving looms and reeds are so artlessly set up that doubtless four times the labor and time are required as would be necessary in Europe for the finishing of a piece of cloth. Nonetheless one must not disdain the Paraguayan cotton cloth, termed *lienzo*, to the degree that Azara did. Several types of *lienzo* are made, differing only in density and in the delicacy of the thread. These fabrics are worked into shirts, undergarments, skirts for both rural women and in general for those of the lower class, made into tablecloths, bedsheets, hand towels, etc. Great luxury predominates in the shirts and undergarments, as well as in the hand towels and women's skirts. A shirt can cost twelve to sixteen piastres and weighs then at the most one and a half ounces. These shirts are as fine as the finest percale, but not as dense. They are adorned at the collar, at the cuffs, and on the chest with pretty embroidery. Instead of a jabot, shirts have a fine lace, likewise made in Paraguay from the locally spun thread. The undergarments are often set with embroidery and lace, displaying the most charming designs, a foot wide at their lower end. A country girl's fine shirt, as well as her skirt, can cost up to twenty and forty piastres, respectively. But in this case it is above all the extent of embroidery that makes these pieces of clothing more expensive. For Paraguay's climate *lienzo* is a most fitting and pleasant cloth to wear against the skin: it protects against cold, and fine *lienzo* only clings too greatly to the skin when one perspires.

Also made from the cotton thread are various types of hammocks, which, since they are long and wide, offer very comfortable and refreshing resting places in the summer. In wealthier homes these hammocks are also items of great luxury, on which the owners spend either much time and labor to create or much money to purchase. I own a very beautifully woven hammock with a hem of artfully worked lace that cost the person who gave it to me more than forty piastres.

Lastly, cotton yarn is employed in making *ponchos* (cloaks) and horse blankets as well; for the latter, wool is mixed in with the cotton occasionally. By the way, this branch of the industry did not come into vogue until most recently after *ponchos* and blankets could no longer be imported from Corrientes, whence previously they had been obtained. This is also one of the advantageous outcomes of Francia's government, since the considerable sums that previously left the country for these objects now promote domestic commercial industry. After several failed attempts, the Paraguayans have finally succeeded in making *ponchos* that are just as beautiful, if not more so, than those found earlier in Corrientes. A *poncho*, when well woven, which in Paraguay one calls *tejido a pala*, is of such a density that rain does not easily penetrate it. On the contrary, when the surface becomes wet, the threads pull together so strongly that the fabric becomes as stiff as leather and water flows off lengthwise.

Note

1. Cultivation of the land has come into vogue in Paraguay only following the Revolution and after this country's trade was devastated, as explained in my *Historical Essay on the Revolution of Paraguay*. [—Author's note.]

Gertrudis Gómez de Avellaneda

Known in her own time as La Peregrina, or "the Wanderer," the Cuban-born Gertrudis Gómez de Avellaneda (1814–73) would become one of Spain's most prolific and celebrated Romantic writers (Aira 2001, 244–46). Avellaneda's talent for versification emerged at the tender age of nine, when she wrote an elaborate neoclassical elegy on the death of her father. Her mother eventually remarried and the family relocated to Spain, where Avellaneda would soon make a name for herself as a poet, novelist, and playwright. Public acclaim for La Peregrina was such that an attempt was made to have her initiated into the famous Real Academia Española, but the customs of the time prohibited admission of a woman. Nonetheless, when Avellaneda and her second husband, Domingo Verdugo, crisscrossed Spain in search of a climate that would prove beneficial to his health, she was revered everywhere they went; the same was true when the couple settled in Cuba in 1859. Over the years, Avellaneda's reputation as a writer has suffered for two reasons. One is that the scandals of her personal life have often overshadowed the serious study of Avellaneda's work. The other is that her most widely read publication, the 1841 novel *Sab*, presents only a somewhat ambivalent critique of chattel slavery as it was practiced in Cuba during Avellaneda's lifetime. The plot revolves around a beautiful creole heiress who becomes engaged to a conniving, upstart Englishman while the devoted slave—Sab—silently pines for her. In the chapter reproduced here, the blooming garden Sab has created for Carlota reminds readers of the "natural" beauty and abundance of Cuba, which contribute to the shining moral and personal qualities of its inhabitants.

***

From *Sab* (1841)

TRANSLATED BY NINA M. SCOTT

Having rested most of the day and all of the night, Carlota awoke at sunrise and, seeing that all still slept, got up out of bed, wishing to breathe the pure dawn air outside. Her indisposition, brought on solely by the fatigue of a sleepless night and the emotional upheavals she had undergone the day before, had disappeared completely after a long and deep sleep, and when she awoke at the sun's first light she felt happy and fortunate, saying to herself: "Enrique is alive and out of all danger; in a week I will have him beside me, loving and happy, and within a few months I will be joined to him by indissoluble bonds."

She put on a light dress and went out silently so as not to wake Teresa. Dawn was fresh and lovely, and the countryside had never seemed to her quite so picturesque and colorful.

When she emerged from the house carrying some kernels of corn in her handkerchief, she was immediately surrounded by innumerable tame birds. The Berber doves, her favorites, and the small, colorful American hens came to pick at the kernels in her skirt and landed fluttering on her shoulders.

A little farther away a peacock ruffled his neck feathers of gray and blue, proudly displaying his magnificent iridescent tail to the first rays of the sun, while the peaceful gander slowly came up to get his portion. The young girl felt very happy at this moment, like a child who encounters her toys after waking from an innocent sleep on her mother's bosom.

Fear of a great misfortune makes us less sensitive to smaller trials. Carlota, having believed her beloved lost to her forever, felt his momentary absence much less keenly. Her soul, exhausted from so many acute pangs, rested with delight on the things which surrounded her, and that incipient, pure day seemed to the maiden's eyes like the peaceful times of her earliest youth.

At the time our story takes place, no great importance was given to gardens in places like Puerto Príncipe; they were hardly known, perhaps because the entire country itself was like a vast and magnificent garden which nature had made and with which no artifice dared to compete. Nevertheless Sab, who knew how much his young mistress loved flowers, had created a small and delightful garden next to Bellavista's main house, toward which the young woman, having fed her favorite birds, now turned her steps.

This little garden adhered neither to the French nor to the English fashion: in laying it out, Sab had followed only his own fancy.

It was a small enclosure protected from the hot south wind by a triple row of tall reeds of a handsome dark green known as *pitos*, which, when gently ruffled by the breeze, produced a soft and melancholy murmur, like that of a gently purling brook. The garden was a perfect square, the other three sides of which were formed by arches of rushes covered by showy festoons of vines and garden balsam, where buzzing hummingbirds as brilliant as emeralds and topazes sipped from red and gold blossoms.

In this small enclosure, Sab had assembled all of Carlota's most beloved flowers. An *astronomía* displayed sumptuous clusters of deep purple blossoms. There were lilies and roses, *clavellinas* and jasmine, the modest violet and the proud sunflower, enamored of the eye of heaven, the changeable pink *malva*, wood sorrel with its pearly blossoms and the *pasionaria*, whose magnificent calyx bears the sacred marks of the Redeemer's passion. In the center of the garden, there was a little pond in which Sab had collected some small, brightly colored fish; encircling the pond was a bench shaded by the broad green leaves of the banana trees.

Carlota ran about the garden filling her white batiste handkerchief with flowers; from time to time she interrupted this task to pursue the colored butterflies which hovered over the blossoms. When fatigued she sat down at the banks of the pond. Her beautiful eyes gradually took on a pensive expression, and she distractedly plucked apart the blossoms she had just chosen so happily, then tossed them into the pond.

Once she was roused from her daydreaming by a slight sound which to her seemed to have been made by the footsteps of someone approaching. Thinking it was Teresa, who had woken up and noticing her absence was coming to fetch her, she called to her several times. No one answered and unconsciously Carlota fell back into her reverie. Not for long, however, for the loveliest and whitest of the butterflies she had seen that morning daringly came to land on her skirt, subsequently fluttering off with provocative flight. Carlota shook her head as though to expel from it a troublesome thought and followed the butterfly with her eyes, seeing it alight on a jasmine whose whiteness it excelled. The young woman got up and darted over to it, but the swift insect evaded her skilled advance and escaped from between her lovely fingers; rapidly fluttering off and stopping at intervals, it led its pursuer on for a long time, mocking her attempts at the very moment that she thought them successful. Tiring a little, Carlota redoubled her efforts, lay in ambush for her swift opponent, kept after it tenaciously, and throwing her handkerchief over it, finally managed to catch it. With the expression of triumph her face became even more beautiful, and with childish glee she peered at the prisoner through an opening in the handkerchief; but with the same inconstancy of the young, she was suddenly no longer amused by the misfortune of her captive. Opening her handkerchief, she took delight in seeing it fly away freely, just as a moment before she had taken pleasure in capturing it.

Seeing her so young, so childlike, so lovely, unreflecting men would never guess that the heart which beat with joy at the captivity and the release of a butterfly would be capable of feelings as strong as they are deep. Ah, they do not know that for superior souls it is necessary to descend from time to time from their elevated heights, that those extraordinary spirits, left unsatisfied by the greatest that the world and life offer them, also need trivial things. If at times they become frivolous and flighty, it is because they feel the need to respect their great gifts and fear to be consumed by them.

In the same way, the current gently spreads its waters over the plants of the field and caresses the flowers which in its impetuous flood it is capable of destroying and uprooting in an instant.

Carlota was interrupted in her innocent amusement by the bustle of the slaves going off to work. She called to them, asking their names one by one and inquiring with enchanting kindness about each one's particular situation, position, and state of being. Delighted, the Blacks responded by showering her with blessings and extolling Don Carlos's goodness and Sab's devotion and benevolence. Carlota enjoyed listening to them and, with words of compassion and affection, divided among them what money she had in her pockets. The slaves went off still blessing her, and she looked after them with brimming eyes.

"Poor unfortunate souls!" she exclaimed. "They judge themselves fortunate because they are not receiving blows and abuse, and they calmly eat the bread of slavery. They judge themselves fortunate, yet their children are slaves before they leave their mother's womb, and they see them sold off like unthinking beasts . . .

Their children, their flesh and blood! When I am Enrique's wife," she added after a moment of silence, "no unhappy soul around me will breathe the poisonous air of slavery. We will give all our Blacks their freedom. What does it matter to be less wealthy? Will we be any less happy because of it? A hut with Enrique is enough for me, and for him there will be no greater riches than my gratitude and my love."

When she finished these words the reeds trembled as though a strong hand had shaken them, and Carlota, startled, left the garden and hurried toward the house.

She had just reached the threshold when behind her she heard a familiar voice wishing her good morning and saw that it was Sab.

"I thought you would have already left for the city," she said to him.

"It seemed to me," said the young man with some agitation, "that I should wait for Your Grace to get up to ask if you had any orders for me."

"I appreciate that, Sab, and will go right now to write to Enrique; I'll give you my letter in a moment."

Carlota went into the house where her father, her sisters, and Teresa slept soundly. As Sab saw her disappear from view, he exclaimed with a deep and melancholy voice, "Why can't your innocent and fervent dreams come true, angel of Heaven? . . . Why did He Who placed you into this world of wretchedness and evil not give this handsome foreigner the mulatto's soul?"

Deeply distressed, he bowed his head and remained lost a while in unhappy thoughts. Subsequently he went to the stable in which were housed his black pony and Enrique's handsome sorrel. Placing his hand on the pony's back, he looked at him with tender eyes.

"Loyal and peaceful animal," he said to him, "you gently carry the weight of this wretched body. Not even the tempest frightens you or induces you to shake it off against the crags. While you respect your worthless burden, this handsome animal rids himself of his, throwing and trampling the fortunate man whose life is cherished and whose death would be mourned. My poor pony! If you were as capable of understanding as you are of affection you would know how much good you could have done to hurl me against the rocks during the storm. No tears would be shed at my death . . . the poor mulatto would be no loss to anyone and you could gallop free over the land or carry a more worthy rider."

The horse lifted its head and looked at him as though wishing to understand him and thereupon licked Sab's hands; by this the animal seemed to be saying "I love you a great deal so as to please you; from no other hand but yours do I gladly accept food."

Domingo F. Sarmiento

Domingo Faustino Sarmiento (1811–88) began his career as a rural schoolteacher and became both president of Argentina and one of the country's greatest proponents of public education. Sarmiento entered politics at a young age, and his outspoken opposition to the dictatorship of Juan Manuel de Rosas led him to flee to Chile, where he wrote his most famous book, *Facundo: Civilization and Barbarism* (1845). *Facundo*, as it is commonly known today, is equal parts biography, history, novel, and sociological treatise. It includes observations about gaucho life and the Argentine countryside, as well as a denunciation of Rosas through the biography of his gaucho lieutenant, the titular Facundo. The excerpt featured here is from chapter 1, which describes Argentina's expansive, empty territories and shows Sarmiento's strong disdain for the unruly, mixed-race horsemen of the interior. *Facundo* argues that the Argentine propensity for "the predominance of brute force, the preponderance of the strongest, authority with no limits and no accountability" is a consequence of the "limitless expanse" of Argentina, whose harsh environments shaped the character of its inhabitants and fostered the "barbarity" of the gauchos and Indians alike. The only solution, according to Sarmiento, is to "civilize" the vast, unsettled expanses of the pampa into modest homesteads, where pioneering families can educate their children in civic and domestic virtues. Curiously, Sarmiento refers to the pampa—a vast expanse of natural grasslands, much like the Great Plains of the midwestern United States—as *el desierto*, an ambiguous term that is often translated as "wilderness" or even "desert."

***

"Physical Aspect of the Argentine Republic, and the Ideas, Customs, and Characters It Engenders" (1845)

TRANSLATED BY KATHLEEN ROSS

> L'étendue des Pampas est si prodigieuse qu'au nord elles son bornées par des bosquets de palmiers, et au midi par des neiges éternelles.[1] —HEAD

The American continent ends to the south in a point, at whose extreme end the Strait of Magellan is formed. To the west, and at a short distance from the Pacific, the Chilean Andes run parallel to the coast. The land that lies to the east of that chain of mountains and to the west of the Atlantic, following the Río de la Plata toward the interior upstream along the Uruguay, is the territory formerly called the United

Provinces of the Río de la Plata, and there, blood is still being shed in order to name it either the Argentine Republic or the Argentine Confederation. To the north are Paraguay, the Gran Chaco, and Bolivia, its alleged borders.

The immense expanse of land is entirely unpopulated at its extreme limits, and it possesses navigable rivers that no fragile little boat has yet plowed. The disease from which the Argentine Republic suffers is its own expanse: the desert wilderness surrounds it on all sides and insinuates into its bowels; solitude, a barren land with no human habitation, in general are the unquestionable borders between one province and another. There, immensity is everywhere: immense plains, immense forests, immense rivers, the horizon always unclear, always confused with the earth amid swift-moving clouds and tenuous mists, which do not allow the point where the world ends and the sky begins to be marked in a far-off perspective. To the south and the north, savages lurk, waiting for moonlit nights to descend, like a pack of hyenas, on the herds that graze the countryside, and on defenseless settlements. In the solitary caravan of wagons slowly traversing the Pampas that stops to rest for a few moments, the crew, gathered around a poor fire, mechanically turn their eyes toward the south at the least murmur of wind blowing the dry grass, to bore their gaze into the profound darkness of the night, searching out the sinister bulks of savage hordes that from one moment to the next can surprise them unprepared. If their ears hear no sound, if their eyes cannot pierce the dark veil that covers this quiet solitude, to be absolutely sure they turn their gaze to the ears of some horse next to the fire, observing if these are at rest and easily folded back. Then their interrupted conversation continues, or they put the half-singed strips of dried beef that are their food into their mouths. If it is not the proximity of savages that worries the man of the countryside, it is the fear of a tiger stalking him, of a viper he might step on. This insecurity in life, which is customary and permanent in the countryside, imprints upon the Argentine character, to my mind, a certain stoic resignation to violent death, making it one of the misfortunes that are inseparable from life, a manner of dying just like any other, and perhaps this may explain, in part, the indifference with which death is given and received, without leaving any deep or lasting impression on those who survive.

The inhabited part of this country, so privileged in riches and containing all manner of climates, may be divided into three distinct physiognomies that imprint different qualities on the populace, according to the way in which it must come to terms with the nature that surrounds it. In the north, melding into the Chaco, a dense forest with impenetrable branches covers expanses we would call unheard of, were there anything unheard of about colossal forms anywhere in the entire expanse of America. In the center, parallel zone, the Pampas and the jungle dispute the land for a long while; the forest dominates in places, then breaks down into sickly, spiny bushes; the jungle appears again thanks to some river that favors it, until in the south the Pampas finally triumph and display their smooth, downy brow, infinite, with no known limit, no noteworthy break. It is an image of the sea on land, the land as it looks on the map, the land still waiting for a command to produce plants and all kinds of seed.

As a notable feature of the physiognomy of this country, one could indicate the agglomeration of navigable rivers that meet in the east, from all points on the horizon, to unite in the Plata and gravely present their stupendous tribute to the ocean, which takes it on the flank, not without visible signs of turbulence and respect. But these immense canals, excavated by the solicitous hand of nature, do not bring about any changes at all in national customs. The son of the Spanish adventurers that colonized the country detests navigation, and feels himself imprisoned within the narrow confines of a boat or launch. When a large river cuts off his path, he calmly undresses, prepares his horse, and directs it to swim toward some barren island out in the distance; arriving there, horse and horseman rest, and from island to island, the crossing is finally completed.

In this manner, the greatest favor that divine providence grants to a people is disdained by the Argentine gaucho, who sees it as an obstacle opposing his movement, rather than the most powerful medium for facilitating it. In this manner, the source of the greatness of nations which brought celebrity to remote Egypt, which made Holland great and is the cause of the rapid development of North America—navigation through rivers or canals—is a dead resource, unexploited by the inhabitant of the margins of the Bermejo, Pilcomayo, Paraná, Paraguay, and Uruguay Rivers. From the Plata, a few little ships with Italian and Genoese crews sail upstream; but this movement goes only a few leagues, and then ceases almost entirely. The instinct for navigation, possessed to such a high degree by the Saxons of the north, was not given to the Spanish. A different spirit is needed to stir up those arteries, in which the vivifying fluids of a nation today lie stagnant. Of all these rivers that should be bringing civilization, power, and wealth to even the most hidden depths of the continent, making Santa Fe, Entre Ríos, Corrientes, Córdoba, Salta, Tucumán, and Jujuy peoples swimming in riches and overflowing with population and culture, there is only one that is fecund in its benefits for those who live on its banks: the Plata, which sums up all of them.

At its mouth are situated two cities: Montevideo and Buenos Aires, today alternately reaping the advantages of their enviable position. Buenos Aires is destined one day to be the most gigantic city of both Americas. With a benign climate, mistress of the navigation of the hundred rivers that flow at its feet, leisurely reclining over an immense territory, and with thirteen interior provinces knowing no other outlet for their products, it already would be the American Babylon, had not the spirit of the Pampas blown over it and the riches that the rivers and provinces must always bring to it in tribute been strangled at their source. It alone, in the vast expanse of Argentina, is in contact with European nations; it alone exploits the advantages of foreign commerce; it alone has power and income. In vain, the provinces have asked it to allow a little bit of European civilization, industry, and immigration to reach them; stupid, colonial policies have turned a deaf ear to this clamor. But the provinces avenged themselves by sending Buenos Aires, in Rosas, much and too much of the barbarism they have to spare . . .

I have indicated this circumstance of the monopolizing position of Buenos Aires to show how in that country there is an organization of the land so central and so unitary, that although Rosas might have cried in good faith: "Confederation or death!" he would have ended up with the Unitarist system that he has established today. We, however, wanted unity in civilization and liberty and have been given unity in barbarism and slavery. But another time will come in which things will return to their normal course. For now, what concerns us is to know that the progress of civilization accrues only in Buenos Aires: the Pampas are a very bad means of bringing and distributing it to the provinces, and later we shall see what results from this. But, beyond all these features peculiar to certain parts of that territory, one general, uniform, and constant trait predominates: whether the land is covered with the lush, colossal vegetation of the tropics, or sickly, spiny, rough bushes reveal the scarce moisture that gives them life, or, finally, whether the Pampas display their clear, monotonous face, the surface of the land is generally flat and unified, without even the sierras of San Luis and Córdoba in the center, and some outlying branches of the Andes in the north, being enough to interrupt this limitless continuity. A new unifying element for the nation that one day will populate those vast solitudes, since it is well known that mountains interposed between countries, and other natural obstacles, maintain the isolation of peoples and preserve their primitive peculiarities. North America is destined to be a federation, less because of the initial independence of its settlements, than because of her broad exposure to the Atlantic and the many routes that lead from it to the interior: the St. Lawrence in the north, the Mississippi in the south, and the immense system of canals in the center. The Argentine Republic is "one and indivisible."

Many philosophers, too, have thought that the plains prepare the way for despotism, in the same way that the mountains have lent support to the forces of liberty. This limitless plain, which from Salta to Buenos Aires and from there to Mendoza, for a distance of more than seven hundred leagues, allows enormous, heavy wagons to roll without meeting a single obstacle on roads where human hands have scarcely needed to cut down more than a few trees and shrubs, this plain constitutes one of the most notable features of the Republic's interior physiognomy. To prepare routes of communication, all that is needed are individual effort and the results of raw nature; even if skill were to lend nature its assistance, even if the forces of society tried to supplant the weakness of the individual, the colossal dimensions of the task would terrify the most enterprising, and the inadequacy of the effort would make it inopportune. So, in the matter of roads, wild nature will make the laws for a long time to come, and the actions of civilization will remain weak and ineffective.

Note

1. "The vastness of the pampas is so prodigious that it is bordered by palm tree forests to the north and eternal snow in the south." This epigraph, attributed by Sarmiento to Francis Bond Head, is nevertheless a quotation from the French translation of Humboldt's *Views of Nature* (1828). A discussion of *Facundo's* quotations can be found in Eva-Lynn Jagoe, 2008. *The End of the World as They Knew It: Writing Experiences of the Argentine South* (Lewisburg, Penn.: Bucknell University Press), 46. [—Eds.]

José María Samper

Born in Honda, Gran Colombia (now Colombia), José María Samper (1828–88) was part of the first generation to grow up in the independent republics of Spanish America. His family benefited substantially from the reforms passed by Tomás Cipriano de Mosquera in the 1840s, particularly the liberalization of the tobacco trade, which enabled them to amass a small fortune during the boom that followed. When the conservatives returned to power in 1858, Samper—lawyer, merchant, politician, and journalist—abandoned South America for Europe, where he wrote five books of musings on politics, art, geography, morality, and other subjects. In the late 1860s, Samper would abandon liberalism altogether. He converted to Catholicism and became a prominent voice among Colombian conservatives, along with his second wife and frequent collaborator, journalist Soledad Acosta Samper. The excerpt included here is from *Essay on the Political Revolutions of the Colombian Republics*, published serially in a London-based magazine in 1861. As the critic Felipe Martínez Pinzón (2016, 57) points out, Samper's writings from this period vent his frustrations at his class's inability to create a disciplined agricultural workforce from a population accustomed to helping themselves to the bounty of tropical nature. In this piece, steeped in the environmental determinism and pseudoscientific racism of the time, Samper laments Spain's inability to colonize the Amazon basin in ways that would lead to a permanent flourishing of civilization in that area. He distinguishes between orderly, peace-loving peoples of the South American highlands and the unruly, ungovernable groups that populate the tropical lowlands and coasts. Like Sarmiento with regard to the pampas, Samper thus saw the jungle itself as an impediment to political, economic, and cultural progress.

*** *

"Former Physical and Social Conditions of the New World" (1861)

TRANSLATED BY GRADY C. WRAY

Life's wonderful exuberance and nature's forces, like its riches—endless and infinitely varied—impose immense difficulties on a disorderly, capricious, and adventurous colonization. In such a world where everything is colossal in nature; where a tree grows from dusk to daybreak; where light functions as an indefatigable worker with prodigious faculties of production; where night and day the earth ferments with feverish and staggering creative power, making felt the exhalation of its accelerated respiration and the palpitations of a fiery pulse; where life is created twice as fast due to the absence of winters and autumns and there is no stopping decomposition, reproduction, and proliferation; where it seems as if creation has not yet finished, and in an incessant delirium of vitality, voluptuousness, and progress, it is inebriated with magnificent possibilities. In such a world, we say that it was not possible to create civilization, except on the condition of concentrating it. There, scarcely can one take a step without the last footprint disappearing under the always invasive wave of a feverish and lustful vegetation that is born, grows, and dies to be reborn one hundred times over in a perpetual tremor of love and forcefulness. Cut open a pathway and tomorrow, if you turn your back, you will find only jungle in its place, a temple of lush green vegetation. Build a house in the wilderness, and if you do not fight hour after hour against the seeds of life that ferment under and all around, in the soil as in the air and light, the relentlessly generous power of nature will quickly expel you from the asylum that you believed was secure. Construct a port, a dike, a bridge, trusting in the calm waters of the waves that lap around it; within a week, if you do not defend your construction head to head, the torrent that has become a river, the cascade that has become formidable falls, and the river, just born, will be transformed into a sea, and suddenly they will demolish all construction in a minute's time.

To the Europeans who are not familiar with the New World, and in order to give them an idea of the physical greatness of the continent, one could tell them: Multiply the Alps by the Pyrenees and the Apennines twenty times, and you will have something similar to the Andes, although with great geological and hydrographic differences. Imagine the Mediterranean, solid, carved out by rivers as large as the Straits of Gibraltar, motionless, whipped by powerful hurricanes and covered with gigantic grasses, with interminable forests of *guadua* bamboo, with palm jungles, colossal vegetation, and plants of all types, and you will have some idea of the pampas of the River Plate and the llanos of the Orinoco region. Imagine Vesuvius and Etna multiplied one hundred times on top of the swarms of snowfalls three times more colossal than Mont Blanc, and you will understand Chimborazo, Cotopaxi, Antisana, and all the snowcapped mountains and volcanoes of Colombia. The Guadarrama, the Nevada, and the Morena mountain ranges of Spain are tiny groups of hills compared with the Colombian mountain ranges. Thus is the proportion of everything.

So, to think about colonizing and exploiting such a world and disseminating forces without foreseeing the consequences of the prodigious exuberance that threatens to devour everything was to compromise the work of colonization from the first. That is what took place. Spain was too weak to monopolize and dominate the world that it had conquered with such supreme ferocity. There is an immense difference and distance between simple conquest—which does not require anything but heroic qualities—and domination, which demands having the genius of administration and numerous elements of a permanent and complicated order.

Spain, a knightly and warrior nation, fanatic and tenacious, and deeply faithful to its traditions, did not have the necessary elasticity (nor did the civilization of that time) to bend or accommodate the novelty, the grandeur, and the exuberance of the Colombian world in order to assimilate it gradually, basing its actions on the related civilizations of Mexico and Guatemala or those of the Chibcha Empire or the Quechuas, or Peruvians, so happily established on the beautiful, fertile, and benign high plateaus of the Andes. Thus, the grandeur, novelty, and exuberance of America were the obstacles of colonization, no less than the imponderable wealth in gold that led to social phenomena that we will analyze later.

If the discovered physical world was so extraordinary, then what were the characteristic conditions of its races and its way of being social? It is important to determine them, if only perfunctorily.

But of course it is necessary to establish a distinction that nature has determined in the distribution of the races. The region of the high plateaus had concentrated efforts of civilization in progress. The hot region of the coasts, of the deep valleys, the pampas, and the llanos were the immense empire of barbarity. In this way the mountainous regions and the hydrography of Colombia were the most secure guides, tracing new societies on top of the base of those that already existed.

The phenomenon was uniform. Cortés, like Alvarado, Quesada and Federmann, Benalcázar and Pizarro, had identical luck. On the coasts and in the deep valleys, there were terrible and mortal battles with bellicose, untamable, and unclothed tribes, essentially hunters, with little or nothing to do with agriculture and without civil life or determined norms of organization. They lived by chance and were entirely nomadic, uncomely tribes lacking nobility, profoundly miserable in their full savage freedom. But upon climbing to the high plateaus of Mexico, to the Venezuelan Andes, to Sogamoso, Bogotá, and Popayán in the Granadian Andes, to Quito, Cuzco, etc., the situation changed entirely.

There, the sweetness of the climates was favorable to the conquistadors, as were the wealth and abundance of agriculture. They found vast cities and innumerable towns and hamlets that gave them protection from the elements; Indigenous armies of forty, eighty, or a hundred thousand that succumbed, almost without combat, to the hundreds of reckless conquistadors. Instead of astuteness, rebel maliciousness, and inflexible resistance from nomadic tribes, those of the high plateaus distinguished themselves by their simple innocence, their blind faith, their sense of hospitality, their love of peace, their sedentary lifestyle, and their sweetness and deference. All victory is a slaughter of lambs because the Indian of the high plateaus does not defend himself; instead he surrenders, kneels down, pleads, cries, and resigns himself to slavery without protest.

What do the conquistadors find in this region? Monuments of notable architecture; rudiments of timekeeping, drawings, arithmetic, and writing; a complete system of sending messages, of taxation, and regular organized communication; bridges, canals, paths, roads, sumptuous temples, prayer rooms, monasteries for virgins, public granaries, opulent and very orderly cities; a full system of civil and penal laws, courts, legislative and administrative counsel, hierarchies in governmental authority, advanced religions, regular and permanent worship and religious orders; recognized and organized marriage and property; flourishing agriculture, very notable industries (particularly that of weaving), excessive use of service and domestic animals; notable progress in civil and military strategy; important arts, such as painting, dissecting, metalworking, fermentation of vegetable substances, etc., whose secrets have been lost.

And all this mixture of civilization's elements was linked to vast confederate systems in which one can see the gradation of tribes, nations, kingdoms, and empires, such as those of the caciques, the *zipas*, the *zaques*,[1] the Incas, and the emperors. And the races? Much more beautiful, robust, and intelligent than those on the coasts and in the hot valleys; hardworking races, fraternal to the point of socialism, sweet and hospitable, susceptible to progress provided that the regime of colonization did not brusquely refute them.

The Spanish monarchs and their representatives in Colombia did not know how to appreciate the polite qualities of these infantile races, eminently accessible to civilization. They knew even less about how to understand the particular genius of the institutions, customs, and traditions of these embryonic nationalities. They wanted to centralize everything, there, where nature, social organization, and the customs were federal; and in this way they suddenly broke the springs and muscles of those societies, condemning them to perish or degenerate. Lacking the genius of colonization, and not having (as occurred later with the Puritans from Scotland in America) any political or social interest that would adhere them to the conquered soil except for a slight interest in collecting and storing gold to return to the opulent metropolises, the Spaniards destroyed at the root the elements of the new, complex society that should have emerged from the Andean high plateaus.

Note

1. The Muisca Confederation was ruled in the south by a leader called a *zipa* and in the north by a *zaque*. [—Eds.]

FOUR
Regionalism and the Export Boom

The first decades of the twentieth century were one of the most devastating periods for Latin American environments and one of the richest and most productive for Latin American environmental literature. The selections in this part and the next respond to the economic, demographic, and ecological transformations associated with the export boom of 1870–1930: part 4 focuses on the body of prose works known as Latin American regionalism and part 5 on the urban poetry and prose of Modernismo. Both, in their ways, are by-products of the export boom, when Latin American economies, some only recently emancipated from the colonial monopolies imposed by Spain and Portugal, were reorganized so as to maximize the output of primary products for sale in Europe and the United States. Rather than developing diversified economies as in the industrializing United States, Latin American countries of the late nineteenth and early twentieth centuries tended to focus on one or two products—oil, rubber, bananas, beef, lumber, coffee beans, and so forth—in high demand elsewhere. As it had since the sixteenth century, the idea of nature as a set of potentially profitable commodities thus continued to have a central role in economic thought as well as cultural imaginaries and narratives of collective identity.

The export boom replicated the colonial past in other ways too. As critic Ericka Beckman (2013, xix) writes, it was marked by "a condition of *non*-independence in the sphere of global market relations," which took the form of economic cycles of boom and bust, growing dependency on foreign imports, and income inequality between a comprador elite and the impoverished underclass. This "condition of *non*-independence"—also referred to as informal imperialism and neocolonialism—was experienced in different ways and to varying degrees throughout Latin America. During much of the nineteenth century, British merchants, entrepreneurs, and bankers had sought to insert themselves into Latin American economic life, filling voids created by the dismantling of the Spanish and Portuguese empires and creating new opportunities, often tied to technology and infrastructure. As the civil wars of the early national period gradually came to an end, Latin American governments undertook expensive public works projects intended to support the expansion of the export sector, such as dredging ports and building railroads, with foreign capital, technology, and expertise.

With the British Empire at its height, Latin Americans, including elites, often found their dealings with British capitalists frustratingly asymmetrical. But the exercise of British power was mild in comparison with that of the United States, which showed less restraint in deploying its armed forces to ensure the preferential treatment of North American businesses. The U.S. intervention in Cuba's independence struggle—later the Spanish-American War—marked "the extension of direct political hegemony in the Caribbean basin" (Halperín Donghi 1993, 163), resulting in political control of Puerto Rico, as well as of the Philippines and Guam. Cuba, though nominally independent, was also strongly dominated by the United States; the Dominican Republic would come under U.S. occupation in 1916. Panama's 1903 secession from Colombia, following an uprising led by officials of the Panama New Canal Company and proclaimed with U.S. naval vessels watching offshore, provided a far-reaching example of the lengths Washington would go to on behalf of U.S. capitalists.

Cuban patriot José Martí perceived before many the growing threat of U.S. imperialism. His 1891 essay "Our America"—"Nuestra América"—urged Latin American elites to set aside the long-established privileges and prejudices that separated them from their compatriots and work together to withstand the menace of the northern colossus. Rethinking national identity based on class and race led Martí to a powerful reconceptualization of the idea of nature and its place in Latin American political thought. Instead of raw materials that can be transformed or converted into spiritual or cultural wealth, nature, in Martí's view—specifically what is local and autochthonous—is the basis of political reason (Castro Herrera 1996).

As Martí's essay suggests, the disadvantageous geopolitical structures of the late nineteenth century reproduced similar structures operating at the national level. Referred to as internal colonialism, or *endocolonialismo*, the exploitation of an internal frontier by relatively privileged socioeconomic groups situated in more metropolitan areas of the same country leads to rapid, often irreversible environmental degradation. During the export boom, the drive to maximize profits led to the ravaging of the continent's interior. Oil drilling led to spills and contamination in Mexico, Venezuela, and Ecuador, while the harvesting of natural rubber led to deforestation and species loss in much of Amazonia. At the same time, the intensity with which monoculture was practiced by producers of bananas and coffee in Central and South America turned agriculture into an essentially extractive practice whereby soil systems were devastated with little thought for regeneration or long-term productivity. In the Brazilian northeast the burning of forest for agriculture and eventually ranching—a practice that began well before the arrival of the Portuguese but accelerated dramatically in the nineteenth century—led to a cycle of devastating droughts and floods. Euclides da Cunha (1902) described the phenomenon in his classic *Backlands: The Canudos Campaign* and cautioned, "Working side by side with the elements, the northeasterly winds, the suction of levels of air, the dog days, wind erosion, sudden storms, man has been a nefarious component of the forces that have been demolishing the climate. If he did not create all this, he did transform it. The ax of the man in the *caatingas* served as a supplement to the scorching sun with his burnings" (51).

Many of the narratives in the canon of Latin American regionalism deal specifically with the hazards and horrors of life on the frontier of capitalist expansion. The economic frontier is represented as a lawless, ruthless space, the principal arena of a savage capitalism that brutalizes and decimates campesinos and Native Americans in a frenzied effort to maximize profits at any cost. Several of the texts presented in this section attest to violent exploitation of laborers on the expanding internal frontier: "The Log-Fishermen," by Uruguayan Horacio Quiroga; Juan Marín's *53rd Parallel South*, about the extermination of the native people in Tierra del Fuego; and Ramón Amaya Amador's *Green Jail*, about the exploitation and environmental hazards endured by workers on the U.S.-owned banana plantations of Honduras. Most infamous of all were the catastrophic human rights abuses associated with the boom in natural rubber, which ravaged Amazonia through the late nineteenth and early twentieth centuries. In some areas of the Amazon, Indigenous populations were reduced by as much as 90 percent, many of the victims tortured to death or murdered outright in the brutal legalized system of debt slavery. That is the subject of José Eustasio Rivera's *The Vortex*, perhaps the most complex and brilliant work of the regionalist canon.

The works of prose fiction collected in part 4 have been gathered under a variety of names and rubrics over the years, each of which frames the texts and shapes interpretative possibilities in subtle but meaningful ways. Most recently, these narratives have come to be known as Latin American regionalism, a relatively capacious term that accommodates both the wealth of novels the genre produced and Quiroga's stories. "Regionalism" foregrounds geography and the relentless geographical impetus behind much of this writing, which has often been published in editions that include a map of the little-known territory in which the principal action takes place. To categorize these narratives under the label "regionalism" is to emphasize the qualities that are most immediately appealing to environmentally minded readers today: their artfully delineated sense of place, created through realistic descriptions of particular landscapes, full of local flora and fauna as well as human beings who speak colorful, rustic, nonstandard varieties of Spanish or Portuguese. The notion of "regionalism" implicitly highlights thoughtful consideration of the ways that the different elements that make up the region interact with one another, forming an ecosystem, a bioregional community, and of the ways that those communities (human and nonhuman) are disturbed by economic activities undertaken on behalf of distant consumers and the financial interests that surround them.

More traditionally, Latin American regionalism has been epitomized by the *novela de la tierra*, a term that emphasizes both its distinctiveness from modernism and its foundational quality. A somewhat derogatory term, as Carlos Alonso (1990, 38) points out, it "could be interpreted metaphorically . . . to describe the position these works are deemed to occupy in the edifice of contemporary Latin American letters: they are considered to be the coarse, unfinished foundation of the structure, whose principal function is to give support to the building erected on them." The "building," of course, was the sophisticated and cosmopolitan "new novel" of the 1960s and '70s, whose authors saw themselves as the literary heirs of William Faulkner, James Joyce, and others. The term *novela de la tierra* is closely related to *novela telúrica*, the "telluric novel." While the terms are semantically similar, the latter more explicitly signals a commitment to the idea that a nation's identity and culture, and sometimes even the physiology of its people, are deeply rooted in the materiality of the space it occupies. Telluric nationalism was an important ideological current throughout much of Latin America in the early twentieth century, particularly in those places where long-settled populations felt threatened by demographic and cultural changes linked to urbanization, technology, and the massive influx of immigrants. Especially in the Río de la Plata, *la novela criolla* is another common name for this manifestation of literary nationalism. Interpreted in this light, the narratives collected here reveal their ambivalent awareness of the complex history of creole identities in the Americas: their self-consciousness about land claims that are not historically legitimate sits uneasily with their plans for environmental stewardship.

Suggestions for Further Reading

Euclides da Cunha. 1902. *Rebellion in the Backlands*, translated by Samuel Putnam. London: Picador, 1995.

Gabriela Mistral. 1922. "Desolation." In *Selected Poems*, translated Ursula K. Le Guin. Albuquerque: University of New Mexico Press, 2003.

Ricardo Güiraldes. 1926. *Don Segundo Sombra*, edited by Gwen Kirkpatrick and translated by Patricia Owen Steiner. Pittsburgh: University of Pittsburgh Press, 1995.

Mário de Andrade. 1928. *Macunaíma*, translated by E. A. Goodland. New York: Random House, 1984.

Rómulo Gallegos. 1929. *Doña Bárbara*, translated by Robert Malloy. Chicago: University of Chicago Press, 2012.

José Martí

"Our America," written by José Martí (1853–95) and first published in the Mexican newspaper *El Partido Liberal* in 1891, is one of the most influential essays in the Latin American canon. One of the great poets associated with the Modernismo movement, Martí was also a leading figure in the independence struggle of his native Cuba. His revolutionary activities on the island as a young man led to a prison sentence in Spain, after which he moved from one Latin American country to another (Mexico, Venezuela, Guatemala) as his outspoken opposition to the dictators of the time required. He spent nearly twenty years in the United States, writing chronicles for the Baltimore *Sun* and the New York *Post* and working as a foreign correspondent for prominent Latin American newspapers. As a result, Martí developed a hemispheric perspective and voice. In "Our America" Martí urges Latin Americans to undertake what would today be described as a process of cultural and economic decolonization. He encourages this work in the name of justice but also with the aim of making Latin American countries internally cohesive enough to withstand the increasing aggression of the United States. "Our America" represents a watershed moment in Latin American environmental thought, deconstructing the set of hierarchical binary oppositions that had structured political theorizations until that time, always implicitly privileging the European: nature/culture, Europe/America. The sentence "The battle is not between civilization and barbarity, but between false erudition and nature" is a direct rejoinder to the central claims of Domingo F. Sarmiento's widely influential political essay, *Facundo: Civilization and Barbarism.*

***

"Our America" (1891)

TRANSLATED BY ESTHER ALLEN

The prideful villager thinks his hometown contains the whole world, and as long as he can stay on as mayor or humiliate the rival who stole his sweetheart or watch his nest egg accumulating in its strongbox he believes the universe to be in good order, unaware of the giants in seven-league boots who can crush him underfoot or the battling comets in the heavens that go through the air devouring the sleeping worlds. Whatever is left of that sleepy hometown in America must awaken. These are not times for going to bed in a sleeping cap, but rather, like Juan de Castellanos's men, with our weapons for a pillow; weapons of the mind, which vanquish all others. Trenches of ideas are worth more than trenches of stone.

A cloud of ideas is a thing no armored prow can smash through. A vital idea set ablaze before the world at the right moment can, like the mystic banner of the last judgment, stop a fleet of battleships. Home-towns that are still strangers to one another must hurry to become acquainted, like men who are about to do battle together. Those who shake their fists at each other like jealous brothers quarreling over a piece of land or the owner of a small house who envies the man with a better one must join hands and interlace them until their two hands are as one. Those who, shielded by a criminal tradition, mutilate, with swords smeared in the same blood that flows through their own veins, the land of a conquered brother whose punishment far exceeds his crimes, must return that land to their brother if they do not wish to be known as a nation of plunderers. The honorable man does not collect his debts of honor in money, at so much per slap. We can no longer be a nation of fluttering leaves, spending our lives in the air, our treetop crowned in flowers, humming or creaking, caressed by the caprices of sunlight or thrashed and felled by tempests. The trees must form ranks to block the seven-league giant! It is the hour of reckoning and of marching in unison, and we must move in lines as compact as the veins of silver that lie at the roots of the Andes.

Only runts whose growth was stunted will lack the necessary valor, for those who have no faith in their land are like men born prematurely. Having no valor themselves, they deny that other men do. Their puny arms, with bracelets and painted nails, the arms of Madrid or of Paris, cannot manage the lofty tree and so they say the tree cannot be climbed. We must load up the ships with these termites who gnaw away at the core of the patria that has nurtured them; if they are Parisians or Madrileños then let them stroll to the Prado by lamplight or go to Tortoni's for an ice. These sons of carpenters who are ashamed that their father was a carpenter! These men born in America who are ashamed of the mother that raised them because she wears an Indian apron, these delinquents who disown their sick mother and leave her alone in her sickbed! Which one is truly a man, he who stays with his mother to nurse her through her illness, or he who forces her to work somewhere out of sight, and lives off her sustenance in corrupted lands, with a worm for his insignia, cursing the bosom that bore him, sporting a sign that says "traitor" on the back of his paper dress-coat? These sons of our America, which must save herself through her Indians, and which is going from less to more, who desert her and take up arms in the armies of North America, which drowns its own Indians in blood and is going from more to less! These delicate creatures who are men but do not want to do men's work! Did Washington, who made that land for them, go and live with the English during the years when he saw the English marching against his own land? These *incroyables* who drag their honor across foreign soil, like the *incroyables* of the French Revolution, dancing, smacking their lips, and deliberately slurring their words!

And in what patria can a man take greater pride than in our long-suffering republics of America, erected among mute masses of Indians upon the bloodied arms of no more than a hundred apostles, to the sound of the book doing battle against the monk's tall candle? Never before have such advanced and consolidated nations been created from such disparate factors in less historical time. The haughty man thinks that because he wields a quick pen or a vivid phrase the earth was made to be his pedestal, and accuses his native republic of irredeemable incompetence because its virgin jungles do not continually provide him with the means of going about the world a famous plutocrat, driving Persian ponies and spilling champagne. The incapacity lies not in the emerging country, which demands forms that are appropriate to it and a grandeur that is useful, but in the leaders who try to rule unique nations, of a singular and violent composition, with laws inherited from four centuries of free practice in the United States and nineteen centuries of monarchy in France. A gaucho's pony cannot be stopped in midbolt by one of Alexander Hamilton's laws. The sluggish blood of the Indian race cannot be quickened by a phrase from Sieyès.[1] To govern well, one must attend closely to the reality of the place that is governed. In America, the good ruler does not need to know how the German or Frenchman is governed, but what elements his own country is composed of and how he can marshal them so as to reach, by means and institutions born from the country itself, the desirable state in which every man knows himself and is active, and all men enjoy the abundance that Nature, for the good of all, has bestowed on the country they make fruitful by their labor and defend with their lives. The government must be born from the country. The spirit of the government must be the spirit of the country. The form of the government must be in harmony with the country's natural constitution. The government is no more than an equilibrium among the country's natural elements.

In America the natural man has triumphed over the imported book. Natural men have triumphed over an artificial intelligentsia. The native mestizo has triumphed over the alien, pure-blooded criollo. The battle is not between civilization and barbarity, but between false erudition and nature. The natural man is good, and esteems and rewards a superior intelligence as long as that intelligence does not use his submission against him or offend him by ignoring him—for that the natural man deems unforgivable, and he is prepared to use force to regain the respect of anyone who wounds his sensibilities or harms his interests. The tyrants of America have come to power by acquiescing to these scorned natural elements and have fallen as soon as they betrayed them. The republics have purged the former tyrannies of their inability to know the true elements of the country, derive the form of government from them, and govern along with them. *Governor*, in a new country, means *Creator . . .*

What a vision we were: the chest of an athlete, the hands of a dandy, and the forehead of a child. We were a whole fancy dress ball, in English trousers, a Parisian waistcoat, a North American overcoat, and a Spanish bullfighter's hat. The Indian circled about us, mute, and went to the mountaintop to christen his children. The Black, pursued from afar, alone and unknown, sang his heart's music in the night, between waves and wild beasts. The campesinos, the men of the land, the creators, rose up in blind indignation against the disdainful city, their own creation. We wore epaulets and judge's robes, in countries that came into the world wearing rope sandals and Indian headbands. The wise thing would have been to pair, with charitable hearts and the audacity of our founders, the Indian headband and the judicial robe, to undam the Indian, make a place for the able Black, and tailor liberty to the bodies of those who rose up and triumphed in its name. What we had was the judge, the general, the man of letters, and the cleric. Our angelic youth, as if struggling from the arms of an octopus, cast their heads into the heavens and fell back with sterile glory, crowned with clouds. The natural people, driven by instinct, blind with triumph, overwhelmed their gilded rulers. No Yankee or European book could furnish the key to the Hispanoamerican enigma. So the people tried hatred instead, and our countries amounted to less and less each year. Weary of useless hatred, of the struggle of book against sword, reason against the monk's taper, city against countryside, the impossible empire of the quarreling urban castes against the tempestuous or inert natural nation, we are beginning, almost unknowingly, to try love. The nations arise and salute one another. "What are we like?" they ask, and begin telling each other what they are like. When a problem arises in Cojimar they no longer seek the solution in Dantzig.[2] The frock-coats are still French, but the thinking begins to be American. The young men of America are rolling up their sleeves and plunging their hands into the dough, and making it rise with the leavening of their sweat. They understand that there is too much imitation, and that salvation lies in creating. *Create* is this generation's password. Make wine from plantains; it may be sour, but it is our wine! It is now understood that a country's form of government must adapt to its natural elements, that absolute ideas, in order not to collapse over an error of form, must be expressed in relative forms; that liberty, in order to be viable, must be sincere and full, that if the republic does not open its arms to all and include all in its progress, it dies.

—*El Partido Liberal* (Mexico City), January 20, 1891

Notes

1. Emmanuel Joseph Sieyès (1748–1836), a French abbot, was among the leading political writers of the French Revolution. [—Eds.]

2. Allen's translation uses "Dantzig" instead of the more conventional "Danzig" for the city now know as Gdansk, Poland. [—Eds.]

Baldomero Lillo

"The Invalids" is one of the stories included in *Sub Terra*, the masterful collection by Chile's Baldomero Lillo (1867–1923). Lillo was born and raised in the city of Lota, center of Chile's coal-mining industry. Beginning in the 1850s the Coal and Industrial Company of Lota had established an extensive infrastructure to support the extraction, sale, and transport of coal. By Lillo's day carbon from Lota fueled factories, trains, and ships all over Chile; it was also a stronghold of socialist organizing (Fraser 2012). Son of a miner, Lillo suffered from whooping cough, which prevented him from working in the mines, but he was employed for a time at the company store and thus became acquainted with the miners and the dangerous conditions in which they worked. Deep underground, often under the sea, miners— including preadolescent boys—spent long days in cramped conditions and darkness, at constant risk of cave-ins and the explosive gas known as *grisú*, or firedamp. Lillo's formal education was patchy at best, but he read voraciously, and the examples of Émile Zola, Bret Harte, and others inspired him to pursue a literary career; their influence is perceived in the stark, somber naturalism of his stories. *Sub Terra* was an immediate success when it was published in 1904; as mining has remained a critical component of Chile's economy and labor politics, the work has not declined in relevance. From an ecocritical standpoint, "The Invalids" is of particular interest because it includes a nonhuman laborer—a broken and dying horse—among those exposed to the hazards of extractive capitalism. The miners' solidarity across species lines implicitly questions the meaning of words like "brutal" and "humane."

✳✳✳

"The Invalids" (1904)

TRANSLATED BY STEVEN DOLPH AND JENNIFER FRENCH

The extraction of a horse from the mine, an uncommon event, had brought to the shaft the workers who emptied the mining carts on the ground and those who had to return the empty ones and set them in the cages.

The workers were all old, useless for the jobs inside the mine, and the horse's return to the brightness of the sun after ten years down there pulling the mineral trains inspired the kind of sympathy one feels toward an old and loyal friend who has shared the suffering of a painful journey.

For many the beast was a reminder of happier days in the narrow quarry, when they buried the fang of the hewer's pickax in the hidden seam with a single blow of a still-exacting hand. Diamond was known to everyone, the generous brute, docile and tireless, who hauled his train of rail trucks morning and night through the sinuous towing galleries. And when the exhaustion of that superhuman labor paralyzed their arms, the passing sight of the horse, white with foam, inspired the men with a second wind, and the human ants would go on drilling with the implacable force of a wave that grain by grain devours the unmoving rock that braves its fury.

They all stood silent before the apparition of the horse, which an incurable limp had rendered useless for any job inside or outside the mine. He would come to an end in the sterile expanse interrupted only in the distance by frail, dusty shrubs, an unchanging and flat gray landscape without a single tree or clump of grass.

There was nothing more dismal than the arid dust of that empty plain, sown with squat mounds of sand so thick and heavy that the winds struggled to push across the naked ground, desperate for moisture.

On a small elevation of the terrain stood the mine's shears, its smokestacks, and its sooty buildings. The miners' houses were laid out across a small depression to the right. Above them a dense mass of black smoke hung closely in the rarefied air, making the inhospitable place even darker.

A suffocating heat radiated from the baked earth, and a faint and impalpable layer of coal dust coated the sweaty faces of the workers resting on their carts and savoring in the silence the momentary respite that the horse's dismissal afforded them.

Following the preliminary clangs, the long pulleys high on the shears began to turn slowly, drawing into their grooves the thin metal cables that the powerful machine then rolled upon a large wheel. A few moments passed and suddenly a dark mass dripping water emerged from the black well and paused several meters above the pithead. A black horse, legs straight and tense, suspended in a web of thick ropes hanging from the cage, teetered over the abyss. From below that grotesque posture made the horse look like a monstrous spider caught in its own web. It swung momentarily and descended softly onto the platform. The workers converged on the bundle and pushed it from the opening of the shaft; then Diamond, quickly freed from his ligatures, raised himself shakily upon his legs and stood, breathing heavily.

Like every other mine worker, he was an animal of short stature. His previously soft coat, now riddled with countless scars, had lost its lustrous jet-black sheen. Deep gashes and festering wounds marked the lash points, and knobby spavins deformed his once-powerful legs. Big in the belly, long-necked and bony-haunched, he had lost all trace of his former handsomeness and strength, and the hairs of his mane had all but disappeared, broken off by the whip, its bloody welts still fresh on his sunken back.

The workers gazed at him in pained surprise. How different he was from the spirited brute they had once known! This was just a pile of ragged meat fit only for feeding the vultures and the buzzards. As the horse stood there, his head bowed, motionless, blinded by the midday light, the oldest of the miners, straightening his angular body, gazed inquisitively around him. His weathered face, its lines firm and severe, expressed a deep solemnity, and his eyes, where his life seemed to have taken refuge, shuttled between the horse and the gathering of his silent comrades, walking ruins that, like broken machines, the mine coughed up every so often from its deep bowels.

The elders gazed curiously at their companion, anticipating another of the strange and incomprehensible speeches that every so often erupted from this miner whom they considered a reservoir of profound intellectual culture, since he always carried in his shirt pocket a torn and filthy book whose reading absorbed his hours of leisure and from which he recited phrases and terms that his listeners found unintelligible.

His usually resigned and tender countenance was transfigured when describing the mistreatment and degradation of the poor, and in those moments his words assumed an oracular or apostolic intonation.

The old man paused momentarily in this thoughtful posture, and then, passing his arm over the neck of the invalid nag, his voice grave and tremulous, as though he were rallying a mob, exclaimed:

"Poor old thing, discarded the moment you break down! Just like the rest of us. Down there there's no difference between men and beasts. The mine sucks us dry and casts us off like a spider pushing from its web the bloodless corpse of the fly that once nourished it. Comrades, this brute is the image of our lives! Like him we are silent, stoically enduring our fate! And yet our strength and power are so immense that nothing under the sun could resist it. If every oppressed person with arms shackled marched against their subjugators, we would crush the pride of the ones who drink our blood and suck the marrow from our bones. In one attack we would scatter them like a hurricane disperses a fistful of straw. They are so few, their number so paltry before the countless armies of brothers in the workshops, in the fields, in the bowels of the earth!"

As he spoke the weathered face of the miner came alive, sparks flew from his eyes, and his body trembled in the grips of his overwhelming excitement. With his head thrown back and his gaze lost in the emptiness, he seemed to glimpse, in the distance, the enormous tide of humanity, advancing across the fields with the heedless flow of the sea that has overrun its ancient barriers. Just as the ocean disperses the sands and erodes the mountains, everything fell before the awesome force of those famished legions waving their ragged garments like flags of extermination, reducing to ashes the palaces and temples that shelter the greed and arrogance behind cruel laws that make beasts of the vast majority of men: like Sisyphus condemned to an eternal task, the wretches labor and struggle, without a flicker of consciousness lighting their enslaved minds, where the idea, that divine seed, could never take root.

The workers stared at the old man with anxious eyes, glowing with the frightened unease of a beast venturing down an unknown path. To those dead souls every new idea was a blasphemy against the creed of servitude they had inherited from their forefathers, and in that comrade whose words so thrilled the young people of the mine, they saw only a rash and unquiet spirit, a fool pretending to defy the immutable laws of fortune.

And when the silhouette of the foreman appeared and came toward them from the far end of the field, everyone hurried to their rail mine wagons. As the men stretched the dry creaking of their exhausted limbs blended with the squeaking of the wheels sliding against the rails.

The old man, his eyes damp and shining, watched the miserable flock disperse. Then he took the horse's gaunt face in his hands and caressed his thin mane, murmuring under his breath:

"Goodbye, friend, you have nothing to envy us. Like you, we walk with a burden that could fall from our shoulders at the slightest disturbance, but we insist on carrying it until our deaths."

And bending over his cart he moved away slowly, saving his strength, a fighter defeated by work and age.

The horse did not take a step, or change its posture at all. The only signs of life on that body covered with ulcers and revolting protuberances were the rhythmic and languid movements of its ears and eyelids. Blinded and dazzled by the bright light that the thin air made all the more radiant and intense, he lowered his head between his forelegs, as if seeking shelter from the luminous arrows that pierced his sensitive pupils, incapable of tolerating any light but from the weak, flickering security lamps.

But the splendor was everywhere and penetrated his closed eyelids triumphantly, further blinding him. Dazed, he took a few steps forward, and his head collided with the plank fence surrounding the platform. He seemed surprised by the obstacle, and perking up his ears sniffed at the wall and snorted warily; he backed up, searching for a way out, and new obstacles appeared in his path; he stumbled around the piles of wood, the rail trucks, and the shear beams like a blind man without a guide. He walked with bent knees as though still navigating the dangers of a conveyance tunnel, fiercely accosted by the multiplying swarm of flies that buzzed around him, undisturbed by the sudden contractions of skin and the febrile twists of his naked tail.

Across his brutish mind skittered the vague notion that he was in an unfamiliar corner of the mine where an impenetrable red veil concealed the things he would recognize.

His time there came to a quick end: a groom appeared with a coil of rope under his arm, approached, threw the halter around his neck, and led the horse along the road, a black strip disappearing into the shimmering, arid field that expanded in every direction to the edge of the horizon.

Diamond limped horribly, and a painful shudder ran across his old, dark hide. From the blue curve of the sky the sun's rays seemed pleased to illuminate the sack of throbbing meat to be pinpointed by the hungry vultures up in the emptiness, faintly visible specks that had nevertheless already spotted that prey offered to them by their lucky star.

The groom stopped at the edge of a downward slope in the landscape. He untied the knot that held the prisoner's soft neck, gave him a hard slap on the thigh to force him on, and turned back to where he had come from.

This slope was covered with a layer of water in the rainy season, but the heat of the summer evaporated it quickly. Some traces of this humidity lingered near the bottom, feeding spiny, gray-colored brush and scattered clumps of thin, dusty grass. Tiny puddles of swampy water hid there, inaccessible to any animal no matter how agile or vigorous it was.

Ravaged by hunger and thirst, Diamond walked a short distance, breathing loudly. Every so often he would bring his lips to the sand and snort forcefully, sending clouds of whitish dust that seemed to boil as they floated just above the scorched earth.

His blindness had not abated, and below his eyelids his contracted pupils only perceived that intense red flame that had taken the place of the now-distant memory of the shadows of the mine.

Suddenly the sky erupted with a piercing buzz followed immediately by a whinny of pain, and the miserable hack took off with a leap, running across the sloping landscape as fast as his deformed legs and weakened state allowed. A dozen large sand flies swarmed above him.

Those fierce enemies gave him no respite, and soon enough he tripped over a wide crevice and his body was left wedged in the fissure. He made a few useless attempts to get up, then stretched out his neck and gave in, convinced of his help-lessness and resigned, passively, like a brute, that death would soon put an end to the pain of his tormented flesh.

The sand flies, now sated with blood, withdrew from their attack and, spar-kling like gemstones from their wings and skeletal plates, cleaved through the warm air and disappeared like golden arrows in the splendid blue sky, its sharp clarity unmarred by even the faintest trace of a cloud.

Gathering shadows, sliding across the ground, began to trace concentric circles around the fallen body. Some twenty large black birds were suspended in the sky, the heavy flapping of the buzzards distinct from the majestic aspect of the vultures, their wings spread wide, motionless, describing immense spirals that tightened slowly around the exhausted body of the horse.

Dark shapes appeared from every corner of the horizon, stragglers hurrying with every flap of their wings toward the feast awaiting them.

Meanwhile the sun descended quickly toward nightfall. With every passing moment the fields took on darker colors and longer shadows. The miners, having finished their chores, abandoned the lugubrious pits like Roman slaves leaving the ergastulum. At the bottom, they crowded around the elevator, forming a compact mass, a knot of heads, legs, and arms woven together that they struggled to untangle when they emerged from the shaft and transformed into a long column marching silently along the road toward the distant dwellings.

The ancient cart driver, sitting on his rail truck, gazed across the fields at the marching workers whose curved torsos still seemed to feel the crushing pressure of the rock walls in the lowest galleries. He stood suddenly, and as the shift bell rang clearly and vibrantly in the still air of the empty countryside, the old man, with a slow and heavy step, joined the column of galley slaves whose lives are worth less to their exploiters than a single clump of the mineral that flows endlessly like a black river from its wellspring.

In the mine, everything held a peaceful silence, and nothing could be felt but the muffled, rhythmic steps of the workers departing. The darkness grew, and in the immense dome above thousands of stars sparkled, their white, iridescent, violet splendor growing as the twilight enveloped the earth in the shadows that herald the darkness of night.

Horacio Quiroga

Once commonly referred to as the South American Poe, Uruguay's Horacio Quiroga (1878–1937) has recently emerged as one of the central figures in the canon of Latin American environmental literature. In the process, readers have come to focus less on the gruesome details and macabre endings that characterize many of his stories and more on the complex and sophisticated ways that Quiroga represents the interrelations of various groups of human beings and the more-than-human nature surrounding them. A disciplined professional writer, Quiroga produced and published more than a hundred stories, many of which appeared first in the newspapers and cultural magazines of Buenos Aires and Montevideo. Some of his best take place in the Misiones region of northeastern Argentina, separated from Paraguay by the Paraná River. Misiones was a place where adventurous settlers could go to try their hand at farming, as Quiroga himself did on a small homestead near the former Jesuit mission at San Ignacio. It was also the site of relatively new forms of extractive capitalism: the multinational *yerba mate* companies whose labor and human rights abuses Rafael Barrett had exposed operated there, as did logging companies that harvested enormous trees and dumped them into the river for transport downstream. Some of Quiroga's most famous stories represent the tropical forest as a deadly, dangerous environment, particularly for those who naively set out seeking adventure and easy money. But in stories like "The Log-Fishmen," Quiroga represents a complex bioregional community at risk of rapid environmental degradation. Here he also conveys the vulnerability of a local worker whom a greedy Englishman hires to "fish" logs from the river illegally.

✳ ✳ ✳

"The Log-Fishermen" (1913)

TRANSLATED BY J. DAVID DANIELSON

The motive was a certain dining-room suite that Mr. Hall didn't have as yet, and he used his phonograph as a lure.

Candiyú saw it in the temporary office of the Yerba Company, where Mr. Hall was operating the machine with the door open.

Candiyú, as a good native, didn't show the least surprise, being content to pull up his horse a bit across the stream of light and look the other way. But since an Englishman at nightfall, in shirtsleeves due to the heat and with a bottle of whiskey beside him, is a hundred times more circumspect than any mestizo, Mr. Hall didn't lift his eyes from the record. So Candiyú, outdone and beguiled, finally brought his horse up to the door, where he leaned his elbow against the threshold.

"Good evening, boss. That's nice music!"

"Yes, it's nice," Mr. Hall replied.

"Nice!" repeated the other. "So much noise!"

"Yes, a lot of noise!" agreed Mr. Hall, who found his visitor's observations not lacking in profundity.

Candiyú admired the new records:

"It costed you a lot, boss?" (Candiyú's Spanish showed traces of Guarani, as Mr. Hall's did of English.)

"Cost . . . what?"

"That talking machine . . . the boys singing."

Mr. Hall's cloudy and inexpressive look became clearer. The commercial accountant was coming to the fore.

"Oh, it costs a lot! . . .You want to buy it?"

"If you wants to sell me . . . ," replied Candiyú just to say something, convinced in advance of the impossibility of such a purchase. But Mr. Hall kept staring at him forcefully, while scrapings flew off the record from the metal trips of the needle.

"I'll sell cheap to you . . . fifty pesos!"

Candiyú shook his head, smiling alternately at the machine and its operator.

"Lots of money! I haven't got it."

"What have you got then?"

The man smiled again, without answering.

"Where you live?" Mr. Hall went on, obviously resolved to unload his gramophone.

"At the port."

"Ah! I know you . . . Your name Candiyú?"

"That's right."

"And you fish for logs?"

"Now and then, some little log that nobody owns."

"I'll sell for logs! . . . Three logs sawed into planks. I'll send a wagon. All right?"

Candiyú was laughing.

"I haven't got any now. And that . . . machinery, is it very tricky to work?"

"No; a button here, and a button there . . . I show you. When you have lumber?"

"Some rise of the river . . . One ought to be coming soon. And what kind of wood you wants?"

"Rosewood. All right?"

"Hum! . . . That kind almost never come down . . . Only when the river really swells. It's nice wood! You likes fine wood, I see."

"And you'll get a fine gramophone. All right?"

The dealing went on to the sound of British tunes, with the native evading the straightaway course and the accountant corralling him in the little circle of precision. At bottom, and granting the heat and the whiskey, the subject of the Crown wasn't making a bad bargain in trading a sorry gramophone for dozens of beautiful planks, while the log-fisherman, in turn, was putting up a few days of usual work against a wonderful little noise machine. So the deal went into effect, subject to an agreed deadline.

Candiyú has been living on the banks of the Paraná for thirty years; and if, after his last attack of fever this past December, his liver can still pass whatever you please, he ought to live on for a few months more. Now he spends his days sitting on his stick-frame cot, with his hat on. Only his hands—livid paws streaked with green, hanging huge from his wrists, as though foregrounded in a photograph—keep moving endlessly, monotonously, trembling like a featherless parrot.

But in those days Candiyú was a different person. Then he had the respectable job of tending someone else's banana grove, and—not quite so legal—that of log-fishing. Ordinarily, and especially when the river rises, there are loose logs that come drifting down from the lumber camps, whether floating off from a pontoon being built, or because some clowning laborer severs a retaining rope with a slash of his machete. Candiyú owned a telescope, and spent his mornings peering at the water, till the whitish outline of a log, standing out against the cape of Itacurubí, sent him out to meet the prey in his rowboat. The task is nothing special if the log is seen in time, because the oar of a man of spirit—pushing or hauling a ten-by-forty timber[1]—is a match for any tugboat.

Up in the Castelhum logging camp, above Puerto Felicidad, the rains had begun, after sixty-five days of total drought that ruined the tires on the hauling wagons. At that moment the company's salable property consisted of seven thousand logs—a fortune and then some. But since a two-ton log doesn't weigh two scruples[2] at a cashier's desk so long as it's not in port, Castelhum and Company were a far piece away from being content.

From Buenos Aires came orders for immediate mobilization; the manager of the camp asked for mules and wagons; they replied that with the money from the first pontoon to come down they could send him the mules, and the manager answered that he'd send them the first pontoon if he got the mules in advance.

There was no way to come to terms. Castelhum went up to the logging site and saw the stock of lumber at the camp, on the bluff above the Ñacanguazú, to the north.

"How much?" Castelhum asked his manager.

"Thirty-five thousand pesos," he answered.

That was the amount needed to move the logs to the Paraná. And without allowing for the untimely season.

Under the rain that joined his rubber cape to his horse in a single stream of water, Castelhum stared lengthily at the whirling river. Then, with a movement of the hooded cape toward the torrent, he asked his companion:

"Will the water rise enough to cover the falls?"

"Yes, if it rains a lot."

"Do you have all your men in camp?"

"Till now I do; I was waiting for orders from you."

"Good," said Castelhum. "I think we're going to come out all right. Listen, Fernández; this afternoon, without delay, I want you to secure the boom at the mouth of the river and start bringing all the logs over here to the bluff. The stream is clean, if you told me right. Tomorrow morning I'm going down to Posadas, and after that, with the first storm that comes, throw the timbers in the stream. Understand? A good rain."

The manager looked at him, with his eyes wide open as could be.

"The line's going to give before a hundred logs come down."

"I know, it doesn't matter. And it'll cost us plenty of pesos. Let's go back and we'll talk it over some more."

Fernández shrugged his shoulders and whistled to the foremen.

For the rest of the day, rainless but drenched in watery calm, the *peones* laid out the chain of logs from one bank to the other at the mouth of the stream, and the tumbling of timbers began at the camp. Castelhum went down to Posadas on flood waters running at seven knots, that had risen seven meters the night before, after coming out of the Guayra.

After a big drought, big rains. At noon began the deluge, and for fifty-two hours straight the bush roared with rain. The stream, risen to a torrent, went on to become a howling avalanche of reddish water. The *peones*, soaked to the bone, their skinny frames revealed by the clothing clinging to their bodies, kept heaving logs down the bluff. Every effort provoked a unanimous cry of encouragement, and when a monstrous log came tumbling down and plunged with a cannon-boom into the water, every one of them let go his ¡*a . . . hijú!* of triumph. And then the wasted striving in the liquid mud, the pike-poles slipping loose, the falls and bruises under the torrential rain. And the fever.

At last, abruptly, the deluge stopped. In the sudden silence round-about you could hear the rain still drumming down on the woods nearby. More muffled and deeper-sounding was the rumbling of the Ñacanguazú. Only a few light drops, and far between, still fell from the depleted sky. But the weather continued sultry, without the slightest gust of wind. It was a time for breathing water, and the workers had barely rested an hour or two when the rain began again—that white, compact, and vertical rain that led to swelling rivers. The work was urgent—wages had gone up commendably—and as the storm went on the *peones* kept on shouting, falling, and tumbling under the icy waters.

At the mouth of the Ñacanguazú the floating barrier held back the first timbers that came down, and, bowed and groaning, withstood many more, till under the irresistible thrust of the logs that struck the boom, like projectiles out of a catapult, the line gave way.

Candiyú watched the river through his telescope, judging that its present swell— which there in San Ignacio was two meters higher than the day before, and had carried off his rowboat in the bargain—was probably a huge flood below Posadas. The timbers had started to come down, cedars or the like, and prudently the fisherman conserved his strength.

That night the water rose another meter, and the next afternoon Candiyú was surprised to see out of the end of his telescope a pack, a veritable throng of loose logs coming around the cape of Itacurubí. Wood that was perfectly dry and loomed up whitish above the water.

That was his place to be. He jumped into his canoe and paddled out to hunt his game.

Now on a swelling of the Upper Paraná a fisherman finds lots of things before getting to his chosen log. Whole trees, of course, ripped sheer from the earth and with their black roots waving in the air, like octopi. Dead cows and mules, along with a good share of wild animals—drowned, shot, or with an arrow still stuck in the belly. Tall cones of ants piled up on a massive root. Maybe a jaguar; all the foam and floating lilies you like—to say nothing of the snakes, of course.

Candiyú dodged, drifted, bumped, and tipped over many more times than necessary till he got to his prize. At last he won it; a blow of his machete laid bare the blood-red grain of the rosewood, and lying up against the log he managed to drift along obliquely with it for a ways. But the branches, the trees, came by ceaselessly, dragging him with them. He changed tactics: roped his prey and then began the mute and truceless struggle, silently throwing his heart into every stroke of the paddle.

A log drifting down on a big swell has enough momentum to make three men hesitate before taking it on. But coupled with his great spirit Candiyú had the experience of twenty years of piracies at low river and high, and besides, he wanted to be the owner of a gramophone.

Nightfall presented him with circumstances entirely to his liking. The river, almost at eye level, was flowing swiftly, with the sleekness of oil. On both sides dense shadows passed and passed again, incessantly. The body of a drowned man bumped into the canoe; Candiyú bent over and saw that his throat was slit. Then there were troublesome visitors, attacking snakes, the same kind that climb up the paddle-wheels of steamboats and on into the passengers' cabins, when the river swells.

The Herculean work went on; his paddle trembled under the water, but he was swept along in spite of everything. At last he gave in; he narrowed the landing angle and gathered the last of his strength in order to get to the edge of the channel, which grazed the towering rocks of the Teyucuaré. For ten minutes the log-fisherman, with his neck-tendons stiff and his chest like stone, did what nobody's ever going to do again to get out of the channel in a swell, with a log in tow. The canoe finally crashed against the rocks and keeled over, just when Candiyú still had strength enough—but no more—to secure the rope and fall on his face on the shore.

A month went by before Mr. Hall got his three dozen planks, but twenty seconds after that he was handing over the gramophone to Candiyú, along with twenty records.

The firm of Castelhum and Company, despite its flotilla of steam-launches, sent out—and for well over thirty days—to retrieve the logs, lost a lot of them. And if some day Castelhum comes to San Ignacio and visits Mr. Hall, he'll sincerely admire the said accountant's dining-room suite, made out of rosewood planks.

Notes

1. In the original, "a ten by forty piece," that is, a log roughly thirty-three feet long by sixteen inches in diameter (ten meters by forty centimeters).
2. Two scruples: less than a tenth of an ounce.

José Eustasio Rivera

A novel written by a poet to document and dramatize the human rights and environmental abuses associated with the exploitation of Amazonian rubber, *The Vortex* (1924) is the most aesthetically complex of the Spanish-American *novelas de la tierra*. José Eustasio Rivera (1888–1928) was a lawyer whose literary career began in 1921 with a collection of sonnets representing the flora and fauna of Colombia's three geographical regions of jungle, highland, and plains. Soon after, he was appointed to a government expedition to investigate rumors that foreigners were exploiting Colombian laborers and illegally harvesting latex from trees on Colombian soil. The commissioners ultimately failed to persuade Colombian officials of the gravity of the situation, but legend has it that Rivera began to compose *The Vortex*, in verse form, while they were floating along the region's waterways in a canoe. The novel is the first-person narrative of Arturo Cova, a well-known poet who flees Bogotá with his lover in order to avoid a scandal. They spend weeks among the rustic society of the plains, then Alicia and another woman are lured into the jungle by the promises of a wealthy rubber trader. As Cova and his friends pursue them, he (and the reader) discover the region's horrifying past, including the deaths of tens of thousands at the hands of gangs that operate with impunity because of their obscurity and ties to powerful international companies. Presented here is the section of the novel traditionally called the "Rubber Tapper's Lament." The speaker, who may be Cova or his friend Clemente Silva, blurs the boundaries between human and vegetal life, imagining the trees as fellow sufferers and subjects.

∗ ∗ ∗

From *The Vortex* (1924)

TRANSLATED BY JOHN CHARLES CHASTEEN

I am a rubber tapper. I live in the fetid river mud, in the solitude of the forest, with my malarial crew, slicing trees that bleed white blood, like the blood of gods. Thousands of miles from my birthplace, I dread all memories of it, because all are sad. My parents? They grew old in poverty, awaiting the return of their absent son. My younger sisters? They waited with patient optimism and trust until no longer young, hoping for a dowry that never materialized.

Sometimes, as I hack at the bleeding bark with my hand ax, I take a notion to vary the arc of its swing just a bit and cut off those worthless fingers that never could hold on to money. What are hands good for, if they don't produce, don't steal, and don't redeem? These hands have wavered when I asked them to end my suffering. And to think that so many denizens of the jungle endure something similar.

Who created the gap that yawns between our aspirations and reality? Why were we given wings to live flightless lives? Poverty and aspiration, stepmother and tyrant, drove us forward, but to no avail. By looking to the heights, we've neglected the most fundamental necessities. Turning to those necessities, we've lost whatever we had gained. As a result, we are heroes only of mediocrity.

The man who saw the resources for a happy life almost within reach has not been able to get rich and leave Amazonia. The man who aimed to win a bride has settled for a concubine. The man who has resisted abuses has been crushed by magnates as impassive as the trees that witness his daily battle against fever, leeches, and insects. I had tried to discount my high hopes, but an exaggerated force lifted them to the stratosphere. High hopes, lost triumphs, forlorn dreams. Look what has become of this poor dreamer!

Slave, don't complain of your toil! Prisoner, don't lament your imprisonment! Little can you imagine this limitless green dungeon, surrounded by immense rivers on all sides. You ignore the torture of watching rays of sun play, at dusk, on the far bank of a river that you'll never be able to cross. The leg irons that bite your flesh are kinder than the leeches that nibble at a rubber tapper's ankles.

I have three hundred rubber trees on my circuit, and to tap them all takes nine days. I've cleared around the base of each tree, cut its shrouds of hanging vines, lacerated a large area of bark, placed buckets for it to drip into, and made an access trail between my circuit and my camp. Patrolling the trail to keep it open, I often come upon a rival tapper or a renegade trying to steal rubber. Then the clang of machetes rings in the forest, and the buckets of white blood often get an admixture of red drops. But no matter. Every drop contributes to the ten liters that the overseers demand of us every day without fail.

Big deal if the fellow who works the next circuit downriver dies of fever! I can imagine him already collapsed in the leaf litter, thrashing at those big, black, stinging flies that won't let him die in peace. He's going to stink so much that I'll have to leave my hut, but not before cleaning out his rubber cache, of course. Someone will do the same with me, as well, when I die. Here I am stealing not to care for my aged parents but to enrich my murderer.

Around the great trunk, I tie a length of caraná vine to collect the latex tears and channel them to the bucket. A cloud of mosquitoes rises into my face to take my blood while my hands are occupied, and a rising vapor blurs my vision. This is a death struggle. I torture the tree and the tree tortures me, until one of us succumbs.

Man is puny, insignificant, and vulnerable in the vastness of the jungle. It would instantly triumph if all natural forces cooperated to wipe us out. But perhaps they can't. Perhaps it isn't yet time for that final, cataclysmic struggle, not yet time to invoke cosmic forces and die in a blaze of glory. But the time will come. Here's a rebellion worthy of Satan's leadership.

I have been a rubber tapper. I am still a rubber tapper. My hand ax cuts wood and can cut flesh.

César Uribe Piedrahita

Colombia's César Uribe Piedrahita (1897–1951) was a painter, sculptor, violinist, scientist, and medical doctor as well as the author of the novels *Toá* (1933) and *Oil Stain* (1935). Intensely devoted to public service and improving the lives of his fellow Colombians, Uribe Piedrahita studied medicine at the University of Antioquia and Harvard, specializing in parasitology and plant toxicology. Upon returning to Colombia, he became director of the National Institute of Hygiene. He traveled throughout the interior, particularly the southern jungles and the eastern plains, collecting plant and animal specimens and treating isolated populations, including Indigenous communities. Uribe Piedrahita became widely known as the developer of Colombia's first antidote for snake venom. He also founded the famous CUP Laboratories in Bogotá, then lost thousands of pages of scientific annotations when the building burned to the ground in the 1948 riots known as El Bogotazo (Ruiza, Fernández, and Tamaro 2019). The selection presented here is an excerpt from *Oil Stain*, a bitter exposé of labor and environmental abuses committed by North American executives operating with the complicity of the Venezuelan dictator Juan Vicente Gómez. Loosely based on the story of the Creole Petroleum Corporation, a U.S.-based multinational created in 1920 to exploit the oil reserves beneath Lake Maracaibo (and later purchased by Standard Oil, today's ExxonMobil), the novel tells the story of an idealistic young physician who takes a job working for a foreign oil company and eventually becomes embroiled in an affair with the bored wife of one of its employees. Interspersed with the narrative are letters exchanged between Dr. Echegorri and his friend, which attest to his growing sense of outrage at the company's interference in national politics.

✳ ✳ ✳

"Mun Hospital" (1935)

TRANSLATED BY PATRICIA GONZÁLEZ

The hospital was a large old ramshackle house, recently painted, with English signs, and it had become the most attractive place in town. Nickel-plated equipment, mysterious colored jars, and white shirt-and-cap nurses, hustling back and forth and shouting in English, had converted it into a hospital.

Highly-paid English speakers such as alcoholic drillers, novice geologists, blacksmiths, and chauffeurs had become the drifting staff of that venture, fulfilling the commitment promised by the companies: "Well-kept modern hospitals will be installed for all employees in the extraction, refinery, and trade of oil, no matter their rank."

"It is very difficult, Mr. McGunn, to deal with Dr. Echegorri. Members of the company's science department brought him here. It seems Dr. Echegorri found a sick expedition traveling up the Apure[1] River. He treated the sick well and left without accepting any remuneration. People from the eastern part of the country tell many tales and oddities about our doctor. He works a lot, or more accurately, he is always working. He is reserved. He refuses to speak English, even though he knows it well, and has almost no accent. Some say he is adventurous, others say he is a fugitive, but I am convinced he is a cultivated man, and above all, a good element for our organization. However, it is difficult to understand the friendship our employee has with suspicious people and well-known enemies of the company, and naturally, of the present government."

"I would like, Mr. Director, to have an interview with Dr. Echegorri in a familiar setting. Please invite him to a 'soirée' at your home."

The conversation of the foreigners gathered at the house of Dr. Bartell, chief of the medical division of the oil company, was lively. Mrs. McGunn was nervously awaiting the arrival of the expected guest. The young wife of the drillers' superintendent was constantly thinking of the adventurous doctor, imagining his life full of romance and wonderful deeds.

"My dear friend:

　　The letters take too long. I am interested in the matter of our colleague Trujillo. I await news. Here they continue to negotiate the B concession. The government provided secret information to 'Bay Oil.' The congress will vote in favor of the proposal. Of course! The secret agents of the oil companies are visiting the town. I am including a photo of a telegram sent by Felssom. I have lots of interesting things to tell you. For now, be content with the clippings included. Tell me about your life; let me know how you are getting on in the oil company. A hug from your colleague,

ALBERTO"

"Doctor Bartell. Is Dr. Echegorri coming? Why is he taking so long?"

The maid brought a card from Echegorri, excusing himself for not coming to the gathering.

"But it is inconceivable for him not to come," said Peggy, in a bad mood. "Couldn't you do something, Mr. Director?"

"I will insist personally. He will not say no to me. We will be back shortly, Mrs. McGunn."

Peggy went out to the spacious hall decorated with orchids and flowering reeds. She contemplated the depths of the night and remembered, as she lay down on the swinging sofa, the few minutes of another dark night, when the silence and darkness got her closer to Dr. Echegorri. Since she arrived at the oil fields, she wanted a romance, some blossoming illusion in her monotonous life. She thought Gustavo could become her solace. Until then, Mrs. McGunn had only met vulgar men, naive simpleton boys, chauffeurs, drillers, and workers from her country's southern oil companies. She understood that if the doctor worked for the company where McGunn worked, she would have him closer, maybe next to her.

"Good evening, everyone. Please excuse me. I truly have not been feeling well. Remnants of my recent expeditions to the upper Orinoco. I had to give in, thanks to the polite insistence of the good Director, and the pleasure of your company . . . No real sacrifice on my part."

. . . "I got the letters you sent . . . It is very interesting to overlap geological maps with political maps. Did you notice? The line of oil towers leaving the town of Zulia coincide with the region in dispute. They are fighting to control prospective zones and areas of exploitation. You will see, the United States against England. But they are not going to fight over it. It's up to the people of the two countries empowered by patriotism. They will deviate the fight to the working class, there as well as here, so they can kill each other. Anderson's presence in Bogotá is significant. He is very dangerous, as well as the other man. Thank you for the newspaper clippings. I am sending you the lists you requested. My health improves slowly. Hugs.

GUSTAVO"

Peggy looked at the coveted guest, pleased with his good manners and gracious words.

"But today for sure you are going to tell us something about your life, Dr. Echegorri. How interesting!"

"I am sorry to insist, there is nothing extraordinary. I must say it again, ma'am, everything they say about me is pure fable. Tropical imaginations . . ."

"I imagine you have considered the offer made to you by the directors of the Anglo-Dutch companies, through me. Naturally, you must be sorry to abandon your present employer. But the position you would hold in my company would be, without a doubt, very high. For the time being, we have convinced the Mun company to allow you to be part of an expedition exploring the western region bordering Colombia. The other part of the commission must visit the Catatumbo[2] region. The proposal no doubt will be very attractive to you since you love adventures and escapades. For us, it would be invaluable, not only because you are a doctor and discrete, but more so because you know the people of the area well. The expedition will be short. Later, you may decide if you want to stay with us or go back to the hospital. What do you say?"

"If it is no longer than two months, I accept, provided that I get written authorization from the head of the hospital."

"Get ready, then. We'll leave within a week."

McGunn shook the doctor's hand. Once in the living room, he made a gesture of success to the director and Peggy.

"Doctor Echegorri, come with me to watch the night. It reminds me of the time I met you at the lakeshore. Have you forgotten?"

"No, I haven't forgotten, nor will I ever. It was a splendid night, silent and warm. The trip back from the lake was magnificent. So many stars!"

"I am very happy you accepted my husband's offer. Naturally, you will visit us frequently. Don't you like to play bridge? No . . . ? What do you like besides trips and work . . . ? Nothing else . . . ? How interesting!"

Gustavo felt Peggy's arm close to him; he inhaled the inciting aroma coming from her youthful body and remained still, eyes semi-open . . . He invited her to the end of the garden, beyond the fence that divided the landscape.

A warm June night. The bushes, brambles, and thorn trees of the forest exhaled their nocturnal fragrances. Bats squeaked, accentuating the silence of the night.

They walked silently, catching shadows with open eyes.

"Dr. Echegorri. Do you like walking at night?"

"A lot. I like traveling the rivers made motionless by the overwhelming darkness. I have seen immense rivers, wider than the Lake Maracaibo itself. I got to know them better traveling alone at night."

"Do you prefer to be alone?"

"Not now."

"Teach me how to pronounce your name . . . Gos-tah-vu . . . Gus-tah-vo . . . ? How does it sound?"

Peggy laughed and squeezed the doctor's arm. The night enveloped them, united them.

"G u s t . . . t a . . . v o . . . !"

***

Oily mud varnishes the few shrubs dragging in the mud. Strong wire fences isolate the many towers, tanks, and powerful motors that make the black blood circulate from the entrails of the earth, through the thick iron arteries, to the belly of the ships. Drop-hammer noises, foul fumes of asphalt residues and multilingual shouts saturate the atmosphere boiling under the sun.

In the oil well La Flor, a dirty mass of men from different parts of the globe gathered: Yankees and Canadians, Armenians, Greeks and Jews, Antilleans and natives from a continent bathed by the Caribbean Sea and the Gulf of Mexico.

With a palpitating rhythm, the giant drill penetrated beneath the earth's crust. There were signs of greasy shale, but the experts never suspected how close the drill was to the repressed abscess about to burst.

The earth roared and shook to its core. The soil shivered and with thundering moans, whistles, and rattles brought up along the tubes, the towers, and up to the sky a black belch that dragged down the drop-hammer, cables, crossbeam, beams, and twisted frames of the giant tower and up-ended the sides of the ironworks, the wires, and broken slabs. It seemed that the jets of oily asphalt were reaching up to the sun.

The turmoil grew among the terrified human mass, which ran against the barbed wires, jumping and dragging themselves amongst the pipe grids, the army of towers, and the line of punctured tanks. Shouts in English were heard: "To the boilers! Put out the fire!"

The air continued to buzz and the earth to groan under the heavy and pestilent rain of cursed oil that covered the landscape, withering the leaves, drowning the trees, and submerging the thousands of insects, worms, and bugs that populated the soil under a gelatinous and sticky mass. The magnificent gush swirled with the wind and fell, spreading thick globs over the houses and roads up to the lake, extending the deadly spill over the surface of the water that turned smooth and metallic, undulating in iridescent, multicolor waves.

The roar of the storm and the anguished bellow from the bowels of the wounded earth continued.

The oil spill continued uninterrupted, covering kilometers of earth, miles of water. Groups of dirty terrified men crowded at the shores of the lake. Gaseous bombs encased in greasy magma smashed against the clouds and scattered their liquid over the heads and backs of the defenseless flock.

The infernal chimney continued to vomit a semi-liquid paste that penetrated crevices and bathed the peaks of the naked hills. The oil filtrated through the pores of the rocks and filled the bosom of the valley.

"Everyone back! Everyone back!" They were shouting in English. "Back! Back!"

The horrific metallic crater kept coughing up the ragged lungs of the earth.

"Back! Everybody! Do not smoke! Back! Back!"

A chain of muted boats, canoes, and rowboats were stationed in a semi-circle guarding the imprecise limits of the oil spill that kept extending more and more over the lake.

"Everyone back! Do not smoke!"

All that was needed was for someone to light a thread of the black slime to transform the earth's foundation into cinders.

"Back! Everyone back!"

And the spill continued to grow.

Notes

1. Apure is the name of both a river in southwestern Venezuela and one of the twenty-three Venezuelan states. The Apure River is one of the major tributaries of the Orinoco.

2. The Catatumbo, a river rising in northern Colombia, flowing into Lake Maracaibo in Venezuela.

Juan Marín

Juan Marín (1900–1963) graduated from the University of Chile with a degree in medical surgery in 1921; he joined the army soon after and made his first trip to Europe in 1929. Around the same time, Marín published a volume of poetry, *Looping*, in the vanguardist style and strongly influenced by his compatriot Vicente Huidobro. In 1932 Marín was stationed at the naval hospital in Punta Arenas, in the remote islands of Chilean Patagonia; it was there that he wrote the work for which he is remembered today, *53rd Parallel South*. The novel takes its name from the latitude line that passes through the southern extremity of Chile and Argentina, just north of the Straits of Magellan. This beautiful, forbidding place, a mix of peninsulas, rocky islands, and blue-green waterways at the southern tip of the Andes, is at once the ends of the earth and a space of often violent encounter for an extremely diverse group of humans: the native Kawésqar and Yaganes (also called Yámanas), British sheep farmers, Yugoslav gold miners, Protestant missionaries, and hunters of seals, otters, and whales. Marín's novel, from which we present the author's synopsis, bears stylistic hallmarks of the vanguardists: his is an imagistic landscape of clean lines and almost surreal dimensions, conveyed in spare and vivid language. The Patagonia of *53rd Parallel South* is also a place of rapid environmental and social deterioration. This is chillingly apparent whenever the narrator's clinical gaze alights on the faces and bodies of Indigenous women and girls, including those forced into prostitution because foreigners have overfished and overhunted the icy waterways, rendering their traditional way of life obsolete.

***

From *53rd Parallel South* (1936)

TRANSLATED BY PATRICIA GONZÁLEZ

During snowy nights, the suffering inhabitants of the colony wander like penitent souls. The icy wind shakes and blows out the humble flames of the lanterns swaying in the vacuum. In a corner of the dome-like sky, the fourfold fixed gaze of the Southern Cross is falling like a spectral aircraft over the horizon. Military men with moustaches and short, red visor caps argue with long-faced Spaniards[1] next to the wretched table; women with bruise-colored hands measure feet of rough cotton,[2] and count "almuds"[3] of beans.

Far away, beyond the smooth trails of the Strait, in the great desert of shifting waters, in the liquid and frothy Sahara of the open sea, little winged boats play

150

hide-and-seek with death, and the skull jumps like a little ivory cosmic roulette ball over each degree of the compass rose.

Bold Portuguese and adventurous Levantines are under the boat's canopy with one hand on the helm and the other on their dagger.

On land, as in the biblical parable, modern farmers scatter seeds of lamb on portions of the continent and over the wild islands. And the woolly grass grows as well as a swelling tide, gray and frizzy over the greenish yellow of the pampas.

Lit by suet flames, uprooted, rude-spoken Yugoslavs weigh gold dust on make-shift scales like new alchemists who have forgotten Faust and adore Shylock.

Sometimes the shadow of the Discoverer descends over the hamlet on a storm-pregnant night, and the tapping of his tall hobnailed boots and the creaking of his leather cape, cured in the whirling wind of desolate corners, is often heard. His rough Lusitanian voice travels the seashell of the storm like a bat's wing:

"Magellan!"

In the glow of fireplaces, bronzed faces with rigid muscles burn charred sticks of memory and take long drinks from the rum of greed, illuminated by the blaze of chimneys. The gold of Porvenir and Port Cutter is as dizzying as the sea of Cape Horn and of dismal Cape Pilar. While the disheveled woman is withdrawn, recounting all the children she had who no longer live, the man writes down on the greasy paper how many sheep his neighbor already has, daubing the pencil on his hardened lips.

On inhospitable beaches, where the cliffs unsparingly resist the salty sea-core that bleeds raging foam, tiny, ruddy-faced men stab each other for a few bottles of grappa or the coveted booty of fur seal.

The Indians naively lunch on sliced meat from the clean-shaven, bilious missionaries while the phlegmatic Englishmen from the ranches practice the singular sport of hunting the long-hair Yaganes.[4] In the barracks, the Captain seasons his breakfast with an indispensable cognac drink and the macabre bugle-call of twenty prisoners skinned alive by the lash in the middle of the patio frosted by a mirage of crystals. Until one fine day, out of pure boredom, the prisoners nail the helpless body of the Captain to the dawn sheets with twenty deadly machete cuts, like a gigantic butterfly without wings in an insect exhibit.

Greasy cards pass from hand to hand in between-decks of schooners going to the islands, or on the wobbling tables of the taverns where otter pelts and women's thighs are traded. The King of Cups and the Jack of Clubs have withstood fifteen years of hunger, cold, and distant visions of the Adriatic sun in the short time between a bottle of rum and a glass of dark beer.

Spanish, Polish, or French women, the shady backwash of the capitals, receive in their grimy beds reeking of antiseptic the woolen covered bodies of Yugoslavian seal hunters, Italian smugglers, and northern captains.

In the meantime, the papers granting deeds to the land rain down from the capital like algebraic "confetti" from a tragic carnival. Notarial streamers pass from hand to hand. It's the dance of the hectares. Life is frenzy: one thousand, ten thousand, one hundred thousand. That guy had them yesterday. This guy has them today. No one will have them tomorrow.

Gold, wool, oil.

From the depths of the earth ascends an oily sickness that breaks through the yellow crust here and there, and the combustible gases poison the breath of men and the wind of mountain canyons. Nevertheless, oil is brought in cans, and artificial wells are drilled as if they were building swimming pools. Shares fly like flocks of birds through the somber halls of metropolitan stock exchanges.

Bank titles, stocks, deeds, records, paper.

But the foreigner who had a small patched sailboat and ten sheep guarded by a dog and wore the same shirt for twenty years, during which he didn't take his boots off to sleep, is now traveling by "pullman" through Europe and writings checks on all the international banks. The little piles of coins kept growing under the dirty mattress, the sheep became countless, the small boats became bigger, and the fences enclosed more and more land under indifferent skies.

On the desolate western coasts, seal hunters approach the boulders armed with rustic clubs amid the Wagnerian symphony of rain, wind, and sea; and the hunters, attentive to the dogs' barking, smash the feline heads with pointed moustaches swimming away in flight between the rocks of the islands.

In the vast prairies, the "camp tenders" sleep with their woolly dogs and pour out their solitary love spasms over the warm bellies of the blank-eyed expressionless sheep, while outside the huts the snow embroiders the dark gown of the night with its white needle.

Englishmen smoking cruel and fragrant pipes remember with alcoholic melancholy the soft autumn that gilds the hills and meadows of "Devonshire," while far in the distance, resembling ants, the woodcutters chop down the virgin forest growing on slopes of inaccessible mountains, with stiff cold faces dripping rain, sunk up to their knees in "peat."[5] They wave the avenging axes to bring down giant trees and roll them down through the echoing gorges to the deep canals. From the top of the mountains, nightmarish amphitheaters that emerged burning in the cosmic night come down zigzagging, roaring, whistling, the blizzard unleashed, the hurricanes phenomenal, the storms howling. And the microscopic world of men, submen and supermen does not cease in its toil. All of it struggles, lives, and dies, dragged by destiny, devouring itself, but ever reborn, each time with more strength.

Strange caravans converge on a hamlet that one day woke up a city, a racial melting pot, a multilingual Babel with strident languages.

The electric piano of the bar lies to men drunk on illusions of fatherland, of home, of a vague and shapeless dream of love and the lips of the autumnal hetaera[6] barely covering her oozing ulcer with lipstick; they give a small bag of gold for the kiss the Indian has never been able, nor ever will be able, to give with her cold oily mouth.

Good sailors head the ships towards the port: "escampavías,"[7] rhythmic schooners with sails like albatross wings, cutters nodding like capricious sea camels, rowboats with broken oars, canoes smelling of seals and "Alacalufe."[8]

They arrive coming from the bad weather, from the fog, and from the night. They come shrouded, like hooded friars under "dominos" of snow; others dismasted, like towns shaken by fantastic earthquakes. Seal hunters from San Felix and Port

Estanislao, woodcutters from Yendegaia, gold diggers from Lenox Island and Picton, farmers from Río Grande and Santa Cruz, Indians from Muñoz Gamero and Mejillones, lighthouse attendants from San Ambrosio and Evangelistas; they come from the sea with pupils ignited by the flame of greed and the embers of a sadistic sensuality.

They are seen on the streets with their boots and pelts, leather hats, pipes, and bushy beards. They come today as they came yesterday, and as they may not come tomorrow. But the hamlet is today a city where palaces with half-closed shutters keep vigil on the larva-infested dream of the ones that agonize in dilapidated huts, machine-gunned by the wind and whipped by the yellow "huasca"[9] of hunger.

Then, the Discoverer's shadow descends on emaciated children with crooked legs and huge hydrocephalic heads; on the tuberculosis-infested ones, snuffed out in the prime of their youth; on the mothers, who spit out their innards on the frozen ground, holding their child against a scrawny breast; on the wretched alcoholics, conquered by delirium, turning away their terrified eyes, in order not to look at what life already showed them long before death.

Over so much misery and so much ugliness, on white nights, the silent shadow of the great sailor falls.

And as the story goes, told by those who have heard the echoing sound of his brackish boots and the rustling of his sea capes, coarse exclamations often escape the thick and bearded mouth of the strong old Portuguese.

We would not like to repeat what those four-hundred-year-old lips say, but we invite the reader to guess after reading these pages of pain, injustice, and death.

Notes

1. In the original *godo*, which is an old insult for Spaniards.

2. *Tocuyo* is a rough cotton burlap.

3. An almud is an old measuring unit. Still used in Chile today, it consists mostly of a wooden box with lines to designate different measurements.

4. The Yaganes were a nomadic Amerindian tribe inhabiting the islands of Patagonia and navigating south of the Magellan Strait. Today they are recognized communities in Punta Arenas and other areas in southern Chile.

5. *Turba*, translated as "peat," is a spongy substance formed due to vegetable matter decomposition. It can be burned like coal.

6. An educated courtesan or mistress in ancient Greece.

7. Type of warship used by the Chilean navy during the late nineteenth and early twentieth centuries.

8. Yámana term for the Kawésqar people, it was adopted by settlers; the name means "mussel eater."

9. In Chile, leather or natural fiber whips to hustle animals pulling carriages.

Graciliano Ramos

The eldest of fifteen or sixteen children, Graciliano Ramos (1892–1953) grew up in Brazil's arid northeast. His parents were small-scale merchants, and the family traveled extensively throughout the region. After graduating from high school, Ramos worked for a time correcting proofs for a newspaper. He moved briefly to Rio de Janeiro but returned to Alagoas to assist his father. In 1927 Ramos was elected mayor of the city of Palmeira dos Indios. He published his first novel, *Caetés*, in 1933; it was followed by *São Bernardo* (1934), *Anguish* (1936), and *Barren Lives* (1938). In 1936 Ramos was arrested on suspicion of subversive activities, spending a year in prison. In 1945, Ramos, one of Brazil's most celebrated writers at the time, joined the Communist Party; he was later elected president of the Brazilian Writers Association. His masterpiece *Barren Lives* tells the story of Fabiano and Vitória as they migrate through the drought-stricken northeast with their two sons, a bird, and a dog in a torturous search for economic opportunity. The region was desertified by unsustainable farming practices stretching back hundreds of years to the time when Indigenous communities first began burning sections of forest for agricultural use; the situation was exacerbated by colonists clearing larger and larger patches of land. *Barren Lives* has long been recognized as an outstanding example of modernist prose. The language is spare, concise, and laconic, a perfect vehicle to convey the harsh reality of a desiccated landscape and the impoverished inner lives of the characters, especially the protagonists' two young sons. Any of its thirteen chapters could stand alone as an independent work of short fiction. The one presented here is chapter 12, "The Birds."

***

"The Birds" (1938)

TRANSLATED BY RALPH EDWARD DIMMICK

The branches of the coral-bean tree down by the water hole were covered with birds of passage. This was a bad sign. In all probability the backland would soon be burnt up. The birds came in flocks; they roosted in the trees along the riverbank; they rested, they drank, and then, since there was nothing there for them to eat, they flew on toward the south. Fabiano and his wife, deeply worried, had visions of misfortunes to come. The sun sucked up the water from the ponds and those cursed birds drank up what was left, trying to kill the stock.

It was Vitória who said this. Fabiano grunted, wrinkled his brow, and found the expression exaggerated. The idea of birds killing oxen and goats! He looked at his wife distrustfully; he thought she was out of her mind. He went to sit on the bench under the shed, and from there he studied the sky, filled with a brightness that boded evil, its clear expanse broken only by the lines of passing birds. A feathered creature kill stock! Vitória must be crazy.

Fabiano stuck out his lower lip and wrinkled his sweaty brow still more deeply: it was impossible for him to understand what his wife meant. He couldn't get it. A little thing like a bird! As the matter seemed obscure to him he refrained from going into it any further. He went into the house, got his haversack, made himself a cigarette, struck the flint against the stone, and took a long drag. He looked in all directions and remained facing north for several minutes, scratching his chin.

"Awful! It's like the end of the world!"

He wouldn't stay there long. In the long-drawn-out silence all that could be heard was the flapping of wings.

What was it that Vitória had said? Her phrase came back to Fabiano's mind, and suddenly its meaning was apparent. The birds of passage drank the water. The stock went thirsty and died. Yes, the birds of passage did kill the cattle. That was right! Thinking the matter over you could see it was so, but Vitória had a complicated way of putting things. Now Fabiano saw what she meant. Forgetting imminent misfortune, he smiled, enchanted at Vitória's cleverness. A person like her was worth her weight in gold. She had ideas, she did! She had brains in her head. She could find a way out of difficult situations. There, hadn't she figured out that the birds of passage were killing the stock? And they were too! At that very hour the branches of the coral-bean tree down by the water hole, though stripped of blossoms and leaves, were a mass of feathers.

Desiring to see it up close he arose, slung his haversack across his chest, and went to get his leather hat and his flintlock. He stepped down from the shed, crossed the yard, and approached the slope, thinking of the dog. Poor thing! Those horrible-looking places had appeared around her mouth, her hair had dropped out, and he had had to kill her. Had he done right? He had never thought about that before. The dog was sick. Could he risk her biting the children? Could he? It was madness to expose the boys to rabies. Poor dog! He shook his head to get her out of his mind. It was that devilish flintlock that brought the image of the little dog back to him. Yes, it was certainly the flintlock. He turned his face away as he passed the stones at the end of the yard where they had found the dog, cold and stiff, her eyes pecked out by the vultures. Taking longer steps he went down the slope and walked across the river flat toward the water hole. There was a wild flapping of wings over the pool of dark water. The branches of the coral-bean tree couldn't even be seen. What a flock of pests! When they came in from the backland they made an end of everything. The stock was going to waste away, and even the thorns would dry up.

He sighed. What was he to do? Flee once more, settle some place else, begin life all over again. He raised his gun and pulled the trigger without even aiming. Five or six birds fell to the ground. The rest took flight and the dry branches appeared in all their nakedness. Little by little they were covered again. There was no end to it.

Fabiano sat down dispiritedly at the edge of the water hole. Slowly he loaded the flintlock with bird shot, but did not use any wadding, so the load would spread and hit many enemies. There was a new report and new birds fell, but this gave Fabiano no pleasure. He had food there for two or three days; if he had enough munition he would have food for weeks and months.

He examined the powder horn and the leather shot holder; he thought of the trip and shuddered. He tried to deceive himself into thinking it wouldn't come about if he didn't provoke it by evil thoughts. He relit his cigarette and sought to distract himself by talking in a low voice. Old Miss Terta was a person who knew a lot about that part of the country. What could be the state of his accounts with the boss? That was something he could never figure out. That business of interest swallowed up everything, and on top of it all the boss acted as if he were doing a favor. Then there was that policeman in khaki—

Fabiano closed his fists and punched himself in the thigh for his bad luck. The devil! There he was, trying to forget one misfortune, and others came crowding upon him. He didn't want to think either of the boss or of the policeman in khaki. But to his despair they insisted on coming to his mind, and he tightened up like a rattlesnake coiling in anger. He was unlucky, the unluckiest fellow in the world. He ought to have struck the policeman in khaki that afternoon; he ought to have carved him up with his machete. But like a good-for-nothing country lout he had pulled in his horns and had showed the policeman the way. He rubbed his sweaty, wrinkled brow. Why bring his shame back to mind, though? He was just a poor devil. But was he determined to go on living like that forever? Worthless and weak, that was what he was. If he hadn't been so timid he would have joined a gang of bandits and would have gone around wreaking destruction. Eventually he would get shot in ambush, or would spend his old age serving out a sentence in jail. This was better, though, than dying by the roadside in the broiling heat, his wife and boys dying too. He ought to have cut the policeman's throat, taking his own good time about doing it. They could put him in jail then, but he would be respected—yes, respected, as a man of guts. The way he was now, nobody could respect him. He wasn't a man; he wasn't anything. He had suffered a beating and had not taken revenge.

"Fabiano, my boy, get your chin up! Get some self-respect! Kill the policeman in khaki! Policemen in khaki are a pack of scoundrels that ought to be put out of the way. Kill the policeman and the people he gets his orders from!"

He began to pant and be thirsty as a result of the energy wasted in his wild gesticulations. Sweat ran down over his red, sunburned face and darkened his ruddy beard. He came down from the bank and bent over the edge of the hole, lapping the brackish water from his cupped hands. A throng of startled birds of passage took flight. Fabiano got up with a flash of indignation in his eyes.

"Dirty, low-down—"

His anger was once again turned against the birds. Sitting back down on the bank, he fired many times into the branches of the coral-bean tree, leaving the ground covered with dead bodies. They would be salted and hung up on a line to dry. He intended to use them for food on the coming journey. He should spend the rest of his money on powder and shot and put in a day there at the water hole, then take to the road. Would he have to move? Although he knew perfectly well he would, he clung to frail hopes. Perhaps the drought wouldn't come; perhaps it would rain.

It was those cursed birds that frightened him. He tried to forget them. But how could he forget them if they were right there, flying about his head, hopping around on the mud, perching on the branches, lying scattered in death on the ground? Were it not for them, the drought would not exist. At least it would not exist just then. It would come later and last a shorter time. As things were, it was beginning now; Fabiano could feel it already. It was just as if it had arrived; he was already suffering the hunger, thirst, and endless fatigue of the trek. A few days earlier he had been calmly making whips and mending fences. Suddenly there was a dark line across the sky, then other lines, thousands of lines uniting to form clouds, and the fearful noise of wings, heralding destruction. He had already suspected something when he saw the springs diminishing, and he had looked with distrust at the whiteness of the long mornings and the sinister redness of the afternoons. Now his suspicions were confirmed.

"Miserable wretches!"

Those cursed birds were the cause of the drought. If he could kill them the drought would be choked off. He moved feverishly, loading the flintlock with fury. His thick, hairy hands, full of blotches and skinned spots, trembled as they moved the ramrod up and down.

"Pests!"

But it was impossible to put an end to that plague. He looked about the countryside and found himself completely isolated. Alone in a world of feathers, full of birds that were going to eat him up. He thought of his wife and sighed. Poor Vitória would again have to carry the tin trunk across the wasteland. It was hard for a woman with her brains to go tramping over the scorched earth, bruising her feet on the stones. The birds of passage were killing the stock. How had Vitória hit on that idea? It was hard. He, Fabiano, no matter how he might rack his brains would never come out with an expression like that. Vitória knew how to figure accounts right; she sat down in the kitchen, consulted piles of different kinds of seeds, representing coins of varying value. And she came out right. The boss's accounts were different, drawn up in ink, against the herdsman, but Fabiano knew that they were wrong and that the boss was trying to cheat him. He did cheat him. But what could he do about it? Fabiano, a luckless half-breed, slept in jail and was beaten. Could he react? He could not. He was just a half-breed. But Vitória's accounts must be right. Poor Vitória. She would never be able to stretch her bones in a real bed, the only thing she truly wanted. Didn't other people sleep in beds? Fearing to wound her feelings, Fabiano would agree with her, though it was just a dream. They couldn't sleep like Christians. And now they were going to be eaten up by the birds of passage.

He got down from the bank, slowly picked up the dead birds, filling his haversack to overflowing with them, and gradually withdrew. He, Vitória, and the two boys would eat the birds.

If the dog were still alive, she would have a feast. Why did he feel such a stab at his heart? The poor dog! He had had to kill her, because she was sick. Then he had gone back to the whips, the fences, and the boss's mixed-up accounts. He walked up the slope and approached the jujubes. At the root of one of them the poor dog loved to wallow, covering herself with twigs and dry leaves. Fabiano sighed. He felt a tremendous weight in his chest. Had he been wrong? He looked at the burnt plain, the hill where the cavies hopped about, and he swore to the catingueira trees and the stones that the animal had rabies and threatened the children. That was why he had killed her. And he had given the matter no further thought at the time.

Here Fabiano's thoughts became mixed up. The idea of the dog mingled with that of the birds of passage, which he failed to distinguish from the drought. He, his wife, and the two boys would be eaten up. Vitória was right; she was smart and saw things a long way off. Fabiano's eyes widened; he wanted to go on admiring her, but his heart was heavy. It felt as big as a bullfrog; it was full of thoughts of the dog. The poor thing, thin and stiff, her eyes pecked out by the vultures!

Passing in front of the jujubes, Fabiano walked more quickly. How could he tell whether the dog's spirit wasn't haunting the place?

Fear was in his soul as he reached the house. It was dusk, and at that hour he always felt a vague terror. He had been discouraged and dejected of late because misfortunes had been many. He would have to consult with Vitória about the trip, get rid of the birds he had shot, explain himself, convince himself he had not done wrong in killing the dog. They would have to abandon the accursed place. Vitória would think just as he did.

Ramón Amaya Amador

Ramón Amaya Amador (1916–66) was a prolific writer and prominent member of the Communist Party of Honduras. Born in Olanchito near the Caribbean coast, he experienced firsthand the social, political, and environmental abuses of the banana industry, which acquired enormous parcels of land that quickly became useless because of the trees' susceptibility to fungal disease. The arrival of sigatoka in the 1930s made banana plantations deadly for human laborers, precisely because it could be effectively combated by frequent application of toxic chemicals (Miller 2007, 129–33). Amaya Amador left his position as a rural schoolteacher to defend Hondurans whose land, livelihoods, and health were being consumed by United Fruit and other U.S.-based corporations. By exposing the relationships between corrupt Honduran officials and United Fruit executives, Amaya Amador's work directly challenged military dictator Tiburcio Carías Andino; he therefore had to flee Honduras soon after the publication of his novel *Green Prison* in 1950. He found refuge in nearby Guatemala until 1954, when a CIA-backed coup removed that country's democratically elected president, Jacobo Árbenz, because of Árbenz's policy of renationalizing unused lands belonging to United Fruit and other companies. Amaya Amador relocated to Argentina. He went home briefly in the late 1950s, then was appointed to represent the Communist Party of Honduras on the *Revista Internacional*, based in Prague. He died in a plane crash near Bratislava, Slovakia (Irving 1997). Amaya Amador left roughly twenty unpublished manuscripts at the time of his death. *Green Prison* is his most celebrated work; it is also the first and most famous example of the *novela bananera*, which takes its place beside the petroleum novel and the rubber-boom novel as a significant subgenre within the regionalist canon.

***

"Green Destiny" (1950)

TRANSLATED BY PATRICIA GONZÁLEZ

The peasants continued to gnaw on their destiny. From dawn till dusk in the banana plantation, watched by creole overseers and foreign bosses, inhaling the "poison" of pesticides, tying sticks, weeding, harvesting almost daily, watering day and night, building, driving tractors, motorcars, or trains, fighting furiously against tropical diseases, against malnutrition, against the misery coiled in barracks and "cuzules,"[1] where vice consorted with lust.

People lived stuck in the plantations as if they were part of them; they were mixed up with, and could be mistaken for, leaves and stalks, machines and animals; they adhered to the land that was fighting the rising natural forest eager to swallow the plantations. It was the confrontation between human and vegetative forces, a necessary struggle to give life to banana plantations and to the wonderfully rich production of fruits. The men went from field to field following the work. Life was the same: cruel and tragic.

The new work that had begun at the beginning of the summer on the other side of the Aguán River[2] was advancing thanks to muscle, motor, and mind. The wild forests and the old haciendas disappeared under the machetes and axes of weeding squads. All the large landowners opted to sell after Sierra and Cantillano set the example by selling first; many barely received the amount needed to pay the lawyer Estanio Párraga for his work in the "state inheritance declarations." Only one man remained indifferent to the hallucination of the dollar: Luncho López, who proudly declared: "I am like a tree with roots that reach deep down into my land." It was his property, and he wandered through it supervising the peons in the sugar cane, banana, and chatal[3] plantations, in the promising cornfields and extensive bean crops; or in the middle of his cattle, where he competed with the cowboys and the milking crew. Three generations of the López family had attended to every inch of the farm land, dark as poor people's bread, but fertile and rich as the womb of a young peasant girl; they were born there, and their ancestors lay underground; *La Dolora* represented his life and his tradition.

After the unpleasant meeting with Mr. Still and *La Central*, Luncho did not go back; it was they, the land buyers, who confronted him in his hacienda; but the will of the old valley man[4] was stronger than the mahogany and guayacan[5] trees of his forests.

"My land is mine! *La Dolora* is my life!"

And the blue-eyed blonde-haired men left upset, coming back another day to hear Luncho's words again: — "I do not sell, I WILL NOT SELL!"

And he did not give in.

It was Estanio Párraga's astute imagination that designed the winning plan that would achieve the objective of the Fruit Company. With admirable subtlety, the lawyer interested the landowner in cultivating bananas in greater quantities, independently; he painted the rosiest economic outcome, achieved without commitments to anyone; better yet, it would be the Company who would benefit by buying all the production of his farms. This way he would be able to keep *La Dolora*.

"You would become a 'small producer.'"[6]

Lawyer Párraga was so persuasive in presenting the advantage and bounty of cultivating bananas exclusively, that Luncho took him seriously. He began talks with Mr. Still, including the Manager of the Fruit Company, coming to an agreement favorable to the landowner. They offered to take all the fruit produced on his farms at a flattering price with no other condition than to allow the Company's railroad to run through his land, as the most efficient transportation method. They also offered to solve his irrigation problem and to control the sigatoka,[7] supplying him all types of materials at cost. Enthused by the new horizon which was opening to his rustic life, the old landowner went back to his land to begin the undertaking that could turn him into a "small producer."

He hired an engineer to divide his lands in small plots and recruited the different groups of peons who would oversee the transformation of the pastures and woodlands of *La Dolora* into one extensive banana plantation. The energy of his youth seemed to have returned to him, and he personally directed the work of the peons. For many weeks, there was continuous activity on his property. The grass cutters came through battling the weeds, destroying grass and fields of herbage, eliminating the wire fences from paths and crossroads; they were followed by young ax cutters who made nature tremble with the echo of their axes falling on the moaning trees, like defeated giants on the back of moist earth. The many guayacan and mahogany trees that filled the ancient forests were given to Mr. Still as useless logs, and not destroyed by fire. The gringo[8] organized a magnificent "bengue"[9] exporting lumber by the cubic foot and producing fabulous earnings, never imagined by Luncho López, who now referred to the foreigners differently.

"These blond men," he would say to attorney Párraga, "are not what I thought. They are civilized people. How mistaken I was at the beginning; yes, it is beneficial to work with these gringos! They are practical entrepreneurs and they have different methods for everything, better than our rudimentary ones. They bring prosperity and labor. I am convinced now that people cannot be judged without knowing them better. Appearances are deceiving."

He made peace with his old friends Sierra and Cantillano, even though he always judged them for selling their land and the crazy way they were squandering their money.

"Me, sell? Never. But I will work the land as long it is mine!"

Things were happening the way Luncho was expecting. Crops and pastures disappeared, leaving only debris; following the burning squad, thousands of voracious tongues of fire consumed everything, producing only coals, black tree trunks, and dispersed ashes. Since the terrain was low, irrigation was done with trenches taking the water from the Aguán; sowing came later.

How joyful was the pure heart of the new "small producer" when the light-green buds sprouted from the fertile rootstalks in his dear land! How much joy he felt during those days when nature spawned the miracle of exuberant vegetal reproduction. Luncho López smiled proudly in the face of his labor, hopeful.

"Here is life," he proclaimed. "Here is the fruit of men's honest labor. The banana trees will rise with God's blessing and the crop will reimburse my expenses and effort. I am putting my land and the happiness of my family at risk. But for men, land and work are the door to a prosperous world."

Under the command of the independent farmer, more than a hundred workers grew a prosperous banana plantation. The day of flowering arrived, the fertilized cones began opening under the sun to give way to the fruits; long, curved banana fingers began to thicken until they became large clusters. It was the celebration of the Honduran earth's reproductive power: magnificent plants and fruits emerged from the warm womb of the land. It was the time to shape the "green gold" with human muscle from the forge on the earth.

One day, leading his men, Luncho witnessed the first cut in his plantation and prepared two fruit carts for the Company to take away, as they had agreed. But that day he had his first disillusion and first dissatisfaction.

He went to *La Central* to talk to Mr. Still, who made excuses.

"López, my friend, forgive me for allowing you to harvest the fruit and not take it; the reason is the lack of ships for transportation; we will let you know when there is a chance."

"But this is not possible, Mr. Still; my farm is ready to harvest and to leave it like that would be my demise."

"We are sorry, but there is nothing we can do. The Company is losing thousands of dollars because of the war."

He returned to his farm disillusioned to confront the ghost of bankruptcy and ruin. What favorable solution could he adopt in such a desperate situation? What to do with that wonderful production of bananas without a market nor a buyer? Disgrace pecked at his heart like a huge vulture; he had invested all his savings in the farm, plus all the revenue obtained through the sale of his cattle. Time went by and the Company did not take one banana cluster from the "small producer." But in the Company plantations, business was as usual, and the harvest of the fruit continued uninterrupted.

One day, Estanio Párraga came to his farm. He found him giving away bananas to the neighbors in town. The presence of the lawyer made him think he was going to elude total ruin, but on the contrary, he was bringing more bad news. The Fruit Company absolutely refused to buy his fruit; no need for it, they had enough. And the Company lawyer finished by saying:

"The Company is notifying you that from now on, it will not provide the chemical materials to cure sigatoka nor the irrigation system for watering."

Facing this series of calamities, Luncho was not able to contain his wrathful impulses and cursed the lawyer, accusing him of evil intent, of encouraging him to undertake the enterprise with the premeditated purpose of ruining him. In the face of this avalanche of drastic accusations, of justified denunciations from the deceived valley man, the lawyer reacted with cynical coldness and shamelessness worthy of a true scoundrel. He didn't even flinch when the honorable man shouted at him:

"Scallywag! Miserable wretch! Swindler!"

The lawyer let him calm down and spoke again in a more flattering tone:

"I do not want to discuss the issue because you are very upset, and you have the right to be. What I can tell you is that you are not defeated yet. You have an acceptable solution: sell the land to the Company."

Hearing that proposition, the innocent Luncho López now understood everything clearly. They had enticed him to undertake banana cultivation to ruin him and for the Company to be in a better position to buy the lands. Now he understood the indecent game of the tycoons and the lawyer, but it was too late to recover his capital, or all the efforts wasted on his farm. Observing the cynicism of Estanio, who dared to smile mockingly, he threw himself on him, punching him in the face, grabbing his neck, and, unable to contain his impulses, with a well-aimed kick ejected him from the house.

As the obese "shyster lawyer" was walking away, Luncho shouted after him:

"Miserable dog! If you ever set foot on my property again, you won't get out alive. Son of one hundred thousand . . ."

Neither Mr. Still nor Estanio returned to *La Dolora* because they knew they would not get anywhere with Luncho, who could become violent. He preferred to go bankrupt than to concede to the gringos. But the third day after he kicked the lawyer off his property, he was visited by the City Commander, who arrived accompanied by a judge, the Colonel of *La Central*, and a sizable entourage.

The visit of those men was a pleasant surprise for Luncho, for the Commander was a friend and an old fellow party member; together, they both supported the last conservative civic campaigns for presidential elections, which brought the ruling Blue party to power. At that time, Luncho had offered for their conservative cause not only his immense moral influence over the peasants of the valley but also his coffer to finance the campaign. Post-election, he went back to his ranch *La Dolora*, working his land to recuperate the thousands of pesos invested in the electoral campaign, unlike most of his companions after the victory. He did not request a state job, nor farms, not even to recuperate the money invested, as was the custom in the national milieu. With all this in mind, the Commander's visit filled him with joy, and he welcomed him with open arms. But soon, all this suddenly changed because the visit of the men, who were his comrades, had an unexpected purpose. The Commander's words, when he spoke, were harsh and laconic:

"I am here as an officer, following the orders of my superiors. The Government understands that the Company has tried to buy your lands and you did not want to sell. I also understand you made a deal to negotiate bananas with the help of the trust, and that you now do not let the Company work in that sector; therefore, the military government orders you to sell *La Dolora*, because the Company needs the land given in concession by the Government. And listen carefully, Luncho: "It is a mi-li-tar-y order!"

Luncho's first reaction was rage and indignation; a bit later, he looked at his old friend thoughtfully, not with rancor, but with pity and sorrow because Luncho was one of the few who believed in the integrity of the man whom they had ascended to the presidency of the Republic. He understood what a military order meant.

"And if I refuse, as I do refuse to sell, what would happen to me?"

"I have strict orders, and if you were my opponent, I would enforce them right away; but we are fellow party members; you have served the party well and that stops me from treating you like all the others; but if you refuse, we have other resources that would release us from any responsibilities, and the result would be the same; you will have to deal with the Law."

"The Law! What do I, or does this have to do with the Law?"

"Who gave you irrigation for the banana plantations you own? Who provided the 'poison'? Who lent you the train track? The Company. How much did you pay for all that? Where are your receipts? The Company has sued you for debt and fraud. How are you going to pay? Luncho, it is better for you to sell *La Dolora*."

"But you know I do not owe the Company anything."

"Yes, but you see, they are recuperating their expenses. They have proof."

There was no name for so much insolence, so much gross injustice, so much pain. For Luncho to truly see the type of men in power was a painful eye-opener; they were nothing more than servile figureheads of foreign monopolies. The political situation of the country was laid out before him undisguised, in all its corruption. And those were his coreligionists, his friends.

"It's justice, legality, an honest government! Alright, Commander, I have been informed and tell Mr. Still that tomorrow, even today if he wants, he can come to receive *La Dolora*. I am assuming, Commander, that I must thank you for not treating me like your opponent. Isn't that right? Express my gratitude to the Government. I now understand how deep the presence of the Company in our country is, and why this regime, which I helped obtain power, is ruling. Make sure you tell your Government that I, Luncho López, feel ashamed to have promoted a gang of public thieves. I could fight legally to defend my rights, but with your kind of justice, I prefer to abandon my hacienda to the gringos. My land was already disgraced by producing the cash to empower the ruling party who now robs me. You may go, gentlemen, *La Dolora* belongs to the Company."

Luncho and his family departed the next day to the city. The attitude of his coreligionist was a mortal blow to his convictions. He left free of hate but carried a deep sorrow in his pure heart.

"Justice! . . . the legalese of my coreligionists . . . My God! What has become of this country? And I believed in honesty . . ."

Estanio Párraga fulfilled his promise. The Company obtained *La Dolora* for next to nothing. Two thousand pesos was given to the old landowner, money his honorable hands would never hold.

Notes

1. *Cuzul*, local term for a small, improvised structure used as a dwelling.

2. The Aguán River, rising in the Department of Yoro in north-central Honduras, flows briefly southward before turning to flow east-northeast to the Caribbean Sea. It passes through the towns of Olanchito and Tocoa, the latter in the Department of Colón.

3. *Chatal*, animal fodder.

4. *Vallero*, valley dweller.

5. *Guayacan*, any of several South and Central American timber trees, typically with strong, dense, hard wood in the genus *Guaiacum*.

6. *Poquitero*, a farmer who grows in smaller quantities.

7. Black sigatoka is a leaf-spot disease of banana plants caused by the ascomycete fungus *Mycosphaerella fijiensis* (Morelet), generally fatal to the plant.

8. *Gringo*, Central and South American slang for U.S. citizens.

9. *Bengue*, colloquial word for side business.

FIVE
Modern Metropoles

The surge in demand for Latin America's export products is one essential feature of the late nineteenth and early twentieth centuries; another is the rapid expansion of the region's principal cities. In reality, urbanization and the export boom are two sides of the same coin. As subsistence agriculture decreased in the countryside, some of the rural population stayed behind, working on the cattle ranches and banana plantations, or harvesting rubber and *yerba mate* in the jungle. Many others migrated to the growing cities, where they hoped to find employment as shop girls or dockworkers, journalists and teachers, or as part of an assembly line in the manufacturing plants that began to appear. The effects of internal migration were compounded by the arrival of hundreds of thousands of immigrants, lured by news of the booming economy. As a result, the capitals of Mexico, Argentina, Cuba, Peru, Chile, and Uruguay all roughly tripled in size between 1895 and 1910; by 1918 the population of Buenos Aires had reached 1.7 million (Halperín Donghi 1993, 179). Like the previous section, this one spans the late nineteenth century and the first three decades of the twentieth, but whereas part 4 focused on the export boom's devastating toll on the human and nonhuman communities of the continent's interior, part 5 brings together a diverse group of responses to the rapid expansion of Latin American cities and the socioeconomic, cultural, and ecological changes it brought about.

To be clear, cities had long been an important feature of Latin American societies. In contrast to the United States, where early settlers established family farms in areas lacking sizable Amerindian populations, the Iberian colonizers located their administrative and economic centers at the site of principal Indigenous cities, which provided labor as well as food and other necessities. Their populations remained fairly constant until the late nineteenth century, when political stability and the export boom set off the demographic shift described above. The transformation of the old colonial capitals—affectionately known as *la Gran Aldea*, "the Great Village"—into the modern metropoles of the twentieth century was not just a question of numbers, however. For women and men, urban living brought new forms of association and entertainment, increased access to new ideas and information, and new possibilities for political action, including socialism, anarchism, and feminism. At the same time, the cities were commonly associated with the rise of a new consumer culture based on access to imported manufactures, especially those of Britain, France, and the United States.

For the poor and working classes, life in the city typically meant the crowded quarters of *conventillos*, or the shantytowns that began to ring major cities in the early twentieth century. Well before industrialization and automobiles produced asphyxiating levels of air pollution, the spike in population density dangerously overburdened the rudimentary sanitation "systems" of most major cities, which in the Americas as well as in Europe generally consisted of tossing human and animal waste into a nearby river or stream. Trash, in most places, simply rotted where it lay, or else was consumed by scavengers. Not surprisingly, the late nineteenth century saw major epidemics in Buenos Aires, Lima, Mexico City, and other urban areas, with death tolls especially high in the crowded neighborhoods populated with immigrants and other recent arrivals.

One response undertaken by Latin America's elites was the so-called Haussmannization of the continent's principal cities. For the landed oligarchy in particular, the export boom brought soaring profits, some of which funded construction of luxurious residences in the cities' more elegant neighborhoods. Following the renovation of Paris (1853–70) implemented by Georges-Eugène Haussmann under Emperor Napoléon III, Latin American elites also undertook a major transformation of their nations' capitals, the effects of which can still be observed today. They improved circulation, erected public works and historical monuments, and created broad avenues and tree-lined parks that lent themselves to various forms of recreation, including the ostentatious display of wealth. Often the desire to "open up" increasingly populous cities was a direct response to the ravages of epidemic diseases, which in Europe and the Americas alike had heightened concerns about public sanitation. The most extreme case was the Mexican capital, where Lake Texcoco had periodically flooded the city with raw sewage since Aztec times. The draining of the lake and the construction of the Gran Canal were considered a major achievement of Porfirio Díaz's thirty-year rule and one of the engineering marvels of the age. As was typical of urban improvement projects of the time, however, the drainage projects displaced the city's poor and working-class inhabitants and took away the source of their livelihood—the lake and the aquatic communities it supported—as well as the floating gardens Mexicans had cultivated for centuries. (Francisco Javier de Clavijero's lavish description of these floating gardens, known as *chinampas*, is featured in part 2.)

The selections included here reflect the environmental and ecological transformations associated with urbanization, as well as the psychological shock experienced by individuals still adjusting to the transition from rural to urban locales. Like the environmental justice movement of today, these writer-activists refuse to separate the politics of race, class, and gender from the politics of waste, access, and contamination. We feature two important feminist writers, the working-class heroine Alfonsina Storni (Argentina) and the more privileged María Luisa Bombal (Chile), as well as socialist Manuel González Prada (Peru) and anarchists Rafael Barrett (Paraguay) and Pierre Quiroule (Argentina). In different ways, they all draw attention to the asymmetrical distribution of environmental pleasure and peril associated with the export boom and the rise of Latin America's modern metropoles. Geographer Neil Smith coined the phrase "uneven development" to describe the linkages between places that benefit unequally from the same economic processes. In this context, uneven development describes the enrichment of the capitals at the expense of the interior but also the construction of splendid mansions in close proximity to the crowded housing of the poor.

We also include works by two writers associated with what is often regarded as Latin America's first autochthonous literary movement, Modernismo. Beginning in 1888, when the Nicaraguan Rubén Darío published a slim book of poetry and prose intriguingly titled *Azul . . .* , the Modernistas undertook a far-reaching renovation of Spanish-language poetry. The Modernistas attempted to use art and literature—above all, poetry—to transcend what they saw as the crass materialism of contemporary life. In this they were inspired by Charles Baudelaire and the French Parnassians, as well as by North American writers Walt Whitman and Edgar Allan Poe. Cosmopolitan, urbane, and explicitly Romantic, Modernismo appears, at least on the surface, to be the polar opposite of earthy, prosaic regionalism, but in some key ways the contrast is more apparent than real. A number of individuals participated in both movements; Uruguay's Horacio Quiroga is one especially prominent example. More fundamentally, regionalists and Modernistas alike reconfigured the binary oppositions between civilization and barbarism, nature and culture they had inherited from previous generations of Latin American intellectuals. As the critic Marie Escalante (2016) points out, the aesthetic philosophy of the Modernistas revolves around the more subtle distinction between nature and artifice, which enables them to perceive the ways that modernity has infringed on nature, modifying and in some cases destroying it.

Finally, we include a founding document of Brazilian modernism, Oswald de Andrade's 1928 "Cannibalist Manifesto." Like Darío and his fellow travelers, Andrade also revises the Eurocentric notion of an ongoing antagonism between the forces of civilization and those of barbarism. Writing when Darío was already an old man, however, Andrade is unconcerned with transcendence, or even subtlety: instead he offers a tongue-in-cheek vindication of the Amazonian natives' mythical anthropophagy as a figure for an aesthetic practice that valorizes Indigenous traditions while "devouring" foreign cultural influences. "We never had speculation," writes Andrade, who became a communist soon after. "But we had divination. We had Politics, which is the science of distribution. And a social system in harmony with the planet."

Suggestions for Further Reading

Federico Gamboa. 1903. *Santa. A Novel of Mexico City*, translated by John Charles Chasteen. Chapel Hill: University of North Carolina Press, 2010.

Enrique Vera y González. 1904. *La estrella del sur: A través del porvenir*. Buenos Aires, Argentina: Instituto Histórico de la Ciudad de Buenos Aires, 2000.

Leopoldo, Lugones. 1906. "Yzur." In *Leopoldo Lugones: Selected Writings*, edited by Gwen Kirkpatrick and translated by Sergio Gabriel Waisman. Oxford: Oxford University Press, 2008.

Climaco, Soto Borda. 1917. *Diana cazadora*. Bogotá: Editorial ABC, 1942.

Martín, Adán. 1928. *The Cardboard House*, translated by Katherine Silver and Rick London. New York: New Directions, 2012.

Rubén Darío

Leader of the Spanish-American literary movement known as Modernismo, Rubén Darío (1867–1916) is celebrated today for his impeccable versification, his formal innovations, vehement rejection of U.S. imperialism, and enduring cultural influence. His life is a story of epic proportions. Raised by a great aunt in León, Nicaragua, Darío read at three, wrote his first verses at ten, and by twelve was famous throughout Central America. Three years later, he rejected a scholarship offered by the Nicaraguan government, which he detested, and went to live in El Salvador. (Darío's mentors hoped the move would prevent him from marrying Rosario Murillo, who became his second wife in 1893 [Aira 2001, 165–67].) He published *Azul . . .*—the book that began Modernismo—in Valparaíso in 1888. Influenced by the French Parnassian movement, Darío's exquisite musicality and pursuit of art for art's sake resonated in an age plagued by materialism and spiritual ennui. He was prolific: the success of *Azul . . .* was followed by *Profane Hymns* (1896) and *Songs of Life and Hope* (1905), among other works. Darío continued his peripatetic existence, working as a newspaper correspondent and forming friendships among the bohemian literati of Paris, Madrid, Buenos Aires, Mexico, New York, and Havana. Literary fame brought a number of diplomatic appointments; nevertheless, Darío was perpetually in financial straits. In his final years he also struggled with alcoholism. The mysticism typical of Darío's late work appears in the poems featured here, "Reincarnations," "The Song of the Pines," "Revelation," and "Philosophy." The poems challenge the distinction between nature and artifice and, more fundamentally, between humanity and nonhuman nature. As translator and critic Steven White (2011, 66–67) writes, Darío suggests that all of nature is intrinsically sacred, a pathway to the divine.

***

Poems (1890–1907)

TRANSLATED BY ANDREW HURLEY, GREG SIMON, AND STEVEN F. WHITE

Reincarnations

First I was a bed of coral,
then a beautiful gem,
then green and hanging ivy on a stem;
then I was an apple,

a lily growing in the fields,
a young girl's lips as she yields,
a skylark singing in the morning;
and now I am like a palm
in Jehovah's light, a soul or a psalm
that is sung to the wind.

Philosophy

Say hello to the sun, spider. Don't feel forlorn.
Offer thanks to God, oh, Toad, that you are alive.
The crab's shell defends itself with a rose's thorn—
a point of resemblance between mollusks and wives.

Enigmas given form—accept what you are;
you can leave responsibility to the Law,
which in turn will leave it to the Omnipotent . . .
(Crickets! Sing the moon! Bears! Dance to your heart's content!)

The Song of the Pines

Pine trees! Brothers on land and in the air,
I love you all! You're sweet, good, and somber.
One might say that you're trees who think and care,
pampered by sunrises, poets, and birds.

The winged sandal must have grazed your brow.
You're masts, proscenia, and a curule chair.
Solar pines! Pines from Italy! How
bathed you are in grace and blue glory there.

Without the sun's gold, you can be gloomy,
covered in glacial mists and dew.
Pines at night in mountains of reverie,
pines from northern climes, you're beautiful, too.

You move like mimes, actors, or a statue,
stretching toward the sweet caress of the sea.
Sacred pines, I will never forget you!
Pines from Naples, loved by flowers and me!

While wandering on my pilgrim's journey,
where I can dream my dreams, I found lovely
pines on Golden Island that granted me
a heartfelt place for you, a place to be.

Loved because they're so sad, so soft and fair,
or for their fragrance like some immense bloom,
for a certain monkish air and long hair:
their sounds, their nests of love, their sap's perfume.

Ancient pines shaken by the wind's presence
in epic poems and loved by the sun!
Lyric pines growing in the Renaissance
and in the soil of some Spanish garden!

Aeolian arms sway together
when a violent gust with its fury
makes silken sounds, sounds of feathers
as it passes, sounds of surf and sea.

There was that night when the hand of Fate
brought the bitter sorrows that enfold me.
The moon used silver on the pine to plate
its blackness. A nightingale consoled me.

We're Romantics. . . . Is there anyone who Is
who isn't? If you've never met the test
of love and pain, or never sung a kiss,
hang yourself from a pine: it's for the best . . .

Not me. The ways of yesterday assure
my longing and my being. I endure
with reveries and shapes as their lover
from far away, heading toward the future.

Revelation

From cliffs that were high and rocky,
my mouth engorged with wind and salt
I launched my cry above the sea

into the infinite cobalt
vision and the blood-red sunset
that myths and miracles exalt.

I drank salt wind and won't forget
the communion of communions
that left my mind's meaning wounded.

Each beating heart and the living cells,
science-fired gut shining within,
constellations and their marvels.

I heard the mountain god begin
to speak with the music he knew—
a concert he played on seven

pipes. And then I shouted, "It's true!
Pan, great god of vitality,
is alive and immortal, too!"

I stared at the peak and could see,
almost, double horns on a head,
a sunlit soul, Pan's devotee.

The single double serpent sped
over waves. It was coiled around
a caduceus transported

by Mercury. I was spellbound
by the thalassic mother, blessed
by this sea of all that I've found.

I saw blue, topaz, amethyst,
gold, pearls, silver, and violet,
and Electra's daughter's conquest.

And I heard the piercing trumpet
as it poured from the triton's shell
and mermaids loved by the poet.

And as one who longs to love well,
I cried out, "Where's the god who brings
forth wheat from mud, and plants that grew

to free this tribe from its wanderings?"
An inner voice said: "I'm with you,
in you, for you: I am All Things."

Julián del Casal

Alongside his Cuban contemporary José Martí, Julián del Casal (1863–93) was one of the principal forerunners of the Modernismo movement. Casal's mother died very young; his father, a wealthy merchant, lost the family fortune and died when Julián was only twenty-one. University-educated, Casal took a mundane position with the island's still-Spanish administration and simultaneously began writing articles for *La Habana Elegante*. Some ill-chosen words about the governor quickly cost Casal his bureaucratic job, however, and from that time on he made a meager living for himself as a journalist and poet. While still a young man, Casal scraped together money for a trip to Madrid that seems to have only underscored his precarious financial situation. Soon after, Casal was diagnosed with tuberculosis. Introverted, isolated, and sick, Casal became devoted to French literature, particularly the poets associated with the symbolist and Parnassian movements. He lived ascetically, dressing always in black like his idol Baudelaire (Aira 2001, 134). Rubén Darío, passing through Havana in 1892, became a close friend. Casal had published his first collection of poetry and prose, *Leaves in the Wind*, in 1890; *Snow* (1894) soon followed. Lacking the brilliant formal inventiveness of Darío and the moral and political optimism of Martí, Casal's aestheticism, cosmopolitanism, and exploration of marginal realities—drugs, mental and bodily illness, death—nonetheless resonate with readers. His ironic, almost perverse animosity toward nonhuman nature is as much a critique of Cuba's bucolic tradition as a profession of faith in artificial beauty. The poem included here, "In the Country," comes from Casal's final collection, *Busts and Rhymes*, which was published posthumously. Casal had prepared the work during a visit at his sister's country house.

***

"In the Country" (1893)

TRANSLATED BY G. J. RACZ

For cities I admit an impure love,
Preferring the illumination of
Gas lamps to age-old sun rays from above.

To languid senses, fresh scents from a wood
Of tall mahoganies smell not so good
As air in any sickly bedroom could.

No forest proudly hailed as tropical
Will ever seem to me more beautiful
Than outskirts of some ancient capital.

The flower that sprouts by country paths, whose light
May seem the earth's own beacon, is by right
Forgotten at a hothouse flower's sight.

More than the birdsong wafting from a tree
Abloom, I find sweet music's harmony
In rhyme, which moves my soul and touches me.

The pure expression on a shepherdess
Could scarcely serve to soften this heart less
While some loose sinner's face inspires *tendresse*.

Go take what golden hues the wheat has donned.
This may be mere caprice, but I'm more fond
Of that rich gold in tresses now dyed blonde.

I don't see how the mist that falls in sheets
To curtain hills most mornings here competes
With mousseline silk, whose test it scarcely meets.

More than the flood cascading from the heights,
I wish to hear mankind bemoan its plights,
Eternally in thrall all days and nights.

The mountain's dewdrops don't come half as near
To reaching this strange soul inside me here
As sobs that bathe an eyelash with a tear.

No, not for starlight's scintillating beam
Would I exchange the iridescent stream
Of any opal, pearl, or diamond's gleam.

Rafael Barrett

Son of an English father and an aristocratic Spanish mother, Rafael Barrett (1876–1910) was raised in belle époque Europe until his quick temper and concern for social justice led to his *desclasamiento*, or formal expulsion from upper-class society. He emigrated to South America, making his way as a teacher, journalist, and political activist. Barrett arrived in Paraguay in 1904 and threw himself into the turbulent politics of a country still recovering from the catastrophic Triple Alliance War of 1864–70. Disenchanted with the veniality and corruption of the two major political parties, Barrett became increasingly radicalized and embraced anarchism before succumbing to tuberculosis at age thirty-four. His voluminous writings, most of which were first published in the periodical press of Asunción, Buenos Aires, and Montevideo, are works of compassion, analysis, and searing social criticism. As Barrett became increasingly alienated from the bourgeois society of Asunción, he supported himself and his family by working as a surveyor, which enabled him to understand the extreme misery to which Paraguay's rural laborers were subjected following the massive liquidation of formerly public agricultural lands. Thousands were lured into the legalized slavery of the *yerba mate* groves in eastern Paraguay, which Barrett documented in chronicles later collected as *What the Yerba Groves Are* (1910) and *The Pain of Paraguay* (1911). In the piece featured here, "Tree Haters" (1907), Barrett criticizes the same class of upwardly mobile businessmen who were enriching themselves through the rapacious exploitation of the displaced campesinos; in this case the target of his critique is not their business ethos so much as their assault on the gracious old trees that once lined the streets of Asunción.

***

"Tree Haters" (1907)

TRANSLATED BY PATRICIA GONZÁLEZ

For an upstart social climber to build his house with money rapidly earned in perhaps honest, although undisclosed, ventures may be acceptable. To build a massive, blood color, vulgar, and dismal brick construction with Spanish tile roof and lattice holes is certainly less so. But it is truly unsettling for the owner to declare: "I am going to uproot all the trees around to make my property look beautiful."

Yes, it seems to be necessary to have it look clean and naked, with its impudent colors polluting the soft hues of the country, the façade shining and foolish. People must say: "This is the new home of Mr. Nobody who became so rich." It is necessary to contemplate without hindrance the monument resulting from Mr. Nobody's success. The trees are not necessary, "they obstruct the view." The eagerness to clean the earth goes beyond vanity, there is more: there is hate, hate towards the trees.

Is it possible? To hate those immovable beings with their noble arms always extended, tirelessly offering us the caress of their shadow, the silent fertility of their fruits, the multifarious and exquisite poetry they raise to the sky? We are assured that dangerous plants do exist. Maybe, but that is no reason to hate them. Our hate condemns them. Perhaps our love would transform and redeem them. Listen to a character from Victor Hugo: "He saw local people very busy uprooting nettles; he looked at the bunch of uprooted plants already dry and said:

"'All this is dead. Nevertheless, this would have been something good if they had known how to use it. When the nettle is young, the leaves make an excellent vegetable; when aged, it has strands and fibers like hemp and linen. Nettle cloth is worth as much as hempen cloth. Furthermore, nettle is a plant that can be harvested twice. And what does the nettle need? Little soil, no care nor cultivation . . . With not much effort, the nettle would be useful but with neglect, it becomes harmful. Then you kill it. How many men are like the nettle!' And after a pause he added: 'My friends, remember this, there are no bad weeds nor bad men, there are just bad cultivators.'"

But more importantly, it is not about cultivation but about sparing the trees. How to appease the assassins? During my travels, there is no place in the Republic where I have not seen the stupid ax of the landowner in action. Even those who have nothing destroy the plants. There is an ever-growing wasteland around the ranches, greater every year, that frightens and saddens. According to an Arab proverb, one of the three missions of every man in the world is to plant a tree. In this case, the son uproots what the father has planted. And it is not for money; I am not referring to those who harvest lumber. That would be an explanation, a merit; we have managed to make greed a virtue. I am referring to those who spend money on devastating the country. They are moved by a *disinterested hate*. And the anxiety increases when the only "improvements" made in the Capital's plazas are uprooting, uprooting, and uprooting trees.

Hate is twice as fierce in a region where summer lasts eight months. The scorching sun is preferred to the sweet presence of a tree. It would seem men are no longer able to feel life in the venerable tree trunks which shake under the iron and collapse with a pitiable crash. It would seem they do not understand that sap is blood and that their victims are engendered in love and in the light. It seems people live enslaved by a vague terror, they fear the forest might shelter delinquents and give life to ghosts. Behind the tree they perceive death. Or else, consumed by an amorphous pain, they want to reproduce around them the desolate desert of their souls.

And then in our soul, irritation transforms into pity. Very desperate, and very deep must be the wound of those who, in resigned silence, have lost that first affection, that fundamental affection that even beasts feel, the holy love for the earth and for the trees.

In *Red and Blue*, Asunción, September 27, 1907

Manuel González Prada

Among of the most progressive Peruvian thinkers of his time, Manuel González Prada (1868–1918) was a prominent Modernista poet as well as a radical social reformer and essayist. Early in life González Prada rebelled against his aristocratic family. He dropped out of the Santo Toribio Seminary to study science and law instead; when his father died he abandoned school altogether and began to write professionally. The years 1871–78 found González Prada at the Tuétame farm in the Mala Valley of southwestern Peru, where he wrote, translated, and experimented with by-products of the yuca root. He also witnessed the exploitation of Indigenous Peruvians by wealthy landowners, which he would later write about extensively. González Prada served in the War of the Pacific (1879–83), then hid in the family home for three years after the fall of Lima. The war further radicalized González Prada, prompting him to found the National Union Party in 1891. The remainder of the 1890s found him in Paris; upon return to Peru he left his own party and increasingly embraced anarchism. In his last years González Prada served as director of the National Library, replacing Ricardo Palma. Affectionately referred to as don Manuel by the generation of Vallejo and Mariátegui, González Prada continued to produce poetry as well as political essays. The poem included here, "Le tour du propiétaire," is from his collection *Exotics* (1911). Using characteristically innovative versification, this poem criticizes the class of absentee landowners, who are completely indifferent to the natural beauty of their rural properties. The French-language title emphasizes the elite's Eurocentric values and their disregard for local values, conditions, and concerns.

✳✳✳

"Le tour du propriétaire" (1911)

TRANSLATED BY G. J. RACZ

(An unrhymed polyrhythm)

With massive, waterproof galoshes on
And decked out in his finest khaki clothes,
      Umbrella (should it rain) in hand
And panama to shield his head from day,
Monsieur bourgeois inspects his sprawling properties,
      Vast rustic holdings and urbane estates.

His stomach full, so well disposed,
   Hot chocolate still digesting as he stands
(How steamy, creamy cocoa can invigorate!),
        He leaves the *confort* of his nest
   And sets out in the open air
At just the hour that demon tempter people call the "noon"
        Casts down those sinful rays of sun
        Upon the unsuspecting world.
The Spring had never spread more joyful happiness about
Or pleasant fragrances or hues in bright array.
        The Earth abloom could only smile
        At that bright firmament ablaze.

   The *bourgeois* hears no sounds: in vain
Do coos of turtledoves die down amid the leafy groves,
Lamenting lives that never are to know of love or Spring,
Or crashes of the surging billows echo from afar
Like wedding vows the Earth below and sky above exchange.

   The *bourgeois* smells no scents: in vain
Does any perfumed resin emanating from tall pines
        Diffuse its comforting and healthful balm
Or leafy, lustful forests' most seductive breath
        Pass like a call to revel in delight.

        The *bourgeois* sees no sights: in vain
        Do Babylonian willows shake when touched
        By any river's sonorous caress
Or white clouds float by wafted on the gentle breeze
Like some eternal jilted bride whose groom is never to appear
Or butterflies sail fluttering by his side —
        Fleet whirlabouts now gaily tinged
With gilded pollen once set off against the lily's white.

        Sweet Nature, you do pour in vain
Your amber syrup, beautifying even more your beauteousness
While offering as a sumptuous gift to men
        Your glorious, Olympian nudity.
The *bourgeois*, though, a real Tartuffe and Harpagon combined,
Can't grasp you, mother void of every hypocritical complaint,
        You, bounteous divinity,
        You, pagan goddess in extreme!

In calculation mid deep thought
About his profits' rise and fall,
The *bourgeois* master notes no sights, no scents, no sounds
As loveliness, light, poetry, and love
Were never products that could figure in his bottom line.

He shoots off sparks and scolds the hapless orchardkeep
Should roses be observed where collard greens
And lettuce ought to grow,
Though he congratulates the gardener and lets out *oh*'s of joy
If, mid the rows where pink carnations and red poppies used to bloom,
He glimpses cabbages.

Pierre Quiroule

Little is known about the life of Pierre Quiroule (1867–1938), the pseudonym of anarchist writer Joaquín Alejo Falconnet. Born in Lyon, Quiroule emigrated from France to Argentina at an early age, the family's journey likely motivated by the misery of France's underclasses, which offered little hope of abating after the failed revolutions of 1848 and 1870. As a teenager in Buenos Aires, he joined a group of anarcho-communists inclined toward tactics of terror and disorganization, but Quiroule's deepest values were aligned with those of Pyotr Kropotkin, the anarchist philosopher who recognized solidarity as an essential human quality. In the early twentieth century, Argentine anarcho-communism was strongly influenced by Italians Errico Malatesta and Pietro Gori, who encouraged local literati, including Leopoldo Lugones, Florencio Sánchez, and Quiroule himself, to adopt a more political stance in their writing. Quiroule collaborated with many publications, including *El Perseguido*, *La Liberté*, and *La Protesta*, writing plays, essays, short stories, novels, and texts of a philosophical and scientific nature. But his most significant work is the 1914 book excerpted here, *The American Anarchist City (A Work of Revolutionary Construction)*. Like Kropotkin, Quiroule was an admirer of medieval European cities; he was also inspired by the long tradition of urban utopias imagined—and in some cases realized—in the Americas (Ainsa 1986). As was the case for the Guarani missions represented in part 2, Quiroule's anarchist utopia was designed for self-sufficiency. All workers were trained in all kinds of work, including agriculture and manufacturing, and production was limited to bare necessities, reducing waste, contamination, and resource use while increasing residents' quality of life. Quiroule's emphasis on a salubrious city resonates with present-day urban ecologists and environmental justice advocates.

***

From *The American Anarchist City* (1914)

TRANSLATED BY ARTHUR DIXON

As the population of the communes was relatively sparse, and its tastes and customs simple, the great enterprises of the age of capitalism, with their mighty plants and factories, were excessive: a few workshops of each variety were quite enough for the production of all that life in the communes demanded, taking into account that, in all trades, this production was limited to items of general utility. For this reason, while veritable armies of workers and countless articles of quite disputable usefulness

were needed to feed the global market before, now only a few individuals were necessary to provide the anarchist city with its essential objects.

Thus, for example, the work of printing had diminished by a tremendous degree
due to the elimination of newspapers and political magazines, of shallow literature,
and of a multitude of pointless printings in the new social organization, such as
commercial flyers, claim forms, etc., which implied a colossal reduction in the production of paper, of inks, of presses, movable types and linotypes, motors and electric
power, etc. Works of carpentry had decreased to an evidently lesser but still appre-
ciable degree, as houses made of glass and wood had no place in their construction.

It is true that the casting of glass for housing required a certain level of supple-
mentary energy, but even still, the economy of time and of people was great, since
this effort totally or partially replaced several important trades: masons, bricklayers,
painters, cart drivers, etc. And so it was with the other professions.

Under these conditions, all communes ceased to be tributaries of other communes and of distant regions because they found within their own territory the
means and resources to develop freely, and since the anarchist youth grew up in
workshops and among machines or mingled with the elders busy tending the land,
when they were not studying in school or taking practical lessons at the four cardinal
points of the region, boys grew into men familiarized with the workings of industrial
and agricultural machinery, abreast of diverse systems and methods of production,
having acquired, little by little, the practice necessary for all labors.

Thus, the son of the emancipated city knew equally how to operate a loom, print
a book, install an electrical system, produce tools, run a bakery, cast houses, etc., just
as he understood physics and chemistry and knew everything relating to agricultural
work, adding to this universal set of skills those of the "chauffeur," or automobile
driver, and even those of the experienced aviator.

This multiplicity of professions and diversity of knowledge allowed them to
collaborate usefully and intelligently in almost all the efforts or endeavors of the
commune, and since the production of things of not-so-pressing use took place only
to the extent that they became necessary, they avoided falling into the danger of
submitting members of the commune to the absurd and odious system of intensive
industrial production adopted in the age of the greatest development and vitality of
capital, in which the worker was doubly the victim of a monstrous social organization that kept him enslaved in body and in spirit; a damnable regime in which gold
reigned insolently over the universe, the individual sacrificed as a burnt offering to
interests, not to those of the masses as they sought to make him believe, given that, as
a unit of said masses, some part of the general production ought to belong to him—
and precisely the opposite occurred—but instead to those of a piddling minority of
privileged parasites, owners of social wealth, who exploited the worker at their whim,
submitting him to an organization of labor both absolutely irrational and built to
atrophy the finest human qualities.

Might we conceive of a condition more miserable and disastrous than that of
these poor pariahs of both sexes who, to earn a paltry daily wage, always insufficient
to obtain life's most essential needs, had to carry out for ten, twelve, fourteen, or
more hours each day grueling and mind-numbing functions or labors, often vile,

humiliating, or demoralizing, always the same, throughout their existence, in dark, wet basements transformed into workshops, or in inadequate conditions, cramped and unhygienic? Labors that consisted, for the seamstress, for example, of remaining seated, rapidly pressing and relieving the foot pedal of the sewing machine, from dawn until late at night, hunched over this amusing and pleasant task: sewing pants and more pants, and, to "rest," opening buttonholes or tying buttons onto eternally identical garments, in exchange for compensation so minuscule that the earnings scarcely exceeded the cost of the thread used and bought by the worker!—For the bottle blower, of desperately pushing the stream of exhaled air over the molten glass, today, tomorrow, and always, until becoming consumptive and unfit for work at the age of thirty:—for the miner, of being entombed in the guts of the earth in order to laboriously extract the black combustible, seeing neither the sun nor the light of day, unable ever to admire the sublime spectacles of nature and exposed to the mortal risk of suffering a horrible death at any moment, in some low and dark gallery, treacherously wounded by the sinister firedamp or drowned in a sudden flood; and all this from father to son and from generation to generation, with no hope of one day escaping so fearfully tragic a fate! . . .—for the bread maker, of tiresomely kneading the nutritive dough, day after day and night after night, until murderous tuberculosis converts him into a sad human ruin, into a walking cadaver;—for the typographer, of invariably repeating the same mechanical movements of the arm over the box, covered in type, before which he stands:—for the tram or train employee, in perforating and handing back to the traveler little scraps of paper or numbered bits of cardboard:—for the "motorman," of stopping the electric coach every one or two minutes before accelerating again the same number of times;—or, like the shop clerk, standing behind the counter for interminable hours of dull inactivity, awaiting the customer, to provide him the objects that he, serving himself without bothering a soul, could take directly from their respective shelves, etc., etc.,—all this, not to mention that "ingenious" division of labor that makes a legion of workers take part in the assembly of certain manufactured objects, such as the needle, among others, that pass through the hands of a hundred twenty different workers before being definitively finished and put on sale! Such irrational labor methods could not survive in anarchist society, where free and varied work replaced the sole profession, that anesthetic of intelligence and of its creative faculties.

Following a course opposite that of capitalist society, in which gold was everything and the individual nothing, in the anarchist commune the individual was everything and gold, dispossessed of its fictitious value and nullified as a factor in social and individual wealth, unnecessary as an agent of commercial transactions or a remunerator of services, had returned to its corresponding place in the scale of metals useful to man, beneath steel and iron.

No low or selfish motive guided the members of anarchist society. Individual effort had a sole end: the good of all, and the activities of all combined harmoniously to create happy and good individualities. None worked with the absurd desire of accumulation, stupidly enslaving the present in fear of the future. The intensification of the joy of living was sought through all means, distancing all causes of pain or bitterness from existence: keeping every one of its units strong, intelligent, and free and in full enjoyment of well-being and health; this was the dominant concern of the anarchist commune.

Four wide diagonal streets gave access from the outside to the square of workshops, warehouses, and stockrooms, which came to be as the heart of the anarchist city: to the North, the diagonal of Harmony; to the South, that of Liberty; to the East, that of Humanity; and to the West, that of Friendship.

These diagonals were, along with the streets of Anarchy and Activity and the path of Abundance, the only true "roads" that crossed the city, placing it in communication with the neighboring towns.

As the new conceptions of existence and the necessities of the young cities were totally distinct from those that had prevailed for the creation and development of the immense cities of the bourgeois age, with their vast and complicated web of streets and communication paths through which thousands of carts and vehicles of all types incessantly circulated, raising clouds of pestilent dust that invaded everything, penetrating even into the very rooms situated—height of aberrations!—on either side of such revolting paths, contaminating the air breathed by the population, thereby exposed to attack by the foulest agents, the most destructive to health, things had proceeded in a manner completely distinct, in every sense and for every purpose.

The traffic of agricultural and other machines leaving the fields or returning to their garage or shed, that of the electromobiles of all types that came and went, bringing or taking cargoes for the provision of the warehouses and stockrooms, or materials needed in the workshops, took place on the aforementioned streets with no need to pass through the inhabited city.

This zone formed an immense park around the industrial city. Its streets, exclusively for pedestrian use, were sandy paths that snaked through the gardens adjacent to each house.

The arrangement of the houses in the city of the Sons of the Sun bore little resemblance to that of the bourgeois city: the distribution of anarchist dwellings was more poetic and rational.

Clusters of chalets emerged here and there from among the shadows of the giant palm trees that opened their splendid parasols over the fine arrows of the pointed roofs, which pierced through the tangled greenery of the climbing jasmines, locked in combat with the spiny rosebushes.

Artistic aerial bridges, from whose balustrades the flowering ivy hung in blooming garlands, connected these lovely dwellings. All around, one could admire a veritable overflowing of roses of all classes and colors, so profuse that, mingling with the little white stars of the fragrant jasmines, they formed veritable cascades of flowers that fell from the balconies to the ground.

In this way, the people of the commune lived in a clean, happy, and healthy city where the air was pure oxygen, not a horrible compound of miasmas and putrefaction.

Alfonsina Storni

At a young age her family's poverty introduced Alfonsina Storni (1892–1938) to the daily humiliations faced by female wage earners in early twentieth-century Argentina. She was a seamstress, a factory worker, and an actress in a small theater company, and before her parents' restaurant business collapsed she waited tables and washed dishes. Storni attended normal school and graduated with a teaching certificate, but she soon found herself pregnant and moved from Rosario to Buenos Aires seeking a more anonymous existence for herself and her son. Against all odds, Storni published her first book of poetry, *The Restless Rosebush*, in 1916; *Sweet Pain* (1918), *Irremediably* (1919), *Languor* (1920), and others followed. Soon Storni was a literary celebrity and a familiar feature of the bohemian intellectual scene in Buenos Aires and Montevideo. While her career flourished, however, Storni's mental and physical health began to decline; she committed suicide at age forty-six by throwing herself into the sea at Mar del Plata. She had managed to produce eight poetry collections and several plays. Her sincere representation of women's emotions, ironic portrayal of men, and honest sensuality established a precedent for modern Latin American women's writing. The four poems featured here contain these characteristic features of Storni's work, while also demonstrating her particular sensitivity to what she perceived as the degraded environment of the modern city. The exception is "You Wish I Were Fair," one of Storni's best-known works. Here, Storni criticizes her contemporaries' racist and sexist ideals and prescribes a direct experience of nonhuman nature to cure her male interlocutor of his hypocrisy.

* * *

Poems (1918–1938)

TRANSLATED BY ORLANDO RICARDO MENES

You Wish I Were Fair

You wish I were dawn,
You wish I were seafoam,
You wish I were nacre.
To be a lily.
Above all others, chaste.
Of faint perfume.
Closed corolla.

Not even a sieved
Moon ray finds me.
Not even a daisy
Can be called my sister.
You wish I were snow,
You wish I were fair,
You wish I were dawn.

You who had all cups
Within easy reach,
Your lips purple
From fruits and honey.
You who wasted away
Banqueting Bacchus
At the feast table
Covered with tendrils.
You who raced to Ruin
In the black garden
Of red-clothed Deceit.
You who preserves
The skeleton whole,
Though I do not yet know
By what miracles
You pretend I am fair
(May God forgive you)
You pretend I am chaste
(May God forgive you)
You pretend I am dawn!

Flee to the forests;
Go to the mountain;
Wipe your mouth;
Live in wood shacks;
Touch the wet earth
With your hands;
Feed your body
With bitter roots;
Drink from the rocks;
Sleep over frost;
Revive tissues
With saltpeter and water.
Talk to birds,
Rise at dawn.
And when your flesh
Has been returned to you,

And you have placed
Inside it your soul
That got entangled
In bedrooms,
Then—good man—
Pretend I am fair,
Pretend I am snow,
Pretend I am chaste.

Sadness

Beside the great city
The river sprawls,
Soft silted. It seems
Motionless, dead, yet
It moves.

Precisely because it is silty,
The river seeks out the sea, blue and limpid,
A heavy body that moves
Without stopping, always another,
Though it seems the same.

Day wanes, and I dream
From this tower, watching the dead
River swell to a vast half-circle,
Disappearing far into the gray
Sea mist that is sometimes sliced
By a white triangle.

Ships and ships pile up
On the port, as if monstrous fish
Had set upon the same prey.

Slum Rosebushes

Of course, since spring has arrived
On the poor houses
Of tin and scrap wood in the outskirts,
You, beautiful climbing bush,
Have covered yourself in roses.

If you were
Like men, O rosebush, you'd no doubt
Prefer for good blooming
Rich houses, their walls luxurious,
And you'd then leave barren
The walls of the poor.

But you're not like this.
The sweet earth
Is enough for you anywhere, and it suits you
The same for luck. Maybe you'd prefer
Those modest hovels where you look
Better as a creeper.
The only decoration that costs nothing
(Good roses, water still falls
from the sky without taxes.)

Beautiful mornings, when you gaze
At open windows,

Your green and juicy arms
Search the glassless space and penetrate
The inside of the room: Good morning,
Your corollas try to say
To the modest bedroom
With their rosy lips.

Buenos Aires Danzón[1]

Buenos Aires, you rise in the autumn sun
over western hillsides cooled by northerlies.
Drunk one afternoon on your yellow
grapes of death, I saw your black bridge—

Puente Alsina—fold into the bellows
of a grand accordion, and to its beat
broken river barges danced your danzón
among ragged lights on the poisonous

Riachuelo, its snaking currents
shedding filaments of blood along
the cluttered cellars. Blocks of moldy

factories, smokestacks spewing breath
from lungs devoured, contorted,
pounding their obsessive wail.

Note

1. More commonly associated with Cuba and Mexico, danzón is a slow, elegant partner dance in syncopated time. Because of danzón's sensual movements and the intimate proximity of dancing couples, conservative elements of the mixed-race societies where it was popular in the early twentieth century considered danzón scandalous. [—Eds.]

Oswald de Andrade

Oswald de Andrade was many things: poet, playwright, and novelist, as well as an intellectual revolutionary, polemicist, and one of the founders of Brazilian Modernism. Born into a wealthy bourgeois family, Andrade was able to travel in Europe during his youth, which introduced him to the early twentieth-century avant-garde artistic and literary trends that influenced so many Latin American writers. After returning to São Paulo, Andrade and other innovative intellectuals planned the 1922 Week of Modern Art, a festival that marked the coalescence of Brazilian Modernism. Inspired by the nationalistic elements of modernism, Andrade attempted to change the traditional Portuguese-inspired aesthetic habits of his contemporaries by returning to what he saw as the "primitive" and authentic expressions of Indigenous Brazilians and encouraging a renewal of Brazilian culture based on its complex heritage. To accomplish this, Andrade formed a splinter group of modernists who embraced the concept he called cultural anthropophagy or cultural cannibalism. This movement, as explained by K. David Jackson (2008, 180), was based on a "model of 'devouring assimilation' of foreign influence under the totem of the cannibal tribes who devoured Europeans," thus creating "a paradoxical telluric and vanguardist model for resolving the dialectic between national and foreign cultural influences." The text featured here is Andrade's "Cannibalist Manifesto," the manifesto for the cultural cannibalism movement that is considered his highest form of aesthetic and literary subversion. Andrade's reductive and ennumerative language is full of natural and folkloric imagery with which he presents a revolutionary statement regarding Brazil's cultural and political history of anticolonial struggle. With phrases such as "It was because we never had grammars, nor collections of old plants. And we never knew what urban, suburban, frontier and continental were," Andrade depicts Brazilian culture as deeply and organically intertwined with non-human nature.

✳✳✳

"Cannibalist Manifesto" (1928)

TRANSLATED BY LESLIE BARY

Cannibalism alone unites us. Socially. Economically. Philosophically.

✳✳✳

The world's single law. Disguised expression of all individualism, of all collectivisms. Of all religions. Of all peace treaties.

***

Tupi or not tupi, that is the question.[1]

***

Down with every catechism. And down with the Gracchi's[2] mother.[3]

***

I am only concerned with what is not mine. Law of Man. Law of the cannibal.

***

We're tired of all the suspicious Catholic husbands who've been given starring roles. Freud put an end to the mystery of Woman and to other horrors of printed psychology.

***

What clashed with the truth was clothing, that raincoat placed between the inner and outer worlds. The reaction against the dressed man. American movies will inform us.

***

Children of the sun, mother of the living. Discovered and loved ferociously with all the hypocrisy of *saudade*,[4] by the immigrants, by slaves, and by the *touristes*. In the land of the Great Snake.[5]

***

It was because we never had grammars, nor collections of old plants. And we never knew what urban, suburban, frontier, and continental were. Lazy in the *mapa-mundi* of Brazil.

A participatory consciousness, a religious rhythmics.

***

Down with all the importers of canned consciousness. The palpable existence of life. And the prelogical mentality for Mr. Lévy-Bruhl to study.[6]

***

We want the Carib Revolution. Greater than the French Revolution. The unification of all productive revolts for the progress of humanity. Without us, Europe wouldn't even have its meager declaration of the rights of man.

The Golden Age heralded by America. The Golden Age. And all the *girls*.

***

Heritage. Contact with the Carib side of Brazil. *Où Villegaignon print terre.*[7] Montaigne. Natural man. Rousseau. From the French Revolution to Romanticism, to the Bolshevik Revolution, to the Surrealist Revolution and Keyserling's technicized barbarian.[8] We push onward.

***

We were never catechized. We live by a somnambulistic law. We made Christ to be born in Bahia. Or in Belém do Pará.

***

But we never permitted the birth of logic among us.

***

Down with Father Vieira.[9] Author of our first loan, to make a commission. The illiterate king had told him: put that on paper, but without a lot of lip. The loan was made. Brazilian sugar was signed away. Vieira left the money in Portugal and brought us the lip.

***

The spirit refuses to conceive a spirit without a body. Anthropomorphism. Need for the cannibalistic vaccine. To maintain our equilibrium, against meridian religions.[10] And against outside inquisitions.

***

We can attend only to the orecular world.

***

We already had justice, the codification of vengeance. Science, the codification of Magic. Cannibalism. The permanent transformation of the Tabu into a totem.[11]

***

Down with the reversible world, and against objectified ideas. Cadaverized. The stop of thought that is dynamic. The individual as victim of the system. Source of classical injustices. Of romantic injustices. And the forgetting of inner conquests.

***

Routes. Routes. Routes. Routes. Routes. Routes. Routes.[12]

***

The Carib instinct.

***

Death and life of all hypotheses. From the equation "Self, part of the Cosmos" to the axiom "Cosmos, part of the Self." Subsistence. Experience. Cannibalism.

***

Down with the vegetable elites. In communication with the soil.

***

We were never catechized. What we really made was Carnaval. The Indian dressed as senator of the Empire. Making believe he's Pitt.[13] Or performing in Alencar's operas,[14] full of worthy Portuguese sentiments.

***

We already had Communism. We already had Surrealist language. The Golden Age.

***

Catiti Catiti
Imara Notiá
Notiá Imara
Ipejú.[15]

***

Magic and life. We had the description and allocation of tangible goods, moral goods, and royal goods.[16] And we knew how to transpose mystery and death with the help of a few grammatical forms.

***

I asked a man what the Law was. He answered that it was the guarantee of the exercise of possibility. That man was named Galli Mathias.[17] I ate him.

* * *

Only where there is mystery is there no determinism. But what does that have to do with us?

* * *

Down with the histories of Man that begin at Cape Finisterre. The undated world. Unrubrified. Without Napoléon. Without Caesar.

* * *

The determination of progress by catalogs and television sets. Only machinery. And blood transfusers.

* * *

Down with the antagonistic sublimations. Brought here in caravels.

* * *

Down with the truth of missionary peoples, defined by the sagacity of a cannibal, the Viscount of Cairu:[18]—It's a lie told again and again.

* * *

But those who came here weren't crusaders. They were fugitives from a civilization we are eating, because we are strong and vindictive like the Jabuti.[19]

* * *

If God is the consciousness of the Uncreated Universe, Guaraci is the mother of the living.[20] Jaci is the mother of plants.[21]

* * *

We never had speculation. But we had divination. We had Politics, which is the science of distribution. And a social system in harmony with the planet.

* * *

The migrations. The flight from tedious states. Against urban scleroses. Against the Conservatories and speculative tedium.

***

From William James and Voronoff.[22] The transfiguration of the Taboo into a totem. Cannibalism.

***

The paterfamilias and the creation of the Morality of the Stork: Real ignorance of things + lack of imagination + sense of authority in the face of curious offspring.

***

One must depart from a profound atheism in order to arrive at the idea of God. But the Carib didn't need to. Because he had Guaraci.

***

The created object reacts like the Fallen Angels. Next, Moses daydreams. What do we have to do with that?

***

Before the Portuguese discovered Brazil, Brazil had discovered happiness.

***

Down with the torch-bearing Indian. The Indian son of Mary, the stepson of Catherine of Medici and the godson of Dom Antonio de Mariz.[23]

***

Joy is the proof of nines.

***

In the matriarchy of Pindorama.[24]

***

Down with Memory as a source of custom. The renewal of personal experience.

***

We are concretists. Ideas take charge, react, and burn people in public squares. Let's get rid of ideas and other paralyses. By means of routes. Believe in signs; believe in sextants and in stars.

***

Down with Goethe, the Gracchi's mother, and the court of Dom João VI.[25]

***

Joy is the proof by nines.

***

The struggle between what we might call the Uncreated and the Creation—illustrated by the permanent contradiction between Man and his Taboo. Everyday love and the capitalist way of life. Cannibalism. Absorption of the sacred enemy. To transform him into a totem. The human adventure. The earthly goal. Even so, only the pure elites managed to realize carnal cannibalism, which carries within itself the highest meaning of life and avoids all the ills identified by Freud—catechist ills. What results is not a sublimation of the sexual instinct. It is the thermometrical scale of the cannibal instinct. Carnal at first, this instinct becomes elective, and creates friendship. When it is affective, it creates love. When it is speculative, it creates science. It takes detours and moves around. At times it is degraded. Low cannibalism, agglomerated with the sins of catechism—envy, usury, calumny, murder. We are acting against this plague of a supposedly cultured and Christianized peoples. Cannibals.

***

Down with Anchieta singing of the eleven thousand virgins of Heaven,[26] in the land of Iracema[27]—the patriarch João Ramalho, founder of São Paulo.[28]

***

Our independence has not yet been proclaimed. An expression typical of Dom João VI: "My son, put this crown on your head, before some adventurer puts it on his!"[29] We expelled the dynasty. We must still expel the Bragantine spirit,[30] the decrees and the snuffbox of Maria da Fonte.[31]

***

Down with the dressed and oppressive social reality registered by Freud—reality without complexes, without madness, without prostitutions, and without penitentiaries, in the matriarchy of Pindorama.

OSWALD DE ANDRADE

In Piratininga, in the 374th Year of the Swallowing of Bishop Sardinha.[32]

Notes

1. In English in original. Tupi is the popular, generic name for the Native Americans of Brazil and also for their language, *nheengatu*.

2. The Gracchi, brothers Tiberius and Gaius, famously advocated for the plebs in second-century Rome. [—Eds.]

3. A student of Greek and Latin literature, Cornelia is said to have been virtuous, austere, and extremely devoted to her sons. In the "Manifesto" she is the bad mother who (in contrast to the mother-goddesses Jaci and Guaraci) brings her children up as subjects of a "civilized" culture.

4. Regarding the "hypocrisy of *saudade*," or "longing," Bendor (2007, 273–74) notes that this passage resonates with the "delicate dialectic of longing for an idealized past and aspiring for a new, modern cultural identity." [—Eds.]

5. The "Great Snake" (*Cobra Grande*) is a water spirit in Amazonian mythology.

6. Lucien Lévy-Bruhl, French philosopher and ethnologist (1857–1939). The "primitive" mentality, according to Lévy-Bruhl, is not a deformation of the "civilized" one but rather a completely different structure of thought. The primitive mind is mystical, collective, and prelogical.

7. Literally, "in the place where Villegaignon took possession of the territory." In Montaigne's essay "Des cannibales," "où Villegaignon print terre" refers to the French mission in Brazil to found, through Villegaignon's 1555 invasion, an "Antarctic France." Montaigne argues in this essay that ritual cannibalism is far less barbaric than many "civilized" European customs. [—Eds.]

8. Count Herman Keyserling, German philosopher, world traveler, and Orientalist (1880–1946). His works propose the (Spenglerian) idea that the Western world must be compenetrated with Eastern philosophy and that Latin America will rise as a world power while Europe declines. Oswald inverts Keyserling's idea that a soulless "technical barbarism" is the sign of the modern world. In Oswald's utopia, primitive man enjoys the fruits of modernization.

9. Antonio Vieira (1608–97), Portuguese Jesuit instrumental in the colonization of Brazil. He came to be known as the Judas of Brazil. In the war between Portugal and the Netherlands over Pernambuco, Vieira negotiated a peace treaty by which Pernambuco was given to the Netherlands so that Portugal would not have to pay the Netherlands to end the war (with money made in Brazil). [Vieira was also one of the founders of the mission system. —Eds.]

10. According to Nunes, "meridian" religions are religions of salvation. *Meridian* as a dividing line seems, in the context of the "Manifesto," to connote the divisions body/soul, native/foreign, and so on, which Oswald is attempting to dismantle.

11. In *Totem and Taboo* (1913, trans. 1918), Freud argues that the shift from "totemistic" to "taboo" systems of morality and religion consolidated paternal authority as the cornerstone of culture. Subjects of the taboo system are "civilized" because they have internalized the paternal rule. Oswald's advocacy of totemistic cannibalism, then, constitutes a rejection of patriarchy and the culture of the (Portuguese) "fathers."

12. The original *roteiros* (from *rotear*, to navigate) can also signify ships' logbooks or pilots' directions.

13. William Pitt (1759–1806), British statesman influential in the formation of colonial policy for India.

14. José de Alencar, Brazilian writer and conservative politician (1829–77). His Indianist novel *O Guarani* (1857) was turned into an opera, with music by Carlos Gomes (1836–96), which opened in the Teatro alla Scala, Milan, December 2, 1870.

15. In a footnote, Oswald provides a Portuguese translation of this Tupi text, running, "New moon, O new moon, blow memories of me into [the man I want]." The note gives the source of this text as *O Selvagem*, an anthropological work by Couto Magalhães, the politician and anthropologist (1836–98).

16. The original here reads, "dos bens físicos, dos bens morais, dos bens dignários." Oswald is playing with legal terms for various kinds of property, so as to ridicule "civilized" European institutions and show that they are superfluous to Brazilian culture.

17. "Galli Mathias" is a pun on *galimatias*, or "nonsense."

18. José de Silva Lisboa, Viscount of Cairu (1756–1835), Brazilian politician. After Dom João VI established his court in Rio de Janeiro (1808) in the wake of Napoléon's invasion of Portugal, the Viscount of Cairu convinced him to open Brazilian ports to "all nations friendly to Portugal."

19. Tortoise of northern Brazil; in the popular culture of the Indians, he is a trickster figure. The jabuti is astute, active, comical, and combative.

20. Tupi sun goddess, mother of all men.

21. Tupi moon goddess, creator of plants.

22. William James, American philosopher (1842–1910), is the author of *Principles of Psychology* (1890), *The Varieties of Religious Experience* (1902), and *A Pluralistic Universe* (1909). Serge Voronoff, Russian-born biologist (1866–1951), is the author of *Étude sur la vieillesse et la rajeunissement par la greffe* (1926) and *La conquête de la vie* (1928), a method of rejuvenation by the grafting of genital glands.

23. Nunes writes that this is a "superimposition of three images: that of the sculpted Indians of the chandeliers of certain Baroque churches, that of the Indian Paraguassu, who went to France in the sixteenth century, accompanied by her husband, the Portuguese Diogo Alvares Correia, and [that of] D[om] Antonio de Mariz, the noble rural lord, father of Ceci, with whom Peri falls in love, in *O Guarani*. Paraguassu was baptized as Saint-Malo. A false version [of the story], spread through schoolbooks, made Catherine of Medici the godmother of this native" ("Le manifeste anthropophage," 189–90n28).

24. Pindorama is the name of Brazil in the Tupi language. It may mean "country or region of palm trees."

25. Dom João VI, King of Portugal (r. 1816–26). As prince regent, he fled the Napoleonic invasion of Portugal (1807) and installed the Portuguese court in Rio de Janeiro (1808–21). He made Brazil a kingdom (1815), equal in status to Portugal, and was Brazil's last colonial monarch before independence (1822).

26. Father Anchieta (1534–97), Jesuit missionary among Indians; known as the Apostle of Brazil and generally considered to be the first Brazilian writer.

27. Indian heroine in Alencar's novel of the same name (1865).

28. João Ramalho was one of the first Portuguese colonizers of Brazil. He was opposed to the Jesuits' founding of São Paulo and organized the Indians' resistance against the missionaries.

29. Dom João VI's son, Dom Pedro I, became emperor of Brazil when independence was declared in 1822. According to tradition Dom João, already sensing that Brazil would separate itself from Portugal, had given Dom Pedro the directions Oswald quotes here before returning to Lisbon in 1821.

30. The Portuguese kings of the period were of the Bragança dynasty.

31. The legendary figure Maria da Fonte became the symbol of a popular rebellion in the Minho (1846) against higher taxation to finance the improvement of roads and reforms in public health.

32. Sardinha was Bishop of Bahia from 1552 to 1556, when he was killed and apparently eaten by the Caltis Indians.

María Luisa Bombal

Chile's María Luisa Bombal (1910–80) was one of the first Latin American authors to break away from realism and write fiction that was instead individualized, introspective, and highly subjective. Born into a rich, aristocratic family, Bombal lived in France after her father's death in 1919; she took a degree from the Sorbonne with a thesis on French writer Prosper Mérimée. After a tumultuous return to Chile, Bombal moved to Buenos Aires, where she lived in the home of her compatriot Pablo Neruda, then serving as consul. In Buenos Aires, Bombal mixed with local literati, including Jorge Luis Borges and Victoria Ocampo; she also met Luigi Pirandello and Federico García Lorca. Eventually Bombal moved to the United States, where she married a French count and frequently wrote in English; she returned to Chile after his death in 1970. Bombal's body of work is spare, and her later publications consist largely of translations and modifications of the two brilliant novellas that she produced and published during the Buenos Aires years, *The House of Mist* (1935) and *The Shrouded Woman* (1937). Profoundly influenced by surrealism, Bombal's evocative, often symbolic prose and subtle psychological analyses of female characters make her one of the early twentieth century's most important writers. The short story presented here, "The Tree," is typical of Bombal's work in the contrast that is drawn between the lifeless, loveless marriage that confines the protagonist and the aestheticized vitality of nonhuman nature. Faced with unbearable loneliness, Brígida personifies the natural features around her, finding solace in the imagined acceptance of birds, the rain, and especially the rubber tree outside her bedroom window.

***

"The Tree" (1939)

TRANSLATED BY RICHARD AND LUCIA CUNNINGHAM

The pianist sits down, coughs from force of habit, and concentrates for a moment. The clusters of lights illuminating the hall gradually dim until they glow like dying embers, whereupon a musical phrase rises in the silence, swells: clear, sharp, and judiciously capricious.

Mozart, maybe, Brígida thinks to herself. As usual, she has forgotten to ask for the program. Mozart—or perhaps Scarlatti . . . She knew so little about music! And it was not because she lacked an ear or the inclination. On the contrary, as a child it had been she who demanded piano lessons; no one needed to impose them on her, as was the case with her sisters. Today, however, her sisters could sight-read perfectly, while she . . . she had abandoned her studies after the first year. The reason for the inconstancy was as simple as it was shameful: she had never been able, never, to learn the key of F. "I don't understand—my memory serves me only to the key of C." And her father's indignation! "Would that I could lay down this burden: a miserable widower with children to educate! My poor Carmen! How she would have suffered with such a daughter! The creature is retarded!"

Brígida was the youngest of six girls—all endowed with different temperaments. She received little attention from her father, for dealing with the other five daughters reduced him to such a perplexed and worn-out state that he preferred to ease his burden by insisting on her feeblemindedness. "I won't struggle any longer—it is useless. Leave her alone. If she chooses not to study, so be it. If she would rather spend her time in the kitchen listening to ghost stories, that is fine with me. If she favors playing with dolls at the age of sixteen, let her play." And so Brígida had kept to her dolls, remaining almost totally ignorant as far as formal education was concerned.

How pleasant it is to be ignorant! Not to know exactly who Mozart was—to ignore his origins, his influences, the particularities of his technique! To simply let oneself be led by the hand, as now . . .

For in truth Mozart leads her—transporting her onto a bridge suspended above crystal water running over a bed of pink sand. She is dressed in white, tilting on one shoulder an open parasol of Chantilly lace, elaborate and fine as a spider's web.

"You look younger every day, Brígida. Yesterday I ran into your husband—I mean, your ex-husband. His hair is now completely white."

But she makes no reply, unwilling to tarry while crossing the bridge Mozart has fabricated toward the garden of her youth.

Tall blossoming spouts in which the water sings. Her eighteen years; her chestnut braids that, unbound, cascaded to her waist; her golden complexion; her dark eyes so wide and questioning. A small mouth with full lips; a sweet smile; and the lightest, most gracious body in the world. Of what was she thinking, seated by the fountain's edge? Of nothing. "She is as silly as she is pretty," they used to say. But she did not mind being silly, nor acting the dunce at parties. One by one, her sisters received proposals of marriage. No one asked her.

Mozart! Now he conducts her to a blue marble staircase on which she descends between two rows of ice lilies. And now he opens a wrought-iron gate of spikes with golden tips so that she may throw herself on Luis, her father's intimate friend. From childhood, she would run to Luis when everyone else abandoned her. He would pick her up and she would encircle his neck between giggles that were like tiny bird cries and kisses she flung like disorderly raindrops on his eyes, his forehead, and his hair—which even then was graying (had he never been young?). "You are a necklace," Luis would say. "You are like a necklace of sparrows."

For which she had married him. Because at the side of that solemn and taciturn man she felt less culpable for being what she was: foolish, playful, and indolent. Yes—now, after so many years, she realizes that she had not married Luis for love; yet she cannot put her finger on why, why she left him so suddenly one day . . .

But at this moment Mozart takes her nervously by the hand, drawing her into a rhythm second by second more urgent—compelling her to retrace her steps across the garden and onto the bridge at a pace that is almost like fleeing. And after stripping her of the parasol and the transparent crinoline, he closes the door on her past with a note at once firm and sweet—leaving her in the concert hall, dressed in black, applauding mechanically as the artificial lights rekindle their flame.

Again shadows, and the prelude of silence.

And now Beethoven begins to stir the lukewarm tide of his notes beneath a vernal moon. How far the sea has retreated! Brígida walks seaward down the beach toward the distant, bright, smooth water; but all at once the sea rises, flowing placidly to meet and envelop her—the gentle waves pushing at her back until they press her cheek against the body of a man. And then the waves recede, leaving her stranded on Luis's chest.

"You have no heart, you have no heart," she used to say to him. His heartbeat was so faint that she could not hear it except in rare and unexpected moments. "You are never with me when you are by my side," she would protest in their bedroom when, before going to sleep, he would ritually open the evening paper. "Why did you marry me?"

"Because you have the eyes of a startled fawn," he would reply, giving her a kiss. And she, abruptly cheerful, would proudly accept the weight of his gray head on her shoulder. Oh, that silvery, radiant hair!

"Luis, you have never told me exactly what color your hair was when you were a boy. Or how your mother felt when you began going gray at the age of fifteen. What did she say? Did she laugh? Cry? And you—were you proud or ashamed? And at school—what did your classmates say? Tell me, Luis, tell me . . ."

"Tomorrow. I am sleepy, Brígida. Very tired. Turn off the light."

Unconsciously, he would turn away from her in sleep; just as she unconsciously sought her husband's shoulder all night long, searching for his breath, groping blindly for protection as an enclosed and thirsty plant bends its tendrils toward warmth and moisture.

In the mornings, when the maid would open the Venetian blinds, Luis was no longer next to her. He had departed quietly without so much as a salutation, for fear the necklace of sparrows would fasten obstinately around his neck. "Five minutes, five minutes, no more. Your office will not disappear if you are five minutes late, Luis."

Her awakenings. Ah, how sad her awakenings! But—it was curious—no sooner had she entered her boudoir than the sadness vanished as if by an enchantment.

Waves crash, clashing far away, murmuring like a sea of leaves. Beethoven? No.

It is the tree outside her dressing-room window. She had only to enter the room to experience an almost overpowering sense of well-being. How hot the bedroom always was of a morning! And what harsh light! By contrast, in the boudoir, even her eyes felt rested, refreshed. The faded cretonne curtains; the tree casting shadows that undulated on the walls like cold, moving water; the mirrors refracting foliage, creating the illusion of a green and infinite forest. How enjoyable that room was! It seemed a world submerged in an aquarium. And how that huge rubber tree chattered! All the birds in the neighborhood took refuge in it. It was the only tree on that narrow, falling street that sloped from one side of the city directly to the river.

"I am busy. I can't be with you . . . Lots of work to do, I won't be home for lunch . . . Hello—yes, I am at the club. An engagement. Eat and go to bed . . . No. I don't know. Better not wait for me, Brígida."

"If only I had friends!" she would sigh. But she bored everyone. "If I tried to be a little less foolish! Yet how does one recover so much lost ground at a single stroke? To be intelligent, you must start very young—isn't that true?"

Her sisters' husbands took them everywhere, but Luis—why had she denied it to herself?—had been ashamed of her, of her ignorance, her shyness, even of her eighteen years. Had he not urged her to pretend that she was at least twenty-one, as though her youth were an embarrassing secret they alone shared?

And at night—he always came to bed so weary! Never paying full attention to what she said. He smiled, yes—a mechanical smile. His caresses were plentiful, but bestowed absentmindedly. Why *had* he married her? To continue their acquaintance, perhaps simply to put the crowning touch on his old friendship with her father.

Maybe life for men was based on a series of established and continuous customs. Rupturing this chain would probably produce disorder, chaos. And after, men would stumble through the streets of the city, roosting on park benches, growing shabbier and more unshaven with each passing day. Luis's life, therefore, was patterned on keeping occupied every minute of the day. Why had she failed to see this sooner? Her father had been right: she *was* retarded.

"I would like to see snow sometime, Luis."

"This summer I will take you to Europe, and since it will be winter there, you shall have your snow."

"I am quite aware that winter in Europe coincides with our summer. I am not *that* stupid!"

At times, to rouse him to the rapture of true love, she would throw herself on him and cover him with kisses: weeping, calling, "Luis, Luis, Luis . . ."

"What? What is the matter? What do you want?"

"Nothing."

"Why do you cry out my name like that, then?"

"No reason. To say your name. I like to say your name."

And he would smile benevolently, pleased with the new game.

Summer came—her first summer as a married woman. Several new business ventures forced Luis to postpone the promised European trip.

"Brígida, the heat will be terrible in Buenos Aires shortly. Why don't you spend the summer on your father's ranch?"

"Alone?"

"I would visit you every week, from Saturday to Monday."

She sat down on the bed, primed to insult him. But she could not find the hurting words. She knew nothing, nothing—not even how to offend.

"What is wrong with you? What are you thinking of, Brígida?"

He was leaning over her, worried, for the first time in their marriage unconcerned about violating his customary punctuality at the office.

"I am sleepy," Brígida had replied childishly, hiding her face in the pillow.

For once, he rang her up at lunchtime from his club. But she had refused to
come to the phone, wielding angrily a weapon she had discovered without thinking:
silence.

That same evening she dined across from him with lowered eyes and nerves
strung tight.

"Are you still angry, Brígida?"

But she did not answer.

"You know perfectly well that I love you. But I can't be with you all the time.
I am a very busy man. When you reach my age, you become a slave to a thousand
obligations."

. . .

"Shall we go out tonight?"

. . .

"No? Very well, I will be patient. Tell me, did Roberto call from Montevideo?"

. . .

"What a lovely dress! Is it new?"

. . .

"Is it new, Brígida? Answer me. Say something."

But she refused to break her silence.

And then the unexpected, the astonishing, the absurd. Luis rises from his
chair and slaps his napkin on the table, slamming the door as he stomps from the
house.

She, too, had gotten to her feet, stunned, trembling with indignation at such
injustice. "And I . . . and I . . ." she stammered, "I, who for almost an entire year . . .
when for the first time I take the liberty of lodging a complaint . . . Ah, I am leaving—I am leaving this very night! I shall never set foot in this house again . . ." And
she jerked open the armoires in her dressing room, strewing clothes furiously in all
directions.

It was then that she heard a banging against the windowpane.

She ran to the window and opened it, not knowing how or whence her courage
came. It was the rubber tree, set in motion by the storm, knocking its branches on
the glass—as though calling her to witness how it twisted and contorted like a fierce
black flame under the burning sky of that summer night.

Heavy rain soon began to lash its cold leaves. How lovely! All night long she
could hear the rain thrashing, splashing through the leaves of the rubber tree like
a thousand tiny rivers sliding down imaginary canals. All night long she heard the
ancient trunk creak and moan, the storm raging outside while she curled into a ball
between the sheets of the wide bed, very close to Luis.

Handfuls of pearls raining on a silver roof. Chopin. *Etudes* by Frédéric Chopin.

How many mornings had she awakened as soon as she sensed that her husband,
now likewise maintaining an obstinate silence, had slipped from bed.

Her dressing room: the window thrown wide, the odor of river and grass floating in that hospitable chamber, and the mirrors wearing a veil of fog.

Chopin intermingles in her turbulent memory with rain hissing through the leaves of the rubber tree like some hidden waterfall—so palpable that even the roses on the curtains seem moist.

What to do in summer when it rains so often? Spend the day in her room feigning sadness, a convalescence? One afternoon Luis had entered timidly. Had sat down stiffly. There was a long silence.

"Then it is true, Brígida? You no longer love me?"

A sudden joy seized her. She might have shouted: "No, no. I love you, Luis, I love you," if he had given her time, if he had not almost immediately added, with his habitual calm: "In any case, I do not think it would be convenient for us to separate, Brígida. Such a move requires much thought."

Her impulse sank as fast as it had surfaced. What was the use of exciting herself! Luis loved her tenderly, with moderation; if he ever came to hate her, it would be a just and prudent hatred. And that was life. She walked to the window and placed her forehead against the cold glass. There was the rubber tree, serenely accepting the pelting rain. The room was fixed in shadow, quiet and ordered. Everything seemed to be held in an eternal and very noble equilibrium. That was life. And there was a certain grandeur in accepting it thus: mediocre, like something definite and irremediable. While underneath it all there seemed to rise a melody of grave and slow words that transfixed her: "Always. Never" . . .

And in this way the hours, days, and years pass. Always! Never! Life! Life!

Collecting herself, she realized that her husband had stolen from the room.

"Always! Never!" . . . And the rain, secret and steady, still whispered in Chopin.

Summer stripped the leaves from its burning calendar. Luminous and blinding pages fell like golden swords; pages also of malignant dampness like breeze from a swamp; pages of furious and brief storms, of hot wind—the wind that carries the "carnation of the air" and hangs it on the huge rubber tree.

Some children used to play hide-and-seek among the enormous, twisted roots that pushed up the paving stones on the sidewalk, and the tree overflowed with laughter and whispering. On those days she would look from the window and clap her hands; but the children dispersed in fear, without noticing the childlike smile of a girl who wanted to join the game.

Alone, she would lean on her elbows at the window for a long time, watching the foliage swaying—a breeze blew along that street which sloped directly to the river—and it was like staring deep into moving water or the dancing flames in a fireplace. One could kill time in this fashion, no need for thought, made foolish by peace of mind.

She lit the first lamp just as the room began to fill with twilight smoke, and the first lamp flickered in the mirrors, multiplying like fireflies eager to hasten the night.

And night after night she dozed beside her husband, suffering at intervals. But when her pain tightened so that it pierced like a knife thrust, when she was besieged by the desire to wake Luis—to hit him or caress him—she tiptoed to her dressing room and opened the window. Immediately the room came alive with discreet sounds and discreet presences, with mysterious footsteps, the fluttering of wings, the sudden rustling of vegetation, the soft chirping of a cricket perched on the bark of the rubber tree under the stars of a hot summer night.

Little by little her fever went down as her bare feet grew cold on the reed mat. She did not know why it was so easy to suffer in that room.

Chopin's melancholy stringing of one *Etude* after another, stringing of one melancholy after another, imperturbably.

And autumn came. The dry leaves hovered an instant before settling on the grass of the narrow garden, on the sidewalk of that sloping street. The leaves came loose and fell . . . The top of the rubber tree remained green but underneath it turned red—darkened like the worn-out lining of a sumptuous evening cape. And now the room seemed to be submerged in a goblet of dull gold.

Lying on the divan, she waited patiently for the dinner hour, and the improbable arrival of Luis. She had resumed speaking to him, had become his again without enthusiasm or anger. She no longer loved him. But she no longer suffered. On the contrary, an unexpected feeling of fulfillment and placidity had taken hold of her. Nothing, no one could now hurt her. It may be that true happiness lies in the conviction that one has irremediably lost happiness. It is only then that we can begin to live without hope or fear, able finally to enjoy all the small pleasures, which are the most lasting.

A thunderous noise, followed by a flash of light from which she recoils, shaking.

The intermission? No. The rubber tree.

Having started work early in the morning without her knowledge, they had felled it with a single stroke of the ax. "The roots were breaking up the sidewalk, and, naturally, the neighborhood committee . . ."

Dazed, she has shielded her eyes with her hands. When she recovers her sight, she stands and looks around. What does she see?

The concert hall suddenly ablaze with light, the audience filing out?

No. She is imprisoned in the web of her past, trapped in the dressing room—which has been invaded by a terrifying white light. It was as if they had ripped off the roof; a crude light entering from every direction, seeping through her very pores, burning her with its coldness. And she saw everything bathed in that cold light: Luis, his wrinkled face, his hands crisscrossed with ropy discolored veins, and the gaudy cretonnes.

Frightened, she runs to the window. The window now opens directly on a narrow street, so narrow that her room almost brushes against a shiny skyscraper. On the ground floor, shop windows and more shop windows, full of bottles. At the corner, a row of automobiles lined up in front of a service station painted red. Some boys in their shirtsleeves are kicking a ball in the middle of the street.

And all that ugliness lay embedded in her mirrors, along with nickel-plated balconies, shabby clotheslines, and canary cages.

They had stolen her intimacy, her secret; she found herself naked in the middle of the street, naked before an old husband who turned his back on her in bed, who had given her no children. She does not understand why, until then, she had not wanted children, how she had resigned herself to the idea of life without children. Nor does she comprehend how for a whole year she had tolerated Luis's laughter, that overcheerful laughter, that false laughter of a man who has trained himself in joviality because it is necessary to laugh on certain occasions.

Lies! Her resignation and serenity were lies; she wanted love, yes, love, and trips and madness, and love, love . . .

"But, Brígida—why are you leaving? Why did you stay so long?" Luis had asked. Now she would have known how to answer him.

"The tree, Luis, the tree! They have cut down the rubber tree."

SIX
Developmentalism

In his inaugural speech of 1949, President Harry S. Truman declared his intention to see the United States "embark on a bold new program for making the benefits of our scientific advances and industrial progress available for the improvement and growth of underdeveloped areas." Surveying the socioeconomic landscape beyond his nation's borders, Truman observed rampant hunger and disease, economic stagnation, and levels of poverty that represented "a handicap and a threat both to them and to more prosperous areas." The threat, more precisely, was Communism, and Truman proposed to contain its spread by using his country's unparalleled resources "to help the free peoples of the world, through their own efforts, to produce more food, more clothing, more materials for housing, and more mechanical power to lighten their burdens." Today Truman's speech is widely cited as one of the first formal articulations of what is known as developmentalism, or *desarrollismo*, a set of ideas so ubiquitous in twentieth-century political and economic thought as to be at times practically invisible. The selections in this part were all produced while *desarrollismo* held sway, a time when Latin Americans of widely divergent ideological commitments agreed that "more food, more clothing, more materials for housing, and more mechanical power" were fundamental ingredients of human happiness and that science and technology should be brought to bear on nature's almost limitless resources so as to provide them.

As Truman proposed, so-called development aid would be one of the central tenets of U.S. foreign policy during the Cold War years, especially through the Kennedy initiative known as the Alliance for Progress, which spent millions of dollars on programs intended to prevent future revolutions like the one that took place in Cuba in 1959. A few years before, the Eisenhower administration had successfully intervened in Guatemala after the democratically elected president, Jacobo Árbenz, had enacted land reform that involved buying back from the United Fruit Company thousands of acres of uncultivated land at the value the company had claimed on a recent tax return. Árbenz was removed from power in a military coup sponsored by the CIA, and his successor quickly restored the company's holdings (Miller 2007, 134). Afterward, the U.S. government continued to provide crucial economic and military support to Latin American governments that pledged to resist the spread of Communism and actively worked to undermine and overthrow those that did not, particularly when the interests of U.S.-owned multinationals were understood to be directly at stake.

Desarrollismo also had a life outside U.S. policy circles. Around the same time that Truman was preparing his speech, the UN-appointed Economic Council on Latin America, led by Argentina's Raúl Prebisch, suggested that the way to build lasting prosperity in the region was to balance the volatility of the export sector, which had long dominated Latin American economies, through industrialization. As historian Tulio Halperín Donghi (1993, 251) has put it, "Only by eschewing the fatal attractions of the doctrine of comparative advantage and striving to create complex, 'mature' economies like those of the industrial countries could Latin Americans equalize their trade relationship with the United States and Europe." *Desarrollismo*, therefore, was closely associated with import-substitution industrialization, which proposed to wean countries off imported manufactures, especially durable goods like automobiles and household appliances, by beginning to produce them locally. Industrialization was seen as indifferent—if not flat-out detrimental—to the economic interests of the traditional land-owning elite and their foreign trade partners, and it quickly became associated with higher wages and higher standards of living for urban workers. This made import-substitution industrialization attractive to populists like Brazil's Getúlio Vargas, as well as more conventional leftists.

As Eduardo Gudynas (2011) has noted, however, *desarrollismo* is linked to nineteenth-century notions of "progress" as a series of European attainments that the rest of the world was expected to emulate as best it could. "Development" and "underdevelopment" are equally Eurocentric notions, inasmuch as they cast the historical effects of colonialism and neocolonialism in terms of the affected societies' inability to provide the same standard of living as that of the consumer societies of the North. Developmentalists are typically uninterested in Indigenous and campesino knowledge; many in fact see rural communities as inherently backward, their traditional cultures an impediment to be overcome for the good of the country. The agricultural methods recommended by developmentalists—be it the Rockefeller Foundation, which helped to stimulate Mexico's so-called Green Revolution in the 1940s, or the Soviet agronomists responsible for Cuba's—favor the intensive use of petrochemicals over the ecologically sustainable farming practices that rural communities had historically developed.

The Latin American political figure most closely associated with developmentalism is Juscelino Kubitschek, president of Brazil from 1955 to 1960, who famously promised his compatriots "a half-century of progress in five years" (Halperín Donghi 1993, 260). Kubitschek's signature accomplishment was to relocate the Brazilian capital from Rio de Janeiro to Brasília, which was designed from the ground up by Lúcio Costa and Oscar Niemeyer. Moving Brazil's seat of government from the colonial city on the southeastern coast to the highlands of the center-western region was intended to redistribute the country's population toward the interior, thereby developing the remote hinterlands. But in practice it provided a textbook example of the perils of the kind of top-down central planning that effectively thwarts the organic social flourishing it is intended to foster (Scott 1998, 117–30).

Brasília may be the most famous of developmentalism's outsize engineering marvels, but it is hardly the only one. Among the most destructive are the "more than 900 large dams over fifteen meters high" that have been built in Latin America, more than half of them in Brazil (Miller 2007, 161). Dams provide 30 percent of Mexico's electricity, 75 percent of Colombia's, and 95 percent of Brazil's, but as Miller notes, dams provide energy where energy is not necessarily needed, and in some cases it takes years before customers are found to absorb the surplus. The human and ecological costs are enormous: upward of half a million people have been displaced by dam building in Mexico and Brazil alone, their homes inundated by artificial reservoirs. In place of irrigated farmland and forests, dams produce poorly oxygenated lakes where few fish survive and many mosquitoes breed, creating new disease risks for humans. In many cases those most immediately affected are Indigenous communities, whose "lifestyles and livelihoods have been drowned for the good of the nation" (161).

The selections gathered here diverge from the developmentalist consensus, documenting its deleterious consequences for Latin American ecosystems and the cultures that depend upon them and offering more open-ended possibilities for relationships between human and nonhuman life. Their ideas are nourished by myriad cultural sources, all of which reject the dominant teleological rationalism. Lydia Cabrera and José María Arguedas were both trained anthropologists, and they utilized their educational backgrounds to convey the complexity and richness of non-Western cultural traditions threatened by the centralizing, homogenizing impetus of the time. Cabrera's 1954 *El monte* (*The Woods*) is referred to as the holy book of Afro-Cuban Santería. In the chapter presented here, Cabrera gathers traditional wisdom and stories about a native tree, the ceiba. We include an excerpt from Arguedas's novel *Deep Rivers* in which the protagonist experiences for the first time the intense spiritual energy of the Pachachaca River. Yet a third anthropologist, Miguel Barnet, produced *Biography of a Runaway Slave* in collaboration with Esteban Montejo, who describes the years he spent alone in the woods, hiding from slave catchers. Written in the aftermath of the Cuban Revolution, Montejo's account emphasizes the satisfactions of a life entirely cut off from capitalist consumerism.

This section also includes one of the great masterworks of twentieth-century poetry, Pablo Neruda's "The Heights of Macchu Picchu." Like Arguedas, the Chilean poet was inspired by the humanized landscape of the Peruvian Andes; but for Neruda, the encounter with Inca ruins sparks thoughts of spiritual rebirth and an intense awareness of the human labor that produces monumental architecture, even that of a pre-Columbian civilization.

Other selections attest to the high cost of two of developmentalism's biggest successes, Mexico and Brazil. As critic Kerstin Oloff (2016) explains, the desiccated, depopulated landscapes of Juan Rulfo's fiction—including "Luvina," republished here in full—evoke the disastrous consequences of the large-scale agricultural experiments of the 1940s. Brazil's Clarice Lispector wrote *The Passion According to G.H.* as her country teetered on the edge of military dictatorship. Her extraordinary imagining of the close encounter between two twentieth-century urbanites— one human, the other a cockroach—destabilizes some of the most fundamental assumptions of Western modernity. Decades later her compatriot, Carlos Drummond de Andrade, wrote "Farewell to the Seven Falls" as the cascades of the Upper Paraná were about to be submerged in the construction of Itaipú Hydroelectric Plant, a joint undertaking of the Brazilian military regime and Paraguay's. Speaking for all the victims of developmentalism's technocratic rationalism, Drummond denounces "a country that is losing its humanity / to become an icy enterprise, nothing more."

Finally, we include fragments from *I, Rigoberta Menchú: An Indian Woman in Guatemala*, which takes up the tragic effects of the 1954 coup against Árbenz. Menchú recounts the illness and death caused by agrochemical use on Guatemala's coffee plantations, as well as the starvation of Indigenous workers. She also describes some of the traditional rituals of her K'iche' people, so that we can better understand the contrast between Western modernity's alienated, rationalistic view of nature and the more integrated, respectful practices of the Maya.

Suggestions for Further Reading

Alejo Carpentier. 1953. *The Lost Steps*, translated by Harriet de Onís. New York: Knopf, 1967.

Julio Ramón Ribeyro. 1955. "The Featherless Buzzards." In *Marginal Voices: Selected Stories*, edited by Dick Gerdes and translated by Dianne Douglas. Austin: University of Texas Press, 1993.

Arnoldo Palacios. 1958. *La selva y la lluvia*. Bogotá: Intermedio, 2010.

Ernesto Cardenal. 1970–1985. "Lights." In *Pluriverse: New and Selected Poems*, edited by Jonathan Cohen and translated by Jonathan Cohen et. al. New York: New Directions, 2009.

Elena Poniatowska. 1988. *Nothing, Nobody: The Voices of the Mexico City Earthquake*, translated by Aurora Camacho de Schmidt. Philadelphia: Temple University Press. 1995.

Pablo Neruda

Ricardo Eliecer Neftalí Reyes (1904–73) grew up in Temuco, in Chile's remote south, where he was taught by Gabriela Mistral—they would both win Nobel Prizes, decades apart—and took the pseudonym Pablo Neruda. Success came early, with *Twenty Love Poems and a Song of Despair* (1924). Neruda continued to write prolifically but soon found himself Chile's consul in Rangoon, Ceylon, and Singapore, an experience that informed *Residence on Earth*. He spent the early 1930s in Spain, where the outbreak of the Civil War permanently ignited Neruda's political conscience. In 1943 Neruda joined the Communist Party, returned to Chile, and was elected senator; he went underground during the anti-Communist scourge a few years later. He renounced his own presidential ambitions to support Salvador Allende, becoming ambassador to France after Allende's win. There he received news of the Nobel Prize and was diagnosed with cancer. Neruda returned to Chile and died, grief-stricken and harassed, after the Pinochet coup. Our selection, "The Heights of Macchu Picchu," was first published in 1947 and subsequently incorporated into the epic *Canto General* (1950). It is based on Neruda's journey to the ruins of the enigmatic Incan city high in the Peruvian Andes. The poet arrives, spiritually exhausted, seeking rejuvenation in the ancient stone. He is attracted by the possibility of connection with the more-than-human, promised by the city's location and his knowledge of pre-Columbian religion. In this Neruda's poem resembles the excerpt from Arguedas's *Deep Rivers* that also appears in this section. But Neruda is impatient with knowledge reserved for priestly castes—even the priestly castes of vanquished races—and asks, "Stone upon stone, and man, where was he?" The conclusion invites the working-class dead, the anonymous laborers who created Macchu Picchu, to speak through the poet's voice.

***

"The Heights of Macchu Picchu" (1947)

TRANSLATED BY JACK SCHMITT

I

From air to air, like an
empty net
I went between the streets and atmosphere, arriving and departing,
in the advent of autumn the outstretched coin
of the leaves, and between springtime and the ears of corn,

all that the greatest love, as within a falling
glove, hands us like a long moon.

(Days of vivid splendor in the inclemency
of corpses: steel transformed
into acid silence:
nights frayed to the last flour:
beleaguered stamens of the nuptial land.)
Someone awaiting me among the violins
discovered a world like an entombed tower
spiraling down beneath all
the harsh sulphur-colored leaves:
farther down, in the gold of geology,
like a sword enveloped in meteors,
I plunged my turbulent and tender hand
into the genital matrix of the earth.

I put my brow amid the deep waves,
descended like a drop amid the sulphurous peace,
and, like a blind man, returned to the jasmine
of the spent human springtime.

II

If the lofty germ is carried from flower to flower
and the rock preserves its flower disseminated
in its hammered suit of diamond and sand,
man crumples the petal of light which he gathers
in determinate deep-sea springs
and drills the quivering metal in his hands.
And all along, amid clothing and mist, upon the sunken table,
like a jumbled quantity, lies the soul:
quartz and vigilance, tears in the ocean
like pools of cold: yet he still
torments it under the habitual rug, rips it
in the hostile vestments of wire.

No: in corridors, air, sea or on roads,
who guards (like red poppies) his blood
without a dagger? Rage has extenuated
the sad trade of the merchant of souls,
and, while at the top of the plum tree, the dew
has left for a thousand years its transparent letter
upon the same branch that awaits it, O heart, O brow crushed
between the autumn cavities.

How many times in the wintry streets of a city or in
a bus or a boat at dusk, or in the deepest
loneliness, a night of revelry beneath the sound
of shadows and bells, in the very grotto of human pleasure
I've tried to stop and seek the eternal unfathomable lode
that I touched before on stone or in the lightning unleashed by a kiss.

(Whatever in grain like a yellow tale
of swollen little breasts keeps repeating a number
perpetually tender in the germinal layers,
and which, always identical, is stripped to ivory,
and whatever in water is a transparent land, a bell
from the distant snows down to the bloody waves.)

I could grasp nothing but a clump of faces or precipitous
masks, like rings of empty gold,
like scattered clothes, offspring of an enraged autumn
that would have made the miserable tree of the frightened races shake.
I had no place to rest my hand,
which, fluid like the water of an impounded spring
or firm as a chunk of anthracite or crystal,
would have returned the warmth or cold of my outstretched hand.
What was man? In what part of his conversation begun
amid shops and whistles, in which of his metallic movements
lived the indestructible, the imperishable, life?

III

Like corn man was husked in the bottomless
granary of forgotten deeds, the miserable course of
events, from one to seven, to eight,
and not one death but many deaths came to each:
every day a little death, dust, maggot, a lamp
quenched in the mire of the slums, a little thick-winged death
entered each man like a short lance,
and man was driven by bread or by knife:
herdsman, child of the seaports, dark captain of the plow,
or rodent of the teeming streets:

all were consumed awaiting their death, their daily ration of death:
and the ominous adversity of each day was like
a black glass from which they drank trembling.

IV

Mighty death invited me many times:
it was like the invisible salt in the waves,
and what its invisible taste disseminated
was like halves of sinking and rising
or vast structures of wind and glacier.
I came to the cutting edge, to the narrows
of the air, to the shroud of agriculture and stone,
to the stellar void of the final steps
and the vertiginous spiraling road:
but, wide sea, O death! you do not come in waves
but in a galloping nocturnal clarity
or like the total numbers of the night.
You never rummaged around in pockets, your visit
was not possible without red vestments:
without an auroral carpet of enclosed silence:
without towering entombed patrimonies of tears.

I could not love in each being a tree
with a little autumn on its back (the death of a thousand leaves),
all the false deaths and resurrections
without land, without abyss:
I've tried to swim in the most expansive lives,
in the most free-flowing estuaries,
and when man went on denying me
and kept blocking path and door so that
my headspring hands could not touch his wounded inexistence,
then I went from street to street and river to river,
city to city and bed to bed,
my brackish mask traversed the desert,
and in the last humiliated homes, without light or fire,
without bread, without stone, without silence, alone,
I rolled on dying of my own death.

V

It was not you, solemn death, iron-plumed bird,
that the poor heir of these rooms
carried, between rushed meals, under his empty skin:
rather a poor petal with its cord exterminated:
an atom from the breast that did not come to combat
or the harsh dew that did not fall on his brow.
It was what could not be revived, a bit
of the little death without peace or territory:

a bone, a bell that died within him.
I raised the bandages dressed in iodine, sank my hands
into the pitiful sorrows killed by death,
and in the wound I found nothing but a chilling gust
that entered through the vague interstices of the soul.

VI

And so I scaled the ladder of the earth
amid the atrocious maze of lost jungles
up to you, Macchu Picchu.
High citadel of terraced stones,
at long last the dwelling of him whom the earth
did not conceal in its slumbering vestments.
In you, as in two parallel lines,
the cradle of lightning and man
was rocked in a wind of thorns.

Mother of stone, sea spray of the condors.

Towering reef of the human dawn.

Spade lost in the primal sand.

This was the dwelling, this is the site:
here the full kernels of corn rose
and fell again like red hailstones.

Here the golden fiber emerged from the vicuña
to clothe love, tombs, mothers,
the king, prayers, warriors.

Here man's feet rested at night
beside the eagle's feet, in the high gory
retreats, and at dawn
they trod the rarefied mist with feet of thunder
and touched lands and stones
until they recognized them in the night or in death.

I behold vestments and hands,
the vestige of water in the sonorous void,
the wall tempered by the touch of a face
that beheld with my eyes the earthen lamps,
that oiled with my hands the vanished
wood: because everything—clothing, skin, vessels,

words, wine, bread—
is gone, fallen to earth.

And the air flowed with orange-blossom
fingers over all the sleeping:
a thousand years of air, months, weeks of air,
of blue wind, of iron cordillera,
like gentle hurricanes of footsteps
polishing the solitary precinct of stone.

VII

O remains of a single abyss, shadows of one gorge—
the deep one—the real, most searing death
attained the scale
of your magnitude,
and from the quarried stones,
from the spires,
from the terraced aqueducts
you tumbled as in autumn
to a single death.
Today the empty air no longer weeps,
no longer knows your feet of clay,
has now forgotten your pitchers that filtered the sky
when the lightning's knives emptied it,
and the powerful tree was eaten away
by the mist and felled by the wind.
It sustained a hand that fell suddenly
from the heights to the end of time.
You are no more, spider hands, fragile
filaments, spun web:
all that you were has fallen: customs, frayed
syllables, masks of dazzling light.

But a permanence of stone and word:
the citadel was raised like a chalice in the hands
of all, the living, the dead, the silent, sustained
by so much death, a wall, from so much life a stroke
of stone petals: the permanent rose, the dwelling:
this Andean reef of glacial colonies.

When the clay-colored hand
turned to clay, when the little eyelids closed,
filled with rough walls, brimming with castles,
and when the entire man was trapped in his hole,

exactitude remained hoisted aloft:
this high site of the human dawn:
the highest vessel that has contained silence:
a life of stone after so many lives.

VIII

Rise up with me, American love.

Kiss the secret stones with me.
The torrential silver of the Urubamba
makes the pollen fly to its yellow cup.
It spans the void of the grapevine,
the petrous plant, the hard wreath
upon the silence of the highland casket.
Come, minuscule life, between the wings
of the earth, while—crystal and cold, pounded air
extracting assailed emeralds—
O, wild water, you run down from the snow.

Love, love, even the abrupt night,
from the sonorous Andean flint
to the dawn's red knees,
contemplates the snow's blind child.

O sonorous threaded Wilkamayu,
when you beat your lineal thunder
to a white froth, like wounded snow,
when your precipitous storm
sings and batters, awakening the sky,
what language do you bring to the ear recently
wrenched from your Andean froth?

Who seized the cold's lightning
and left it shackled in the heights,
dispersed in its glacial tears,
smitten in its swift swords,
hammering its embattled stamens,
borne on its warrior's bed,
startled in its rocky end?

What are your tormented sparks saying?
Did your secret insurgent lightning
once journey charged with words?
Who keeps on shattering frozen syllables,

black languages, golden banners,
deep mouths, muffled cries,
in your slender arterial waters?
Who keeps on cutting floral eyelids
that come to gaze from the earth?
Who hurls down the dead clusters
that fell in your cascade hands
to strip the night stripped
in the coal of geology?

Who flings the branch down from its bonds?
Who once again entombs farewells?

Love, love, never touch the brink
or worship the sunken head:
let time attain its stature
in its salon of shattered headsprings,
and, between the swift water and the walls,
gather the air from the gorge,
the parallel sheets of the wind,
the cordilleras' blind canal,
the harsh greeting of the dew,
and, rise up, flower by flower, through the dense growth,
treading the hurtling serpent.

In the steep zone—forest and stone,
mist of green stars, radiant jungle—
Mantur explodes like a blinding lake
or a new layer of silence.

Come to my very heart, to my dawn,
up to the crowned solitudes.
The dead kingdom is still alive.

And over the Sundial the sanguinary shadow
of the condor crosses like a black ship.

IX

Sidereal eagle, vineyard of mist.
Lost bastion, blind scimitar.
Spangled waistband, solemn bread.
Torrential stairway, immense eyelid.
Triangular tunic, stone pollen.
Granite lamp, stone bread.

Mineral serpent, stone rose.
Entombed ship, stone headspring.
Moonhorse, stone light.
Equinoctial square, stone vapor.
Ultimate geometry, stone book.
Tympanum fashioned amid the squalls.
Madrepore of sunken time.
Rampart tempered by fingers.
Ceiling assailed by feathers.
Mirror bouquets, stormy foundations.
Thrones toppled by the vine.
Regime of the enraged claw.
Hurricane sustained on the slopes.
Immobile cataract of turquoise.
Patriarchal bell of the sleeping.
Hitching ring of the tamed snows.
Iron recumbent upon its statues.
Inaccessible dark tempest.
Puma hands, bloodstained rock.
Towering sombrero, snowy dispute.
Night raised on fingers and roots.
Window of the mists, hardened dove.
Nocturnal plant, statue of thunder.
Essential cordillera, searoof.
Architecture of lost eagles.
Skyrope, heavenly bee.
Bloody level, man-made star.
Mineral bubble, quartz moon.
Andean serpent, brow of amaranth.
Cupola of silence, pure land.
Seabride, tree of cathedrals.
Cluster of salt, black-winged cherry tree.
Snow-capped teeth, cold thunderbolt.
Scored moon, menacing stone.
Headdresses of the cold, action of the air.
Volcano of hands, obscure cataract.
Silver wave, pointer of time.

X

Stone upon stone, and man, where was he?
Air upon air, and man, where was he?
Time upon time, and man, where was he?
Were you too a broken shard
of inconclusive man, of empty raptor,

who on the streets today, on the trails,
on the dead autumn leaves, keeps
tearing away at the heart right up to the grave?
Poor hand, foot, poor life . . .
Did the days of light
unraveled in you, like raindrops
on the banners of a feast day,
give petal by petal of their dark food
to the empty mouth?
                        Hunger, coral of mankind,
hunger, secret plant, woodcutters' stump,
hunger, did the edge of your reef rise up
to these high suspended towers?

I want to know, salt of the roads,
show me the spoon—architecture, let me
scratch at the stamens of stone with a little stick,
ascend the rungs of the air up to the void,
scrape the innards until I touch mankind.

Macchu Picchu, did you put
stone upon stone and, at the base, tatters?
Coal upon coal and, at the bottom, tears?
Fire in gold and, within it, the trembling
drop of red blood?
Bring me back the slave that you buried!
Shake from the earth the hard bread
of the poor wretch, show me
the slave's clothing and his window.
Tell me how he slept when he lived.
Tell me if his sleep was
harsh, gaping, like a black chasm
worn by fatigue upon the wall.
The wall, the wall! If upon his sleep
each layer of stone weighed down, and if he fell beneath it
as beneath a moon, with his dream!
Ancient America, sunken bride,
your fingers too,
on leaving the jungle for the high void of the gods,
beneath the nuptial standards of light and decorum,
mingling with the thunder of drums and spears,
your fingers, your fingers too,
which the abstract rose, the cold line, and
the crimson breast of the new grain transferred
to the fabric of radiant substance, to the hard cavities—

did you, entombed America, did you too store in the depths
of your bitter intestine, like an eagle, hunger?

XI

Through the hazy splendor,
through the stone night, let me plunge my hand,
and let the aged heart of the forsaken beat in me
like a bird captive for a thousand years!
Let me forget, today, this joy, which is greater than the sea,
because man is greater than the sea and its islands,
and we must fall into him as into a well to emerge from the bottom
with a bouquet of secret water and sunken truths.
Let me forget, great stone, the powerful proportion,
the transcendent measure, the honeycombed stones,
and from the square let me today run
my hand over the hypotenuse of rough blood and sackcloth.
When, like a horseshoe of red elytra, the frenzied condor
beats my temples in the order of its flight,
and the hurricane of cruel feathers sweeps the somber dust
from the diagonal steps, I do not see the swift brute,
I do not see the blind cycle of its claws,
I see the man of old, the servant, asleep in the fields,
I see a body, a thousand bodies, a man, a thousand women,
black with rain and night, beneath the black squall,
with the heavy stone of the statue:
Juan Stonecutter, son of Wiracocha,
Juan Coldeater, son of a green star,
Juan Barefoot, grandson of turquoise,
rise up to be born with me, my brother.

XII

Rise up to be born with me, my brother.

Give me your hand from the deep
zone of your disseminated sorrow.
You'll not return from the bottom of the rocks.
You'll not return from subterranean time.
Your stiff voice will not return.
Your drilled eyes will not return.
Behold me from the depths of the earth,
laborer, weaver, silent herdsman:
tamer of the tutelary guanacos:
mason of the defied scaffold:

bearer of the Andean tears:
jeweler with your fingers crushed:
tiller trembling in the seed:
potter spilt in your clay:
bring to the cup of this new life, brothers,
all your timeless buried sorrows.
Show me your blood and your furrow,
tell me: I was punished here,
because the jewel did not shine or the earth
did not surrender the gemstone or kernel on time:
show me the stone on which you fell
and the wood on which you were crucified,
strike the old flintstones,
the old lamps, the whips sticking
throughout the centuries to your wounds
and the war clubs glistening red.
I've come to speak through your dead mouths.
Throughout the earth join all
the silent scattered lips
and from the depths speak to me all night long,
as if I were anchored with you,
tell me everything, chain by chain,
link by link, and step by step,
sharpen the knives that you've kept,
put them in my breast and in my hand,
like a river of yellow lightning,
like a river of buried jaguars,
and let me weep hours, days, years,
blind ages, stellar centuries.

Give me silence, water, hope.

Give me struggle, iron, volcanoes.

Cling to my body like magnets.

Hasten to my veins and to my mouth.

Speak through my words and my blood.

Juan Rulfo

Although his complete works constitute a scant three hundred pages, Juan Rulfo (1917–85) is considered one of the finest writers of twentieth-century Latin America. His novel *Pedro Páramo* (1955) and the short stories collected in *The Plain in Flames* (1953) exemplify the ambiguous combination of folklore and realism known as magical realism; they have been enormously influential in Rulfo's native Mexico as well as other parts of the Americas. During Rulfo's childhood in rural Jalisco, the wealth and connections of his landowning family did little to insulate them against the widespread violence of the Mexican Revolution and the Cristero Rebellion of 1926–29. His father was murdered in 1923 as a result of a dispute regarding grazing rights, and his mother died a few years later; several of his father's siblings were also killed in what Rulfo would later describe as "a geographic devastation" (Boldy 2016, 9). Readers of Rulfo's work have traditionally emphasized his astonishing aesthetic treatment of motifs such as madness, patriarchy, poverty, and corruption, all of them closely connected to the violence unleashed by the revolution. More recently, however, scholars have begun to turn their attention to the specifically environmental devastation that presents itself in many of his narratives. The critic Kerstin Oloff (2016, 80), for one, has productively linked Rulfo's characteristically arid, barren landscapes to the modernization of Mexico's agricultural systems in the mid-twentieth century, the so-called Mexican miracle that resulted in widespread soil loss and desertification. The selection presented here is "Luvina," from *The Plain in Flames*.

***

"Luvina" (1953)

TRANSLATED BY ILAN STAVANS WITH HAROLD AUGENBRAUM

Of all the high ranges in the south, the one in Luvina is the highest and rockiest. It's full of that gray stone from which they make lime, but in Luvina they don't make lime from it nor do they put it to any good use. They call it crude stone there, and the incline that rises toward Luvina is called Crude Stone Hill. The wind and sun have taken care of breaking it down, so the earth around there is white and shining, as if it were bedewed with morning dew; though all this is just words, because in Luvina the days are as cold as the nights and the dew grows thick in the sky before it manages to reach the earth.

. . . And the earth is steep. It slashes everywhere into deep ravines, so far down that they disappear, that's how far down they go. People in Luvina say dreams rise out of those ravines; but the only thing I ever saw rise up from there was the wind, whirling, as if it had been imprisoned down below in reed pipes. A wind that doesn't even let bittersweet grow: those sad little plants can barely live, holding on for all they're worth to the side of the cliffs in these hills, as if they were smeared onto the earth. Only at times, where there's a little shade, hidden among the rocks, can the *chicalote* bloom with its white poppies. But the *chicalote* soon withers. Then one hears it scratching the air with its thorny branches, making a noise like a knife on a whetstone.

"You'll see that wind blowing over Luvina. It's gray. They say that's because it carries volcanic sand; but the truth is, it's a black air. You'll see. It settles on Luvina, clinging to things as if it were biting them. And on many days it carries off the roofs of houses as if it were carrying off a straw hat, leaving the walls unprotected and bare. Then it scratches, as if it had nails: one hears it morning and night, hour after hour, without rest, scraping the walls, tearing off strips of soil, gouging under the doors with its pointy spade, until one feels it roiling inside oneself, as if it were trying to rattle the hinges of our very bones. You'll see."

The man who was talking remained quiet for a while, looking outside.

The sound of the river passing its rising waters over the *camichín* boughs reached them; the rumor of the air softly moving the almond-tree leaves, and the screams of the children playing in the little space illuminated by the light coming out of the store.

Termites came in and bounced against the oil lamp, falling to the ground with their wings scorched. And night still advanced outside.

"Hey, Camilo, give us two more beers!" the man went on. Then he added:

"Something else, señor. In Luvina you'll never see a blue sky. The whole horizon is colorless; always cloudy with a caliginous stain that never disappears. The whole ridge bald, without a single tree, without a single green thing for your eyes to rest on; everything enveloped in the ash-cloud of lime. You'll see: those hills, their lights darkened as if they were dead, and Luvina at the very top, crowning it with its white houses as if it were the crown of a dead man . . ."

The children's screams got closer until they were inside the store. That made the man stand up, go to the door, and say to them: "Get away from here! Stop interrupting! Go on playing, but without making a ruckus."

Then, heading back to the table, he sat down and said:

"So yes, as I was saying. It rains very little there. By midyear a bunch of storms arrive and lash the earth, ripping it up, leaving nothing but a sea of stones floating on the crust. Then it's nice to see how the clouds crawl along, the way they wander from one hill to another making noise as if they were swollen bladders; ricocheting and thundering just as if they were breaking apart on the edge of the ravines. But after ten or twelve days they leave and don't come back until the following year, and sometimes it happens they don't come back for a few years . . ."

". . . Yes, rain is scarce. Little or next to nothing, to the point that the earth, in addition to being dry and shrunken like old leather, is full of cracks and that thing they call "*pasojos de agua*" there, which are nothing but dirt clods hardened into sharp-edged stones that pierce your feet when you walk, as if the land itself had grown thorns there. As if it were like that."

He drank the beer until only foam bubbles were left in the bottle and then went on talking:

"No matter how you look at it, Luvina is a very sad place. Now that you're going there, you'll see what I mean. I would say it's the place where sadness nests. Where smiles are unknown, as if everyone's faces had gone stiff. And, if you want, you can see that sadness at every turn. The wind that blows there stirs it up but never carries it away. It's there, as if it had been born there. You can even taste it and feel it, because it's always on you, pressed against you, and because it's oppressive like a great poultice on your heart's living flesh.

". . . People there say that when the moon is full, they see the shape of the figure of the wind wandering the streets of Luvina, dragging a black blanket; but the thing I always came to see, when the moon was out in Luvina, was the image of despair . . . always.

"But drink your beer. I see you haven't even tried it. Drink. Or perhaps you don't like it as it is, at room temperature. There's no other option here. I know it tastes bad like that; that it takes on a flavor like donkey's pee. You get used to it around here. Keep in mind that over there you can't even get this. You'll miss it when you get to Luvina. Over there you won't be able to get anything but mescal, which people make with an herb called *hojasé,* and after the first few swallows you'll be going round and round as if you had been beaten up. Better drink your beer. I know what I'm talking about."

Outside you could still hear the river struggle. The rumor of wind. Children playing. It seemed as if it were still early in the night.

Once again the man had gone to look out the door and had come back.

Now he was saying:

"It's easy to look at things from over here, merely recalled from memory, where there's no similarity. But I have no problem going on telling you what I know in regard to Luvina. I lived there. I left my life there . . . I went to that place with my illusions intact and came back old and used up. And now you're going there . . . All right. I seem to remember the beginning. I put myself in your shoes and think . . . Look, when I first got to Luvina . . . But first can I have your beer? I see you're not paying any attention to it. And it'll be good for me. It's healing for me. I feel as if my head were being rinsed with camphor oil . . . Well, as I was telling you, when I first arrived in Luvina, the mule driver that took us there didn't even want the beasts to rest. As soon as we were on the ground, he turned around:

" 'I'm going back' he said.

" 'Wait, you won't let your animals take a rest? They're beaten up.'

" 'They would end up even more messed up here,' he said. 'I better get back.'

"And he left, dropping us at Crude Stone Hill, spurring his horses as if he were fleeing from a place of the devil.

"We, my wife and three children, remained there, standing in the middle of the plaza, with all our belongings in our arms. In the middle of that place where you heard only the wind . . .

"Nothing but the plaza, without a single plant to break the wind. We stayed there.

"Then I asked my wife:

"'What country are we in, Agripina?'

"And she shrugged her shoulders.

"'Well, if you don't mind, go look for someplace to eat and someplace to spend the night. We'll wait for you here,' I said to her.

"She took the youngest of our children and left. But she didn't come back.

"At dusk, when the sun lit up only the hilltops, we went looking for her. We walked along the narrow streets of Luvina, until we found her inside the church: sitting right in the middle of that lonely church, with the child asleep between her legs.

"'What are you doing here, Agripina?'

"'I came in to pray,' she said to us.

"'What for?' I asked.

"She shrugged her shoulders.

"There was nothing to pray to there. It was an empty shack, with no doors, just some open galleries and a broken ceiling through which the air filtered like a sieve.

"'Where's the inn?'

"'There is no inn.'

"'And the hostel?'

"'There is no hostel.'

"' Did you see anyone? Does anyone live here?' I asked her.

"'Yes, right opposite . . . Some women . . . I can still see them. Look, behind the cracks in that door I see the eyes watching us, shining . . . They have been staring at us . . . Look at them. I see the shining balls of their eyes . . . But they have nothing to give us to eat. Without even sticking their heads out, they told me there's no food in this town . . . Then I came here to pray, to ask God on our behalf.'

"' Why didn't you come back? We were waiting for you.'

"'I came here to pray. I haven't finished yet.'

"'What country is this, Agripina?'

"And she shrugged her shoulders again.

"That night we settled down to sleep in a corner of the church, behind the dismantled altar. Even there you could feel the wind, though not quite as strong. We kept hearing it passing above us, with its long howls; we kept hearing it coming in and going out through the hollow concavities of the doors; hitting the crosses in the stations of the cross with its hands of wind: big, strong crosses made of mesquite wood that hung from the walls over the length of the church, tied with wires that grated each time the wind shook them as if it were the grating of teeth.

"The children were crying because they were too frightened to sleep. And my wife was trying to hold them all in her arms. Hugging her bouquet of children. And I was there, not knowing what to do.

"The wind calmed down a bit before sunrise. Later on it came back. But there was a moment at dawn when everything became still, as if the sky and the earth had joined together, crushing all sounds with their weight . . . You could hear the children breathing, now more relaxed. I could hear my wife breathing heavily next to me:

"'What's that?' she said to me.

"'What's what?' I asked her.

"'That. That noise.'

"'It's silence. Go to sleep. Rest, even if only a little bit, because it will be dawn soon.'

"But soon I heard it, too. It was like bats flitting in the darkness, very close to us. Like bats with their long wings sweeping against the floor. I got up and the sounds of wings beating became stronger, as if the colony of bats had been frightened and they were flying toward the holes in the doors. Then I tiptoed over there, feeling that muffled whispering in front of me. I stopped in the doorway and I saw them. I saw all the women of Luvina with water jugs on their shoulders, with their shawls hanging from their heads and their dark silhouettes against the black depths of the night.

"'What do you want?' I asked them. 'What are you looking for at this time of night?'

"One of them responded:

"'We're going to get water.'

"I saw them standing in front of me, watching me. Then, as if they were shadows, they started walking down the street with their black water jars.

"No, I'll never forget that first night I spent in Luvina.

". . . Don't you think this deserves another drink? If only so I can get rid of the bad taste of the memory."

"I believe you asked me how many years I was in Luvina, right? . . . Truth is, I don't know. I lost any sense of time once the fever got me all turned around; but it must have been an eternity . . . And that's because time is very long there. No one keeps count of hours, nor is anyone interested in how the years mount up. Days start and end. Then night comes. Just day and night until the day you die, which for them is a kind of hope.

"You must think I'm harping on the same idea. And yes, it's true, señor . . . To sit on the doorstep, watching the sun rise and set, raising and lowering your head, until the springs go slack and then everything comes to a halt, without time, as if one lived forever in eternity. That's what the old men do over there.

"Because only old people live in Luvina and those who aren't yet born, as people say . . . And women with no strength, just skin and bones, they're so thin. The children who were born there have left . . . No sooner do they see the light of dawn than they become men. As people say, they jump from their mother's breast to the hoe and they disappear from Luvina. That's how things are there.

"Only very old men remain and abandoned women, or women with a husband who is God only knows where . . . They return every so often like the storms I was telling you about; you can hear the whole town whispering when they come back and something like a grunt when they leave . . . They leave behind a sack of provisions for the old and plant another child in their wife's womb, and then no one knows anything about them again until next year, and sometimes never . . . That's the custom. Over there it's called the law, but it's the same thing. Their children spend their lives working for their parents the way they did for theirs and as who knows how many before them behaved in accordance with that law . . .

"Meanwhile, the old people wait for them and for the day of their death, sitting in their doorways, with their arms at their sides, moved only by the grace that is a child's gratitude . . . Alone, in that solitude of Luvina.

"One day I tried convincing them to go elsewhere, where the soil was good. 'Let's leave this place,' I said. 'We'll find a way to settle somewhere else. The government will help us.'

"They listened to me without batting an eye, looking at me from the depths of their eyes, from which only a little light emerges from deep inside.

"'You say the government will help us, professor? Are you acquainted with the government?'

"I told them I was.

"'We know it, too. It so happens that we do. What we know nothing about is the government's mother.'

"I told them it was the fatherland. They shook their heads to say no. And they laughed. It was the only time I saw the people from Luvina laugh. They bared their ruined teeth and told me no, the government had no mother.

"And you know what? They're right. The government man only remembers them when one of his young men has done something wrong down here. Then he sends to Luvina for him and they kill him. Beyond that, they don't even know that they exist.

"'You want to tell us we should leave Luvina because, according to you, it's enough being hungry with no need to be,' they said to me. 'But if we leave, who'll carry our dead? They live here and we can't leave them behind.'

"And they're still there. You'll see them once you get there. Chewing dry mesquite pulp and swallowing their saliva in order to outwit hunger. You'll see them passing by like shadows, hugging the walls of houses, almost dragged along by the wind.

"'Don't you hear that wind?' I finally told them. 'It'll be the end of you.'

"'You endure what you have to endure. It's God's mandate,' they answered me. 'It's bad when the wind stops blowing. When that happens, the sun presses close to Luvina and sucks our blood and the little water we have in our hides. The wind makes the sun stay up there. It's better that way.'

"I said nothing more. I left Luvina and I haven't gone back nor do I think I will.

". . . But look at the somersaults the world is doing. You're going there now, in a few hours. It's probably fifteen years since I was told the same thing: 'You're going to San Juan Luvina.'

"In those days I was strong. I was full of ideas . . . You know that ideas infuse us all. And one goes with a burden on one's shoulders to make something out of one's self. But it didn't work out in Luvina. I did the experiment and it came undone . . .

"San Juan Luvina. The name sounded celestial to me. But it's Purgatory. A moribund place where even the dogs have died and there's not even anyone to bark at the silence; because the moment one gets used to the winds that blow there, one hears nothing but that silence that exists in all solitudes. And that uses you all up. Look at me. It used me up. You're going, and you'll understand what I'm saying very soon . . .

"What do you think if we ask that man to put together some *mezcalitos* for us? With beer one needs to get up all the time and that interrupts the conversation. Listen, Camilo, send us over some mezcals right away!

"So yes, as I was telling you . . ."

But he didn't say anything. He kept staring at a fixed point on the table where the termites, now without wings, circled like naked little worms.

Outside one could hear the night advancing. The water of the river splashing against the trunks of the *camichines*. The already distant shouting of children. Through the small sky of the doorway one could see the stars.

The man who was watching the termites slumped over the table and fell asleep.

Lydia Cabrera

Writer and ethnographer Lydia Cabrera (1899–1991) is one of the major figures of Cuban literature, best known for her work on Afro-Cuban traditions, folklore, and religions. Like many upper-class Cubans of the time, Cabrera grew up surrounded by Black servants, and it was from them that she first experienced the rich tradition of Afro-Cuban storytelling. At twenty-seven she left the island to study painting in Paris. She spent the next decade in Europe, mingling with other intellectuals—Paul Valéry, Federico García Lorca, Pablo Neruda, Miguel Ángel Asturias, Gabriela Mistral, and Wilfrido Lam—who were interested in the so-called primitive cultures of Africa and Latin America. Cabrera became especially close to Venezuelan novelist Teresa de la Parra, and it was to entertain de la Parra, dying of tuberculosis, that she wrote down the stories that became *Contes nègres de Cuba*, or *Black Stories from Cuba* (Aira 2001, 107). Upon returning to the island, Cabrera was encouraged by her brother-in-law, ethnographer Fernando Ortiz, to more systematically pursue her interest in the culture and religions of Cuba's Afro-descended populations. The result was *El monte* (1954), a monumental compendium of the knowledge, ceremonies, stories, and practices of Black Cubans and the first major anthropological study of Afro-Cuban religions. It features Santería, which combines elements of Catholicism with Yoruba belief in natural deities called orishas. Cabrera's book, translated as *The Bush*, *The Wilderness*, or *The Woods*, emphasizes the relationship between nature and the sacred, delving into the ways that the divine is present in plants, animals, and the environment. Our excerpt focuses on the ceiba tree, venerated throughout Cuba because of an ancient Yoruba belief in the supernatural powers of the similar African teak.

***

"The Ceiba Tree" (1954)

TRANSLATED BY PATRICIA GONZÁLEZ

> "Ceiba, you are my mother; give me shade."

The ceiba tree, like the royal palm tree, is the most characteristic on the island and the sacred tree par excellence. If we didn't already know that all the spirits, the ancestors, the African "saints"[1] of all nations brought to Cuba, and the Catholic saints gravitate towards the ceiba and inhabit it permanently, we would wonder if there was an independent cult to the ceiba as shown by the extreme devotion dedicated to the ceiba by both Blacks and whites.

The ceiba was also known as "the throne of Sanfán Kón, the Saint Barbara of China" by Chinese imported during the colonial time, and today by their descendants.

If we ask a white peasant, a "guajiro,"[2] about the mysticism the ceiba inspires all over the country, he invariably would say that "it is blessed," and that his elders taught him to worship it because "it is the most sacred and the greatest in the world." And everybody will repeat the same: "The ceiba is Holy!" "It is the tree of the Virgin Mary." "It is the tree of the Almighty" or of "the power of God," it is the "mystery tree." Evidence of such strength is demonstrated when the natural elements, when unleashed, respect its power: the fiercest hurricane does not demolish nor break the ceiba, nor does lightning destroy it.

"Lightning respects the ceiba tree and nothing else."

Chop down a ceiba tree? What an outrage! The ceiba tree must not be chopped nor burnt. Nobody ventures to demolish one of those imposing trees, dry centenarians feared and adored by all in the countryside, without previously presenting offerings, consulting the orishas, and taking all precautions. It is understandable why Black and white peasants living in close quarters with each other see that solemn, majestic, huge tree as the material manifestation of some powerful divinity. This Ceiba divinity simply strikes a chord deep down in all humans, responding to either an atavism or an ancient religious instinct.

"The ceiba is a saint: Iroko."[3] "It's the Immaculate Conception." "It holds Arému,[4] the Virgin of Mercy of the Arará,[5] and Yémmu.[6]

Sometimes the explanations of my elderly informants are confusing. The ceiba is a "seat of Iroko, who is there present"; and the Immaculate Conception "comes to the ceiba" and lives in it. Others assured me that "Iroko is the same ceiba." Also, "Babá[7] is in the ceiba." "The ceiba belongs to Oggún and Orichaoko." Alternatively, it belongs to "Obbá and Changó."

"Aggayú[8] is also ceiba." Once the tree is consecrated, it will be known as Iroko.

My centenarian friend Addié, from Matanzas, entrusted herself to the ceiba every morning, "because to live one must have the protection of the mighty mother ceiba." "Whether you want it or not," as the Ocha[9] chant says: "You must invoke Iroko," because the death spirits, the okús,[10] are greeted in the ceiba; the deceased rest there."

Blacks of Congolese heritage call it nkunia house Sambi (tree house of God); nkunia Lembán, nkunia mabúngu, Ñangue, Gúndu (Mama Ungundu), Naribé, Sánda, Fiame, Nfúmba and Fumbe (deceased), Mamá Fumbe. Those that claim to be Lukumí[11] called it: Arabbá, Iroko, Elúwere, Asabá. (Iggi-Arabbá) Iggi-Olorun.[12] (Tree of God).

Some elders agree, explaining to me that Cuba did not have iroko, which is a kind of African mahogany, and that the Lukumís gave the name "arabá" to the French rubber tree (also called gógó by Sandoval). Nevertheless, the ceiba reminded them of iroko and they "consecrated" it and gave it the name used in Africa for the immense, very similar tree venerated all over the coast of Guinea.[13] The same thing happened with many other trees.

"Even though the ceiba is not a legitimate iroko, it is considered one; and it is known sometimes as iroko and others as arabbá." "In this context, the ceiba is like Obbáburo:[14] an African tree where a festivity takes place."

"Iroko belongs to the saint Oddúa,[15] who lives high on top." Iroko is Olofi's[16] body; the holiest and most mysterious tree." However, Iroko or Iroke, "pure Lukumí from Oyó," "called Loko in Dajomi [Dahomey]," is the orisha who owns the ceiba, "an old male saint; he has a woman called Abomán, who also lives in the ceiba, and a sister called Ondó." The ceiba is commonly called Iroko, like the orisha.

The dance of Iroko is done with a cane beautifully covered with necklaces and a broom decorated with red and white beads. This saint worshipped on the ceiba tree belongs to the lineage of Naná Burukú and Ayánu, Saint Lazarus, both Lukumí and Arará.[17] "But Iroko does not come down [possess a person] like Oro, the one that snores." Santeros[18] parade a young bull around the tree with lit candles before beheading it as sacrifice. In the meantime, roosters, hens, Florida ducks, and white turkeys are also sacrificed. Every month, a young white rooster is offered. Others say the ceiba tree belongs to Aggayú,[19] "the strong-armed one," and not to Abanlá, the purest virgin, but all agree that all orishas "go" to the ceiba, and all, Aggayusolá, Changó, Naná, all of them are worshipped near the ceiba; including Dádda Awuru Maggalá, Gebioso, the oldest Changó of the Arará.

Mayomberos[20] call the ceiba "Fortune World" and "Beautiful Girl" sometimes "as an endearment or to tease it." "Because the ceiba is holy and blessed, it is understood it can never be used for something bad"; "the ceiba sheds tears when a bad deed is intended," which happens when the tree trunk is oozing, it is advising the magus:[21] "Do not not perform that bad deed because it is not good for your soul." But . . . God allows everything. "God says, matters of men do not concern me. Let them deal with it. I do not get involved in anything." So, the ceiba can both kill and bring to life. The power of the ceiba can grant most requests, but, as we all know, it all depends on rendering ritual fees.

Here is an essential offering to earn the goodwill and assistance of Mother Ceiba. Cook sixteen eggs, draw a cross with cacao butter on the earth under the tree, in the direction where the sun rises. Over the cross place the peeled eggs, and the petition is repeated every time you place one egg. At the end you add, "I wish that you grant me my request in so many days" ("it is advisable to set a term"), but the prayer becomes more effective if you place an old penny next to each egg. "To appease an enemy and to stop them from hurting us, cook four or eight eggs, smear them with cocoa butter, almond oil, and a calming balm, cover them with cotton, and at sunset, take the offering and place it under the roots of the ceiba while calling the name of the person you want to pacify. One must speak with Obatalá,[22] who is right there sitting on her throne and she, the peacemaker, tames and changes that enemy." . . .

"Once there was a very poor man who had many children. Night found him in the countryside away from home; tired, but not wanting to get home empty-handed, he cuddled to rest on a ceiba tree branch. He fell asleep. It was around midnight, the hour when the ceibas walk, and he was awakened by a noise. The noise was a huge black mass walking towards him; he remained quiet where he was, and it was another ceiba getting closer.

The ceibas greeted each other:

"Malembe Nguei, Malembe Mpolo."

"Kindiambo, kilienso guatuka nguie?" (What is new?)

"What's new? Well you know, I live in front of the Mayor's palace," one ceiba tells the other one, starting to move its roots to also begin a walk, "and the Mayor has been crying nonstop since yesterday, like a woman, because his daughter búta ndumba! (Beautiful Girl) is dying from a disease with no cure except with this one remedy."

"Which one?"—asked the other ceiba.

"She must be wrapped with a new sheet and kept three hours over a pot filled with boiling milk, cinnamon, and honey, absorbing the vapors from the milk and praying musakala múnbansa musu kuenda sanga ntiba karidi fuyánde . . . then the girl will live."

"It is true," said the ceiba. "That is the remedy. Where are you going now?"

"I am going to see my aunt."

"I am going to see my sister."

"Good lúmbo . . ."

The ceiba was unaware it had a man hidden on a branch, because when he arrived the ceiba was asleep. The man left quietly, not making any noise, but he had heard enough . . .

At night ceibas wake up around midnight and go out visiting, having gatherings and entertainments. Those two stayed talking until late, and the poor man, kíangana, kíangana, kíangana, arrived at the Mayor's palace and waited by the door until dawn. He said he was a doctor who only cured extreme cases, and the Mayor brought him in.

"If you cure my daughter, I will make you rich. If my daughter dies, I will have your head off."

The man saw the sick girl; he prayed and did everything he heard from the ceiba. The young woman sweated profusely over the pot of boiling milk! Three hours later he wrapped her well to keep her warm, and the girl went back to bed. She was breathing better and better. He ordered the windows, closed for many days, to be opened. Sunrays entered; the sick girl opened her eyes. She was already cured. The Mayor tells the poor man: "I want you to be my family doctor."

"Mayor, sir, I can only cure those with no cure."

They put him inside a carriage, filled it with money, and he went home. "Now, let's buy everything!"

"Due to those rare occasions, some poor fellow becomes rich from one day to the next."

Notes

1. In Cuban Spanish "santo" refers to diverse African deities, as well as to the Catholic saints.

2. In Cuba, a person who lives and works in the countryside, peasant, farmer; usually a white farmer.

3. Yoruba name given to the orisha represented by the ceiba tree in Cuba.

4. Name given to the first male child, implying something precious.

5. Arará is a minority group in Cuba (especially in the provinces of La Habana and Matanzas) who descend from Fon, Ewe, Popo, Mahi, and other ethnic groups of Dahomey, Republic of Benin.

6. Yémmu, Afro-Cuban orisha, wife of Obatalá and mother of all orishas.

7. Father, referring to the Afro-Cuban orisha Obatalá.

8. Oggún, Orichaoko, Obbá, Changó, and Aggayú are orishas worshipped in Cuba.

9. Name given to the Yoruba religion in Cuba.

10. Ikú is the name given to death in Yoruba.

11. Name given in Cuba to the descendants of Yoruba speakers from West Africa.

12. Olorun is the sun and a powerful orisha. In Lukumí, Oru is sun.

13. Guinea refers to the African continent.

14. Obba means king; communities in Africa gather around a sacred tree.

15. Oddúa is an orisha representing the secrets and mysteries of death. Sometimes referred to as an avatar of Obatalá.

16. Olofi, supreme god for the Yoruba.

17. Saint Lazarus is the Catholic saint representing Babalú-Ayé, the skin-infected orisha worshipped on December 16–17 by Cubans from Yoruba and Arará lineage. Naná Burukú is his mother.

18. Initiates of the Lukumí Ocha system.

19. Yoruba orisha, represented by a volcano.

20. Practitioners of Palo Monte, also known as Regla Congo, an Afro-Cuban religion of Bantú origin.

21. Translator's note: I have chosen "magus" for "brujo," or wizard.

22. Peaceful Yoruba orisha, represented by male and female avatars.

José María Arguedas

José María Arguedas (1911–69) was a Peruvian writer and anthropologist whose work reflects his deep affective connection to the Andean Quechua community and his commitment to the vitality of Indigenous cultures. Born in Andahuaylas in the Peruvian cordillera, Arguedas lost his mother at an early age. He suffered mistreatment at the hands of his stepmother and stepbrother and was subsequently raised by two Quechua households. Arguedas thus spent key years of his childhood speaking primarily Quechua, which he considered his native language; he also imbibed Quechua ethical values and appreciation for nature. The deeply personal body of literature that Arguedas produced before committing suicide in 1969 demonstrates both his appreciation for Andean Indigenous cultures and his sensitivity to Peru's long history of colonial oppression, exploitation, and racial violence. He is celebrated in particular for his ability to evoke in Spanish the metaphorical registers and syntax of Quechua. Arguedas's major works of fiction include *Of All Bloods* (1964) and *The Fox from Up Above and the Fox from Down Below* (1971); he was also an accomplished anthropologist. For many readers, however, Arguedas's greatest achievement is his semiautobiographical novel of 1958, *Deep Rivers*, one of the earliest and most sensitive works of magical realism in Latin American fiction. The excerpt presented here is the fifth chapter, "Bridge over the World," in which the narrator recollects his experience at a boarding school run by hypocritical and narrow-minded Catholic priests. Romantic fantasies and sojourns to the surrounding countryside provide a desperately needed respite from an institution in which older, wealthier boys—members of the creole elite—are tacitly permitted to sexually abuse an intellectually disabled woman who works there.

***

"Bridge over the World" (1958)

TRANSLATED BY FRANCES HORNING BARRACLOUGH

I looked forward to Sundays, when I set out on long walks in the country. On other days I banished the evil from my mind by thinking of my father, by inventing great deeds to try to accomplish when I became a man, or by letting my thoughts dwell on that young girl with the beautiful countenance who lived in the cruel village of the *capuli* orchards. And as I recalled her image, other younger girls would come into my mind, one of whom might perhaps pay more attention to me and be able to divine and take for her own my dreams, my memories of journeys, of the rivers and mountains I had seen, of the sheer cliffs and wide plains populated with lakes that I had crossed. But she should be small and slender with blue eyes and braids.

But on many afternoons I, too, would follow the bigger boys to the inner courtyard and contaminate myself watching them. They were like goblins, like the monsters who appear in nightmares, moving their hairy arms and legs. When I returned from the dark courtyard the expressions of some of them, the anguished, smothered, burning sounds they made as they moaned or howled triumphantly, followed me. There was still light at that hour; the setting sun illumined the rooftops. The sky, yellow as honey, seemed to be aflame. And we had nowhere to go. The walls, the ground, the doors, our clothes, the sky at that hour—so strange and shallow, like a hard roof of golden light—all seemed contaminated, lost, or full of anger. No thought, no memory could penetrate the mortal isolation that separated me from the world at such times. I, who felt as if even the things owned by others were mine. The first time I saw a line of beautiful weeping willows shimmering on the bank of a stream I could not believe that those trees might belong to someone else. The rivers were always mine, the bushes that grew on the mountain slopes, the village houses with their red roofs streaked with lime, the blue fields of alfalfa, the beloved valleys filled with maize. But at the time I'd return from the courtyard, at dusk, this maternal image of the world would fall from my eyes. And at nightfall my feelings of loneliness and isolation grew more intense. Even though I was surrounded by boys my own age and by other people, the dormitory was more frightening and desolate than the deep gorge of Los Molinos, where I had once been abandoned by my father when he was being pursued.[1]

The valley of Los Molinos was a rather steep-walled canyon, through the depths of which a little river flowed between giant boulders and spiky shrubs. The water swirled under the rocks. In the still pools, almost hidden in the shadow of the rocks, swam some swift, silvery, needlelike fish. Five stone mills, ranked one below another in the least precipitous part of the gorge, were turned by the same water. The water came through a narrow aqueduct of stone and lime which the Spaniards had made, cutting long tunnels through the living rock. The road uniting the valley with the nearest towns was almost as narrow as the aqueduct and, like it, clung to the face of the cliff, with long sections under a roof of rock; horsemen had to bend over there and could see the river rushing through the bottom of the ravine. The soil was yellow and sticky. In the rainy season the road stayed closed; even mountain goats slipped in the yellow clay. The sun rose late and disappeared soon after midday. Its rays crept slowly up the rocky walls of the canyon, rising like a warm liquid. And so, while the mountain peaks were alight, the valley of Los Molinos was left in shadow.

In that gorge I lived, abandoned, for several months; I wept aloud at night; I wanted to leave but feared the road, with its dark stretches tunneled through the living rock, and the narrow trail, a mere trace in the yellow clay which, in the blackness of the night, seemed aglow with a soft, hazy, blinding light. I'd get up at moonrise. The mill gear thundered; the immense river boulders crowned with dry bushes awaited me and I could not get by them. The little bridge of eucalyptus trunks covered with yellow dirt shook at the first tread of the traveler.

But even there, in that chill gorge that buried its inhabitants, alone, in the care of a feeble, old, almost blind Indian, I never lost hope. The fish in the pools, the great sun that sped across the sky, the goldfinches that hovered over the threshing floors, and the mills that laboriously ground out the flour, the dust-covered shrouds on the crosses hanging on the mill wall, the riverbed, tangled and wild as it was—all of these gave me courage. I lived trembling with fear, not because I had been left behind but because the gorge was so dark and until then I had always lived in level valleys bright with maternal fields of maize, and I needed companionship to conquer my fear and explore calmly and fearlessly the boulders, tunnels, and enormous upended rocks of that gloomy, uninhabited riverbed.

I recalled this, recalled it and relived it in moments of great loneliness. But what I really experienced those nights in the dormitory was a feeling of horror, not as if I had once again fallen into the gloomy, isolated gorge of Los Molinos, but rather into an ever wider and deeper crevasse in the ice, where no voice or encouragement from the busy world could reach me.

That was why I dashed out of school on Sundays to go walking through the fields until I'd become dazed by the fiery heat of the valley.

I'd go down the road to the sugar cane fields, seeking the big river. As I descended, the road became dustier and the heat more intense. The *pisonayes* formed patches of woodlands; the pepper trees became taller and thicker trunked. The Peruvian pepper tree, which in the warm mountains is translucent, with musical red seeds that chime like tiny cymbals when the wind blows, was here in the depths of the blazing valley transformed into a tall, large-crowned tree, covered with dirt, seemingly overcome with sleep, its fruit blurred by the dust, submerged, as I was, in the dense, scorched air.

Sometimes I managed, after hours of walking, to reach the river. I would come to it just as I was feeling sore and exhausted, and would contemplate it, as I stood on the side of the great bridge, leaning against one of the stone crosses that are set up on top of the central pillars.

A smooth bend of the river, the awesome Pachachaca, appeared before me, winding round the base of a cliff on which only blue-flowered vines were growing. The large migratory parrots use that cliff as a resting place; they cling to the vines and their shrieking calls come down from on high.

The calm, rippling current of the river flows slowly eastward; the long boughs of the *chachacomo* bushes graze the surface of its waters, are swept under, and spring back violently on freeing themselves from the current. It looks like a river of molten steel, blue and smiling, despite its solemnity and depth. A chill wind flows over the top of the bridge.

The Pachachaca bridge was built by the Spaniards. Its two high arches are supported by pillars of stone and lime, as powerful as the river. The abutments that canalize the waters are built upon the rocks and oblige the river to go rushing and tumbling along through the imposed channels. On the pillars of the arches, the river breaks and divides; the water rises to lap at the wall, tries to climb it, and then rushes headlong through the spans of the bridge. At dusk, the spray that splashes from the columns forms fleeting rainbows that swirl in the wind.

I didn't know if I loved the river or the bridge more. But both of them cleansed my soul, flooding it with courage and heroic dreams. All of the mournful images, doubts, and evil memories were erased from my mind.

And thus renewed and brought back to myself, I would return to town, resolutely climbing the dreadful slope, holding mental conversations with my old distant friends, Don Maywa, Don Demetrio Pumaylly, and Don Pedro Kokchi . . . those who had brought me up and made my heart like their own.

For many days afterward I felt alone, completely isolated. I felt I should be like the great river, crossing the land, cutting through the rocks, undetainably and serenely flowing through mountains and forests, and entering the sea accompanied by a huge nation of birds that sang from the heavens.

On those days I didn't need my little friends. I was exalted by my decision to march along invincibly.

"Like you, Pachachaca River!" I would say to myself.

And I could go into the dark courtyard, walk back and forth across its dusty ground, go up to the board fence, and return to the light of the main courtyard, feeling prouder and calmer. I even pitied the feeble-minded woman; I grieved to remember how she was beaten and fought over with implacable brutality, how they banged her head against the board fence and the base of the toilets, and how she fled down the passageway, running like a hunted bear. And the poor young men who pursued her, and then defiled themselves to the point of feeling the need to flagellate themselves and cry out under the weight of repentance.

Yes! I must be like that clear, imperturbable river, like its conquering waters. Like you, Pachachaca! Handsome, glossy-maned steed, who runs undetainably and unceasingly along the deepest of earthly roads!

Note

1. For years, during Arguedas's childhood, his father suffered from political persecution.

Clarice Lispector

Born in western Ukraine, Clarice Lispector (1920–77) suffered, in her early years, famine, war, and violent antisemitism. When the family arrived in northeastern Brazil in 1922, Clarice's father made a meager living selling rags; her mother died a few years later. Despite the family's poverty, Clarice and her sister were encouraged to pursue educational opportunities their parents had been denied (Moser 2015). She entered law school at the University of Brazil but left to work as a journalist, at which she excelled. At twenty-three Lispector published her first novel, *Near the Wild Heart*, and was celebrated as a major talent in the modernist style of Joyce and Woolf. Despite such success, she married and left Brazil to accompany her diplomat husband on postings in Italy and the United States. Unhappy in the relationship, Lispector missed Brazil and her work as a journalist, but financial security enabled her to continue writing while raising two children. Her career reignited when the family settled in Rio de Janeiro in the early 1960s. Lispector's many novels and story collections—among them *The Chandelier* (1946), *The Besieged City* (1949), *The Passion According to G.H.* (1964), *The Stream of Life* (1973), *The Hour of the Star* (1977), and *Family Ties* (1960)—consistently ignored social problems, preferring to focus instead on the self and its reactions to external objects and events. These existential speculations are written in a brilliantly inventive, lyrical, and metaphorical style using interior monologues and stream of consciousness. In this selection from *The Passion According to G.H.*, the death of a cockroach sparks a metaphysical crisis and an expansion of consciousness beyond humanity.

***

From *The Passion According to G.H.* (1964)

TRANSLATED BY IDRA NOVEY

Each eye reproduced the entire cockroach.

—Pardon me for giving you this, hand holding mine, but I don't want this for myself! take that roach, I don't want what I saw.

There I was open-mouthed and offended and withdrawn—faced with the dusty being looking back at me. Take what I saw: because what I was seeing with an embarrassment so painful and so frightened and so innocent, what I was seeing was life looking back at me.

How else could I describe that crude and horrible, raw matter and dry plasma, that was there, as I shrank into myself with dry nausea, I falling centuries and centuries inside a mud—it was mud, and not even dried mud but mud still damp and still alive, it was a mud in which the roots of my identity were still shifting with unbearable slowness.

Take it, take all this for yourself, I don't want to be a living person! I'm disgusted and amazed by myself, thick mud slowly oozing.

That's what it was—so that's what it was. Because I'd looked at the living roach and was discovering inside it the identity of my deepest life. In a difficult demolition, hard and narrow paths were opening within me.

I looked at it, at the roach: I hated it so much that I was going over to its side, feeling solidarity with it, since I couldn't stand being left alone with my aggression.

And all of a sudden I moaned out loud, this time I heard my moan. Because rising to my surface like pus was my truest matter—and with fright and loathing I was feeling that "I-being" was coming from a source far prior to the human source and, with horror, much greater than the human.

Opening in me, with the slowness of stone doors, opening in me was the wide life of silence, the same that was in the fixed sun, the same that was in the immobilized roach. And that could be the same as in me! if I had the courage to abandon . . . to abandon my feelings? If I had the courage to abandon hope.

Hope for what? For the first time I was astonished to feel that I'd based an entire hope on becoming something that I was not. The hope—what other name could I give it?—that for the first time I now was going to abandon, out of courage and mortal curiosity. Had hope, in my prior life, been based upon a truth? With childlike surprise, I was starting to doubt it.

To find out what I really could hope for, would I first have to pass through my truth? To what extent had I invented a destiny now, while subterraneously living from another?

I closed my eyes, waiting for the astonishment to pass, waiting for my panting to calm to the point that it was no longer that awful moan that I'd heard as if coming from the bottom of a dry, deep cistern, as the cockroach was a creature of a dry cistern. I was still feeling, at an incalculable distance within me, that moan that was no longer reaching my throat.

This is madness, I thought with my eyes closed. But it was so undeniable feeling that birth from inside the dust—that all I could do was follow something I was well aware wasn't madness, it was, my God, the worse truth, the horrible one. But why horrible? Because without words it contradicted everything I used to think also without words.

I waited for the astonishment to pass, for health to return. But I was realizing, in an immemorial effort of memory, that I had felt this astonishment before: it was the same one I had experienced when I saw my own blood outside of me, and I had marveled at it. Since the blood I was seeing outside of me, that blood I was drawn to with such wonder: it was mine.

I didn't want to open my eyes, I didn't want to keep on seeing. It was important not to forget the rules and the laws, to remember that without the rules and laws there would be no order, I had to not forget them and defend them in order to defend myself.

But it was already too late for me to hold myself back.

The first bind had already involuntarily burst, and I was breaking loose from the law, though I intuited that I was going to enter the hell of living matter—what kind of hell awaited me? but I had to go. I had to sink into my soul's damnation, curiosity was consuming me.

So I opened my eyes all at once, and saw the full endless vastness of the room, that room that was vibrating in silence, laboratory of hell.

The room, the unknown room. My entrance into it was finally complete.

The entrance to this room had a single passageway, and a narrow one: through the cockroach. The cockroach that was filling the room with finally open vibration, the vibrations of its rattlesnake tails in the desert. Through a painstaking route, I had reached the deep incision in the wall that was that room—and the crevice created a vast, natural hollow hall as in a cave.

Naked, as if prepared for the entrance of a single person. And whoever entered would be transformed into a "she" or "he." I was the one the room called "she." An I had gone in which the room had given a dimension of she. As if I too were the other side of the cube, the side that goes unseen when looked at straight on.

And in my great dilation, I was in the desert. How can I explain it to you? in the desert as I'd never been before. It was a desert that was calling me as a monotonous and remote canticle calls. I was being seduced. And I was going toward that promising madness. But my fear wasn't that of someone going toward madness, but toward a truth—my fear was of having a truth that I'd come not to want, an infamizing truth that would make me crawl along and be on the roach's level. My first contact with truths always defamed me.

—Hold my hand, because I feel that I'm going. I'm going once again toward the most divine primary life, I'm going toward a hell of raw life. Don't let me see because I'm close to seeing the nucleus of life—and, through the cockroach that even now I'm seeing again, through this specimen of calm living horror, I'm afraid that in this nucleus I'll no longer know what hope is.

The cockroach is pure seduction. Cilia, blinking cilia that keep calling.

I too, who was slowly reducing myself to whatever in me was irreducible, I too had thousands of blinking cilia, and with my cilia I move forward, I protozoan, pure protein. Hold my hand, I reached the irreducible with the inevitability of a death-knell—I sense that all this is ancient and vast, I sense in the hieroglyph of the slow roach the writing of the Far East. And in this desert of great seductions, the creatures: I and the living roach. Life, my love, is a great seduction in which all that exists seduces. That room that was deserted and for that reason primally alive. I had reached the nothing, and the nothing was living and moist.

Esteban Montejo

Esteban Montejo (1860–1973) was a slave on a Cuban sugar plantation, a fugitive in the forest, a soldier in the war for national independence, and a hired hand in the rural economy of the early twentieth century. After the 1959 revolution he also became the subject of a book, *Biography of a Runaway Slave*, written by anthropologist Miguel Barnet on the basis of many hours of recorded interviews with Montejo. Their collaboration produced one of only two firsthand accounts of the life of an enslaved person in Latin America. *Biography of a Runaway Slave* is also one of the richest and most expansive representations of a Black Latin American's experience of nonhuman nature in the nineteenth century. While the text is undoubtedly informed by the ideals and concerns of the Cuban Revolution and its aftermath, the excerpt presented here nevertheless stands as a much-needed counterpoint to representations of plantation ecology and relations between the enslaved and nonhuman nature produced by white elites such as André João Antonil and Gertrudis González de Avellaneda. Like Cabrera's ethnographic book *The Woods*, "Life in the Woods" represents the forest as a refuge from the dehumanizing violence of the plantation. The chapter recalls the years Montejo spent alone after escaping from captivity, hiding in the wilderness to avoid being taken by slave hunters. Anecdotes from life on the plantation are interwoven with recollections of hunting and foraging in the woods and on nearby farms. Montejo describes his former self as "half wild" and utterly self-sufficient, living in intimate contact with bats, birds, and other creatures and treating his ailments with medicinal plants. Montejo's satisfaction regarding his years in the woods stands in contrast to his life as a waged laborer, which painfully re-creates the conditions of slavery.

***

"Life in the Woods" (1966)

TRANSLATED BY W. NICK HILL

I have never forgotten the first time I tried to run away. That time I failed and spent a number of years enslaved by the fear they would put the shackles on me again. But I had the spirit of a cimarrón in me, and it didn't go away. I kept quiet about things so nobody could betray me because I was always thinking about escaping. It went round and round in my head and wouldn't leave me in peace. It was an idea that never left me and sometimes even sapped my energy. The old Blacks were not kindly towards running away. The women even less so. Runaways, there weren't many. People were afraid of the woods. They said that if some slaves escaped, they would be caught anyway. But for me that idea went around in my head more than any other. I always had the fantasy that I would enjoy being in the forest. And I knew that working in the fields was like living in hell. You couldn't do anything on your own. Everything depended on the master's orders.

One day I began to watch the overseer. I had already been studying him. That dog got stuck in my eyes, and I couldn't get him out. I think he was a Spaniard. I remember that he was tall and never took his hat off. All the Blacks had respect for him because one of the whippings he gave could strip the skin off of just about anybody. The thing is, one day I was riled up, and I don't know what got into me, but I was mad, and just seeing him set me off.

I whistled at him from a distance, and he looked around and then turned his back. That's when I picked up a rock and threw it at his head. I know it hit him because he shouted for someone to grab me. But he never saw me again because that day I made it into the woods.

I traveled many days without any clear direction. I was sort of lost. I had never left the plantation. I walked uphill and downhill, all around. I know I got to a farm near Siguanea, where I had no choice but to camp. My feet were full of blisters and my hands were swollen. I camped under a tree. I stayed there no more than four or five days. All I had to do was hear the first human voice close by, and I would take off fast. It would have been real shitty if you got caught right after escaping.

I came to hide in a cave for a time. I lived there for a year and a half. I went in there thinking that I would have to walk less and because the pigs from around the farms, the plots, and the small landholdings used to come to a kind of swamp just outside the mouth of the cave. They went to take a bath and wallow around. I caught them easy enough because big bunches of them came. Every week I had a pig. That cave was very big and dark like the mouth of the wolf. It was called Guajabán. It was near the town of Remedios. It was dangerous because it had no way out. You had to go in through the entrance and leave by the entrance. My curiosity really poked me to find a way out. But I preferred to remain in the mouth of the cave on account of the snakes. The majases are very dangerous beasts. They are found in caves and in the woods. Their breath can't be felt, but they knock people down with it, and then they put people to sleep to suck out their blood. That's why I always stayed alert and lit a fire to scare them away. If you fall asleep in a cave, be ready for the wake. I didn't want to see a majá, not even from a distance. The Congos, and this is true, told me that those snakes lived more than a thousand years. And as they approached two thousand, they became serpents again, and they would return to the ocean to live like any other fish.

Inside, the cave was like a house. A little darker, naturally. Oh, and dung, yes, the smell of bat dung. I walked on it because it was as soft as a mattress. The bats led a life of freedom in the caves. They were and are the masters of them. All over the world it's like that. Since no one kills them, they live a long time. Not as long as the snakes, for sure. The dung they drop works afterward as fertilizer. It becomes dust, and it's thrown on the ground to make pasture for animals and to fertilize crops.

One time that place nearly burned up. I lit a fire, and it spread all through the cave. The bat shit was to blame. After slavery I told the story to a Congo. The story that I had lived with the bats, and that joker, they could sometimes be more jokers than you might imagine, he said: "Listen here, boy, you know nothin'. In my country that thing what you call a bat is big like a pigeon." I knew that was a tall tale. They fooled nearly everyone with those stories. But I heard it, and smiled inside.

The cave was quiet. The only sound always there was the bats going: "Chwee, chwee, chwee." They didn't know how to sing. But they talked to each other and understood each other. I saw that one would say "Chewy, chewy, chewy," and the bunch would go wherever he went. They were very united about things. Bats have no wings. They're nothing but a cloth with a little black head, very dirty, and if you get up real close, you'll see they look like rats. In the cave I was summering, you might say. What I really liked was the woods, and after a year and a half I left that darkness behind. I took to the footpaths. I went into the woods in Siguanea again. I spent a long time there. I took care of myself like a spoiled child. I didn't want to be chained to slavery again. For me that was disgusting. I've always thought so. Slavery was a nuisance. I still think so today.

I was careful about all the sounds I made. And of the fires. If I left a track, they could follow my path and catch me. I climbed up and down so many hills that my legs and arms got as hard as sticks. Little by little I got to know the woods. And I was getting to like them. Sometimes I would forget I was a cimarrón, and I would start to whistle. Early on I used to whistle to get over the fear. They say that when you whistle, you chase away the evil spirits. But being a cimarrón in the woods you had to be on the lookout. I didn't start whistling again because the guajiros, or the slave catchers, could come. Since the cimarrón was a slave who had escaped, the masters sent a posse of rancheadores after them. Mean guajiros with hunting dogs so they could drag you out of the woods in their jaws. I never ran into any of them. I never seen one of those dogs up close. They were trained to catch Blacks. If a dog saw a Black man, he ran after him. If by chance I heard one barking nearby, I took my clothes right off because the dog can't smell anybody naked like that. When I see a dog now, nothing happens, but if I seen one then, all of me you would see would be my heels. I've never been attracted to dogs. To my mind they have wicked instincts . . .

All the leaves in the woods have uses. Tobacco or mulberry leaves work for bites. Whenever I saw that the bite of some bug was going to get swollen up on me, I took hold of the tobacco leaf, and I chewed it well. Then I put it on the bite, and the swelling went down. Often when it was cold, an ache seeped into my bones. It was a dry pain that didn't go away. To rid myself of it I made a brew of rosemary leaves, and it went away right then. The cold also gave me a bad cough. The sniffles and a cough was what I got. That was when I picked a big leaf and put it on my chest. I never found out the name of that leaf, but it gave off a whitish liquid that was very warm. That soothed my cough. When I got very cold my eyes would water up, and they itched in a very bothersome way. The same thing happened to me with the sun. In that case I would put out a few leaves of the itamo plant to catch the dew, and the next day clean my eyes with them. Itamo is the best thing there is for that.

Nowadays what they sell in the pharmacy is itamo. What happens is that they put it in little jars, and it seems like something else. As one gets old, the thing with your eyes goes away. I haven't suffered from itching for many years.

I smoked the leaf of the macaw tree. I made well-rolled, tightly-packed cigars with it. After I left the woods, I didn't smoke tobacco any more, but while I was a cimarrón, I smoked it all the time.

And I drank coffee. I made coffee with guanina leaf. I had to grind the leaf with a bottle. After it was well broken up, I boiled it, and then it was coffee. You could always put a little wild honey in it to give it flavor. With the honey the coffee gave strength to the body. You're always fortified when you live in the woods.

Carlos Drummond de Andrade

Carlos Drummond de Andrade (1902–87) was one of Brazil's most important and accomplished poets. Born into a landowning family in Minas Gerais, Drummond attended secondary school in Belo Horizonte and became licensed in pharmacy in 1925. By the late 1920s he was active in literary and intellectual circles. Drummond published his first collection of poems, *Some Poetry*, in 1930; dedicated to Mario de Andrade, it opens with the famous "Seven-Sided Poem." Drummond was one of a group of young poets who were developing a Brazilian modernist style based on the use of colloquial language and unconventional syntax in free verse. In the mid-1930s Drummond moved to Rio de Janeiro, where he spent several decades working for the Brazilian government, ultimately serving as director of the National Historical and Artistic Heritage Service. Meanwhile, Drummond produced roughly fifteen volumes of poetry and a half dozen collections of *crônicas*, a short, informal genre of journalism. The poem presented here is "Farewell to the Seven Falls." It was written while the dictatorships of Brazil and Paraguay were building Itaipú Dam, a massive hydroelectric power plant on the Paraná River. The creation of the artificial lake that feeds Itaipú displaced tens of thousands of residents and drastically altered regional ecosystems. The project also destroyed one of South America's most stunning topographical features, the massive cataracts known to Brazilians as the Seven Falls and to Paraguayans as Guairá Falls. Amid the outpouring of grief and rage, Drummond published his poem in large type on a full page in the newspaper *Journal do Brasil*. Soon after the submerged rock was dynamited to ensure smooth transit of the river, destroying the falls forever.

***

"Farewell to the Seven Falls" (1982)

TRANSLATED BY CHARLES A. PERRONE

> Seven ladies have come my way,
> And all seven have come to kiss me. —ALPHONSUS DE GUIMARAENS

> Here in times past hymns did resound. —RAIMUNDO CORREIA

Seven falls have come my way,
and all seven have vanished.

The roar of the waterfalls comes to an end,
and with that, the memory of the Indians, shattered,
no longer arouses the slightest shiver.
The dead Spaniards, the dead pioneers,
the extinguished fires
of the royal city of Guaira will be joined
by the seven ghosts of the waters murdered
at the hands of men, masters of the planet.

Here in times past did voices resound
of an imaginative Nature, fertile
in theatrical stagings of dreams
offered to man with no contracts.
A beauty-unto-itself, a fantastic design embodied
in bubblings and black clouds of aerial contour,
would show itself, disrobe, consecrate freely
coitus before enraptured human eyes.
All the architecture, all the engineering
of distant Egyptians and Assyrians
could never hope to create such a monument.

And it is being dismantled
by the ungrateful meddling of technocrats.
Here seven visions, seven sculptures
with liquid profiles
dissolve in the midst of computerized calculations
of a country that is losing its humanity
to become an icy enterprise, nothing more.

Movement is made into a dam,
turbulence is made into the silence
of a business, a hydroelectric project.
Let us offer all the comforts
that tariffed light and power generate
at the cost of another benefit that is priceless
that is irreplaceable, impoverishing life
under the fierce illusion of enriching it.
Seven herds of water, seven white bulls,
of billions of intermingled white bulls,
sink into a lake, and in the void
that no form will ever fill, what is left
except the gestureless pain of Nature,
the silenced censure
the curse that time will unfailingly bring?

Come ye foreign peoples, come ye Brazilian
brothers of all countenances
come see and keep
no longer the natural work of art
today a melancholic postcard
but rather its specter still bedewed
with iridescent pearls of foam and ire,
passing, flying around
between destroyed suspension bridges
and the useless weeping of things,
tears powerless to stir remorse,
no confessed burning guilt.
("We assume responsibility!"
We are building a great Brazil!")
And yada yada blah blah blah . . .

Seven falls came our way,
and, ah, we knew not how to love them,
and all seven were killed,
and all seven vanish in the air,
seven ghosts, seven crimes
of the living pummeling life
that will never be reborn.

Rigoberta Menchú

A member of the K'iche' Maya ethnic group of Guatemala's north-central highlands, Rigoberta Menchú (b. 1959) received the 1992 Nobel Peace Prize in recognition of her role in Guatemala's national reconciliation following decades of civil war, a conflict stretching back to the 1954 overthrow of Jacobo Árbenz in a coup backed by the CIA. Menchú became known internationally after the publication of *I, Rigoberta Menchú: An Indian Woman in Guatemala*, in 1983. The book was coproduced with anthropologist Elisabeth Burgos, based on a weeklong series of interviews that Burgos transcribed, edited, and arranged in a format resembling that of a European-style memoir or autobiography. It more properly belongs to the Latin American genre known as *testimonio*, which refers to a firsthand account produced in order to draw attention to a critical situation of political or socioeconomic injustice. Menchú's account has been the subject of controversy since the 1999 publication of *Rigoberta Menchú and the Story of All Poor Guatemalans*, by U.S. anthropologist David Stoll. Stoll reported certain factual inconsistencies between Menchú's narrative and information provided by other members of her community; more generally, Stoll takes issue with Menchú's framing of the conflict in patterns of landownership stretching back to the colonial period. Menchú's defenders continue to assert the fundamental validity of her account within a larger historical narrative of land and natural-resource usurpation, political and cultural disenfranchisement, and genocidal violence. The selections here come from the early ethnographic sections of the book, which describe the abusive working conditions on the coffee plantation, including the farmers' use of toxic chemicals and their effects on the workers, in stark contrast to Mayan relations with the land and with nonhuman nature more broadly.

***

From *I, Rigoberta Menchú: An Indian Woman in Guatemala* (1983)

TRANSLATED BY ANN WRIGHT

Chapter VII. Death of Her Little Brother in the *Finca*. Difficulty of Communicating with Other Indians

We'd been in the *finca* for fifteen days, when one of my brothers died from malnutrition. My mother had to miss some days' work to bury him. Two of my brothers died in the *finca*. The first, he was the eldest, was called Felipe. I never knew him.

He died when my mother started working. They'd sprayed the coffee with pesticide by plane while we were working, as they usually did, and my brother couldn't stand the fumes and died of intoxication. The second one, I did see die. His name was Nicolás. He died when I was eight. He was the youngest of all of us, the one my mother used to carry about. He was two then. When my little brother started crying, crying, crying, my mother didn't know what to do with him because his belly was swollen by malnutrition too. His belly was enormous and my mother didn't know what to do about it. The time came when my mother couldn't spend any more time with him or they'd take her job away from her. My brother had been ill from the day we arrived in the *finca*, very ill. My mother kept on working and so did we. He lasted fifteen days and then went into his death throes, and we didn't know what to do. Our neighbours from our village had gone to different *fincas*, there were only two with us. We weren't all together. We didn't know what to do because in our group we were with people from other communities who spoke different languages. We couldn't talk to them. We couldn't speak Spanish either. We couldn't understand each other and we needed help. Who was there to turn to? There was no-one we could count on, least of all the overseer, he might even throw us out of the *finca*. We couldn't count on the owner, we didn't even know who he was since he always did everything through intermediaries: the overseers, the contracting agents etc. So that's how it was. When my mother needed help to bury my brother, we couldn't talk to anyone, we couldn't communicate, and she was desolate at the sight of my brother's body. I remember only being able to communicate with the others through signs. Most of them have had the same experiences; every day they're stuck in situations in which they can't call on help from outside and have to help each other. But it was very difficult. I remember also wanting to make friends with the children who lived in our shed with us—we were three hundred . . . four hundred people working in the *finca*—but we couldn't get to know each other.

Chapter X. The Natural World. The Earth, Mother of Man

From very small children we receive an education which is very different from white children, *ladinos*. We Indians have more contact with nature. That's why they call us polytheistic. But we're not polytheistic . . . or if we are, it's good, because it's our culture, our customs. We worship—or rather not worship but respect—a lot of things to do with the natural world, the most important things for us. For instance, to us, water is sacred. Our parents tell us when we're very small not to waste water, even when we have it. Water is pure, clean, and gives life to man. Without water we cannot survive, nor could our ancestors have survived. The idea that water is sacred is in us children, and we never stop thinking of it as something pure. The same goes for the earth. Our parents tell us: "Children, the earth is the mother of man, because she gives him food." This is especially true for us whose life is based on the crops we grow. Our people eat maize, beans and plants. We can't eat ham, or cheese, or things made with equipment, with machines. So we think of the earth as the mother of man, and our parents teach us to respect the earth. We must only harm the earth when we are in need. This is why, before we sow our maize, we have to ask the earth's permission.

Pom, copal, is a sacred ingredient for our people. We use it to express our feelings for the earth, so that she will allow us to cultivate her. *Copal* is the resin of a tree. It has a smell like incense. We burn it and it gives off a very strong smell: a smoke with a very rich, delicious aroma. We use the candle, water and lime a great deal in our ceremonies. We use candles to represent the earth, water and maize, which is the food of man. We believe (and this has been passed down to us by our ancestors) that our people are made of maize. We're made of white maize and yellow maize. We must remember this. We put a candle out for man, as the son of the natural world, the universe, and the members of the family join together in prayer. The prayers usually ask the earth for permission to plant our crops at sowing time, to give us a good harvest, and then to give thanks with all our might, with all our being, for a good harvest.

The prayers and ceremonies are for the whole community. We pray to our ancestors, reciting their prayers which have been known to us for a long time—a very, very long time. We evoke the representatives of the animal world; we say the names of dogs. We say the names of the earth, the God of the earth, and the God of water. Then we say the name of the heart of the sky—the Sun. Our grandfathers say we must ask the sun to shine on all its children: the trees, animals, water, man. We ask it to shine on our enemies. To us an enemy is someone who steals or goes into prostitution. So, you see, it's a different world. This is how we make our pleas and our promises. It doesn't refer so much to the real world, but it includes part of our reality. A prayer is made up of all this. We make a definite plea to the earth. We say: "Mother Earth, you who gives us food, whose children we are and on whom we depend, please make this produce you give us flourish and make our children and our animals grow . . . ," and other things as well. Or we say: "We make our vows for ten days so that you concede us permission, your permission, Mother Earth, who are sacred, to feed us and give our children what they need. We do not abuse you, we only beg your permission, you who are part of the natural world and part of the family of our parents and our grandparents." This means we believe, for instance, that the sun is our grandfather, that he is a member of our family. "We respect you and love you and ask that you love us as we love you"—those prayers are specially for the earth. For the sun, we say: "Heart of the sky, you are our father, we ask you to give your warmth and light to our animals, our maize, our beans, our plants, so that they may grow and our children may eat." We evoke the colour of the sun, and this has a special importance for us because this is how we want our children to live—like a light which shines, which shines with generosity. It means a warm heart and it means strength, life-giving strength. It's something you never lose and you find it everywhere. So when we evoke the colour of the sun, it's like evoking all the elements which go to make up our life. The sun, as the channel to the one God, receives the plea from his children that they should never violate the rights of all the other beings which surround them. This is how we renew our prayer which says that men, the children of the one God, must respect the life of the trees, the birds, the animals around us. We say the names of birds and animals—cows, horses, dogs, cats. All these. We mention them all. We must respect the life of every single one of them. We must respect the life, the purity, the sacredness, which is water. We must respect the one God, the heart of the sky, which is the sun. We must not do evil while the sun shines upon his children. This is a promise. Then we promise to respect the life of the one creature, which is man. This is very important. We say: "We cannot harm the life of one of your children, we are your children. We cannot kill any of your creatures, neither trees nor animals." Then we offer up a sheep or chickens, because we believe sheep to be sacred animals, quiet animals, saintly animals, animals which don't harm other animals. They are the most tranquil animals that exist, like birds. So the community chooses certain small animals for the feast after the ceremonies.

SEVEN

Neoliberalism and Globalization

The concept of globalization conventionally refers to processes of international economic integration that accelerated significantly in the 1980s and '90s. Globalization was stimulated, economically, by the drop in transport costs after the oil crisis of the previous decade; technologically, by the emergence of the internet, email, and cell-phone communications; and politically, by the privatization of public companies and resources and the deregulation of industries and financial markets associated with neoliberalism. The idea of development, the focus of the previous section, does not entirely disappear from public discourse in Latin America, but the strong, activist state that formerly had a central role in economic decision-making is replaced by the famous "invisible hand" of capitalist markets. In fact, the debt crises faced by several of the region's formerly powerful states during the 1980s and '90s resulted in economic austerity measures that eroded workers' rights and intensified exploitation of natural resources in those countries. The selections gathered here demonstrate some of globalization's most baleful impacts on the human and nonhuman communities of Latin America but also the emergence of a new global environmental consciousness, including linkages among activists in locations around the world and a growing awareness of the human and ecological costs of modernization.

Unlike previous economic linkages, globalization is understood to be multi-nodal, meaning that commodities, money, and people now follow diverse and ever-changing pathways as they "flow" around the world. This is true to an extent: as new centers of economic power have arisen in some parts of the postcolonial world, particularly in Asia and the oil-rich Middle East, the spread of the internet and other forms of electronic communication have simultaneously enabled a powerful new South-South intellectual and cultural dialogue to emerge, in some cases effectively bypassing the former metropolitan centers of Western Europe and the United States. But if the structures of domination of the old, colonial world have become a bit less visible, hardly have they gone away. As the critic Mary Louise Pratt (2002, 3) points out in her powerful critique of the concept of globalization and its central metaphor, in recent years the world's wealth has flowed faster than ever from poor countries into rich ones, especially the United States. This perverse financial flow—or, as Pratt wryly suggests, "drainage" —has taken place amid a global crisis of human uprootedness spurred by political violence, lack of economic opportunity, natural disasters, and other manifestations of environmental degradation in the Global South.

One of neoliberalism's most important proponents was Ronald Reagan, president of the United States from 1981 to 1989. Reagan popularized the concepts of "laissez-faire" and "trickle-down" economics, arguing at home that markets work best without outside intervention and that society as a whole benefits from policies that most obviously and immediately benefit the rich. Meanwhile in Central America, Reagan's foreign-policy team worked assiduously to bring down the governments of people who thought otherwise. In some Southern Cone countries, neoliberal economic policies were forcibly imposed by military dictatorships that tortured and terrorized the opposition out of existence and then proceeded to privatize and deregulate formerly national industries and other resources. In the case of Chile, one of the most brazenly murderous dictators in the history of Latin America, General Augusto Pinochet (in office 1973–90), turned away from both industrialization and mining in order to focus Chile's economy on export agriculture (Halperín Donghi 1993, 349). The results of that decision, made on the advice of Milton Friedman and his disciples at the University of Chicago, can be observed every day at grocery stores across the United States, which sell apples, grapes, and other produce that travels all the way from the southern hemisphere in order to provide off-season fruits to consumers. This is what sociologist Fernando Mires (1990, 62–63) refers to as "the economics of the absurd": a mode of collective decision-making so rigidly quantitative that it cannot methodologically account for nonquantifiable values, even values as seemingly fundamental as the future fertility of the soil, or the thriving—even survival—of human communities and nonhuman nature.

As the name suggests, neoliberalism is a throwback to the economic philosophy of the nineteenth and early twentieth centuries. Not surprisingly, the environmental impact of globalization bears a certain resemblance to that of the export boom of the early twentieth century, Latin America's previous experiment with free-market economics and the law of comparative advantage. Under globalization, as environmental historian J. R. McNeill (2000, 320) writes, "economic integration focused the dispersed demand of millions upon limited zones of supply. These zones were often sparsely populated frontiers, where the human touch had hitherto been light and where social restraints upon rapacity were few. The result was rapid exhaustion of commodities and transformation of ecologies." What McNeill refers to as frontier economics ran rampant in the Amazon rain forest during the wild rubber boom of the early twentieth century and took off on a previously inconceivable scale during the early 1980s, when international demand for beef and agricultural products led to the burning of hundreds of thousands of square miles. At night the orange glow of thousands of fires in the Brazilian state of Rondônia was visible to astronauts floating in the newly launched space shuttle, and the images they recorded—like the famous Blue Marble photo of 1972—touched off a new era in planetary consciousness as well as new political battles over who has the right to make decisions about the rain forest's future (Benjamin 2003).

In addition to the governments of Brazil, Colombia, Ecuador, and Peru, the contenders—to borrow the language of Ramachandra Guha and Joan Martínez-Alier (2013, 11–15)—were "ecosystem people," local communities committed to the defense of long-standing, sustainable practices; "omnivores," individuals and groups whose greater economic wherewithal enables them to utilize natural resources harvested from a larger area; and the increasingly prominent conservation organizations emanating from the United States and Europe. All of these groups had a role in the heroic life of Chico Mendes, the Brazilian rubber tapper and labor activist who became one of Latin America's most prominent "environmental martyrs" (the term belongs to critic Rob Nixon [2017]) when he was murdered by a rancher named Darci Alves da Silva in December 1988. We include among the selections gathered here an excerpt from Mendes's final interview, published posthumously as *Fight for the Forest* in 1989. Mendes's book, the outcry over his assassination, and the involvement of Sting, U2, and other rock stars called widespread international attention to the first United Nations Earth Summit, which was held in Rio de Janeiro in 1992.

The 1992 Earth Summit also brought new visibility to the political and environmental activism of Amerindian peoples and the knowledge on which it is based, an important step toward the decolonization of knowledge that is also reflected in Latin American literature of the time. This section features poetry by Juan Carlos Galeano, a non-Indigenous Amazonian writer who engages deeply and creatively with Native American traditions. Like Nicaragua's Esthela Calderón, whose wonderful ethnobotanical poems are also included here, Galeano draws on Amerindian culture and traditions in ways that are substantially different from the magical realism that emerged as a mainstream literary current during the high-water mark of developmentalism. For Galeano and Calderón, Amerindian ontologies are not atavistic reminders of the premodern margins of Latin American societies but rather active and vital forms of knowledge and culture in the present, the site of alternative, even oppositional modernities.

A critique of the Western concept of modernity and its guiding role in Latin American political and intellectual life is at the heart of Octavio Paz's 1990 Nobel lecture, "In Search of the Present." Beginning with his self-imposed exile from the walled garden of his family's home in suburban Mexico City, Paz abjures his own (and others') relentless pursuit of an ideal that is felt to be ineluctably elsewhere, perpetually postponed. For Paz, the pursuit of modernity is unavoidably linked to the degradation of environments and the immanent exhaustion of natural resources, both in Latin America and around the world.

Finally, trash. In the 1990s, Latin America's sprawling landfills became key visual signifiers of the gross disparities of wealth and poverty both within the region and around the world, reminders of the vast amounts of waste produced by contemporary consumer societies, and affirmations of the survival strategies developed by individuals living within the informal economy. In the selections from Fernando Contreras Castro's *Única Looking Out to Sea* and Gioconda Belli's *Waslala* presented here, the garbage dump is the principal axis around which the narratives develop. For Contreras Castro, the group of people living in a landfill on the outskirts of the capital of San José represent the disposable people of neoliberalism, those for whom the stripped-down state has no purpose and no need (Bales 2012). In *Waslala*, on the other hand, the far-off First World exports nuclear waste and hazardous material to a small, impoverished town, an ecological sacrifice zone where modernity's arrival signifies the absence of any future at all (Lerner 2010).

Suggestions for Further Reading

César Calvo. 1981. *The Three Halves of Ino Moxo: Teachings of the Wizard of the Upper Amazon*, translated by Kenneth A. Symington. Rochester, Vt.: Inner Traditions International, 1995.

Anacristina Rossi. 1992. *La loca de Gandoca / The Madwoman of Gandoca*, translated by Terry J. Martin. Lewiston, N.Y.: Edwin Mellen Press, 2006.

Rodrigo Rey Rosa. 1994. *Lo que soñó Sebastián*. Barcelona: Seix Barral, 1994.

Mempo Giardinelli. 1995. *An Impossible Balance*, translated by Gustavo Pellón. Newark, Del.: Juan de la Cuesta, 2010.

Julian Joven [pseudonym of Cristian Molina]. 2014. *Un pequeño mundo enfermo*. Mar del Plata, Argentina: La Bola Editora, 2014.

Chico Mendes

Francisco Alves Mendes Filho (1944–88), better known as Chico Mendes, is among the most influential of the individuals Rob Nixon (2017) calls environmental martyrs, those who have lost their lives defending forests in Latin America and throughout the Global South. Born on a Brazilian rubber plantation, Mendes began working as a rubber tapper at age nine. He became active in trade unions seeking to protect the rubber groves of the Amazon from unrestrained economic development in the form of deforestation, road building, and cattle ranching. The rubber tappers' struggle, originally articulated as an effort to preserve their own livelihoods, eventually became part of a larger struggle for Indigenous rights and environmental protection in the Amazon basin. As Mendes himself eloquently said, "At first I thought I was fighting to save rubber trees, then I thought I was fighting to save the Amazon rainforest. Now I realize I am fighting for humanity" (Haberman 2016). Mendes became an international cause célèbre when his advocacy work came to the attention of the World Wildlife Fund and the Environmental Defense Fund, which tried to convince the Inter-American Development Bank and other institutions to take up the rubber tappers' demand to create extractive preserves in the Amazon. Despite that visibility, Mendes was assassinated at his home in Xapuri by Darci Alves da Silva on December 22, 1988. The killer was the son of Darly Alves da Silva, who had recently purchased land belonging to a preserve that Mendes and his fellow trade unionists attempted to protect by blocking the access roads. The selection presented here is from Mendes's last major interview, published in 1989 as *Fight for the Forest*.

∗∗∗

"The Landowners Strike Back" (1989)

TRANSLATED BY CHRIS WHITEHOUSE

We know we face powerful opposition. As well as the landowners and businessmen who dominate the Amazon region, we are up against the power of those who voted against land reform in the Constituent Assembly. The voting power of these people in Congress has been a problem for us and has encouraged the growth of the right-wing landowners' movement, the Rural Democratic Union (UDR). The defeat of the land reform proposal was a big victory for the landowners and land speculators. Now, since the establishment of the UDR in Acre, we've got a real fight on our hands. However, we also believe our movement has never been stronger.

You can already see how strong the UDR is in Acre—it's just organised its first cattle auction to raise funds. We know, through people who have been to UDR meetings here, that their aim is to destroy the Xapuri union by striking at the grass-roots organisations of the Xapuri rubber tappers. They think if they can defeat Xapuri they can impose their terms on the whole state and further afield in the Amazon region as well. The Governor of Acre himself told me this. Just to give you an idea, it was after the UDR's official launch here in Acre that the first drops of blood were spilt in Xapuri.

The Government Takes Sides

There was a time when the state government seemed to be paying a lot of attention to environmental problems and to the rubber tappers.[1] But we soon realized it was just putting on a show of defending the environment so the international banks and other international organizations would approve its development projects.

We can't see how the authorities can say they defend the ecological system while at the same time deploying police to protect those who are destroying the forest. That happened, for example, in the case of the Ecuador rubber estate where there were many nut and rubber trees. The Governor was warned several times about what was going on there. In fact, I personally warned him and suggested he go and look at what was happening for himself. I told him he was being very hasty in sending police there. Fifty hectares of virgin forest were cut down, but thanks to the pressure, thanks to the hundreds of telegrams sent to the Governor by national and international organizations, we managed to get him to withdraw the police from the area and so saved about 300 hectares of forest.

In the area they destroyed there, the last harvest produced 1,400 cans of brazil nuts,[2] a good crop. We challenged the owner of the land and the Governor himself to work out the annual income per hectare produced by forest products such as brazil nuts and rubber and then compare it with that produced by grazing cattle there. They refused because they knew we could prove the income from one hectare of forest is 20 times greater than when the forest is cleared and given over to cattle.

We quoted decree law 7.511 of 30 July 1986 and regulation 486 of 28 October 1986, which prohibit the cutting down and sale of brazil nut and rubber trees and the deforestation of hillsides. There were two hillsides in the area being cut down on the Ecuador rubber estate and the law was completely flouted. After the second *empate*,[3] when the rubber tappers managed to stop work going ahead, the local IBDF representative appeared and without even inspecting what was going on, told the landowner he could go ahead and clear the forest. He gave the landowner a license even though the landowner did not present, as he should have done, a written plan for managing the area.

Another law—I can't remember its number—says you can only clear up to 50 hectares of forest without presenting a forestry management plan. Further on it adds that it's forbidden to cut down any area of forest on hillsides or where there is a concentration of brazil nut and rubber trees. None of these laws were respected. The Governor himself didn't even consider them and the IBDF certainly didn't.

We do have a good relationship with the Acre Technology Foundation (FUN-TAC), which is a state government agency.[4] They really understand how difficult the lives of rubber tappers are and recognize that deforestation is a problem. But despite the good relationship we've got with FUNTAC, we have no confidence left in the state government. How can we believe a Governor who says he defends the forest, and visits Rio and Japan to talk about defending the forest, but who then orders the police to go and protect the people who are destroying it? He ought to be using the political power that his office gives him. If he used his power in favor of the workers he'd certainly get their support.

Holding Back Progress

People have used all kinds of arguments against us. The landowners say we're holding back progress and harming the country's economy. They say rubber is not important to the economy and the future lies with cattle raising. Others say the Amazon is a vast expanse of uninhabited territory and that it should be developed. All kinds of reactionary arguments are used against us. Our enemies work hard at putting forward their arguments to try and undermine our own. However, the national press has now started to realize that the defense of the Amazon is really an issue.

But anyway, we can deal with the arguments that are used against us. To those who say Acre should be producing food, we say there is plenty of land for that. What are the big colonization projects supposed to be producing? Anyway, all it needs is for the government to develop an agricultural policy that takes into consideration the region's small farmers. There should be no problem about growing enough food.

The rubber tappers aren't saying that nobody should lay a finger on the Amazon. No. We've got our own proposals for organizing production. The rubber tappers and the Indians have always grown their subsistence crops but they've never threatened the existence of the forest. It's the deforestation carried out by the big landowners to open up pasture for their cattle that is threatening the forest. Often, these people are just speculating with the land. What happens in Xapuri and other parts of the Amazon is that these people cut down 10,000 hectares, turn half of it into pasture for their cattle and let the other half grow wild. They are really just involved in land speculation.

The landowners use all the economic power at their disposal. They bribe the authorities; it's common knowledge that they've bought off the IBDF staff in the Amazon region. They also use the law. They request policy protection for the workers hired to cut down the trees, saying it is their land so they can do whatever they like with it. They accuse the rubber tappers of trespassing when we try and stop deforestation. They turn to the courts for support and protection, claiming the land is private property. But the rubber tappers have been here for centuries!

There has been less pressure from the police in the last two years because we are able to present reasoned arguments to them. When we organize an *empate*, the main argument we use is that the law is being flouted by the landowners and our *empate* is only trying to make sure the law is respected.

The other tactic the landowners use, and it's a very effective one, is to use hired guns to intimidate us. Our movement's leaders, not just myself but quite a few others as well, have been threatened a lot this year. We are all on the death list of the UDR's assassination squads. Here in Xapuri, these squads are led by Darli and Alvarino Alves da Silva, owners of the Parana and other ranches round here. They lead a gang of about 30 gunmen—I say 30 because we've counted them as they patrol the town. Things have changed recently because we managed to get an arrest warrant issued in Umuarama, in the state of Parana, for the two of them. I don't know whether it was the federal police, but somebody tipped them off. Now they're both in hiding and have said they'll only give themselves up when I'm dead.

We are sure this will be the landowners' main tactic from now on. They are going to fight our movement with violence and intimidation. There's no doubt in our minds about that. The level of violence that has been common in the south of the state of Para is already spreading to Xapuri, to Acre.

Rich Men's Law

The law has always been on the side of the rich. One of our problems is how to cope with this bias in the judicial system. We often turn to it for support but it always sides with the landowners. This year the police even refused to carry out an inquiry into who shot the rubber tappers who were camped out outside the IBDF offices on 27 May 1988. The gunmen were recognized and are well known around here and witnesses have made statements to the police, but they haven't done a thing.

In the case of Ivair's death,[5] it is obvious who hired the assassins. We don't know who the killers were but we know who paid them.

Now, if you know who is behind a crime, you can easily get hold of the people responsible for carrying it out. The person who hired the killers was Cícero Tenório Cavalcanti, a candidate of the PMDB party. This is common knowledge and people have made statements to the police to this effect, but no progress has been made on the case and Cícero Cavalcanti hasn't even had to make a statement to the police.

Notes

1. The reference is to the administration of Flaviano Melo, governor of the state of Acre from 1987 to 1990. Melo represented the old local elite who controlled the rubber industry, and whose dominance was being challenged by a new elite of ranchers, mostly newcomers to Acre.

2. *Seringueiros* (rubber tappers) trade Brazil nuts using old 30-liter paraffin cans as the measure.

3. On the meaning of the Portuguese term *empate*, Tony Gross (1989, 2) writes, "In the early 1970s the Xapuri Rural Workers' Union was founded, and Chico was soon elected its president. A modest and unpretentious man, he was nevertheless a natural leader. As the conflicts over land intensified, the union developed the technique of the *empate*, sometimes translated as 'stalemate' or 'standoff.' During the dry season ranchers hire laborers to clear the forest for pasture. Just before the rains come in September the cleared areas are fired. Faced with eviction and loss of

livelihood, the rubber tappers began to assemble *en masse* at sites about to be cleared, preventing the clearing and persuading the laborers to lay down their chainsaws and go home. Over the last ten years during the months of June, July, and August the forests of the upper Acre valley have been the scene of numerous *empates*." [—Eds.]

4. FUNTAC was created by the Flaviano Melo government in the belief that Acre had a future in forestry, but it was abandoned by subsequent governments.

5. Ivair Higino de Almeida, age twenty-six, member of the Xapuri Rural Workers' Union and prospective Workers' Party candidate for the November 1988 municipal elections, was assassinated in a roadside ambush outside Xapuri on June 18, 1988.

Octavio Paz

Octavio Paz (1914–98), principally a poet but also highly regarded as a cultural critic and essayist, was one of the twentieth century's most influential writers. Paz was born in Mexico City to a family of creole intellectuals whose fortune was lost in the 1910 Revolution. Acquiring a love of literature from his grandfather's private library, Paz published his first poetry collection at nineteen. In 1937 he traveled to Spain and France, where he met André Breton and other leading figures of the surrealist movement, who would come to exert a strong influence on him. After working on literary magazines, in 1945 Paz became a diplomat, acting as Mexico's ambassador in several countries; experiences in India and Japan were especially consequential for his intellectual and aesthetic development. Given that cosmopolitan orientation, it is not surprising that Paz is widely recognized as an instrumental figure in the modernization of poetry in Spanish. Paz published prolifically; his most significant works include the long poem *Sunstone* (1957) and book-length essay *The Labyrinth of Solitude* (1950). He also founded and directed numerous cultural magazines over decades. Politically and ideologically, Paz often found himself at odds with much of the Latin American intelligentsia. After having supported the Republican side in the Spanish Civil War, Paz became increasingly outspoken about human rights abuses by left-wing movements and governments, especially the Soviet Union and Cuba. Presented here is Paz's speech upon winning the Nobel Prize in 1990, "In Search of the Present." The speech represents a watershed moment as one of the region's most famous (and controversial) intellectuals calls into question long-standing aspirations to modernization and progress, citing environmental degradation as one of his principal concerns.

***

"In Search of the Present" (1990)

TRANSLATED BY ANTHONY STANTON

The consciousness of being separate is a constant feature of our spiritual history. Separation is sometimes experienced as a wound that marks an internal division, an anguished awareness that invites self-examination; at other times it appears as a challenge, a spur that incites us to action, to go forth and encounter others and the outside world. It is true that the feeling of separation is universal and not peculiar to Spanish Americans. It is born at the very moment of our birth: as we are wrenched from the Whole we fall into an alien land. This experience becomes a wound that never heals. It is the unfathomable depth of every man; all our ventures and exploits, all our acts and dreams, are bridges designed to overcome the separation and reunite us with the world and our fellow-beings. Each man's life and the collective history of mankind can thus be seen as attempts to reconstruct the original situation . . .

The feeling of separation is bound up with the oldest and vaguest of my memories: the first cry, the first scare. Like every child I built emotional bridges in the imagination to link me to the world and to other people. I lived in a town on the outskirts of Mexico City, in an old dilapidated house that had a jungle-like garden and a great room full of books. First games and first lessons. The garden soon became the center of my world; the library, an enchanted cave. I used to read and play with my cousins and schoolmates. There was a fig tree, temple of vegetation, four pine trees, three ash trees, a nightshade, a pomegranate tree, wild grass and prickly plants that produced purple grazes. Adobe walls. Time was elastic; space was a spinning wheel. All time, past or future, real or imaginary, was pure presence. Space transformed itself ceaselessly. The beyond was here, all was here: a valley, a mountain, a distant country, the neighbors' patio. Books with pictures, especially history books, eagerly leafed through, supplied images of deserts and jungles, palaces and hovels, warriors and princesses, beggars and kings. We were shipwrecked with Sinbad and with Robinson, we fought with d'Artagnan, we took Valencia with the Cid. How I would have liked to stay forever on the Isle of Calypso! In summer the green branches of the fig tree would sway like the sails of a caravel or a pirate ship. High up on the mast, swept by the wind, I could make out islands and continents, lands that vanished as soon as they became tangible. The world was limitless yet it was always within reach; time was a pliable substance that weaved an unbroken present.

When was the spell broken? Gradually rather than suddenly. It is hard to accept being betrayed by a friend, deceived by the woman we love, or that the idea of freedom is the mask of a tyrant. What we call "finding out" is a slow and tricky process because we ourselves are the accomplices of our errors and deceptions. Nevertheless, I can remember fairly clearly an incident that was the first sign, although it was quickly forgotten. I must have been about six when one of my cousins who was a little older showed me a North American magazine with a photograph of soldiers marching along a huge avenue, probably in New York. "They've returned from the war" she said. This handful of words disturbed me, as if they foreshadowed the end of the world or the Second Coming of Christ. I vaguely knew that somewhere far away a war had ended a few years earlier and that the soldiers were marching to celebrate their victory. For me, that war had taken place in another time, not here and now. The photo refuted me. I felt literally dislodged from the present.

From that moment time began to fracture more and more. And there was a plurality of spaces. The experience repeated itself more and more frequently. Any piece of news, a harmless phrase, the headline in a newspaper: everything proved the outside world's existence and my own unreality. I felt that the world was splitting and that I did not inhabit the present. My present was disintegrating: real time was somewhere else. My time, the time of the garden, the fig tree, the games with friends, the drowsiness among the plants at three in the afternoon under the sun, a fig torn open (black and red like a live coal but one that is sweet and fresh): this was a fictitious time. In spite of what my senses told me, the time from over there, belonging to the others, was the real one, the time of the real present. I accepted the inevitable: I became an adult. That was how my expulsion from the present began.

It may seem paradoxical to say that we have been expelled from the present, but it is a feeling we have all had at some moment. Some of us experienced it first as a condemnation, later transformed into consciousness and action. The search for the present is neither the pursuit of an earthly paradise nor that of a timeless eternity: it is the search for a real reality. For us, as Spanish Americans, the real present was not in our own countries: it was the time lived by others, by the English, the French and the Germans. It was the time of New York, Paris, London. We had to go and look for it and bring it back home. These years were also the years of my discovery of literature. I began writing poems. I did not know what made me write them: I was moved by an inner need that is difficult to define. Only now have I understood that there was a secret relationship between what I have called my expulsion from the present and the writing of poetry . . .

What is modernity? First of all it is an ambiguous term: there are as many types of modernity as there are societies. Each has its own. The word's meaning is uncertain and arbitrary, like the name of the period that precedes it, the Middle Ages. If we are modern when compared to medieval times, are we perhaps the Middle Ages of a future modernity? Is a name that changes with time a real name? Modernity is a word in search of its meaning. Is it an idea, a mirage or a moment of history? Are we the children of modernity or its creators? Nobody knows for sure. It doesn't matter much: we follow it, we pursue it. For me at that time modernity was fused with the present or rather produced it: the present was its last supreme flower . . .

For us, as Latin Americans, the search for poetic modernity runs historically parallel to the repeated attempts to modernize our countries. This tendency begins at the end of the eighteenth century and includes Spain herself. The United States was born into modernity and by 1830 was already, as de Tocqueville observed, the womb of the future; we were born at a moment when Spain and Portugal were moving away from modernity. This is why there was frequent talk of "Europeanizing" our countries: the modern was outside and had to be imported . . .

Modern man has defined himself as a historical being. Other societies chose to define themselves in terms of values and ideas different from change: the Greeks venerated the *polis* and the circle yet were unaware of progress; like all the Stoics, Seneca was much concerned about the eternal return; Saint Augustine believed that the end of the world was imminent; Saint Thomas constructed a scale of the degrees of being, linking the smallest creature to the Creator, and so on. One after the other these ideas and beliefs were abandoned. It seems to me that the same decline is beginning to affect our idea of Progress and, as a result, our vision of time, of history and of ourselves. We are witnessing the twilight of the future. The decline of the idea of modernity and the popularity of a notion as dubious as that of "postmodernism" are phenomena that affect not only literature and the arts: we are experiencing the crisis of the essential ideas and beliefs that have guided mankind for over two centuries. I have dealt with this matter at length elsewhere. Here I can only offer a brief summary.

In the first place, the concept of a process open to infinity and synonymous with endless progress has been called into question. I need hardly mention what everybody knows: natural resources are finite and will run out one day. In addition, we have inflicted what may be irreparable damage on the natural environment and our own species is endangered. Finally, science and technology, the instruments of progress, have shown with alarming clarity that they can easily become destructive forces. The existence of nuclear weapons is a refutation of the idea that progress is inherent in history. This refutation, I add, can only be called devastating.

In the second place, we have the fate of the historical subject, mankind, in the twentieth century. Seldom have nations or individuals suffered so much: two world wars, tyrannies spread over five continents, the atomic bomb and the proliferation of one of the cruellest and most lethal institutions known by man: the concentration camp. Modern technology has provided countless benefits, but it is impossible to close our eyes when confronted by slaughter, torture, humiliation, degradation, and other wrongs inflicted on millions of innocent people in our century.

In the third place, the belief in the necessity of progress has been shaken. For our grandparents and our parents, the ruins of history (corpses, desolate battlefields, devastated cities) did not invalidate the underlying goodness of the historical process. The scaffolds and tyrannies, the conflicts and savage civil wars were the price to be paid for progress, the blood money to be offered to the god of history. A god? Yes, reason itself deified and prodigal in cruel acts of cunning, according to Hegel. The alleged rationality of history has vanished. In the very domain of order, regularity and coherence (in pure sciences like physics) the old notions of accident and catastrophe have reappeared. This disturbing resurrection reminds me of the terrors that marked the advent of the millennium, and the anguish of the Aztecs at the end of each cosmic cycle.

The last element in this hasty enumeration is the collapse of all the philosophical and historical hypotheses that claimed to reveal the laws governing the course of history. The believers, confident that they held the keys to history, erected powerful states over pyramids of corpses. These arrogant constructions, destined in theory to liberate men, were very quickly transformed into gigantic prisons. Today we have seen them fall, overthrown not by their ideological enemies but by the impatience and the desire for freedom of the new generations. Is this the end of all Utopias? It is rather the end of the idea of history as a phenomenon, the outcome of which can be known in advance. Historical determinism has been a costly and bloodstained fantasy. History is unpredictable because its agent, mankind, is the personification of indeterminism.

This short review shows that we are very probably at the end of a historical period and at the beginning of another. The end of the Modern Age or just a mutation? It is difficult to tell. In any case, the collapse of Utopian schemes has left a great void, not in the countries where this ideology has proved to have failed but in those where many embraced it with enthusiasm and hope. For the first time in history mankind lives in a sort of spiritual wilderness and not, as before, in the shadow of those religious and political systems that consoled us at the same time as they oppressed us. Although all societies are historical, each one has lived under the guidance and inspiration of a set of metahistorical beliefs and ideas. Ours is the first age that is ready to live without a metahistorical doctrine; whether they be religious or philosophical, moral or aesthetic, our absolutes are not collective but private. It is a dangerous experience. It is also impossible to know whether the tensions and conflicts unleashed in this privatization of ideas, practices and beliefs that belonged traditionally to the public domain will not end up by destroying the social fabric. Men could then become possessed once more by ancient religious fury or by fanatical nationalism. It would be terrible if the fall of the abstract idol of ideology were to foreshadow the resurrection of the buried passions of tribes, sects and churches. The signs, unfortunately, are disturbing.

Fernando Contreras Castro

Fernando Contreras Castro is one of Costa Rica's most prominent writers. Born (1963) in San Ramón, in the Alajuela province, Contreras Castro has published seven books, including short stories, novels, and essays. He teaches literature at the University of Costa Rica. Contreras Castro is part of what is often referred to as Costa Rica's disenchanted generation of writers and intellectuals. Emerging in the mid-1980s, their work typically expresses frustration with the Costa Rican model of government and a desire to address the concerns of the country's marginalized populations, particularly the rural and urban poor. For environmentally attuned writers like Contreras Castro and his contemporary Anacristina Rossi, the contradictions associated with Costa Rica's commitment to the sustainable tourism industry are a particular target of criticism. The selection presented here is a fragment from Contreras Castro's first published novel, *Única Looking Out to Sea*. The book was an immediate success upon its publication in 1993 and has subsequently become recommended reading for the Costa Rican secondary-school system. Set in a fictional garbage dump on the outskirts of a Costa Rican city, *Única*'s central theme is the problem of waste: both the vast amount of garbage produced each day by consumption-driven capitalist societies and the idea that certain "unproductive" members of the same societies are also somehow disposable, like the individuals who end up inhabiting the landfill. Contreras Castro calls these people *buzos*, or "divers," since they find what they need to survive by sifting through a toxic "sea" of trash. Contreras Castro's novel has helped to shed light on the millions of people around the world in similar situations.

***

From *Única Looking Out to Sea* (1993)

TRANSLATED BY ROSE SCHREIBER-STAINTHORP

If there had once been a river, and that river had been blue, all that was left now was a dead sea, its tides propelled by the two tractors laboring, dawn to dusk, under the city's daily surge of eight hundred tons of trash.

From far away, but not too far, one could make out the hollow shell of hill—its insides ripped away to create an open pit for the landfill. Sunk into the clay-rich soil, a chain link fence at the base of the hill restricted access to the dump, separating it from the surrounding Río Azul neighborhood. The fence, which also ran alongside the town school, did nothing to stifle the putrid stench emanating from the dump, oozing into people's homes, cloaking the entire town in a thick, viscid atmosphere. It was inescapable—a heaviness that would persist long after the landfill was shut down, the festering juices distilled from mounds upon mounds of compacted trash having been seeping into the subsoil for decades, like a black tide brimming up through the lacerated surface of the earth.

Toward nighttime, some of the divers gathered at Única's shack to eat. Each brought what they could and Única, in her maternal way, distributed the rations among them.

Momboñombo, who was still struggling to eat, felt stronger now that he knew he was finally one of them. He had grown more adept at keeping his food down.

Earlier, Única had introduced him to the community of divers with great fanfare, only to be met by their overwhelming indifference. Since then, some of the divers greeted him without so much as raising their eyes, more fixated on their plates than on the newly arrived. A few of the divers preferred to eat with their hands, the rest used the utensils Única distributed at the beginning of each meal and collected at the end.

"Everything turns up here, Mr. Momboñombo. Everything you see here, spoons, forks, knives, plates, all of it, I scavenged it."

El Bacán interrupted Única with one of his timeworn speeches:

"When the sun sets, Mr. Momboñombo, that's when the table's set. We bring our undisposables from home. You know that word? Some people'll say 'disposables'—I read that, doesn't sound right to me. Undisposables is better. You dispose it when you got it, undispose it when it's gone. Everything those trucks bring to the landfill, it's undisposables, Mr. Momboñombo; but if people really do say disposables, then I'd guess you'd say disposables is what we bring . . ."

Momboñombo listened to him in silence, merely nodding his head. It was something that had struck him as strange about El Bacán. He seemed so childlike, boyish, his rubber shoes, orange on one foot, blue on the other, the way he moved his hands, his affectionate gaze . . . El Bacán was just a boy!

Única, having realized how precocious he was as a child, taught him to read at an early age. By the time he was four, he was already cultivating an unchecked passion for reading. The only problem was that he was soon learning hundreds of new words that Única didn't know and couldn't explain to him. He read whatever he got his hands on—newspapers thrown away once the headlines, like the editorials, began showing signs of rot, out-of-date porn magazines, household appliance manuals, old books—in short, anything legible that made its way to the dump. El Bacán's lexicon was full of words that were just as mysterious to him as they were to the other divers; and although he wielded them well, which made it seem as though he understood them perfectly, down to their etymological roots, in reality he had no idea what the words meant. But the other divers didn't know that. To them, he seemed oddly enlightened and they listened dutifully, giving him what little attention they could muster.

This was Única's secret; she'd always known there was something about her son that kept him from maturing. Far from tormenting her, the idea seemed to please her. After all, it was comforting to know she'd always have her five- or six-year-old son by her side, his brief outbursts of adolescence few and far between.

After the meal, the divers retired to their hovels. Nights at the landfill—so long as they weren't abruptly punctuated by the arrival of garbage trucks during heavy season—were dark, silent nights. Further back, past the edge of the landfill, a few patches of vegetation had managed to survive and it was there, with the onset of evening, that the last remaining insects would buzz and chirp, lulling the divers to sleep, reassuring them there was still life on the hill.

After three weeks of living at the garbage dump, Momboñombo still struggled to sleep. The asthma that afflicted the rest of the divers had begun to affect him too. The three of them slept on two makeshift beds where, at times, Única Oconitrillo's cough was so powerful it seemed she might burst and El Bacán murmured soft, meaningless baby prattle. To breathe, Momboñombo opted to sleep sitting up, but it was no use. The smell of moist indigestion, garbage-choked earth, was relentless.

Momboñombo Moñagallo was new to the landfill, which explained why he could still smell it. He understood, however, that with each passing minute, the hot breath at the mouth of the landfill was burning through his sense of smell. Day after day, he found himself increasingly unable to distinguish between the thousands upon thousands of smells that, together, constitute the stench of decay.

Whatever traces of urbanity he had left, he was willing to overcome them to adapt to his new life, never mind that it wasn't the life he'd chosen. When he first arrived at the landfill, he hadn't intended to become a diver; it was simply a more dramatic form of suicide. And yet, with Única's warm ministrations and El Bacán's tender demeanor he was beginning to believe, slowly but surely, that life could still be meaningful. Ultimately, identicide had been better than suicide.

He'd destroyed his identity, gotten rid of his name, of the house he'd had for a few short years, his government ID, his memories, everything gone; the day he'd arrived at the landfill was the day his unemployment payments had ended, and he could no longer feign the part of citizenry.

He'd never had a career, never learned a trade.

Instead, he'd worked as a security guard, first at construction sites and later at someone's seaside estate. Then, when he was close to forty, the Main Library hired him to be a *huachiman* . . . A watchman.

Since then, he'd spent his nights wandering the shelving racks, sleeping by day, reading by night to stay awake. He read every night for twenty-six years until, finally, he accused the library of racketeering with Despish Paper, a private toilet paper company, to whom they'd been selling books for six colones a ton.

He was so appalled he'd threatened to take the story to the press.

"Just what we need! The same paper used for printing humanity's hopes and dreams, we'll be writing on it with our asses!"

So many books sent to such an ignoble end. Among them, some very old, very rare editions, the loss of which was irreparable—records from late eighteenth-century Carthage, world literature, all of it sold with about as much consideration as the priest and the barber.

The watchman reported the case and lost his job. Having never received the state's social guarantees, Momboñombo didn't consider himself Costa Rican. There was no pension waiting for him and the unemployment payments lasted a mere two months; after that, he seemed to suddenly grow old, or rather, he realized he was already too old to start anew.

Sixty-six years aren't that many, but sixty-six years of hardship—that was enough to make Momboñombo an old man.

Gioconda Belli

The colorful life of Gioconda Belli (b. 1948) occupies the center of two major books, the 1988 novel *The Inhabited Woman* and her 2000 memoir, *The Country Under My Skin*. Having grown up in a rich and conventional Nicaraguan family, in 1970 Belli joined the Sandinista National Liberation Front in its struggle against the Somoza dictatorship, which had brutalized and exploited the country for decades. She worked underground until 1975, at which point she was forced into exile in Mexico and Costa Rica. After the Sandinista victory of 1979, Belli held important positions in the socialist government, including director of official communications. She has subsequently distanced herself from the Sandinista government of Daniel Ortega, becoming one of the most outspoken critics of its plans to build a transoceanic canal in Nicaragua. Over the years Belli has maintained an active career as a poet. In 1978 she won the prestigious Casa de las Américas Prize for poetry alongside fellow Central American Claribel Alegría. Belli's poetry, like her prose works, makes an explicit commitment to women's empowerment and emancipation, especially the liberation of female sexuality from patriarchal repression. As early as *The Inhabited Woman*, Belli's dedication to women's emancipation within revolutionary political struggle has been linked to a deep sensitivity to nonhuman nature. The selection presented here is an excerpt from *Waslala* (1996), which takes place in the dystopian present, a time when Central American countries are ruled by armed gangs instead of civil administrations. The most valuable export product is oxygen from the region's forests, and the "off-shoring" of North American hazardous waste is part of the international balance of trade.

✳✳✳

From *Waslala* (1996)

TRANSLATED BY ROSE SCHREIBER-STAINTHORP

They left the hotel at nightfall. The warm wind blowing off the lake simply heightened the humidity in the air. Melisandra, her arms crossed, tightened her blouse and curled up against the side of the vehicle, attempting to shield herself from the wind billowing through the hoodless jeep. Raphael was seated up front beside Morris. Seen from behind, their heads looked like two strange, exotic flower bulbs. They were talking about the Espada brothers, but their words kept getting swept away with the wind. Only when the road curved and sound traveled back in her direction could Melisandra briefly make out a syllable or two before they slipped past her.

She could have leaned forward but chose not to. Instead, she preferred to rest the back of her neck against the cold metal jutting from the seat upholstery and stare up into the now dark sky. Joaquin wouldn't have agreed with Raphael about the Espada brothers. For him, there were just two types of people and the Espadas were on the opposing side. It was a simple but effective Manichaeism. Yet for Raphael, it was always more complicated and maybe that's what made him so attractive: he wanted to understand people's deeper motives, not judge them based on appearances, and not immediately relegate them to one side or another. For him, good and bad were an intrinsic part of everything and everyone. No doubt, it was a way of looking at the world that could easily turn him into a mere spectator, unable to fully immerse himself in anything. It put him at risk of paralysis, skepticism. Raphael didn't necessarily have the strength that other people had, the kind that comes from following through with certain principles.

She felt sick, nervous, suddenly frightened, desperate to close her eyes and wake up somewhere safe. Years later, she would recall her feelings as a kind of premonition. The vehicle crossed through the iron gate at the school's entrance. Before they pulled up, Morris paused to look down at the dock lit by floodlights. The barge rocked to and fro on the water while a group of sturdy young men unloaded the containers. The school building, however, was dark, silent. It was a strange contrast, thought Melisandra as she walked inside. She'd imagined the interior of the building to be like the dock; she wasn't prepared for these incongruously dark hallways, the lights off, filled with a heavy stupor and the empty echo of their footsteps on their way to Engracia's rooms.

Morris rushed ahead. He scanned the surroundings, clearly eager to find some explanation of what he too found surprising. By the time they arrived at Engracia's rooms, they'd broken into a run, for no other reason than the bizarre silence.

Morris turned on the lights and made his way around the furniture. The parrot, jolted awake, began flying clumsily around the room, cawing and flapping its unsteady wings that Engracia had clipped to keep it from escaping. Instinctively, Melisandra went to stand beside Raphael, and, unsure of what to do next, she crossed her arms again. They waited for Morris to finish scouring the rooms. When he returned, he said Engracia was nowhere to be found. It was definitely strange.

"I think we're getting too worried," Raphael said. "This doesn't look violent. If something happened, they'd have realized it down at the dock. Engracia and the boys are here, they've got to be. We probably just can't hear them—this place is huge," he added, sounding unconvinced. He stepped into the hallway and peered off into the patios, hoping to discern something, anything, through the dark.

Melisandra was first to spot the lights shining through the window.

"Morris, Morris!" she called, "come see this."

It was hard to say what it was. It was at the back of the patio, close to the incinerator, and it was glowing: small, bright, circular objects in motion that emitted an unfamiliar, bluish light.

"Oh god," Morris exclaimed, "what the hell is that?"

A sudden gust of wind delivered the sound of laughter. Then, hardly a moment later, Raphael called out to them from the patio. They rushed downstairs.

"I think they're over there," said Raphael, "by the light. I heard voices. I think I heard Engracia's."

Morris activated the light on his metallic arm and the three of them began making their way toward the incinerator, past piles of garbage and junk.

Morris didn't want to think what he'd been thinking. But he couldn't stop. It was impossible. He circled the large, square body of an industrial cooler, surrounded on all sides by mounds of cast-off refrigerators. He was careful not to trip over the rusted-out engines. Morris reached out his arm to alert Melisandra, whose quick breathing he could hear close by. The palm trees swayed in the wind, their leaves rasping against one another. Again he heard laughter. The sky was clouded over. A thin half-moon, almost like an arched brow or the crisp stroke of an unfamiliar alphabet, appeared briefly in the dark sky before disappearing again, shrouded by thick mounds of clouds rolling overhead. He didn't want to think what he'd been thinking. It must be a mistake. He felt a pain at the top of his stomach. The idea that what he was thinking—which he didn't want to think—could be true made the acid in his stomach churn. He concentrated on not tripping. It was hard. The patio was difficult to navigate even in broad daylight. Rusted pipes, rods, sheets of metal were scattered throughout. He'd told Engracia repeatedly. One of these days they should clean it up. It was dangerous. He wondered if the boys were wearing the masks and costumes he'd brought them. Melisandra didn't say anything. Morris looked back and saw her and Raphael at a short distance, advancing slowly. He signaled for them to hurry. The light from his arm wasn't enough for the three of them and he couldn't stop to shine the light behind him. They were close. The voices, the laughter, were clearer now. The silhouette of the incinerator loomed larger, concealing the palms at the back. They could hear the palm tree blades whipping against one another in the wind.

He thought he saw her. He thought he saw her face, bright and recognizable, distinct from all the rest. They were gathered in a circle around a phosphorescent blaze. Men and women, illuminated. Boys. Their hands, their faces, gave off a blue-tinged glow. Someone was bending down, pulling arms flecked with light out of a metal vessel at the center. Morris didn't want to think what he'd been thinking, but now, from where he stood—so close he was almost there—he couldn't stop.

He emerged from the shadows. His eyes scanned their glowing bodies and he made his way up to the vessel, a sturdy metal cylinder. As a silence fell over the group, like children caught red-handed, he submerged his metal arm in the phosphorescent dust.

Engracia approached him. She was coated in it, much more so than anyone else—even the outer layer of her hair was shining. Her teeth. She resembled a mythical Medusa. Don't ruin it for us, she said, you look like someone died—it's phosphorescent paint, that's all. We're just having a good time, she added.

Morris removed his metallic arm and glanced at the gauges on the dashboard. Then he turned toward Engracia and struck her. Her head spun from side to side. One. Two. Three. Four times. The boys pounced on him. Morris hit one of them. He heard the heavy crunch of bones as the boy fell to the ground. Raphael, Josué, and the others rushed to contain him. Now there were light particles on his shirt, on his shoes. Engracia hadn't made a sound. She must know, thought Morris. Suddenly exhausted, he let himself fall to the ground, his limp body signaling to the boys that they needn't contain him anymore. He dropped his head in his hands, defeated, alone, surrounded on all sides by phosphorescent faces, arms, hands, and voices that still called him professor yet demanded an explanation, why had he done that, they were just having fun—good, innocent fun. They must think I'm crazy, thought Morris. That's why they didn't fight back. Even Engracia was approaching him now. For the first time since he'd known her, he could make out the aura of loneliness that enveloped her, a translucent but impenetrable wall.

He looked at them dolefully, embarrassed by his own reaction. Waves of rage swept up and down his body, like a pendulum swaying uncontrollably in his chest. I told them, he thought, I said it all the time.

The group looked at him expectantly, frightened. Morris felt himself overtaken by a sudden, heavy exhaustion. He didn't want to cry but he let out a hoarse sob. "They'll think I'm crazy," he thought. He reached out his arm to touch Engracia, the Medusa.

"I'm so sorry," he said at last, "Forgive me, I didn't mean to do that. But I've always said we need to be careful. Precisely to avoid accidents like this. This bright dust isn't a joke, it's caesium 137. It's a radioactive isotope. The lethal dosage is somewhere between five hundred and six hundred rems. I'm guessing everyone received at least that much. All of you are going to get incredibly sick. In a few hours, you'll start vomiting, you'll have a fever, headache, burns, your skin will start to sear. You'll lose intercellular fluid and electrolytes, there'll be damage to your spinal bone marrow, your hair will fall out . . . What idiocy, oh god, so idiotic!"

He lost his composure as he spoke. He stood up, newly overcome by rage, fists clenched. Once again, he submerged his metallic arm in the cylinder. No one said anything. Josué, who hadn't touched the dust, was sitting on a washing machine, staring fixedly at his nails. Engracia walked around and around the circle. The boys remained seated on the ground. Morris removed his arm and looked at the dashboard.

"No one survives this much exposure," he said. "They'd have to receive electrolytes intravenously."

"How much time do we have?" asked Engracia.

"One, maybe two weeks," said Morris. "Two weeks if we're lucky . . . Where did you find it?"

"We broke the cylinder from the machine," said one of the boys, pointing toward a corner of the patio.

Morris didn't need to get closer, he could tell what it was. It was a machine that, until recently, had been used to treat cancer patients with radiation; but now, with gene therapy, they could isolate and neutralize genes in newborns, so the machines were obsolete.

Raphael left the circle. He took Melisandra's arm and guided her off to the side. Morris sat back on the ground. He sobbed, his face buried in his arm. The others listened to him cry in silence. It seemed as if Engracia might approach him, but instead she looked down at her big, radiant hands and stayed put. "Poor thing," Morris thought, lifting his head. His fury had left him. He stood up and opened his arms to Engracia. She tried to step away. You'll get contaminated too, she said, it's better if you don't touch me. He seemed not to hear. With his metallic arm, Morris drew Engracia toward him, embraced her, held her close. He kissed her face with long, deliberate kisses, each one leaving particles of light on his lips. It was like a hole had pierced the night, thought Melisandra, and for a moment, the world around them seemed crystal clear, the nighttime texture of the air torn open by enormous fireflies. They looked so beautiful. Engracia resembling an ancient deity, terrible and magnanimous, newly returned after an otherworldly journey. The boys magnificent and sprightly, androgynous ephebes from a sacred forest. Everyone's movements seemed to flow and ripple, they moved weightlessly through the thickness of the night, at once negating and affirming the darkness. It was difficult to imagine something so beautiful could be so deadly, that death was shrouded in fantastic, iridescent colors and supernatural, angelic faces, faces whose contours were illuminated by the light in their bones, their cartilage, the orbits of their eyes, as if a torch lit their blood from within, the light shining from inside each of their bodies. Maybe the beauty blinded them, thought Melisandra. They didn't think about the consequences. They got carried away, spellbound by the dust on their skin, transfigured into mythical creatures. And how can you blame them, thought Raphael. How can you blame them in this wasteland of junk and trash—they thought they found the very essence of light, of course they wanted to possess it. It's exactly what an alchemist or a magician would have done, overwhelmed by the need to transform or forget—however briefly—the opaque, imperfect human condition.

At the center of the circle, Morris and Engracia remained locked in embrace, their slow movements resembling a kind of ritual dance of silence. Suddenly, Engracia pulled away and turned to face the group.

"We have to sing," she scolded them, clapping her hands as if to break the trance they'd fallen into. "The best way to cure ourselves is to sing. Josué, go bring your guitar."

Morris walked over to the metal container. He stared determinedly into the glowing light and then, before they could stop him, he leaned over the container and in quick, deliberate movements, like a euphoric miner covering himself head to toe in gold dust, he scooped up the light and painted his face, his good arm, his hair, his chest.

Subcomandante Marcos

Subcomandante Marcos was the leader of the Zapatista National Liberation Army (EZLN), based in Chiapas, Mexico, and a global icon for Indigenous cultural and political rights. While he has never officially disclosed his real identity, many have identified Marcos as Rafael Sebastián Guillén Vicente (b. 1957), a former professor at the Autonomous Metropolitan University in Mexico City. Guillén resigned from teaching in 1984 and soon after withdrew to the mountains of Chiapas to work with Mayan peasants. On New Year's Day 1994—the same day that the North American Free Trade Agreement went into effect—Subcomandante Marcos made headlines by leading an EZLN military offensive that seized several towns in southern Chiapas. Quick retaliation from the government led to the EZLN's retreat into the Lacandón jungle. Marcos, however, had already roused national leftist support, as was evident when more than a hundred thousand people demonstrated in Mexico City. Much of his fame and notoriety came from his written work: over many long years of hiding in the jungle, Marcos wrote frequent letters to the public that were published in newspapers and later online. Full of humor and erudition, the letters present extensive political critiques organized around topics including human and Indigenous rights, neoliberalism and globalization, and environmental degradation. The selection presented here is one of Marcos's public letters from 1999. It is addressed to José Saramago, the Portuguese novelist awarded the Nobel Prize the previous year. Marcos applies metaphors from Saramago's own work and frames the fight for Indigenous land rights as a struggle against capitalist globalization, advocating for the protection of the Lacandón jungle and nearby areas as essential for both environmental and cultural diversity.

* * *

A Letter from Subcomandante Marcos to Saramago (1999)

TRANSLATED BY ROSE SCHREIBER-STAINTHORP

To: José Saramago, Planet Earth

From: SubMarcos, Mountains of Southeastern Mexico

Don José,

I write in the hope these lines will reach you while your feet are still traversing Indigenous ground. I mean to send my regards, of course—regards that are not only for you, they're also for Pilar—but not only that. Above all, I send my regard for your words, your restless, irreverent words, which you wave like a sword, leaving cuts and scrapes no ointment can soothe.

But—and I believe I said this already—the purpose of this letter isn't just to send my regards. There's something I want to tell you and something I want to ask you for. I'll have you know that the sea put a copy of your book, *This World and the Other*, into my hands. I began reading it back to front; this, around here, is the strictest test of whether a book should be kept close to us. If we can start a book at the end or from anywhere in the middle, then it's a book we should always keep close. I know that as literary criteria go, it seems a bit eccentric, but it's how we know which books share the humidity, the sleepless nights, the swish of an armed helicopter's blades, the purr of a bomber plane, the constant howl of tank engines, the impertinence of so many cockroaches, the webs relentlessly woven by spiders big and small, the inevitable comings and goings of ants. Among those books (which I won't discuss here since the Mexican government might consider them subversive, and, moreover, I think Cervantes, Shakespeare, García Lorca, Neruda, Hernández, Cortázar, Sor Juana, and countless others have more than enough titles and honors already, adding "political criminal" strikes me as a tad excessive), I now include *This World and the Other*.

But the purpose of this letter isn't to discuss books whose pain resonates here. It just so happens that the other day I was leafing back and forth through the pages of your book and my eyes settled on a text called "Blue for Mars." The plot is simple: you've spent the past ten years living on Mars and you've come to realize that aliens don't have wars, don't differentiate between city and countryside, and a whole bunch of other alien things. But here's the problem: there are only two colors on Mars, black and white, and all the shades in between. The aliens think they need to discover other colors in order to be truly happy. You wonder if you should bring them blue. And this brings us to the purpose of this letter, which is that, here, Zapatistas are fighting for a world that welcomes all colors and allows those colors to be what they are—different.

I go back to leafing through the book and land on "The Smile," which rebels against the notion that "smile" can be defined as an intransitive verb and a soundless facial expression. And I realize it's true, not only is "smile" not an intransitive verb, it's actually extremely transitive. Take Ezequiel (Tojolabal, three years old); his smile isn't so much a smile as it is a doorway (a doorway into his childhood self, Indigenous and Zapatista, and a doorway into the adult world, Indigenous and Zapatista, that fights for Ezequiel and other children like him—fights for them to have open, transitive doors, instead of closed, intransitive ones). Although, come to think of it, I'm not so sure: is "door" an intransitive verb? A question best left to linguists.

I keep leafing through the book and my eyes settle on "Black Snow," which is a meditation on the traces of death in a little boy's drawing, the little boy having decided that nature should be an ally to human grief, share its burden (joy too, I think, but that's not in the text). And, once again, this brings us to the purpose of this letter because—not to take us off track—Yeniperr (Tojolabal, five years old) just stopped by to show me her drawing and in it, the sky is blue (exactly as the aliens would have wanted), but instead of birds, there are helicopters, and the earth—the one in Yeniperr's drawing—is covered in mountains. but instead of flowers, the earth sprouts balaclavas. Needless to say, Yeniperr was only showing me the drawing so we could "trade" it for the chocolate almond candy sitting on my table. I've been jealously guarding that chocolate almond candy as if it were the last one, not only because it is, effectively, the last one, although by and large for that very reason. In any case, Yeniperr walked off with the chocolate almond candy and I got the drawing with the blue sky, helicopters instead of birds, and an earth that sprouts balaclavas instead of flowers. I'm sure the aliens wouldn't have wanted this kind of blue, full of helicopters and balaclavas. I put the drawing aside to continue flipping through the pages of the book, and that's when I find what I was looking for (of course, I didn't know what I was looking for until I found it). There it was:

"Silence is black, fertile land, a rich soil for being, a quiet melody in the sunlight. Words fall upon silence. All words. Good words and bad words. The wheat and the chaff. But only wheat gives us bread."

"Silence is black, fertile land." True. But there's more. This war of ours, which has been steadily unfolding between the government and Indian nations, is a war over that silence, that land. And it's true: because of this war, good and bad words have settled here. Each speaks of the land differently.

Because when someone from the Mexican government says "land," it comes after "buy" or "sell." Because for the rich and powerful, land is just a commodity.

And when a Zapatista says "land," it doesn't come after anything else. No, it comes alongside words such as "homeland," "mother," "house," "school," "history," and "wisdom."

Because for us, Indigenous Zapatistas, the earth is blue. And it is also yellow and red and black and white and brown and purple and orange and green (aliens, by the way, turn green with envy just knowing we have all these colors here on earth), and the earth, like Ezequiel's smile, is also a transitive doorway (linguistics be damned), and if the earth is overrun by helicopters instead of birds, balaclavas instead of flowers, then that's precisely why the Indigenous Zapatistas need to defend the land against those who treat it like a commodity, unable to see the land for what it truly is: an open door, made of all colors.

Of course, in a place like Chiapas, the powerful see the earth as more than just a commodity. For the globalization traffickers, this land is a "mine," one they can exploit till it runs dry. In Chiapaneca Indian land, the "mine" has oil. The government won't acknowledge the real motivations driving its war: it desperately wants to take possession of the mine. But the government doesn't want to exploit the land themselves, they want to sell it.

In the Marqués de Comillas region, in the Lacandón jungle, there's a potential oil reserve with an estimated 1,498 million barrels of crude, sprawled over 2,250 square kilometers. In the Ocosingo region, they want to claim a potential reserve with an estimated 2,178 million barrels of crude, covering 5,550 square kilometers, and they already have plans to drill 21 exploratory wells. In the early nineties, Petróleos Mexicanos (Pemex) said it was going to invest in this whole oil-rich region—they called it the Ocosingo-Lacantún Exploratory Macro-Project, and it included Ocosingo and Marqués de Comillas. It was worth 2.7 billion pesos in 1991—roughly the equivalent of a billion dollars today (*El Financiero*).

So, at the very least, that "mine" contains 3,500 million barrels of crude. At today's prices, that's worth 80 billion dollars—that's 80 times more than their "initial investment." But the government doesn't want to extract the oil themselves; instead, they want to sell the land to foreign buyers. And megacorporations are interested, with the kind of interest that's worth several zeros more than 80 billion dollars. Because they're the ones with the real studies—they know how much potential oil is actually sitting beneath the Lacandón jungle.

Biodiversity, water, petroleum. Those are the riches of Montes Azules, a biosphere reserve at the heart of the Lacandón jungle. Even so, conditions at the nature reserve continue to deteriorate, and given the state's plans to build the San Quintín–Amador Hernández Highway right through the Perla River valley, it's at risk of being split in two.

Meanwhile, the jungle along the upper Usumacinta River basin and Tulujah River basin was officially recognized as protected forest. And yet, Marqués de Comillas and the northern part of the jungle were left unprotected, and Pemex considers this area a primary region for exploration. Of course, other national and transnational companies are involved as well.

Pemex acknowledges that prior to 1995, it explored a dozen or so oil deposits in the region, and earlier, in the 1980s, it clashed with the then-Secretariat of Ecology and Urban Development over the environmental damage caused by its road construction, use of explosives, and mining in the jungle. The National Ecology Institute (INE) argues that continued encroachment into the rain forest and subsequent changes in land use are the primary "threats" facing Montes Azules today; they also state that construction of the Southern Border Highway, as well as oil exploration and production, have increased the pace of deforestation. Add to this a series of reforestation efforts backed by Semarnap, which claims these efforts and the recent involvement of the Mexican Army were planned as far back as 1995 and that reforestation species (mahogany, lemon verbena, and pink poui) were chosen because they were "the hardest hit by logging and the most difficult to reestablish." And yet, biologists and other specialists support passive forest restoration, which gives the land time to rest, not active reforestation. They've also asked, "Why aren't local communities involved in these projects? It's them, not the soldiers, who know this land better than anyone" (*El Financiero*).

As if this weren't enough, the Montes Azules biosphere is facing a further threat: planned construction of the San Quintín–Amador Hernández-Perla valley highway. The Perla River flows into Montes Azules and the planned route would split the reserve in two. But it's not just the San Quintín–Amador Hernández-Perla valley highway that's threatening the reserve's ecosystem. There's also the military presence. Soldiers from the National Defense Army have gone into the communities of El Guanal and Amador Hernández and cleared a sizable amount of land in order to build two helipads. Now, helicopters from San Quintín have been bringing in more troops, provisions, hatchets, rolls of barbed wire mesh, on top of tripod machine guns, flamethrowers, defoliant chemicals, barrels upon barrels of tear gas, and alcohol.

Which is why your book, Mr. Saramago, along with Chiapaneca land struggles and the war between profit and transitive doorways, brings me to the Tzeltal community in Amador Hernández. There, for more than four months now, Indigenous Zapatistas have stood their ground against elite forces from the National Defense Army. Each day, the Zapatistas go before the soldiers and offer their blessings, they teach them about politics, they sing the national anthem. To "protect" soldiers from the dangerous ideas espoused by Zapatistas, the lead general of the military invasion has installed up to eight high-powered loudspeakers. Apparently, the general likes to play music by the pianist Richard Clayderman; whenever the Zapatistas sing the Mexican national anthem, the soldiers blast Clayderman at full volume to drown out these words: "But if some enemy outlander should dare to profane your ground with his sole, think, oh beloved fatherland, that heaven has given you a soldier in every son."

Amador Hernández: a community in which the paradoxes of Mexico's southeastern war are glaringly apparent. There, the Indigenous sing their national anthem and defend their land, their open door to all colors. There, government soldiers make themselves deaf, struggling to drown out the words that expose them for what they are: a front line for globalization.

Yes, in Amador Hernández, you can see the war for what it truly is: on one side are soldiers, surrounded by barbed wire fences, trenches, machine guns, flamethrowers, shields, and gas expellers; on the other, a crowd of Indigenous men, women, children, and elderly, all of them short in stature, their skin the color of the earth, brandishing no other weapon than words, sung and written. Because in the end, when the soldiers turned the speakers to full volume, the Zapatistas fell silent and held up signs with the very words—written in large, unsteady letters—they had intended to speak. The noise made it impossible to hear but not to see, so the general ordered his troops to cover their eyes. More than one soldier peered out from under his blindfolded eyes to read the fateful messages inscribed on these signs: "This land belongs to our dead ancestors. How will you kill our dead?"

Don José:

You say both wheat and chaff fall upon the land, but only wheat produces bread. You're right. Here we say: cynicism and rebellion fall upon the land, but only rebellion gives us a future.

I just read an article in which you, speaking from Guadalajara, state that your calling is to say and do things that upset the government. So, Don José, this is the favor I want to ask of you: when no one is looking, take a fistful of this soil beneath your feet, discreetly pour it into a plastic bag, and place that bag in your left pocket. As you travel far and wide around this world, make sure to stop every now and then and reach casually into your pocket and pull out a small handful of dirt and let that dirt fall to the earth and land where it may. Don't worry about how much to take, just so long as it's enough to scatter some of our soil around the world.

Even though science may not be able to explain it, rebellion is contagious. And not just that. For five hundred years, we've known that rebellion is not only contagious, but bountiful: it births a future.

So. You have my regards and now I believe that rebellion is likewise a transitive word.

From the mountains in southeastern Mexico,
Subcomandante Insurgente Marcos,
Mexico, December 1999

P.S. Durito sends his regards to Ms. Pilar (he calls her "Pilarica"—which, I keep telling him, is rude) and asked if Pilar can send some of the coffee she makes. I told him it's better if she sends nuts. Durito, annoyed, said there aren't nuts in Lanzarote. Of course there are, I said. Nuts are like colors, you find them all over the world.

Eduardo del Llano

Cuba's Eduardo del Llano is internationally known for stories and films that employ satirical humor to portray realities of life in contemporary Cuba. Born (1962) in Moscow, del Llano studied art and literature at the University of Havana, where he has subsequently taught Latin American art and photography. The first film to which he contributed screenwriting, Daniel Díaz Torres's *Alice in Wondertown* (1991), is a political allegory about the day-to-day absurdity of life under the Castro regime. It was labeled counterrevolutionary and blocked after four days of screenings with record-high attendance (French 1991). Since that time, del Llano has remained a prolific writer of novels, short stories, and screenplays. He has also become an important director of independent films, regularly taking advantage of online distribution opportunities for work that is not shown publically in Cuba. Del Llano has won major national and international prizes, including the Sundance Award for best script (*Life Is to Whistle*, 1998) and the Alejo Carpentier Award for best novel (*The Enemy*, 2018). Del Llano's films are often based on his own stories and novels. He has to date produced fifteen short films featuring a recurring character named Nicanor O'Donnell, an antihero well known among Cubans. In "Greenpeace," the story presented here, Nicanor is defense attorney for three Cuban environmentalists. Despite their best intentions, the trio end up accused of a slew of crimes against the government. The characters' casual use of racist language is both a faithful reflection of contemporary culture in many American environments and an uncomfortable reminder of the lingering legacies of colonialism and Black slavery, even in a society theoretically based on socialist principles of equality.

***

"Greenpeace" (2000)

TRANSLATED BY ROSE SCHREIBER-STAINTHORP

Rigoberto *Gravilla* Molina, Prisciliano *Sangre'e mono* Jiménez, and Bárbaro *Negro-emierda* Casas[2] were huddled glumly together in a corner of their cell when an officer—who seemed to embody all three—opened the door, stepping aside as he motioned me in.

"Yell if they give you trouble," he cautioned. "I'll be close by, watching a telenovela. Last night's ending was unbelievable."

Sure, I said, and the officer walked off. I positioned my chair in front of the three detainees, sat down, and gave them a commiserating look. They stared back, somewhat reluctantly, with the kind of evasiveness you see on guys lined up at a sperm bank.

"My name is Nicanor O'Donnell," I told them, "I'm your lawyer. I want the three of you to tell me exactly what happened, down to the last detail. Just like you'd tell a friend."

For a few minutes no one spoke. Sure, they'd have reacted quicker if I was the detective—you don't win with the state, so it's better to just go along to get along. But I'm guessing my politeness made me look weak, and, when you've got scores to settle, it's easier to make weak people pay.

"Have they been treating you well?"

"They treat us like criminals," said Gravilla, his voice quivering at the implied injustice. "And nothing you do is going to change it. The trial will be a joke, like always."

"So you're saying you're innocent."

The three of them stared back at me, their expressions belligerent.

"What do you think?"

"Look, all I know is you've all been charged with damage to cultural heritage, sabotage, dissemination of seditious propaganda, illegal attempt to sacrifice livestock, assault on a government farm manager, and usurpation of authority, to name a few. If you can convince me you're not guilty, I'll work on convincing the judge."

"Usurpation of authority—what's that?"

"It means the three of you were wearing military uniforms when they caught you trying to kill the cow."

"We weren't killing any fucking cows!" screeched Sangre'e mono. "They don't get it, we were saving them! All they saw were three guys dressed like soldiers beating up another guy, at night, in the woods, with a cow, and they assume we're a bunch of delinquents."

I nodded to show I agreed—people are very superficial and taken by appearances.

"Either way, I don't get it," I added. "Why don't you start from the beginning? I'm in no rush. You can have all the cigarettes you want."

They weren't shy with the cigarettes. Gravilla didn't seem convinced it was worth it, but Sangre'e mono and Negroemierda were eager to re-create things for me, somewhat more eloquently than the fragmented, hijacked version I'd gotten from the detective who'd led the interrogation. And then—even though I hadn't wanted it, I'd accepted the case more out of a sense of duty—I found myself completely captivated by their story. I even handed the guard some money to go buy more cigarettes.

Three months earlier, Gravilla had organized a group meeting at his cramped, makeshift barbacoa—the kind you see in houses sometimes.

Sangre'e mono had been in jail for possessing foreign currency—this was back when foreign currency was illegal. And Negroemierda, he'd spent the night behind bars for the two smacks he'd given a mulatta in public. Still, though, neither of them was a born-and-bred criminal. All three had bailed on their jobs and were getting by as "entrepreneurs"—which meant they sold T-shirts, soap, and cassette tapes. In Belén, it's what everyone did.

Belén is the kind of neighborhood where syllogisms and distinctions fall apart. In some sense, everyone is within the law, but they're also outside it too. Geographically, it's the most densely populated part of the city, and yet it still retains its village spirit. It's also the poorest part of the city and the furthest removed from nature—there are no trees, no flowers, and there's not enough water. Sure, it's a historic neighborhood, but people in Belén are forced to live day-to-day. And so, with all that plus Sangre'e mono's and Negroemierda's folkloric inability to get anywhere on time, they showed up at Gravilla's place five minutes early.

"So what's the big mystery, Gravilla?" They asked together, having just finished a round of drinks, which, for them, was equivalent to five o'clock tea.

"It's not money," Rigoberto clarified, "it's something else. Let's just get that out of the way, so you two don't start sharpening your teeth."

Sangre'e mono and Negroemierda stayed silent. The three of them had been friends since before they could walk, and, over the years, Gravilla had developed a reputation as an ideologue. Whatever he was about to say, they knew it'd be worth listening to.

Their host walked over to the window and returned holding a flowerpot, inside of which was a dead fern. He placed the container at the center of the group and looked from one to the other gravely. There was a speculative silence.

"Marijuana?" asked Sangre'e mono. His nostrils twitched like a guinea pig's.

"No, you idiot," said Gravilla. "It's a fern. Well, a dead fern. It belonged to my old lady, she left it to me. The week after she went, so did the fern."

The other two exchanged glances. They'd already paid their full, by-the-book respects to Gravilla—for his mother's death, obviously.

"Religion?" Negroemierda suggested, "you're saying your old lady's spirit killed a tiny plant?"

"No wonder they call you Negroemierda. Fuck. Weren't you watching TV last night? You must've because there was no blackout, no power spike, so no reason not to."

"You mean the telenovela?"

"No. The show about us killing the environment."

His guests blinked at him, seeming unsure.

"I saw it," Sangre'e mono said, nodding, "but I don't get it. Why don't you just spell it out for us, Gravilla? You want to sell plants to tourists?"

"I want us," began Gravilla, careful to stress each word, "to form an Environmental Brigade."

It was as if, at a meeting for the UN Security Council, all the interpreters were on strike. Negroemierda remained rooted to the spot, impassive, but Sangre'e mono recoiled and bolted for the door.

"Are you crazy, man? I'm not going back to the hole, and definitely not for political shit. If you're trying to plant bombs or start fires, you're on your own. I'm out."

"Sit down, Prisciliano," ordered Gravilla, "Fucking grass eater—you want to crawl around on all fours the rest of your life? An Ecological Brigade has nothing to do with politics."

Thrown off guard at the sound of his given name, Sangre'e mono obeyed. He crossed himself, glancing furtively around the room.

"Listen up, it makes sense. Right before my old lady died, one of the things I promised her was I wouldn't go back to the hole, not even for fingerprints. So no, I don't want any trouble either. But I'm not about to spend my life selling soap, or whatever other bullshit to German gringas. No, gentlemen, there are more important things in life, things that affect everyone. You know thousands of plants and animals disappear every day?"

"What, they get stolen?" inferred Negroemierda.

"No, fuckwit, they die. They go extinct. When's the last time you saw a parrot not in a cage? They're not even on Isla de Pinos anymore. My grandpa used to hunt deer in the mountains, but you don't find them there these days. And hutias? And think about it, compared to other places, Cuba isn't even that bad. There are hardly any whales left, you know. Or tigers, or that Chinese bear, the what's-it-called, the black and white one with circles around its eyes. You think the Almendares River is dirty? Well, that's what the whole ocean is like."

"It's true," Sangre'e mono conceded. "I went to the beach on Sunday and a piece of crap was floating in the water."

"See? And what about the trees? Without trees, there's no air, the hole in the ozone will just get bigger, and we'll be charred out of existence. Fuck, ever since my old lady and the fern died, I've been thinking. The scraps, the easy stuff, that won't get us anywhere, we have to think big, gentlemen, think big or the world'll get too small."

Negroemierda, who'd been nodding his head for the past minute, continued to do so. Sangre'e mono lit a cigarette, then gestured aggressively and launched into a barrage of objections.

"And what the fuck are we going to do about it, Gravilla? It's the government's problem. They regulate everything here; you get a group together, doesn't matter what it is—maybe you're just drinking fucking soda—and they're on your back about it. What are we going to live off anyway, if we spend all our time in the Scatological Brigade?"

"Ecological. Ecology is a science—it studies how to keep plants and animals alive. There are ecologists all over the world these days. They're called Greens, they've got political parties."

"Political parties? And you're saying this to calm me down? Shiiit . . ."

"Let me speak, asshole. We're not going to do anything wrong, okay? Wherever someone's killing plants for no reason, we swoop in, talk'em out of it. If someone's trying to abandon an animal or making it suffer, we take out the little fucker's tooth. The government doesn't have to know. What'll we live off of? Man, for now, we'll just do what we've been doing. You can tell someone not to cut down a tree and then sell'em a T-shirt. No ideological contradictions there. The important thing is we'll know we're doing things that protect the environment."

Having finished speaking, Gravilla passed around the bottle of liquor. Negroemierda took a slow, deliberate sip before patting his host on the shoulder.

"Man, as far as I'm concerned, I can bailar this bomba. Fuck it, it's a nice idea, reminds me of when we were little pioneers. Maybe we'll even get some decent gigs and stop dealing soap. You think I should go to the foundry? See if they've got something for me?"

"Definitely," said Gravilla.

The following Sunday, the very first independent Environmental Brigade of Cuba (well, maybe just the city, or at the very least, Belén) began actively contributing to society. In the days following the constitutive meeting and leading up to the weekend, Negroemierda, elected Chief Information Officer, cut out and archived whatever mildly relevant material he could find, including an old edition of *Robin Hood*. From his research, ecologists were clearly a noble, thriving force in the civilized world, and Greenpeace—which they'd taken on as the family crest—had ships and planes and offices. Sangre'e mono thought they should have a name (something less threatening than Brigade), and he offered a few, wide-ranging suggestions that went from *Green Lightning* to *José Martí*. There was even a verse from Lorca. Gravilla said no, they didn't need a name, and Negroemierda, who was a pushover, agreed.

For their debut that Sunday, Gravilla planned an offensive to help stray animals. Together they gathered fifty cats, eighteen dogs, four mice, one pond slider turtle, twelve lizards, six chickens, and approximately ninety cockroaches. The cockroaches were unquestionably Sangre'e mono's doing, and once they were back at Brigade headquarters, he was admonished by Gravilla.

"Don't be an animal, 'Mono. Cockroaches are a pest."

"So? You didn't say there were rules. You said we had to protect all the animals. It's not the cockroach's fault it's a cockroach and likes crawling on people."

"Well, we need priorities. Pond sliders could go extinct, cockroaches won't. In fact, there's more and more cockroaches every day. Put'em outside. And give the mice to the cats."

"Sounds like an ethical dilemma," said Negroemierda, who'd been reading a lot the past few days, "we're just going to kill the mice? The cats might have eaten them anyway, or not, but if we straight up give them to the cats, they'll definitely get eaten, and personally, I think this whole thing's fucked if we're the ones killing rodents and altering the ecological balance."

"Fine. The mice get a head start. Put a meter between the cats and the mice and then release them. And since we're on the subject of ethical dilemmas, go return the chickens."

"They're stray chickens," Negroemierda said defensively, but when the other two looked him up and down, he backed down, "Well, sort of, in a way. There was a house along the fence."

In the end, they put in fifty pesos each—monthly dues, said Gravilla—and bought two pounds of dried milk for the dogs, cats, and reptiles. The reptiles, frankly unimpressed by the Green initiative, quickly began creeping and crawling their way to freedom. But the rest of the animals seemed thankful to be fed. One cat did scratch Sangre'e mono, however.

"So now what?" asked the wounded Sangre'e mono. "Do we sell T-shirts to buy food for the dogs and cats every week?"

"It's a symbolic act, animal. We're a Brigade, we do what we can."

"Stop calling me a fucking animal, man. I thought we're supposed to defend them. We can't use that word as an insult."

Negroemierda soon found a job as a security guard at the foundry and he took a mound of books with him to read at his post. Within a week, he'd begun telling the others that Buddha forbade killing anything that breathed and that, ultimately, this prohibition led to exhausting secular debates about whether a disciple of Siddhartha could rightfully step on an ant since, for all anyone knew, the ant could be a wise spirit reincarnated. Hoping to avoid logical quagmires, Gravilla suggested they define protected species as animals more than five centimeters long, domestic or otherwise, that didn't carry diseases and weren't being raised for end-of-year celebrations. And this, more or less, became the Brigade's official policy with regard to local fauna.

For Gravilla, whose environmentalism had sprung from a fern of familial importance, it was the flora that was especially important. Thus, the following Sunday he took his entourage to Vedado, where a group of neighbors had organized a collective, volunteer bush pruning. Once they delivered their fiery philippic against the wrongdoers, the Brigade was met by the unexpected accusation that they were sabotaging CDR efforts, and, ultimately, the threat of calling the police. The Brigade opted for tactical retreat, but they returned that very night, and, while the CDR watchman was snoring away, they dug up the mutilated bushes, took them to the Havana Forest, and planted them there.

Two months after the initial founding assembly, the Brigade had developed a renowned list of action items, the likes of which included the following:

1. Conscientious lambastement of an old man, the owner of a horse-drawn wagon, for allowing thirty children—at two pesos per capita—to ride said wagon around the block, at undeniable physical and, presumably, moral injury to the animal. Henceforth, the old man would limit wagon rides to ten children, albeit at six pesos a ticket. The children's parents complained, the old man blamed the Brigade, but the whole thing ended right there and then since the horse died that same day, the result of a monstrously sized hernia.

2. A trip to the seaside to pick up cans and other trash. The garbage, stuffed into six plastic sacks, was hauled away by the three commandos plus a handful of young women they casually met on the beach. It was deposited at an illicit dumping ground in the neighborhood and set on fire. The collateral damage included two singed clotheslines and three fully carbonized cats, one of which was Sangre'e mono's prior assailant. Subsequently, the carcasses were smuggled into the Zoo and, as a sort of offering, thrown into the tiger pen.

3. Shearing of the neighbor's pet husky, the idea being that the dog days of Cuban summer must be torture for a creature native to Alaska. The husky's owner tried to protest and, in return, was given an explanation and a punch, just not in that order. Then, to make up for it, said owner was sold a steeply discounted T-shirt.

4. Tree planting in overly urbanized and polluted zones, such as their own neighborhood, Belén. Given the lack of ad hoc terrain, the Brigade chose to rip out a few sections of sidewalk, haul in dirt from an empty lot, and plant their seedlings in the newly formed green space. Ferns, mostly. Children caught pulling up the saplings were immediately and severely reprimanded.

Etcetera, and lengthy etcetera.

After two months, Negroemierda lost his job; the others, meanwhile, had failed to find one. With the T-shirt and soap business all but neglected, they could barely afford their monthly dues. Their environmental fervor, on the other hand, had reached new heights on the mercury column. Perhaps no other virus is quite as contagious as doing social good, and the sheer volume of evil activates, animates. Just look at the state of the earth—from any angle—and you'll see.

"I was thinking," Negroemierda said one day (he'd become the true intellectual of the movement now that Gravilla was increasingly consumed by operational affairs), "fuck, man. We still don't have anything that identifies us. It's time to play hard. This shit has been a long time coming—first the ascetics, then Robin Hood, Rousseau, the hippies. All of them wanted to go back to nature. To live green. We're Greens. We need a uniform, something we can wear on environmental missions."

"A uniform . . . ," mused Sangre'e mono. "I know someone who could get us a few meters of green polyester, but it's not cheap."

"We don't need it," said Gravilla, "gentlemen, with three military uniforms, we're set. I've got two spares, from my time in the Reserves."

"And I've got another one," announced Negroemierda, "see? This is what I'm saying, we need to start with our image. We could get furry little almiquis[2] embroidered on the pockets. Maybe grow our hair out, become vegetarians. You know, the whole naturistic vibe. But it won't work unless we up our game. We have to make people really feel it, then they'll start talking about us."

His proposal to restrict their diet to the vegetable kingdom was not well received, but his other proposals were. By the third month, a troupe of hairy, bearded eccentrics, dressed in newly fitted olive-green uniforms, began making waves in wider Havana. Especially after someone claimed to have seen them wandering around Plaza de la Catedral the night before a tree fern, ten meters tall, was transplanted right into the middle of the square.

The barbacoa was rechristened General Headquarters, and it opened a public service office. Whoever wanted to could report someone for animal or plant cruelty or unconscionable environmental damage. Gravilla and Negroemierda attempted to enroll in an International Environmental Policy Workshop, but, for unknown reasons, their applications were rejected. It subsequently fell to Sangre'e mono to contact foreign activists, but on the second night, there was a police raid outside the hotel and he barely got away.

The Brigade was not a political faction. But only they knew that. When Sangre'e mono's girlfriend found out about their plans to pour concrete down the drain pipes at the Almendares River and fill the chimney at a plastics factory with shit, she left him, saying she saw nothing in his future but steel bars. Thinking they were spies or provocateurs, their neighbors in Belén stopped greeting them. In response, the trio began distributing posters that read TO SURVIVE IN CUBA, WE MUST KEEP CUBA CLEAN.

It was around then, at the peak of *underground* fame, that a sympathizer, of which there were a few, showed up at General Headquarters to report a dark conspiracy between a government farm administrator and some local criminals. Apparently, the administrator was letting criminals slaughter state cows in return for a hefty share of the profits. And, he said, the following night they were planning on killing a Holstein, a record-setting milker.

"We have to save her," said Gravilla excitedly. "A single life is worth more than all the possessions of the richest man in the world."

And that night the Brigade took a blood oath and Gravilla said Negroemierda was right, they should be vegetarians, and maybe they shouldn't even eat plants, because a true environmentalist should ultimately surpass Buddha. And they meditated, and almost levitated, and then they went to the cowshed and ambushed the administrator and began beating him, which is when the police arrived because the sympathizer—who'd been the owner of the asshole cat that scratched Sangre'e mono, the one that got burnt to a crisp—had set them up, and all it takes is three guys dressed like military beating up another guy, at night, in the woods, with a cow, and they assume they're a bunch of delinquents, Mr. Lawyer O'Donnell.

It was three in the morning and Negroemierda was on the last cigarette.

"The uniforms, that's where we went wrong," he concluded, "We got a little crazy. But fuck, Mr. O'Donnell, there's so much that needs doing . . . Where are the kids going to play, huh? Have you thought about that?"

I didn't respond. Gravilla, facing the wall, seemed to be sleeping. He hadn't said a word during Sangre'e mono's and Negroemierda's lengthy retelling. Sangre'e mono was openly weeping.

"Can you help us?" he asked, sniffling loudly.

"A little," I said, "but it won't be easy."

The prison guard reappeared at the door.

"You're not bored yet, Mr. Lawyer? You should get some rest. You missed the best episode."

"I'm leaving now," I said, and stared quietly at the three environmentalists. Three marginal men with no work history and enough charges for ten life sentences. The overwhelming image of defeat. I stood up.

"If you need anything now, maybe I can get it for you. More cigarettes?"

They didn't answer. I walked to the door. Just as I was about to leave, Gravilla spoke.

"There's something I want."

I turned. The expression on his face was difficult to define, halfway between imploring and amused.

"So long as it's within my reach," I responded.

"I'm sure it is. A fern. Could you bring me a fern? A small one."

"I'll do my best," I said, and left.

July 4, 1996

Notes

1. The nicknames of the three characters—Gravilla (gravel), Sangre'e mono (monkey-blood), and Negroemierda (shitty Black)—reflect the island's history of slavery and racialized identities. [—Eds.]

2. The almiqui or Cuban solenedon is a small, nocturnal burrowing animal endemic to the island. Rare and considered endangered, the almiqui's venom is poisonous. [—Eds.]

Esthela Calderón

León, Nicaragua, is where Rubén Darío breathed his last and where the poet Esthela Calderón was born (1970) and raised. Calderón is a tireless promoter of Nicaraguan culture, as well as an accomplished poet, novelist, and painter. She resides in upstate New York and teaches Latin American literature and creative writing at St. Lawrence University. Calderón is the author of the historical novel *Eight Sides of a Coin* (2008) as well as, with Steven F. White, of *Culture and Customs of Nicaragua* (2008). But Calderón is best known for her poetry, in particular the environmental and ethnobotanical poems of *Breeze of a Vital Current* (2010), *My Grandfather's Bones* (2013), and other works. Calderón attributes her deep appreciation for nonhuman nature to her Nicaraguan childhood. "As a child I learned the uses of plants like the *mango mechudo*, whose leaves, boiled in water, reduce inflammation, *limonaria*, which cures tooth-aches, and valeria, to induce sleep. Every time my thoughts took me back to the first verses that my mother taught me" (White 2014, 289). On one level, her poetry is an impressive catalog of plant species, filled with names and images that deepen our knowledge of the natural world and make visible the tremendous variety that exists. On another level, we find in her poetry a unique literary contribution to ethnobotany that deals not only with the practical, physical uses of plants but also with their mysterious connection to the human.

✳✳✳

Poems (2008–2012)

TRANSLATED BY STEVEN F. WHITE

The Woman I Could Have Been

If they'd let me make
each part of my body,
I would have chosen the strength of trees.

My feet would be sculpted from Laurel
and my legs would come from two solid trunks
of Pochote
so I'd never get tired as I carried my memory.

I'd mold my hips
with bronzed rhythms of Mahogany.
And with them I'd scare away disgrace
during days and nights of indifference.

My womb would become a husk,
a warm home where a Cacao tree grows,
and a pair of climbing vines would be my arms
so they could be outside and way beyond me,
holding me with the hands of a Guarumo.

If they'd let me make
each part of my body,
I would have chosen the varied
colors of plants and fruit.

With the Malinche's red,
I'd paint my lips for the labyrinth of battles.
I'd cover my body
with the color of sinful Nísperos.
And two black Tamarind seeds
would light my eyes.

The Guanacaste would give me two ears as a gift,
the Grosella, its round fruit for my nose.
And the Guava's little white pillows would be my teeth.

The wild Passionfruit's tangled vines
with Jalacate flowers would be my hair,
and a duo of small Mandarines
would sing happily on my chest.

If they'd allowed me to construct my heart,
I would have carved it from the flesh of an Oak
and added the flowers of all the Madreados in May,
a slice of obstinate Cactus,
the insufferable tolerance of a Poppy,
and something from the Orchid's cold gaze.

If they'd allowed me to make
each part of my body,
I would have chosen flowers that smell like sleep.

My tongue would turn into the Madrones' complaints
and the Corozos' Stations of the Cross.

My mouth would have the breath of Brugmansias.
Then I could die, transparent and awake,
longing for the slow passage of a star,
imagining myself now as the woman I could have been.

A bunch of Everlasting as a brain
and thick liquid from Hibiscus flowers for blood.

Seed of I Don't Know What

One November day in hurricane winds,
I was hurled into the void.
What could have been my home was left behind.
I flew, pushed by fury,
And fury itself became my sister.
I came and went,
making fun of a whirlpool here,
and learning how to whistle there.
I quickly learned to live
with the chains of the air.
It cost nothing to breathe deeply
and admire the imperturbable majesty of rivers
that decipher the consciousness of stones.
I sensed the vertigo of a mountain of Birches
and the symphony of Coyotes
as they howled in a labyrinth of tree trunks.
I landed on a carpet of black tulips.
Seed of I don't know what, that's what I've decided to call myself,
sister of fury and agony.

Talking with My Worms

Last night, I talked with the worms
who will eat my eyes, my tongue and my ears
one of these days, perhaps in the near future.
For now, they're eating Poppies and Guanábana roots,
killing time until my body falls
then curls up in its house of Pine.
They say it won't hurt:
a tickling around my toenails
and maybe a little shiver in my guts
will be the only hint of their meticulous work.
They've promised to merge me with the earth,
slide me over the butterflies' colors
and make me rain as golden sugar

on the roof of the room where I keep my books.
They'll move their fervent mouths
until they strip away the pulp from my hands.
Gray and white bones will be the fortune
I bequeath between the boards.
In the brain splashed across the canvas
of a lasting poem,
they'll decipher it all, letter by letter,
until they reach the trees, stones and flowers.
They say I'll return in the musical bark and deep voice of an Espavel tree
or in the Chilamates' spiral-bound siestas.
This dream about my worms
is the most prudent thing I've been able to write
about life.

Juan Carlos Galeano

Raised in the area of the Caquetá River, in the Amazon basin of Colombia, Juan Carlos Galeano (b. 1958) has created a body of poetry, prose, and film that reflects his long political and aesthetic engagement with the diverse societies of the rain forest. Galeano, an environmental activist, poet, and professor at Florida State University, is a witness to both the deleterious effects of deforestation for agriculture and cattle ranching—especially the displacement of originary peoples—and to the transformative possibilities of Amazonian cultures, Indigenous and mestizo alike. Amazonia's stories, and the systems of knowledge and cosmologies of Amazonian cultures, would become the focus of years of travel and fieldwork for Galeano, as well as the subject of much of his artistic work. His 2009 *Folktales of the Amazon* includes stories from seven different countries and presents a series of narratives about the relationships among people, plants, animals, and other supernatural beings. Galeano's poetic style has also been influenced by the stories he collects. The selections presented here come from his 2014 collection of poetry *Yakumama (and Other Mythical Beings)*. Rooted in Indigenous and creole traditions, the poems depict a transformational world in which identities are profoundly unstable, sometimes hilariously so. Plants express desire, fear, and resentment; creatures shape-shift; and curses fly, particularly when humans enter the jungle without heeding its warning. The Western distinction between nature and society is all but unknown here. Exploring the supernatural and highly sensorial realm of Galeano's Amazon, then, we experience the awe of an encounter with a world that is at once grand, incomprehensible, and deeply vulnerable.

***

Poems (2014)

TRANSLATED BY JAMES KIMBRELL AND REBECCA MORGAN

Curupira

With one foot pointing ahead and the other pointing behind, the Curupira walks
      through the jungle and tends to the animals, braiding the young palm
      trees' hair.

Hunters swap the Curupira cigars for his secrets.

The Curupira puffs the cigars; animals, trees, and fruits appear in the path of
      his smoke.

But the men shouldn't make off with all the animals, trees, and fruits.

The Curupira could blow smoke so the animals, trees, and fruits disappear.

Blow all his smoke and make the paths vanish.

He could also tell the animals his secrets for hunting men.

Dark Shamans

for Neil L. Whitehead, in memoriam

Píííímatíchupíríí, whistle the Dark Ones with their blade-lips, signaling any harm
      that speeds toward people.

The leaves turn yellow, white, black, and then yellow again.

The Dark Ones sip their victims' juices through silver straws.

Píííímatíchupíríí, they whistle as they slip away, smelling of tiger lard and leaving
      no other trace.

Because of the Dark Ones a man's hand shrivels up, or he loses his job.

Some little flowers are wrong if they think the Dark Ones are harmless.

If it weren't for mothers' prayers and music from the radio, the Dark Ones would
      squelch the happiness of many.

Cantagalo

"Cantagalo once was a city on dry land."

A paradise city at the bottom of the river.

Those who live along the riverbanks say you can hear dogs barking, roosters
      crowing and music in the streets.

Mothers of the river manufacture pure air under the water

and fruits that appear by themselves on the tables that grow in their fields.

Pain and thorns are left behind on the trail, far from Cantagalo.

There is nothing more beautiful than pearl houses with boas for hammocks where love-wrecked pink dolphins play around.

"If there is a heaven up there, there should be one down here," say the songs coming from the water.

"Come live with us," call the dolphins as they smile at the young girls in their dreams.

Lupuna

A tree famous for his ability to do good or evil, but mostly evil.

His mother sleeps in the belly of his trunk with one eye wide open, one shut.

If someone wants to do evil to an enemy, they tack a picture to the Lupuna's trunk.

No one, calling to clouds, should beat the trunk of a Lupuna.

Nor should anyone turn the Lupuna's soul into pressboard.

Effortlessly, when the Lupuna gets upset, his mother lets fly all manner of darts and arrows.

You should greet the Lupuna and take him presents every now and then.

To those who don't respect the Lupuna and piss beside his trunk, the Lupuna will balloon their bellies with water until they burst.

EIGHT
End Times: Climate Change and Mass Extinction

The earth is currently undergoing what scientists refer to as a mass-extinction event, the dying off of an extraordinary number of species in a very short time. As Elizabeth Kolbert (2014, 19) writes in her Pulitzer Prize–winning book *The Sixth Extinction*, five similarly massive episodes of biotic attrition have occurred "in the three-and-a-half-billion-year history of life on earth"; the most recent one was triggered by the asteroid that wiped out the dinosaurs sixty-five million years ago. Species are now disappearing at anywhere from a thousand to ten thousand times the normal background rate, and scientists estimate that from 25 to 75 percent of existing species will be lost over the next century. The causes of the Sixth Extinction are multiple and complex, but they all stem from human activity: pollution, habitat loss, mobility (so-called invasive species), and, above all, anthropogenic climate change. "We" — or at least those of us whose lifestyles are based on fossil-fuel consumption, industrial agriculture, and other processes resulting in the emission of heat-trapping carbon dioxide that becomes stored in the earth's atmosphere — have changed the chemical and biological composition of environments around the world so radically and so quickly that adaptations developed over millions of years of evolutionary history are useless to species' survival, and sometimes fatal (17). The writers brought together in this final section help us to mourn the irreparable losses of the Sixth Extinction while also documenting and adamantly protesting the unequal distribution of ecological risk and responsibility in our time.

The first decades of the twentieth-first century have seen important political and socioeconomic developments in Latin America. The massive dislocations caused by neoliberal economic policies in the 1980s and '90s prompted the rise of the so-called New Left in Latin American politics, beginning with Hugo Chávez's election as president of Venezuela in 1998. Chávez was soon joined by left-leaning leaders in Brazil, Argentina, Chile, Bolivia, Ecuador, Uruguay, and Paraguay, a veritable "pink tide" that promised to counteract neoimperialistic economic policies of the United States and the world's major financial institutions by restoring redistributive programs in their countries.

The rise of the New Left was especially remarkable in the Andean region, where Evo Morales became Bolivia's first head of state of Indigenous descent (and the region's second, after Benito Juárez in nineteenth-century Mexico). Morales and Ecuador's Rafael Correa were both elected in part on the basis of an important alliance of Indigenous and environmentalist support. In 2008 Ecuador became the first country in the world to constitutionally enshrine the rights of nature. Based on the Indigenous Andean concept of *sumac kawsay*, which translates roughly to "the good way of living," the constitution guarantees Ecuadorans' right to potable water, healthy sustainable food consistent with their identities and cultural traditions, and the right to live in a safe, unpolluted environment. Even more radically, article 71 of the constitution invokes Pachamama, the earth/mother of traditional Andean belief, stating that "Nature, or Pacha Mama, where life is reproduced and occurs, has the right to integral respect for its existence and for the maintenance and regeneration of its life cycles, structure, functions and evolutionary processes." Bolivia soon followed suit.

Despite that promise, however, the history of the New Left in power has been marked by contradiction and rising popular discontent. During the first few years, the rapid expansion of China's economy provided important opportunities for Latin American governments to raise revenues for social justice initiatives including housing, health care, and education. Those same opportunities made it extremely difficult for Ecuador and Bolivia to maintain their commitment to Indigenous and environmentalist constituencies. In practice, the rights of nature have been regularly sacrificed to neoextractivist economic policies. In Venezuela, the important socioeconomic initiatives undertaken by the Bolivarian Revolution ran aground with the worldwide collapse of oil prices: after Chávez dismantled the country's agricultural system, his successor, Nicolás Maduro, has turned armed militias against a starving and irate population. Frustrations following the downturn of China's economy have led to the resurgence of right-wing governments in Argentina, Brazil, and Paraguay.

Meanwhile, drug trafficking fueled by demand in the United States has led to an increase in violence and corruption, especially in Mexico and Central America. As economic globalization continues to produce strong incentives for the extraction of natural resources, a dangerous situation has arisen for the individuals and communities that have dared to protest the destruction of their environments. As reported in the *Guardian*, environmental activists are killed around the world every week, many of them in Latin America, "where the abundance of resources is often in inverse proportion to the authority of the law or environmental regulation" (Watts 2018). The list of those murdered includes Honduras's Berta Cáceres (d. 2016), whose Goldman Prize acceptance speech is featured among the selections in this part. Cáceres was a leader of the four-thousand-member Lenca people, who successfully prevented the world's largest dam-building company, Sinohydro, from constructing a hydroelectric dam on the Gualcarque River.

Belgian philosopher Isabelle Stengers (2015) offers a simple observation with terrifying implications: "we are more badly equipped than ever for putting to work the solutions defined as necessary" (10) to avoid the most devastating possibilities associated with global climate change—mass extinction in the oceans and on land; sea-level rise that drowns islands and coastal cities; the widespread collapse of agricultural systems; and the reoccurrence of massive hurricanes and other "natural" disasters—all of which will create human upheaval, conflict, and suffering on a previously unprecedented scale. According to Stengers, the inadequacy of our culture and our politics was already self-evident in the response to Hurricane Katrina, which struck the city of New Orleans in 2005: "the poor abandoned whilst the rich found shelter" (25). As demonstrated by the U.S. government's grossly insufficient response to Hurricanes Irma and María—now known to have caused the deaths of more than four thousand people in Puerto Rico—the situation has only gotten worse. Donald Trump won the U.S. presidency in 2016 in part on the assurance that he would invalidate President Barack Obama's commitment to the 2015 Paris Agreement and roll back decades of environmental protections. Throughout much of the Americas, we now face a political landscape in which the most powerful institutions are multinational corporations.

The COVID-19 pandemic that began in late 2019 offers other alarming lessons about governments' inability to control the dangers unleashed by humankind's changing relations with nonhuman nature. As environmental historian Donald Worster (2020) points out, a growing number of biologists who study disease outbreaks have found that epidemics often follow a "disturbance in ecological relations," humans being the principal disturbing force. People are causing animals sickness as we alter their habitats and disorganize their lives, especially by turning wild ecosystems into more simplified agricultural regimes (Worster 2020). Industrial agriculture, considered the "biggest single cause of declining biodiversity and species extinction on the planet" is making "old, relatively harmless viruses that had been generalists into deadly specialists that live on a narrowing biotic spectrum" (Worster 2020). While we have been practicing agriculture for thousands of years, we are now doing it more aggressively because of the economic benefit of the increased food demand, which could not happen without the connivance of agribusiness and corporate farmers in the global trade world. The novel coronavirus, which is believed to have leapt from bats to human beings, possibly in China, before spreading around the globe on cruise ships, airplanes, and other vectors of human creation, has underscored our species' shared vulnerability to ecological imbalance, even as mortality rates remain disproportionately high among communities of color throughout the United States and in much of the world. While some have cheered the temporary reduction in air pollution as people responded to lock-down orders around the planet, the larger environmental crisis and the losses it entails thus far show no sign of abating.

Capitalist institutions, as one group of authors puts it, send "a constant barrage of messages asking us to *forget*—that is, to allow a few private owners and public officials with their eyes focused on short-term gains to pretend that environmental devastation does not exist" (Tsing et al. 2017, 1). The selections gathered in this part resist the capitalist imperative to forget. Some, like the poetry of Mexico's Homero Aridjis and José Emilio Pacheco, are works of mourning that treat the animal species conservation biologists refer to as "ghosts" because their extinction in the wild is already irreversible. In a world of induced obliviousness, to mourn the losses of the Anthropocene is at once a necessary prelude to politics and a political act in itself. As Donna Haraway (2016, 39) writes, "Grief is a path to understanding entangled shared living and dying; human beings must grieve with, because we are in and of this fabric of undoing. Without sustained remembrance, we cannot learn to live with ghosts and so cannot think." Humans, as Haraway points out, following the work of Thom van Dooren, are not the only species that grieve the loss of their kin; to mingle our grief with other animals, as Pacheco and Aridjis do, is to recognize ourselves and other species as mutually dependent subjects.

Other selections here are also populated with ghosts and spirits, including "the traces of more-than-human histories through which ecologies are made and unmade" (Tsing et al. 2017, 1). Such is the case with Mayra Montero's 1997 novel *In the Palm of Darkness*, about a herpetologist hunting for Haiti's disappearing frogs. Ghosts and spirits also haunt Samanta Schweblin's *Fever Dream* (2014), an eco-gothic horror story about the unpredictable aftermath of pesticide poisoning. These mysterious presences are reminders of the reality of beings and powers whose existence defies human understanding. The papal encyclical of 2015, issued by the first Catholic pope from Latin America, raises similar themes from within the spiritual tradition of the Roman Catholic Church.

Non-Western articulations also feature prominently in this section. Aridjis's poems incorporate traces of Amerindian knowledge, suggesting the resonance between our unfolding ecological disaster and the Spanish conquest of Mexico/Tenochtitlán. We also feature two poems by Jaime Huenún, a Mapuche writer from Chile's southern territory. Huenún's "Ceremony of Love" and "Ceremony of Death" are contributions to the decolonization of knowledge, a project that now seems increasingly essential to the continued survival of our species as a whole. At the same time, Huenún's work subtly presses back on the catastrophism of our times. As the critic Macarena Gómez-Barris (2017, 4) writes, if we intend to "decolonize the Anthropocene," it will be necessary to "catalogu[e] life otherwise, or the emergent and heterogeneous forms of living that are not about destruction or mere survival within the extractive zone, but about the creation of emergent alternatives." For Huenún and other Indigenous intellectuals, "the paradigm of 'no future' has already taken place and we are on the other side of the colonial catastrophe" (4).

Finally, we conclude with three poems by Peruvian Eduardo Chirinos, originally published in the collection *Thirty-Five Biology Lessons (and Three Didactic Stories)*. The "didactic stories" reproduced here are all about extinction events: the asteroid that wiped out the dinosaurs, the volcanic eruption that triggered an ice age seventy thousand years ago, and the more recent nuclear disaster at Chernobyl, in the former Soviet Union. These beautiful poems, written while the poet himself was struggling with cancer, demonstrate a spirit of tenderness, irony, and gentle curiosity as Chirinos addresses a radically, rapidly changing world and the life-forms emerging within it.

Suggestions for Further Reading

Luis Sepúlveda. 1989. *Mundo del fin del mundo*. Barcelona: Tusquets, 1994.

Sylvia Iparraguirre. 1998. *Tierra del Fuego*, translated by Hardie St. Martin. Willimantic, Conn.: Curbstone, 2000.

Sônia Bridi. 2012. *Diário do clima: Efeitos do aquecimento global—um relato em cinco continentes*. São Paulo: Globolivros, 2012.

Jaime Luis Huenún Villa. 2014. *Poetry of the Earth: Trilingual Mapuche Anthology*, edited by Jaime Luis Huenún Villa and translated by Víctor Cifuentes Palacios, Juan Garrido Salgado, Steve Brock and Sergio Holas. Carendale, Queensland, Australia: Interactive Press, 2014.

Liliana Colanzi. 2016. *Our Dead World*, translated by Jessica Sequeira. Victoria, Tex.: Dalkey Archive Press, 2017.

José Emilio Pacheco

José Emilio Pacheco (1939–2014) was among the most important writers of his generation. His poetry is characterized by clarity, precision, and balance, with limited ornamentation; if Pacheco's great overarching theme is time, his work also addresses social and environmental issues in his native Mexico, especially pollution, poverty, and government bureaucracy. Pacheco produced his first works of poetry, *Elements of Night* and *Fire's Repose* in the 1950s and '60s, and he remained prolific in subsequent decades. In addition to poems, Pacheco wrote novels, including *You Will Die Far from Here* (1967); he also produced acclaimed anthologies of Mexican and Latin American poetry and taught literature at several U.S. universities. In 2009, Pacheco received the prestigious Cervantes Prize in recognition of his lifetime achievement. *An Ark for the Next Millennium*, published in 1993, is an anthology of animal poems Pacheco wrote over the course of nearly thirty years. The collection takes inspiration from the medieval genre of the bestiary, in which allegories of real or imaginary animals are used for moral or religious purposes. As the critic María Rosa Olivera-Williams points out (1998), Pacheco's *Ark* resembles the traditional bestiary in that it, too, is a collective effort. The poetry, which incorporates copious citations from earlier published work, is richly illustrated by painter Francisco Toledo; the version presented here, furthermore, was translated by Margaret Sayers Peden. In these poems, Pacheco examines the human world through the eyes of animals and the animal world through the eyes of humans, and he connects the two worlds both symbolically and materially. As a result, environmental apocalypse becomes a shared experience as animals and the violent natural world they face become at once poetic subjects and tools for reflection on the most ruthless species of all: the human.

***

Poems (1993)

TRANSLATED BY MARGARET SAYERS PEDEN

Equation to the First Degree, with Unknown Quantity

In the city's last river, through error
or spectral incongruity, suddenly
I saw a dying fish. It was gasping,
poisoned by filthy water as lethal as
the air we breathe. What frenzy in

the ring of its lips
the gaping zero of its mouth.
Nothingness perhaps,
word beyond expression,
the last voice
of nature in the valley.
The fish's only recourse was
a choice between asphyxias.
That double agony haunts me,
the dying water and its habitant:
    its doleful eyes on me,
    its will to be heard,
    its irrevocable sentence.
I will never know what it tried to tell me,
that voiceless fish that spoke only the
omnipotent language of our mother, death.

Whales

Large floating tribes
    migrations
icebergs of flesh and blood
    doleful islands

Through the sad night of the deep
    resounds
their elegy and farewell
    because the sea
has been dispossessed of its whales

Survivors from a different apocalypse
    they adopted the shape of fish
without becoming like them

They must surface to breathe
    covered with millenary algae
and then
    the cruel, explosive harpoon
gluts itself on them

And all the sea becomes
    a sea of blood
as they are towed to the factory ship
    to make lipstick

soap   oil
and dog food

His eyes [are] like the eyelids of the morning.
Out of his nostrils goeth smoke,
like that of a pot heated and boiling.
In his neck strength shall dwell,
and want goeth before his face.*

*Based on Job 41:18–22 (King James Version).

Augury

Until just recently I was awakened by the sound of birds.
Today I realized they're no longer there. Those signs of life
are gone. Without them, things seem much drearier. I
wonder what may have killed them—pollution? noise?
starving city dwellers? Or maybe the birds realized that
Mexico City is dying, and have flown away before the
final ruin.

Baboon Babble

Born here in this cage, the first lesson
I, the baboon, learned was that
in every direction I look this world is
        bars and more bars.
Everything I see is striped
like the bars of a tiger's pelt.
They say somewhere there are free monkeys.
        I have seen nothing
but an infinity of kindred prisoners,
        always behind bars.
        At night I dream
of a jungle bristling with bars.
I live only to be stared at.
The throng they call people comes here.
They like to tease me. They enjoy it
when my rage rattles the bars.
        My freedom is my cage.
        Only dead
will I be carried outside these brutal bars.

Homero Aridjis

Born (1940) to a Greek father and Mexican mother in Michoacán, Mexico, Homero Aridjis is an indefatigable playwright, novelist, and poet, as well as an internationally recognized environmental activist. In reality, it is practically impossible to separate Aridjis's activism from his creative work. While he has lived in and out of Mexico, including as ambassador to the Netherlands and Switzerland, and as a professor at multiple U.S. institutions, Aridjis for many decades now has been a prominent and widely respected figure of Mexican culture and politics. He was a founding member of the Mexican National Advisory Council for Environmental Sustainability; he is also founder and president of the Group of One Hundred, an advocacy group that convenes influential artists and intellectuals to fight against air pollution, species loss, and other issues of concern. They are especially known for their work to preserve the oyamel fir forests of the Monarch Butterfly Biosphere Reserve in central Mexico, where millions of monarchs spend the winter months before beginning their multigenerational migration to the United States and Canada. Aridjis's poetry merges elements from the Bible, Greek mythology, and Mexican history. Since the 1980s, his poems have often revolved around visions of environmental collapse due to human neglect of the natural world. Representing the planet as a Garden of Eden entrusted to humanity, Aridjis introduces the idea of apocalypse, not as the divine judgment of Judeo-Christian tradition but as a gradual act of a human race that has become oblivious to its deep dependence on the more-than-human world surrounding it.

***

Poems (1994–2014)

TRANSLATED BY GEORGE MCWHIRTER

Uncreation

the world made
man came
with an ax
a bow
a gun
a harpoon
a bomb
armed from head to foot

to the teeth with evil intent
he killed the rabbit
he killed the eagle
he killed the tiger
he killed the whale
he killed off man

The Last Night of the World

I believed it was the last night of the world
and the angels of light and dark would appear
on the horizon and many would go down
in mortal conflict. In the battle
between the hosts of good and evil,
man would be made spectator; the golds
from the sundered day tumble from the clouds.

But it was not the last night of the world,
only one more night that would not come back to the world.
Standing at the window of a room that looked out
over a few gray houses and a vanished river,
an angel was thinking about the bodies of water that had been.
It heard the story of its lost childhood in the distance,
the river ran through yesterday, which is the future running backwards.

The virgin, a Mazahua Indian, was begging in the street,
but nobody would give a dime to help her
because there was a street full of Mazahua women
and it would take a sack of coins to give to all.
And because this nobody had holes in his pockets
and bony legs. The street was a concrete
loneliness lost in other lonelinesses of concrete.

It made my head ache to see what men had done
to the water and the birds,
to the life and the trees along the avenue.
It made my head ache to see my shadow in the street
and to know that down every road and every moment
the end of the world drew nigh. A beggar
with shining eyes was pursuing me.

In the shop windows of men, there were
stuffed animals and plastic fruit,
photographs of the Earth when it was still blue;
of woods, long before their ruination.

Hungering after memory, but for myself
more, I turned a corner, seeking to come upon
that double of mine, the beggar, by surprise.

I met an angel with big feet
reading the paper under the muddied moon,
the golden prints of his feet were embossed on the sidewalk.
ANGELS INVADE THE CITY—
was the news of the day;
OUR VIRGINS LOVE-CRAZED BY ANGELS—
was yesterday's.

Then, unwilling and unenthused,
I unwalked all the roads,
as if the love of the beings I knew
had deserted the streets of the Earth.
Then, on reaching my home,
like the angel at the window, I put
my ear to hearing the water of the vanished river.

The Hunt for the Red Jaguar

To Chloe and Eva Sophia

We tracked the jaguar all night.
Now and then, he paused to observe us
with the eyes of a drunken sun. Elusive.
When we closed in, he was gone.

We went after him as in pursuit of a myth.
All the animals had died,
those not dead had been caged.
We were only missing the red jaguar.

We set out in pursuit of him at nightfall.
We lit up his face in the fastness.
The preyed-upon predator, we identified him
by the black spots on his solar coat.

Us, we burned copal,
set traps in his path.
We danced his dance
in feline face masks.

We summoned serpents
out of myth and history,
those who pour phantoms from their maws
into the land of the living.

His amber-yellow eyes
never stopped staring
through the bushes at
our eyes besotted with greed.

We raved out loud,
we had projects on hand,
a hotel to be built here, a golf course there,
a road, a discotheque.

Walking on the *k'an che*,
those stones that talk in the night,
we heard his deep-voiced
growls, the roars.

Along the macheted trail
the white dogs barked at him
under the dried-up tree
where he was perched.

We went after him as far as the Cave.
In its labyrinth of entrances and exits
he lost us. Navigator of the nothing,
down the underground river he sailed on a log.

We hunted him through woodland and savannah,
through mangrove and mountain. His soul
traveled through the Milky Way. From the fangs
of the Plumed Serpent, Venus hung like a pearl.

He called upon his ancestral gods in the savannah,
howling at the death of the Jungle,
the Animals and Trees
in the Era of Extinction.

Yellow with light the old Tree
of the World was not far off.
With its necklace of mirrors and jade
was the Serpent conceived in the sea.

At the site of the Black Dream
the opened sarcophagus clanged,
out of it spirits emerge
talking like you and I.

"He's going to come down here, the shadow
is leaping at us," said the hunter.
But he did not come down, for the Jaguar god
went home to his throne of black stone in Chichén Itzá.

There, while gorging on his prey,
we took him. We transferred him to a zoo.
Along all the spillways of noise
streams of cars tore down on us.

The provoker of eclipses,
Lord of the Starry Night,
the Jaguar god, now
clapped into a cage.

Images of Butterflies

In the twilight mountains the earth dark boat

In the nocturnal sky empty of butterflies

Space butterfly-less as man void of images

Under the full moon white clusters of silence

All have gone, only I stay on

chasing the shadows of butterflies under the full moon

Mayra Montero

Born (1952) in Havana, Cuba, Mayra Montero and her family resettled in Puerto Rico not long after the Revolution. She studied journalism in Puerto Rico and Mexico, becoming an acclaimed news correspondent and journalist. Montero continues to produce reportage and a weekly column, as well as prose fiction. As a student, she came into contact with the Haitian community in Puerto Rico, learning about their traditions and contemporary reality through university professors and her own travels to the Dominican Republic and Haiti, where she witnessed the struggles of migrant laborers. These experiences are prominent in Montero's short stories and novels, which explore a wide Caribbean geography and cultural practices ranging from the sugar harvest to voodoo. She is the author of ten books, including the 1997 novel *Tú la oscuridad*, translated into English as *In the Palm of Darkness*. Inspired by the mysterious worldwide disappearance of frog species, the novel traces the fictional journey of an American academic, Victor Grigg, who travels to the mountains of Haiti in search of the *grenouille du sang*, the rare "blood frog" that he fears has gone extinct. Accompanying Victor is Thierry Adrien, a native Haitian knowledgeable of the occult and of local fauna. In this excerpt from the novel, Victor continues his search after a beating from the infamous Macoute, a special operations group of the military government, and presents himself for a meeting with a Haitian herpetologist, Dr. Emile Boukaka. Just as the novel presents a meeting and fusion of cultures, so too does it bring into conversation diverse systems of environmental knowledge in pursuit of an ecological mystery that has evaded Western science.

✳✳✳

"Indian Hut" (1997)

TRANSLATED BY EDITH GROSSMAN

We didn't go to Jérémie that week or the next week either. We left twenty days later, on a Tuesday, after I'd seen the doctor recommended by the embassy. He was an elderly Haitian, very short and somewhat brusque, who spent a long time palpating my bones and examining me with a stethoscope. He also drew blood samples, and with the results in hand he came to tell me I was cured.

My recuperation took longer than expected because of an enlarged vein, a kind of dark-green tumor at the height of my knee, a hard, painful ball that would not go down for days. I used the time to research the species mentioned by Thierry. *Osteopilus dominicencis* was the scientific name for a variety of toad that was fairly common on Hispaniola. It could be white, and then it was called *crapaud blanc*, or brown, and then the name changed to *crapaud brun*. What was known in Haiti as the *bilan* was simply the *Diodon holacanthus*, a spine-covered fish also called the guanabana fish. As for the *crapaud de mer*, I learned it was the *Sphoeroides testudineus*, the most poisonous species in these waters.

One afternoon a man came to see me in the company of the hotel manager: He said he was from the police and wanted details of the assault; he asked if I suspected anyone or wanted to file a complaint. I thought it prudent to say I could hardly remember a thing, and suspected no one. I added that all I wanted was to recover so I could travel to Jérémie, and somehow I let him know that I wouldn't go back to the Mont des Enfants Perdus.

He seemed satisfied, and promised that the investigation would continue and they'd keep me informed; the manager only bowed his head, he was a distinguished-looking mulatto with a quiet voice who did not wish to intervene more than absolutely necessary. When they left I decided to call Martha. I had been waiting for the right moment, it was New Year's Eve, a date that intimidates me and that I loathe with all my heart, which is why I felt like placing the call. It took them more than a quarter of an hour to connect me, and when I finally heard her voice, something very strange happened, I became disoriented for a second and asked who I was talking to; very discreetly she said, "It's me," she recognized my voice right away and was self-assured enough to wait and say nothing. "It's Victor," I said in a strangled voice. She didn't speak right away, first she cleared her throat: "You vanish like a ghost and now suddenly you reappear."

I told her about the theft of the letters and the report for Vaughan Patterson, but as I spoke I noticed that my words sounded false, as if I were inventing an excuse, a wild story, something even I had trouble believing. I didn't mention the beating; I would have liked to cause her concern but the entire incident was rather humiliating and I wasn't sure what effect it would have on her.

For a long time Martha didn't say a word, she was listening to me, I suppose, and then she interrupted: "Listen, I have something to tell you." It was my turn to be silent, and I felt the vein in my knee begin to throb; I moved my leg and the throbbing stopped. "I wrote you a letter," she continued, "and I want to know where to send it." I waited a few seconds, I thought about asking her just to tell me what it was, to do it on the phone, a single blow, rapid and precise. Instead I said I was staying at the Oloffson Hotel but in a few days I'd be leaving for Jérémie, and the best thing was to write to me in care of the embassy; I gave her the address and she repeated it to make sure she had it right. Then she gave me some messages left by my colleagues; Patterson had called too, trying to locate me, but Martha couldn't help him very much: "I told him I didn't know anything about you." At this point the conversation languished and ended as abruptly as it had begun, with no good wishes for the new year; neither one of us wanted to mention it, that would have been too much. When I hung up I was filled with a kind of shame, or mute rage; I regretted not asking what I clearly was obliged to ask. In situations like this a man has to know certain details. I picked up the receiver to call her again but hung up immediately. In situations like this a man needs all his self-control.

By the time I could finally walk again, Thierry had located Dr. Emile Boukaka, a surgeon and an amateur herpetologist. Months earlier I had read one of his articles in *Froglog* on the decline of amphibians; it was a brief piece but I made a file for it and decided to write to him. I never imagined at the time that I would meet him face-to-face in Port-au-Prince. He sent me his card through Thierry, fine gray stock with gray-blue lettering; I called and we made an appointment.

The day before we were to leave for Jérémie, I went to number 77 rue Victor Severe, a brick house that had no shingle. Only at the top of the stairs, a few steps made of shoddy cement, rough cement that scraped at the soles of my shoes, did I see a nameplate: EMILE BOUKAKA, CABINET. I rang the bell and a neatly dressed girl opened the door, led me straight to her small desk, and we both remained standing while she looked for my name in an old appointment book. Then she asked me to have a seat. At that hour there were no patients, and since there were no magazines or newspapers either, I concentrated on a large poster, stained with mildew, that hung directly in front of me:

> *Toad, that under cold stone*
> *Days and nights hast thirty-one*
> *Swelter'd venom sleeping got,*
> *Boil thou first i' the charmed pot.*

Next to the poster was a kind of bulletin board with a number of postcards pinned to the cork. I went over to look at them, they were from all over the world, France for the most part, but also some unexpected places, Bombay, for example, Nagasaki, Buenos Aires, even Bafatá. The girl had left the room, and out of curiosity I took down some cards: most were simply greetings and regards, or data related to the disappearance of some amphibian. One, however, attracted my attention more than the others: Under a shelter three naked Indian women were squatting down and cooking, and behind them a very old man, who was naked as well, stared belligerently into the camera. The card seemed very old, and it was hand-painted; in one corner, in tiny letters, was the caption: INDIAN HUT, BENI, BOLIVIA.

On the other side were a few lines written in a mix of English and French:

"*De Pérou, une photo de mes cher anthropophages. Kisses to Duval, is he still in Port-au-Prince?*"

It was signed at the bottom with the initials C. Y.

I looked for a date but didn't see one, I replaced it, and at that moment was startled by a honeyed-almond voice, almost a woman's voice:

"*Et bien*, where are the blessed frogs going?"

I had thought that Emile Boukaka was a mulatto; nobody had told me so but I had an image of him as a tall, gray-haired light-skinned man with spectacles, more self-conscious, less chubby and tropical than he actually was. Boukaka wore a green shirt with hibiscus flowers on it, and he was absolutely black, intensely black, the skin on his arms gleamed as if he had been born in Africa. His hair and beard were somewhat reddish, and he had an enormous round, flat face, a face like a Mexican (or Bolivian?) tortilla patted into shape by naked Indian women. There, in the fat circle of that face, his nose, his bulging eyes, his thick half-smiling lips seemed to be dancing.

"They're all going to leave us," he added. "I know you're looking for the *grenouille du sang*."

I smiled, and Boukaka gestured for me to follow him. He led me down a hallway filled with night photographs; I recognized some species, most were from the Amazon. Then we came to an office painted yellow; more photos were hanging there, and I stopped in front of an imposing, gigantic, purple image: It was the *Eleutherodactylus sanguineus*.

"They're leaving or they're hiding," he insisted. "Or they're simply letting themselves die. Nothing is clear, nobody wants to talk about it."

"I do," I said. "I came to talk to you."

He showed me a copy of a report he had been working on for several years. He took out more photographs, opened a cabinet and showed me fifteen or twenty preserved frogs. The *grenouille du sang* was not among them, though he said he had often seen it when he was a boy, and later, in his youth, he had caught one. His father, who had also been a physician and a student of batrachians, used to take him along on his expeditions to the Mont des Enfants Perdus. But those had been different times, before the place had been turned into the hell it later became.

"Nowadays no one would even think about going on that mountain," he added.

"I did," I replied, with some irony, "and so did the guide who works with me. His name is Thierry Adrien and he worked with Jasper Wilbur more than thirty years ago."

"That Thierry . . ." Boukaka murmured, not finishing the sentence. "I didn't know Wilbur, but he was a good friend of my father's. He died suddenly, and my father was the one who went to Jérémie to collect his things."

I was about to ask if he knew the circumstances of Jasper Wilbur's death, but decided I shouldn't distract him or change the subject. Then I spoke to him about Casetaches Hill, we discussed for some time the possibility of finding *Eleutherodactylus sanguineus* there, not more than a handful of individuals but I'd settle for a single frog so I could keep my promise to Vaughan Patterson. Boukaka shook his head and I attempted to persuade him. They'd said, for example, that the Wyoming toad had disappeared. Dr. Baxter, who discovered it, was the first to raise the alarm, and then in 1983 his assistants admitted there was nothing else to do, nowhere else to look. I had put it in my file of extinct species. And had kept it there until 1987, when a fisherman saw it in a pond south of Laramie. True, it was just one colony with fewer than a hundred members. But it was the *Bufo hemiophyrs*, no doubt about it, Baxter's favorite animal. They say the man wept when he saw it again.

"Do you know what the farmers say on Gonâve Island?"

Boukaka circled the room and stopped right behind me; it was difficult for me to hear and accept that voice, a thin, musical thread, and not be able to look into his face.

"They say that Agwé Taroyo, the god of waters, has called the frogs down to the bottom. They say they have seen them leave: Freshwater animals diving into the sea, and the ones that don't have the time or strength to reach the meeting place are digging holes in the ground to hide, or letting themselves die along the way."

Boukaka came back into view, holding a pipe in his mouth; the pipe was cold, and he sat down again at his desk and began to fill it with tobacco.

"It seems absurd, doesn't it? . . . Well, some fishermen from Corail who were casting their nets near Petite Cayemite reported pulling hundreds of dead frogs from the water, and when they came to the beach, a little rocky beach on the island, they found the birds devouring thousands of other frogs. That was two weeks ago."

The aroma was very strong, cinnamon mixed with something else I couldn't identify: perhaps anise or mint; I had a hunch it might have been eucalyptus.

"Do you know what a voodoo song says, a song they sing to greet Damballah Wedó?"

I shook my head, I thought Boukaka's almond voice was a singer's voice. It didn't go with his face, or his bus driver's belly, or the sparse hairs of his beard, a meager beard that surely had stopped growing.

"Damballah is a silent deity, the only mute god in the pantheon. The song goes like this: 'Toad, give your voice to the serpent, the frogs will show you the way to the moon, when Damballah desires it, the great flight will begin.'"

Boukaka lowered his head, he seemed exhausted; the smell of his pipe began to make me feel tired too.

"The great flight has begun," he repeated. "You people invent excuses: acid rain, herbicides, deforestation. But the frogs are disappearing from places where none of that has happened."

I wondered who he meant by "you people." You people, the professional herpetologists. Or you people, the biologists who hold their conferences in Canterbury, in Nashville, in Brasília, hold them behind closed doors and walk out more perplexed than when they came in. You people, fearful, finicky people, incapable of looking at the dark, recalcitrant, atemporal side of the decline.

"I have no excuses," I said. "Nobody knows what's going on."

We spent more time talking about other species; I made an effort to handle with some grace the enormous quantity of data provided by Boukaka. I was amazed by his capacity for detail, his precision, I can even say his erudition. When we said good-bye he shook my hand; I was about to tell him that he reminded me of a famous musician, I had been trying to think who it was he resembled and then I looked into his eyes and decided it was Thelonious Monk. It may have been irrelevant but I remembered a composition of Monk's that wasn't played too often: "See You Later, Beautiful Frog."

"What I've learned, I learned in books," Boukaka said emphatically from the door. "But what I know, everything I know, I took from fire and water, from water and flame: One puts out the other."

On that overcast Tuesday in the middle of January when we finally set out for Jérémie, I still had not received Martha's letter, but I had no doubt what it would say.

Thierry was driving, telling me a love story, his fingers clutching at the steering wheel, his eyes fixed on the road, not much more than a rutted trail. He spoke in a very sweet voice, he didn't even look as old. Suddenly he said something that struck me: A man never knows when the grief begins that will last forever. I looked at him and saw a tear running down his cheek.

"Not grief, not joy," I said very quietly. "A man never knows anything, Thierry, that's his affliction."

Jaime Luis Huenún

Jaime Luis Huenún (b. 1967) is a poet of Huilliche-Chilean descent. Huenún is frequently identified as a Mapuche poet; the term, which literally means "people of the land," refers to the four originary peoples of Chile and southwestern Argentina, one of which is the Huilliche. His work is steeped in Huilliche culture and the Mapudungun language. Huenún, who grew up in Osorno, south of Valdivia and Araucanía, has described his poetic idiom as "soaked in the Indian and mestizo waters" of his origin; it is "a mechanism of cultural and political resistance rather than a merely individual lyric expression or inquiry" (Huenún 2014, 225). Huenún was a child when a CIA-backed coup replaced the democratically elected socialist Salvador Allende with the military dictatorship of General Augusto Pinochet in 1973. For his people, the Pinochet years brought economic initiatives that encouraged logging and intensive agricultural activity on communal lands, coupled with draconian anti-terrorist laws that remain in force today, severely limiting the Mapuches' ability to advocate for their right to reclaim lands lost during the dictatorship. The connection of the Mapuche to nature, ancestral myths, and the fight against the loss of identity all appear as central themes in Huenún's work, which simultaneously affirms Mapuche experience and nature-based cosmology and acts as a form of collective memory. The selections presented here, both from *Ceremonies* (1998), exemplify an ethos of deep cultural resistance to ethnocide and environmental degradation alike.

***

Poems (1998)

TRANSLATED BY JOHN BIERHORST

Ceremony of Love

The Indian trees last night made love: *mañio* and *ulmo*, *pellín* and *hualle*[1]
tineo and *lingue* node to node made love[2]
with tenderness, the *peumos*[3]
barks darkened, the *coigües*[4] especially
roots, tufts, and sprouts kissed lovingly
the arousal of birds already stirred
by the plumes of their
own warbling loves.

Even *winka*[5] shoots buried themselves
as lovers, and Indian waters then
opened their springs, giving birth, sip by sip
calling out to each other: good water, excellent,
yes but violated we are the waters
Rahue, the weeping ones, Pilmaiquén,[6] the fruitful ones, the midwives, yet joyful
the arroyos that pass through
the mountains and hills like rabbits.

And doves the same love promptly coupled,
the green
wellsprings Inallao, the strong
honey Huaiquipán,[7] the swift
eyes Llanquilef[8], the thrush
breasts Relequeo, the black hair Huilitraro *quillay*,[9]
the new beech trees Paillamanque.

Huilliche[10] love, last night they loved intensely
in all the Indian groves
under perpetual ripe native skies
they made love, mounded
like rupturing waters, like *anchimallén*[11] on fire, in the fragrant dawn
they made love, seeds
sweetening like
vessels filled with *muday*.[12]

Ceremony of Death

> . . . raised their bloodied
> hands to the sky . . . —EL PROGRESO (OSORNO), 21 OCTOBER 1912

UNO (FORRAHUE)

We didn't speak Chilean, my friend,
what they call Castillian:
Copihue, yes, *copihue* blanco, *copihue* rojo,[13]
flor de *michai*,[14]
chilco[15] nuevo.
We didn't know the Virgin or Christ,
father,
or God in the Highest.
We played in the field, throwing horse manure at each other,
stole honeycombs from the *ulmos* (and from the flies)
and mushrooms from the *hualles* of the pampa,

watched our sisters bathing nude
in the arroyo with handfuls of soap wood.
It was bad.
Yes.
It's what brought envy and lawsuits and carbines,
it's why the deer and the fish became shy.
It was bad, my friend, bad.
The raw heart of a lamb, we ate it warm
at the *lepun*,[16]
we prayed in Huilliche to the laurel branches
at our shaman's side,
with fire we killed anyone who set a demon
against another's body and against another's soul.
We spit out the words: Witch devil! Go, get away!
and the thickest woods
concealed the owl.
It was bad, bad.
In the old days, friend, the natives did not know
how to live, we did not know.
Women became pregnant in the dark and in the light,
and children were brought up by the grace
of forests and rivers.
And so it was, dear Mama, so it was:
suddenly the stars no longer
ignited our blood,
and we were forced to hide like foxes
in mountains and gullies.

Notes

1. Notes to "Ceremony of Love" and "Ceremony of Death" are based on the glossary provided in *Ül: Four Mapuche Poets*, ed. Cecilia Vicuña, trans. John Bierhorst (Pittsburgh: Americas Society/Latin American Literary Review Press, 1998), 147–49. *Mañío*, Prince Albert's yew (*Saxegothaea conspicua*), an evergreen tree fifteen to twenty meters in height; *ulmo*, the heartleaf eucryphia, a stout tree reaching forty meters in height (*Eucryphia cordifolia*); *pellín*, oak; *hualle*, an evergreen beech, or oak (*Nothofagus obliqua*) also called *pellín coyam*, reaching about forty meters in height. [—Eds.]

2. *Tineo*, a stout tree five to twelve meters in height (*Weinmannia trichosperma*) used in the lumber industry; *lingue*, a tree twenty to twenty-five meters in height with a luxuriant spherical crown (*Persea lingue*).

3. *Peumo*, an evergreen tree, member of the laurel family, four to ten meters in height (*Cryptocarya alba*).

4. *Coigüe*, a large beech reaching forty-five meters in height (*Nothofagus dombeyi*).

5. *Winka*, foreigner.

6. Rahue, river that passes through the city of Osorno; Pilmaiquén, river that passes through the province of Osorno.

7. Huaiquipán, family name.

8. Llanquilef, family name.

9. Huilitraro, family name; *quillay*, an evergreen shrub, the soap bark tree (*Quillaja saponaria*).

10. Huilliche, southern Mapuche community located between Valdivia and the island of Chiloé.

11. *Anchimallén*, a demon who appears in the form of a pygmy.

12. *Muday*, chicha, or beer, fermented beverage made from corn, wheat, barley, or potatoes mixed with wheat.

13. *Copihue*, Chilebells (*Lapageria rosea*) or its vine, adopted by Chileans as their national flower; the blossoms are reddish, typically, or white.

14. *Michai*, an evergreen shrub (*Berberis actinacantha*).

15. *Chilco*, a shrub (*Fuschia magellanica*).

16. *Lepun*, a ritual of the coast dwellers (Huilliche).

Samanta Schweblin

When Samanta Schweblin (b. 1978) was twelve years old, she stopped talking for a full year in response to an argument with a friend. As a result, she later said, "When I stopped talking, language exploded—in the best possible way. I was constantly reading, I started writing, and my interior world was enormous" (Rollenhagen 2019). The literary fiction of this important new Argentine writer is characterized by a refined sensitivity to language and an ability to create vivid and shocking subjective worlds. Her work was first recognized in 2001 by a prize from Argentina's National Arts Fund, then in 2008 the Cuban government awarded Schweblin the Casa de las Américas Prize for the story collection *The Fury of Plagues*. The selection presented here is an excerpt from the opening pages of Schweblin's 2014 novel *Distancia de rescate*, translated into English by Megan McDowell as *Fever Dream* and subsequently nominated for the International Man Booker Prize. The narrative represents a conversation between a boy named David, whose lines are in italics, and Amanda, who lies dying in a hospital bed. At David's insistence, Amanda recounts the conversation she had with his mother, Carla, a few days earlier. This is the beginning of a rigorous and ingeniously plotted environmental horror story in which the virulent toxins of industrial agriculture produce unspeakable harm. As Jia Tolentino (2017) wrote for the *New Yorker*, the design of Schweblin's *Fever Dream* "is at once so enigmatic and so disciplined that the book feels as if it belongs to a new literary genre altogether." This makes it an appropriate vehicle to convey the strange and ubiquitous sense of dread swirling in the present.

***

From *Fever Dream* (2014)

TRANSLATED BY MEGAN MCDOWELL

I cross the yard. When I skirt the pool, I look in the window toward the dining room to be sure that my daughter, Nina, is still asleep, hugging her big stuffed mole. I get into the car on the passenger side. I sit, but I leave the door open and roll the window down, because it's very hot. Carla's big bun is drooping a little, coming undone on one side. She leans against the backrest, aware that I'm there now, beside her once again, and she looks at me.

"If I tell you," she says, "you won't want me to visit anymore."

I think about what to say, something like "Now Carla, come on, don't be silly," but instead I look at her toes, tense on the brakes, her long legs, her thin but strong arms. I'm disconcerted that a woman ten years older than me is so much more beautiful.

"If I tell you," she says, "you won't want him to play with Nina."

"But Carla, come on, how could I not want that."

"You won't, Amanda," she says, and her eyes fill with tears.

"What's his name?"

"David."

"Is he yours? Is he your son?"

She nods. That son is you, David.

I know. Go on.

She wipes away her tears with her knuckles, and her gold bracelets jangle. I had never seen you, but when I'd mentioned to Mr. Geser, the caretaker of our rental house, that I'd made friends with Carla, he asked right away if I'd met you yet. Then Carla says:

"He was mine. Not anymore."

I look at her, confused.

"He doesn't belong to me anymore."

"Carla, children are forever."

"No, dear," she says. She has long nails, and she points at me, her finger level with my eyes.

Then I remember my husband's cigarettes, and I open the glove compartment and hand them to her with a lighter. She practically snatches them from my hand, and the perfume of her sunscreen wafts between us.

"When David was born, he was the light of my life, he was my sun."

"Of course he was," I say, and I realize I need to be quiet now.

"The first time they put him in my arms, I was so anxious. I was convinced he was missing a finger." She holds the cigarette between her lips, smiling at the memory, and she lights it. "The nurse said sometimes that happens with the anesthesia, it can make you a little paranoid. I swear, until I counted all ten of his fingers twice, I wasn't convinced everything had turned out all right. What I wouldn't give now for David to simply be missing a finger."

"What's wrong with David?"

"But back then he was a delight, Amanda, I'm telling you: my moon and stars. He smiled all day long. His favorite thing was to be outside. He was crazy about the playground, even when he was tiny. You see how around here you can't go for a walk with a stroller. In town you can, but from here to the playground you have to go between the big estates and the shanties along the train tracks. It's a mess with all the mud, but he liked going so much that until he was three I'd carry him there, all twelve blocks. When he caught sight of the slide he'd start to shout. Where's the ashtray in this car?"

It's under the dashboard. I pull out the base and hand it to her.

"Then David got sick, when he was that age, more or less, about six years ago. It was a difficult time. I'd started working at Sotomayor's farm. It was the first job I'd worked in my life. I did the accounting, which really wasn't anything like accounting. I just filed papers and helped him add, but it kept me entertained. I went around town on errands, all dressed up. It's different for you, coming from the capital, but around here you need an excuse for a little glamour, and the job was the perfect pretext."

"What about your husband?"

"Omar bred horses. Yes, that's right. He was a different guy back then, Omar."

"I think I saw him yesterday when Nina and I were out walking. He drove by in the pickup, but when we waved he didn't wave back."

"Yes, that's Omar these days," says Carla, shaking her head. "When I met him he still smiled, and he bred racehorses. He kept them on the other side of town, past the lake, but when I got pregnant he moved everything to where we are now. Our house used to be my parents'. Omar said that when he hit it big, we'd be loaded and we could redo everything. I wanted to carpet the floors. Yes, it's crazy living where I do, but oh, I really wanted it. Omar had two spectacular mares that had given birth to a couple of big winners. They'd been sold and were running races—still do—at Palermo and San Isidro. Later, two more fillies were born, and a colt; I don't remember any of their names. To do well in that business you have to have a good stallion, and Omar got hold of the best. He fenced in part of the land for the mares, built a corral behind it for the foals, planted alfalfa, and then he could take his time building the stable. The deal was that Omar would borrow the stallion for two or three days, and later, when the foals were sold, a fourth of the money went to the stallion's owner. That's a lot of money, because if the stallion is good and the foals are well taken care of, each of them goes for between 200,000 and 250,000 pesos. Anyway, one time we had that precious horse with us. Omar watched him all day long, followed him around like a zombie to keep track of how many times he mounted each mare. He wouldn't leave the house until I got back from Sotomayor's, and then it was my turn, though I would just take a look out the kitchen window at him every once in a while, as you can imagine. So one afternoon I'm washing the dishes and I realize I haven't seen the stallion in a while. I go to the other window, then to another that looks out behind the house, and nothing: the mares are there, but no sign of the stallion. I pick David up, who by then had taken his first steps and had been following me around the house that whole time, and I go outside. There's only so much searching you can do, either a horse is there or it's not. Evidently, for some reason he'd jumped the fence. It's rare, but it happens. I went to the stable praying to God he'd be there, but he wasn't. Then my eyes fell on the stream and I felt a spark of hope; it's small but it runs in a hollow, a horse could be drinking water and you wouldn't even see it from the house. I remember David asking what was happening. I was still carrying him, he was hugging my neck and his voice was clipped by the long strides I was taking, bouncing him side to side. 'There, Mom!' said David. And there was the stallion, drinking water from the stream. David doesn't call me Mom anymore. We went toward it, and David wanted me to put him down. I told him not to go near the horse, and I went toward the animal, taking short little steps. Sometimes he moved away, but I was patient, and after a while he started to trust me. I managed to get hold of the reins. It was such a relief, I remember it perfectly, I sighed and said out loud, 'If I lost you, I'd lose the house too, you jerk.' See, Amanda, this is like the finger I'd thought David was missing. You say, 'Losing the house would be the worst,' and later there are worse things and you would give the house and even your life just to go back to that moment and let go of the damned animal's reins."

I hear the slam of the screen door from the living room and both of us turn toward the house. Nina is in the doorway, hugging her stuffed mole. She's sleepy, so sleepy it doesn't even scare her when she doesn't see us anywhere. She takes a few steps, and without letting go of the stuffed animal she grabs the railing and concentrates on going down the three porch steps until she's on the grass. Carla leans back in the seat and watches her in the rearview mirror, silent. Nina looks down at her feet. She has a new habit since we got here, and she's doing it now: pulling up the grass by clenching it between her toes.

"David had knelt down in the stream, his shoes were soaked. He'd put his hands in the water and was sucking on his fingers. Then I saw the dead bird. It was very close to David, just a step away. I got scared and yelled at him, and then he got scared, too. He jumped up and fell backward onto his bottom from the fear. My poor David. I went over to him dragging the horse, who neighed and didn't want to follow me, and somehow I picked him up with just one hand and I fought with both of them until we made it back up the hill. I didn't tell Omar about any of it. What for? The screwup was over and done with, fixed. But the next morning the horse was lying down. 'He's not there,' said Omar. 'He escaped,' and I was about to tell him that he'd already escaped once, but then he saw the horse lying in the pasture. 'Shit,' he said. The stallion's eyelids were so swollen you couldn't see his eyes. His lips, nostrils, and his whole mouth were so puffy he looked like a different animal, a monstrosity. He barely had the strength to whinny in pain, and Omar said his heart was pounding like a locomotive. He made an urgent call to the vet. Some neighbors came over, everyone was worried and running back and forth, but I went into the house desperate, and I picked up David, who was still sleeping in his crib, and I locked myself in my room, in bed with him in my arms, to pray. To pray like a crazy woman, pray like I'd never prayed in my life. You'll be wondering why I didn't run to the clinic instead of locking myself in the bedroom, but sometimes there's not enough time to confirm the disaster at hand. Whatever the horse had drunk my David had drunk too, and if the horse was dying then David didn't have a chance. I knew it with utter clarity, because I had already heard and seen too many things in this town: I had a few hours, or maybe minutes, to find a solution that wasn't waiting half an hour for some rural doctor who wouldn't even make it to the clinic in time. I needed someone to save my son's life, whatever the cost."

I steal another look at Nina, who is now taking a few steps toward the pool.

"It's just that sometimes the eyes you have aren't enough, Amanda. I don't know how I didn't see it—why the hell was I worrying about a goddamn horse instead of my son?"

I'm wondering whether what happened to Carla could happen to me. I always imagine the worst-case scenario. Right now, for instance, I'm calculating how long it would take me to jump out of the car and reach Nina if she suddenly ran and leapt into the pool. I call it the "rescue distance": that's what I've named the variable distance separating me from my daughter, and I spend half the day calculating it, though I always risk more than I should.

Berta Cáceres

Like Chico Mendes, Honduran Berta Cáceres (1973–2016) is one of Latin America's environmental martyrs (Nixon 2017), a tenacious fighter for the human and environmental rights of Indigenous peoples. The daughter of a midwife and social activist who provided care to refugees from El Salvador, Cáceres from an early age focused on community service and grassroots organizing. In 1993 she cofounded the National Council of Popular and Indigenous Organizations of Honduras, which coordinates more than two hundred communities of her Indigenous Lenca people in the protection of their rights against the intertwined systems of domination of capitalism, patriarchy, and racism. Most famously, Cáceres was instrumental in a ten-year campaign that successfully prevented the Chinese-owned Sinohydro conglomerate from building the Agua Zarca Dam on the Gualcarque River, a spiritual home for many Lenca as well as a vital source of food and water. Cáceres described the economic policy established by the military government that came to power in the 2009 coup as a "predatory energy model," since approximately 30 percent of the country's land was designated for mining and energy development at great cost to collective and human rights (Colotti 2016). Honduras is known as the most dangerous country in the world for activists: since the 2009 coup more than one hundred twenty environmental and land activists have been murdered with almost complete impunity for the killers (Goldman Environmental Foundation, n.d.). Cáceres herself was added to this number in 2016, when she was murdered in an attack that independent investigations have linked to the government and to hydroelectric company officials.

***

Goldman Environmental Prize Acceptance Speech (2015)

In our world-views, we are beings who come from the Earth, from the water and from the corn. The Lenca people are ancestral guardians of the rivers, in turn protected by the spirits of young girls, who teach us that giving our lives in various ways for the protection of the rivers is giving our lives for the well-being of humanity and of this planet. COPINH,[1] walking alongside people struggling for their emancipation, validates this commitment to continue protecting our waters, the rivers, our shared resources and nature in general, as well as our rights as a people. Let us wake up! Let us wake up, humankind! We're out of time. We must shake our conscience free of the rapacious capitalism, racism, and patriarchy that will only assure our own self-destruction. The Gualcarque River has called upon us, as have other gravely threatened rivers. We must answer their call. Our Mother Earth—militarized, fenced in, poisoned, a place where basic rights are systematically violated—demands that we take action. Let us build societies that are able to coexist in a dignified way, in a way that protects life. Let us come together and remain hopeful as we defend and care for the blood of this Earth and of its spirits. I dedicate this award to all the rebels out there, to my mother, to the Lenca people, to Río Blanco, and to the martyrs who gave their lives in the struggle to defend our natural resources. Thank you very much.

Note

1. COPINH stands for Consejo Cívico de Organizaciones Populares e Indígenas de Honduras. In English the same organization is known as the National Council of Popular and Indigenous Organizations of Honduras. [—Eds.]

Pope Francis

Argentinean cardinal José Mario Bergoglio (b. 1936) assumed the papacy in 2013 as Pope Francis, becoming the first pope from the western hemisphere, the first from the Global South, and the first from the Jesuit order. The name he chose signals the pope's deep admiration for Saint Francis of Assisi, patron saint of ecology. Saint Francis is known for his efforts to emulate Christ, to repudiate material comforts, and to incorporate all of nature into Christian practice and theology. As cardinal, Bergoglio made a reputation for himself as an advocate for the poor who eschewed the typical privileges of the Church hierarchy by using public transportation and living in a small apartment during the Argentinean economic crisis in 2001. As pope, he has continued to live relatively modestly and to advocate on behalf of the world's poor. *Laudato Si'*, issued in 2015, is Pope Francis's second encyclical, which is a formal letter addressed to the whole of the Roman Catholic Church. The pope's ongoing commitment to the poor dovetails with an equally deep concern for the environment, so that the neglect of both emerges as a moral issue Christians are called to resolve. The encyclical, the title of which means "Praise Be to You" in Latin, outlines major global threats to environmental integrity, including pollution, climate change, and excessive use of water and other natural resources, and it connects these to the moral degradation of human relationships and society itself. Pope Francis thus calls for "integral ecology": environmental activism that addresses the social dimensions of environmental issues, including the needs of the poor and the "ecological debt" that rich societies of the North have incurred relative to the Global South.

***

From *Laudato Si'* (2015)

Global Inequality

The human environment and the natural environment deteriorate together; we cannot adequately combat environmental degradation unless we attend to causes related to human and social degradation. In fact, the deterioration of the environment and of society affects the most vulnerable people on the planet: "Both everyday experience and scientific research show that the gravest effects of all attacks on the environment are suffered by the poorest."[1] For example, the depletion of fishing reserves especially hurts small fishing communities without the means to replace those resources; water pollution particularly affects the poor who cannot buy bottled water; and rises in the sea level mainly affect impoverished coastal populations who have nowhere else to go. The impact of present imbalances is also seen in the premature death of many of the poor, in conflicts sparked by the shortage of resources, and in any number of other problems which are insufficiently represented on global agendas.[2]

It needs to be said that, generally speaking, there is little in the way of clear awareness of problems which especially affect the excluded. Yet they are the majority of the planet's population, billions of people. These days, they are mentioned in international political and economic discussions, but one often has the impression that their problems are brought up as an afterthought, a question which gets added almost out of duty or in a tangential way, if not treated merely as collateral damage. Indeed, when all is said and done, they frequently remain at the bottom of the pile. This is due partly to the fact that many professionals, opinion makers, communications media and centers of power, being located in affluent urban areas, are far removed from the poor, with little direct contact with their problems. They live and reason from the comfortable position of a high level of development and a quality of life well beyond the reach of the majority of the world's population. This lack of physical contact and encounter, encouraged at times by the disintegration of our cities, can lead to a numbing of conscience and to tendentious analyses which neglect parts of reality. At times this attitude exists side by side with a "green" rhetoric. Today, however, we have to realize that a true ecological approach *always* becomes a social approach; it must integrate questions of justice in debates on the environment, so as to hear *both the cry of the earth and the cry of the poor.*

Instead of resolving the problems of the poor and thinking of how the world can be different, some can only propose a reduction in the birth rate. At times, developing countries face forms of international pressure which make economic assistance contingent on certain policies of "reproductive health." Yet "while it is true that an unequal distribution of the population and of available resources creates obstacles to development and a sustainable use of the environment, it must nonetheless be recognized that demographic growth is fully compatible with an integral and shared development."[3] To blame population growth instead of extreme and selective consumerism on the part of some is one way of refusing to face the issues. It is an attempt to legitimize the present model of distribution, where a minority believes that it has the right to consume in a way which can never be universalized, since the planet could not even contain the waste products of such consumption. Besides, we know that approximately a third of all food produced is discarded, and "whenever food is thrown out it is as if it were stolen from the table of the poor."[4] Still, attention needs to be paid to imbalances in population density, on both national and global levels, since a rise in consumption would lead to complex regional situations as a result of the interplay between problems linked to environmental pollution, transport, waste treatment, loss of resources and quality of life.

Inequity affects not only individuals but entire countries; it compels us to consider an ethics of international relations. A true "ecological debt" exists, particularly between the Global North and South, connected to commercial imbalances with effects on the environment, and the disproportionate use of natural resources by certain countries over long periods of time. The export of raw materials to satisfy markets in the industrialized north has caused harm locally, as for example in mercury pollution in gold mining or sulphur dioxide pollution in copper mining. There is a pressing need to calculate the use of environmental space throughout the world for depositing gas residues which have been accumulating for two centuries and have created a situation which currently affects all the countries of the world. The warming caused by huge consumption on the part of some rich countries has repercussions on the poorest areas of the world, especially Africa, where a rise in temperature, together with drought, has proved devastating for farming. There is also the damage caused by the export of solid waste and toxic liquids to developing countries, and by the pollution produced by companies which operate in less developed countries in ways they could never do at home, in the countries in which they raise their capital: "We note that often the businesses which operate this way are multinationals. They do here what they would never do in developed countries or the so-called first world. Generally, after ceasing their activity and withdrawing, they leave behind great human and environmental liabilities such as unemployment, abandoned towns, the depletion of natural reserves, deforestation, the impoverishment of agriculture and local stock breeding, open pits, riven hills, polluted rivers and a handful of social works which are no longer sustainable."[5]

The Wisdom of the Biblical Accounts

The creation accounts in the book of Genesis contain, in their own symbolic and narrative language, profound teachings about human existence and its historical reality. They suggest that human life is grounded in three fundamental and closely intertwined relationships: with God, with our neighbor and with the earth itself. According to the Bible, these three vital relationships have been broken, both outwardly and within us. This rupture is sin. The harmony between the Creator, humanity and creation as a whole was disrupted by our presuming to take the place of God and refusing to acknowledge our creaturely limitations. This in turn distorted our mandate to "have dominion" over the earth (Gen 1:28), to "till it and keep it" (Gen 2:15). As a result, the originally harmonious relationship between human beings and nature became conflictual (Gen 3:17–19). It is significant that the harmony which Saint Francis of Assisi experienced with all creatures was seen as a healing of that rupture. Saint Bonaventure held that, through universal reconciliation with every creature, Saint Francis in some way returned to the state of original innocence.[6] This is a far cry from our situation today, where sin is manifest in all its destructive power in wars, the various forms of violence and abuse, the abandonment of the most vulnerable, and attacks on nature.

We are not God. The earth was here before us and it has been given to us. This allows us to respond to the charge that Judaeo-Christian thinking, on the basis of the Genesis account which grants man "dominion" over the earth (Gen 1:28), has encouraged the unbridled exploitation of nature by painting him as domineering and destructive by nature. This is not a correct interpretation of the Bible as understood by the Church. Although it is true that we Christians have at times incorrectly interpreted the Scriptures, nowadays we must forcefully reject the notion that our being created in God's image and given dominion over the earth justifies absolute domination over other creatures. The biblical texts are to be read in their context, with an appropriate hermeneutic, recognizing that they tell us to "till and keep" the garden of the world (Gen 2:15). "Tilling" refers to cultivating, ploughing or working, while "keeping" means caring, protecting, overseeing and preserving. This implies a relationship of mutual responsibility between human beings and nature. Each community can take from the bounty of the earth whatever it needs for subsistence, but it also has the duty to protect the earth and to ensure its fruitfulness for coming generations. "The earth is the Lord's" (Ps 24:1); to him belongs "the earth with all that is within it" (Dt 10:14). Thus God rejects every claim to absolute ownership: "The land shall not be sold in perpetuity, for the land is mine; for you are strangers and sojourners with me" (Lev 25:23).

This responsibility for God's earth means that human beings, endowed with intelligence, must respect the laws of nature and the delicate equilibria existing between the creatures of this world, for "he commanded and they were created; and he established them for ever and ever; he fixed their bounds and he set a law which cannot pass away" (Ps 148:5b–6). The laws found in the Bible dwell on relationships, not only among individuals but also with other living beings. "You shall not see your brother's donkey or his ox fallen down by the way and withhold your help . . . If you chance to come upon a bird's nest in any tree or on the ground, with young ones or eggs and the mother sitting upon the young or upon the eggs; you shall not take the mother with the young" (Dt 22:4, 6). Along these same lines, rest on the seventh day is meant not only for human beings, but also so "that your ox and your donkey may have rest" (Ex 23:12). Clearly, the Bible has no place for a tyrannical anthropocentrism unconcerned for other creatures.

Together with our obligation to use the earth's goods responsibly, we are called to recognize that other living beings have a value of their own in God's eyes: "by their mere existence they bless him and give him glory," and indeed, "the Lord rejoices in all his works" (Ps 104:31). By virtue of our unique dignity and our gift of intelligence, we are called to respect creation and its inherent laws, for "the Lord by wisdom founded the earth" (Prov 3:19). In our time, the Church does not simply state that other creatures are completely subordinated to the good of human beings, as if they have no worth in themselves and can be treated as we wish. The German bishops have taught that, where other creatures are concerned, "we can speak of the priority of *being* over that of *being useful*."[7] The Catechism clearly and forcefully criticizes a distorted anthropocentrism: "Each creature possesses its own particular goodness and perfection . . . Each of the various creatures, willed in its own being, reflects in its own way a ray of God's infinite wisdom and goodness. Man must therefore respect the particular goodness of every creature, to avoid any disordered use of things."[8]

Notes

1. Bolivian Bishops' Conference, Pastoral Letter on the Environment and Human Development in Bolivia *El universo, don de Dios para la vida* (March 23, 2012), 17.

2. Compare German Bishops' Conference, Commission for Social Issues, *Der Klimawandel: Brennpunkt globaler, intergenerationeller und ökologischer Gerechtigkeit* (September 2006), 28–30.

3. Pontifical Council for Justice and Peace, *Compendium of the Social Doctrine of the Church*, 483.

4. *Catechesis* (June 5, 2013): *Insegnamenti* 1/1 (2013), 280.

5. Bishops of the Patagonia-Comahue Region (Argentina), *Christmas Message* (December 2009), 2.

6. Bonaventure, *The Major Legend of Saint Francis*, VIII, 1, in *Francis of Assisi: Early Documents*, vol. 2, New York-London-Manila, 2000, 586.

7. German Bishops' Conference, *Zukunft der Schöpfung-Zukunft er Menschheit. Einklärung der Deutschen Bischofskonferenz zu Fragen der Umwelt und der Energieversorgung* (1980), II, 2.

8. *Catechism of the Catholic Church*, 339.

Eduardo Chirinos

Eduardo Alejandro Chirinos Arrieta was a distinguished Peruvian poet, as well as a literary critic and professor at the University of Montana. Born in Lima in 1960, he was educated there before moving to the United States with his wife, Jannine Montauban, so that both could undertake doctoral training in Spanish and Latin American literature at Rutgers University. Chirinos wrote eighteen books of poetry, many of which have been translated into English by longtime collaborator G. J. Racz. Playful, tender, erudite, and inventive, his work has received many accolades and awards over the years, among them the Casa de las Américas Prize—one of Latin America's highest literary honors—which was given to *A Brief History of Music* by the Cuban government in 2001. Animals of all kinds were one of Chirinos's favorite subjects and appear repeatedly throughout his extensive body of work, if never more poignantly than in *Thirty-Five Zoology Lessons and Other Didactic Poems*, written during the long battle with cancer that ended in February 2016. The poems presented here, "The K/T Boundary Chronicle," "The Toba Chronicle," and "The Chernobyl Chronicle" are the "didactic poems" referred to in the title of the collection. We have selected them to conclude this final section of *The Latin American Ecocultural Reader* because the poems exemplify the spirit of resilience that is needed in our profoundly uncertain times. They practice the ancient art of lamentation for what is irreparably lost, and in doing so interrupt the call to forgetfulness that is ubiquitous in a society dominated by consumer capitalism. Wedding science to poetry, they also urge us to wonder and curiosity about life on earth, including what comes next.

❋❋❋

Poems (2013)

TRANSLATED BY G. J. RACZ

The K/T Boundary Chronicle

Geologists recount how, sixty-five million years ago,
intense volcanic activity occurred in what is today India:
approximately four hundred thousand square miles were
        covered
by lava (the so-called Deccan Traps), which had
a dire effect on the climate.

        The night these events transpired,

paleontologists say, was responsible for the extinction of the
dinosaurs, the end of their reign on the face of the planet.

Geophysicists tell it a different way. The same number
of years ago, an enormous meteorite (or maybe a comet)
struck the earth. The impact pulverized the meteorite
(or comet), spreading its ash over the globe
and darkening the atmosphere. Geologists assure us

this ash was iridium and that the imprint of so enormous a spheroid
can be found in Mexico, in a crater northeast of the Yucatán
called Chicxulub. The hole is some thirty miles deep
and one hundred ten in diameter.
       Its impact
was two million times stronger than the "Tsar
Bomba," a Soviet horror during the Cold War years.

The noise must have deafened all living creatures,
the same ones that had to contend with tsunamis,
fires, and a nuclear winter created by ash
that blotted out the sun.
     The Cretaceous-Tertiary Boundary
(or "K/T Boundary," as scientists call it)
resulted in the disappearance of several animal species
and many plants, a phenomenon that gravely
affected the food chain.
      In short order
the K/T Boundary marked the end of the dinosaur era
and the beginning of the age of mammals, which
were then minuscule, shrew-sized beings.

Following this disaster, the mammals had the world
all to themselves—and they took advantage. They grew in size
and branched out with dazzling speed, occupying geological spaces
left by triceratops, tyrannosaurus rex, and other creatures
we remember now through children's toys.

The Toba Chronicle

Some seventy thousand years ago, scientists say,
a volcanic winter darkened the earth.
An eruption north of Sumatra
released so much sulfur into the air, so many particles
of sulfuric acid, that the temperature of the globe
plummeted drastically, bringing about a new

ice age. This glacial period, scientists explain,
lasted about a thousand years: hundreds of animal
species disappeared, entire continents suffered deforestation,
and the human race was brought to the brink of extinction.

This was the so-called Toba catastrophe.

These days, Toba is a pleasant, lovely lake.
The fifteen thousand survivors left on earth
were undoubtedly not aware of this.
                                I can hardly imagine the scene:
it's as if the population of the entire world were
reduced to one neighborhood in some sparsely inhabited city
or the sum total of students at the University of Montana.

Yet one day the frost slowly began to melt,
the sulfur dispersed into the air, and the particles
of sulfuric acid increased the supply of nutrients
the earth needed. New plants and trees
greeted the sun as an ally of life.
The survivors, meanwhile, looked to making
babies, inventing gods, and domesticating animals.

History records other eruptions
(in Peru, Indonesia, and the Philippines), all
violent, all catastrophic, but none
as terrible as the one in Toba, north of Sumatra.

An eruption like that, scientists assure us,
occurs once every million years. We still have
a ways to go, so there's nothing to worry about.

The Chernobyl Chronicle

Zoologists recount how, in days of old,
bison wandered freely through the forests of Europe.
It makes sense, since you can see drawings of them in the caves of Altamira,
         Lascaux, and Chauvet
that look just like the kind that roamed American plains
before they were slaughtered by Buffalo Bill and his henchmen.

Historians recount how, in the Middle Ages,
kings and noblemen protected the European variety.
They bred the animal in special parks and used it as a sort of decoration
in the gardens surrounding their palaces. You know the rest:

the overhunting, the extension of arable lands, the two world
wars. Only in the Caucasus and Poland's Białowieża
Forest did wild herds continue to exist.
The last bison in the Caucasus died in 1919 while the Russian
Revolution raged on, and only about fifty specimens remained
in Białowieża before the Second World War. That's where history ends.

Until the disaster in Chernobyl occurred.

That explosion freed 500 times more radioactive material into the air
than the atom bomb at Hiroshima and resulted in the evacuation of 116,000
souls (not to mention thirty-one deaths). It also sent a radioactive cloud
parading its shadow over thirteen countries before the wall came down.
This fact is important: today Chernobyl is divided between
the Ukraine and Belarus, now a pristine region of forests
and swamps. Who'd have thought that, after this disaster, it would
go back to being what it was before Stalin's machinations?

But, getting back to the bison . . .

The evacuation of Chernobyl entailed residents leaving
the area and abandoning their homes, fields, steel factories, and nuclear plants.
Nature thus liberated, the beaver returned to its lodge, the eagle to its aerie, and
        the wolf to monitoring the explosion
of rabbits and deer. Bison on the brink of extinction resurfaced as well,
only to face the winter's raw cold and the summer's unbearable heat.

Biologists relate that all these animals live in constant
danger, that their bodies are contaminated with
radioactive material such as europium oxide, uranium oxide,
zirconium alloys, and God knows what other toxins.
The creatures are unaware of this, though, all happy
in that slice of heaven Europe has conceded them.

Me, I love bison. Half an hour from my house
there's a reserve where they graze in relative freedom.
I'm talking about American buffalo, of course.
The European kind I've seen at the zoo in Madrid
and in a documentary where a stampeding herd scares off
wolves in order to stand watch over one of its dead.

Ainsa, Fernando. 1986. "La ciudad anarquista americana (estudio de una utopía libertaria)." *Cahiers du monde hispanique et luso-brésilien*, no. 46:65–78. *Contrecultures, utopies et dissidences en Amérique latine.*

Aira, César. 2001. *Diccionario de autores latinoamericanos.* Buenos Aires: Emecé.

Alonso, Carlos J. 1990. *The Spanish American Regional Novel: Modernity and Autochthony.* Cambridge: Cambridge University Press.

Arias, Santa. 2009. "Geografía, imperio e iglesia bajo la huella de la Ilustración." In *Poéticas de lo criollo*, edited by Juan M. Vitulli and David Solodkow, 331–52. Buenos Aires: Corregidor.

Arnold, A. James, et al. 1994. *A History of Literature in the Caribbean.* Amsterdam: Benjamins.

Avelar, Idelber. 2013. "Amerindian Perspectivism and Non-Human Rights." *Alter/nativas: Latin American Cultural Studies Journal* 1. https://alternativas.osu.edu/assets/files/essays%201/idelberavelar.pdf.

———. 2014. "On Amerindian Perspectivism and the Critique of Anthropocentrism." *Revista de Estudios Hispánicos* 48, no. 1 (March): 105–21.

Balderston, Daniel, and Mike Gonzalez. 2004. *Encyclopedia of Latin American and Caribbean Literature, 1900–2003.* London: Routledge.

Bales, Kevin. 2012. *Disposable People: New Slavery in the Global Economy.* Berkeley: University of California Press.

Barrera-Osorio, Antonio. 2006. *Experiencing Nature: The Spanish American Empire and the Early Scientific Revolution.* Austin: University of Texas Press.

Beck, Ulrich. 1999. *World Risk Society.* Cambridge: Polity Press.

Beckman, Ericka. 2013. *Capital Fictions: The Literature of Latin America's Export Age.* Minneapolis: University of Minnesota Press.

Bendor, Roy. 2007. "On Cannibalists and Sociolinguistics: Cultural Cannibalism as a Critical Theory of Hybridity." In *Linguistic Identity in Postcolonial Multilingual Spaces*, edited by Eric A. Anchimbe, 265–84. New Castle, U.K.: Cambridge Scholars Publishing.

Benjamin, Marina. 2003. *Rocket Dreams: How the Space Age Shaped Our Vision of a World Beyond.* New York: Simon and Schuster.

Benjamin, Walter. 1969. "Theses on the Philosophy of History." In *Illuminations*, edited by Hannah Arendt, 253–64. New York: Schocken Books.

Boldy, Steven. 2016. *A Companion to Juan Rulfo.* Rochester, N.Y.: Boydell and Brewer.

Bongie, Chris. 1998. *Islands and Exiles: The Creole Identities of Post/Colonial Literature.* Stanford, Calif.: Stanford University Press.

Briggs, Ronald. 2010. *Tropes of Enlightenment in the Age of Bolívar: Simón Rodríguez and the American Essay at Revolution*. Nashville, Tenn.: Vanderbilt University Press.

Buell, Lawrence. 1998. "Toxic Discourse." *Critical Inquiry* 24, no. 3 (Spring): 639–65.

Cañizares-Esguerra, Jorge. 2006a. *Nature, Empire, and Nation: Explorations of the History of Science in the Iberian World*. Stanford, Calif.: Stanford University Press.

———. 2006b. *Puritan Conquistadors: Iberianizing the Atlantic, 1550–1700*. Stanford, Calif.: Stanford University Press.

Castro Herrera, Guillermo. 1996. *Naturaleza y sociedad en la historia de América Latina*. Panama City: CELA.

Chakrabarty, Dipesh. 2009. "The Climate of History: Four Theses." *Critical Inquiry* 35, no. 2 (Winter): 197–222.

Coates, Timothy J. 2012. Introduction to *Brazil at the Dawn of the Eighteenth Century*, by André João Antonil. Translated by Timothy J. Coates and Stuart B. Schwartz. Dartmouth, Mass.: Tagus Press at UMass Dartmouth.

Colotti, Geraldina. 2016. "El legado de Berta Cáceres, en una de sus últimas entrevistas." *Agencia Paco Urondo*, July 3, 2016. http://www.agenciapacourondo.com.ar /patria-grande/el-legado-de-berta-caceres-en-una-de-sus-ultimas-entrevistas.

Coronil, Fernando. 1997. *The Magical State: Nature, Money, and Modernity in Venezuela*. Chicago: University of Chicago Press.

Coupe, Laurence. 2000. *The Green Studies Reader*. New York: Routledge.

Crosby, Alfred W. 1972. *The Columbian Exchange: Biological and Cultural Consequences of 1492*. Westport, Conn.: Greenwood Press.

da Cunha, Euclides. 2010. *Backlands: The Canudos Campaign*. Translated by Elizabeth Lowe. London: Penguin Books.

Davies, Catherine. 2007. "Troped Out of History: Women, Gender, and Nation in the Poetry of Andrés Bello." *Bulletin of Hispanic Studies* 84, no. 1 (January): 99–111.

de la Cadena, Marisol. 2010. "Indigenous Cosmopolitics in the Andes." *Cultural Anthropology* 25, no. 2 (April): 334–70.

del Llano, Eduardo. n.d. "Biografía." Sitio oficial de Eduardo del Llano. https:// eduardodelllano.wordpress.com/biografia/.

DeLoughrey, Elizabeth. 2011. "Yam, Roots, and Rot: Allegories of the Provision Ground." *Small Axe* 15, no. 1 (March): 58–75.

DeLoughrey, Elizabeth, and George B. Handley. 2011. *Postcolonial Ecologies: Literature of the Environment*. New York: Oxford University Press.

Descartes, René. 1999. "Discourse on the Method for Guiding One's Reason and Searching for Truth in the Sciences." In *Discourse on Method and Related Writings*, translated by Desmond M. Clarke, 1–54. London: Penguin Books.

Descola, Philippe. 2013. *Beyond Nature and Culture*. Translated by Janet Lloyd. Chicago: University of Chicago Press.

"Eduardo del Llano, nueva víctima de la censura en la TV cubana." 2017. CubaNet, November 2, 2017. https://www.cubanet.org/cultura/eduardo-del-llano-nueva -victima-de-la-censura-en-la-tv-cubana/.

Elliott, J. H. 1970. *The Old World and the New: 1492–1650*. Cambridge: Cambridge University Press.

Escalante, Marie. 2016. *La naturaleza como artificio: Representaciones de lo natural en el modernismo*. Madrid: Iberoamericana / Vervuert.

Escobar, Arturo. 2003. "'Mundos y conocimientos de otro modo': El programa de investigación de modernidad/colonialidad latinoamericano." *Tabula Rasa*, no. 1 (January–December): 51–86.

———. 2008. *Territories of Difference: Place, Movements, Life*, Redes. Durham, N.C.: Duke University Press.

Ferrando, Roberto. 1957. "Fernández de Oviedo y el conocimiento del Mar del Sur." *Revista de Indias* (January): 469–82.

Fink, Sheri. 2018. "Puerto Rico's Hurricane María Death Toll Could Exceed 4,000, New Study Estimates." *New York Times*, May 29, 2018. https://www.nytimes.com /2018/05/29/us/puerto-rico-deaths-hurricane.html.

Flys Junquera, Carmen, José Manuel Marrero Henríquez, and Julia Barella Vigal. 2010. *Ecocríticas: Literatura y medioambiente*. Madrid: Iberoamericana / Verveurt.

Foucault, Michel. 1970. *The Order of Things: An Archaeology of the Human Sciences*. New York: Random House.

———. 2003. *"Society Must Be Defended": Lectures at the Collège de France, 1975–76*. Edited by Mauro Bertani and Alessandro Fontana. Translated by David Macey. New York: Picador.

Fraser, Benjain. 2012. "Baldomero Lillo's Underground Literary Modernism." *The Latin Americanist*, 56: 75–99.

French, Howard W. 1991. "Havana Journal: A Film Is Banished, but Its Sly Grin Still Lingers." *New York Times*, June 29, 1991. https://www.nytimes.com/1991/06/29 /world/havana-journal-a-film-is-banished-but-its-sly-grin-still-lingers.html.

French, Jennifer L. 2005. *Nature, Neo-Colonialism, and the Spanish American Regional Writers*. Lebanon, N.H.: University Press of New England.

Gan, Elaine, Anna Tsing, Heather Swanson, and Nils Bubandt. 2017. "Introduction: Haunted Landscapes of the Anthropocene." In *Arts of Living on a Damaged Planet: Ghosts of the Anthropocene*, edited by Anna Tsing, Heather Swanson, Elaine Gan, and Nils Bubandt. Minneapolis: University of Minnesota Press.

Garrard, Greg. 2004. *Ecocriticism*. London: Routledge.

Gerbi, Antonello. 1973. *The Dispute of the New World: The History of a Polemic, 1750–1900*. Translated by Jeremy Moyle. Pittsburgh: University of Pittsburgh Press.

Gleijeses, Piero. 1992. *Shattered Hope: The Guatemalan Revolution and the United States, 1944–1954*. Princeton, N.J.: Princeton University Press.

Glotfelty, Cheryll. 1996. "Introduction: Literary Studies in an Age of Environmental Crisis." In *The Ecocriticism Reader: Landmarks in Literary Ecology*, edited by Cheryll Glotfelty and Harold Fromm, xv–xxxvii. Athens: University of Georgia Press.

Goldman Environmental Foundation. n.d. "Berta Cáceres." Goldmanprize.org. Accessed June 3, 2018. https://www.goldmanprize.org/recipient/berta-caceres/.

Gómez-Barris, Macarena. 2017. *The Extractive Zone: Social Ecologies and Decolonial Perspectives*. Durham, N.C.: Duke University Press.

Greenblatt, Stephen. 2005. *Renaissance Self-Fashioning: From More to Shakespeare*. Chicago: University of Chicago Press.

Gross, Tony. 1989. "Introduction." *Fight for the Forest,* by Chico Mendes and Tony Gross. London: Latin American Bureau.

Gudynas, Eduardo. 2011. "Desarrollismo, extractivismo, y post-extractivismo." In *El desarrollo en cuestión: Reflexiones desde América Latina,* coordinated by Fernanda Wanderley, 379–410. La Paz: Oxfam and CIDES UMSA.

———. 2015. *Derechos de la naturaleza: Ética biocéntrica y políticas ambientales.* Buenos Aires: Tinta Limón.

Guha, Ramachandra, and Joan Martínez-Alier. 2013. *Varieties of Environmentalism: Essays North and South.* New York: Earthscan.

Haberman, Clyde. 2016. "The Lasting Legacy of a Fighter for the Amazon." *New York Times,* November 27, 2016. https://www.nytimes.com/2016/11/27/us/chico -mendes-amazon-retro-report.html.

Halperín Donghi, Tulio. 1993. *The Contemporary History of Latin America.* Edited and translated by John Charles Chasteen. Durham, N.C.: Duke University Press.

Haraway, Donna J. 2016. *Staying with the Trouble: Making Kin in the Chthulucene.* Durham, N.C.: Duke University Press.

Harrison, Robert Pogue. 1992. *Forests: The Shadow of Civilization.* Chicago: University of Chicago Press.

Harvey, David. 2005. *A Brief History of Neoliberalism.* Oxford: Oxford University Press.

———. 2008. Foreword to *Uneven Development: Nature, Capital, and the Production of Space,* by Neil Smith, vii–x. Athens: University of Georgia Press.

Heffes, Gisela. 2013. *Políticas de la destrucción/Poéticas de la preservación: Apuntes para una lectura (eco) critica del medio ambiente en América Latina.* Buenos Aires: Beatriz Viterbo.

Huenún, Jaime Luis. 2015. "La poesía es un arma ensangrentada en la memoria." In *El consumo de lo que somos. Muestra de poesía ecológica hispánica contemporánea,* edited by Steven F. White, 223–26. Madrid: Ediciones Amargord.

Iñigo Clavo, María. 2016. "Modernity vs. Epistemodiversity." e-flux journal no. 73, May 2016. https://www.e-flux.com/journal/73/60475/modernity-vs -epistemodiversity/.

Irving, Evelyn Uhrhan. 1997. Review of *Jacinta Peralta,* by Ramón Amaya Amador. *World Literature Today* 71, no. 4 (Autumn 1997): 759.

Jackson, K. David. 2008. "Andrade, Oswald de (1890–1954)." In *Encyclopedia of Latin American History and Culture,* 2nd ed., edited by Jay Kinsbruner and Erick D. Langer, 1:180. New York: Scribner's.

Eva-Lynn Jagoe, 2008. *The End of the World as They Knew It: Writing Experiences of the Argentine South* (Lewisburg, Penn.: Bucknell University Press).

Jameson, Fredric. 1991. *Postmodernism, or, The Cultural Logic of Late Capitalism.* Durham, N.C.: Duke University Press.

Jáuregui, Carlos A. 2008. *Canibalia: Canibalismo, calibanismo, antropofagia cultural y consumo en América Latina.* Madrid: Iberoamericana / Vervuert.

Jones, Sonia Harrison. 2013. *Alfonsina Storni.* Halifax, Can.: Erser and Pond.

"Juan Marín (1900–1963)." 2018. In *Memoria chilena/Biblioteca Nacional de Chile.* Accessed May 14, 2019. http://www.memoriachilena.gob.cl/602/w3-article-3490.html.

Kahn, Peter H., Jr. 2002. "Children's Affiliations with Nature: Structure, Development, and the Problem of Environmental Generational Amnesia." In *Children and Nature: Psychological, Sociocultural, and Evolutionary Investigations*, edited by Peter H. Kahn Jr. and Stephen Kellert, 93–116. Cambridge, Mass.: MIT Press.

Kilpatrick, Frederick A. 1931. *A History of the Argentine Republic*. Cambridge: Cambridge University Press.

Kolbert, Elizabeth. 2014. *The Sixth Extinction: An Unnatural History*. New York: Holt.

Kovel, Joel. 2013. *The Enemy of Nature: The End of Capitalism or the End of the World?* London: Zed Books.

Latour, Bruno. 1993. *We Have Never Been Modern*. Translated by Catherine Porter. Cambridge, Mass.: Harvard University Press.

Lerner, Steve. 2010. *Sacrifice Zones: The Front Lines of Toxic Chemical Exposure in the United States*. Cambridge, Mass.: MIT Press.

Lindstrom, Naomi. 1994. *Twentieth-Century Spanish American Fiction*. Austin: University of Texas Press.

MacCormack, Sabine. 1991. *Religion in the Andes: Vision and Imagination in Early Colonial Peru*. Princeton, N.J.: Princeton University Press.

Mann, Charles. 2005. *1491: New Revelations of the Americas Before Columbus*. New York: Knopf.

Marcone, Jorge. 1998a. "Cultural Criticism and Sustainable Development in Amazonia: A Reading from the Spanish-American Romance of the Jungle." *Hispanic Journal* 19, no. 2 (Fall): 281–94.

———. 1998b. "Del retorno a lo natural: *La serpiente de oro*, la 'novela de la selva' y la crítica ecológica." *Hispania: A Journal Devoted to the Teaching of Spanish and Portuguese* 81, no. 2 (May): 299–308.

———. 2000. "Jungle Fever: Primitivism in Environmentalism; Rómulo Gallegos's *Canaima* and the Romance of the Jungle." In *Primitivism and Identity in Latin America: Essays on Art, Literature, and Culture*, edited by Erik Camayd-Freixas and José Eduardo González, 157–72. Tucson: University of Arizona Press.

Marder, Michael. 2013. *Plant Thinking: A Philosophy of Vegetal Life*. New York: Columbia University Press.

Martínez-Alier, Joan. 2002. *The Environmentalism of the Poor: A Study of Ecological Conflicts and Valuation*. Cheltenham, U.K.: Edward Elgar.

Martínez Pinzón, Felipe. 2016. *Una cultura de invernadero: Trópico y civilización en Colombia (1808–1929)*. Madrid: Iberoamericana / Vervuert.

Mazzotti, José Antonio. 2000. "Introducción. Las agencias criollas y la ambigüedad 'colonial' de las letras hispanoamericanas." In *Agencias criollas: La ambigüedad 'colonial' en las letras hispanoamericanas*, edited by José Antonio Mazzotti, 5–33. Pittsburgh: Iberoamericana.

McFarlane, Anthony. 2014. *War and Independence in Spanish America*. London: Routledge.

McGregor, James H. 2015. *Back to the Garden: Nature and the Mediterranean World from Prehistory to the Present*. New Haven, Conn.: Yale University Press.

McNeill, J. R. 2000. *Something New Under the Sun: An Environmental History of the Twentieth-Century World*. New York: Norton.

Meadows, Donella H., Jørgen Randers, and Dennis L. Meadows. 2004. *Limits to Growth: The Thirty-Year Update*. White River Junction, Vt.: Chelsea Green Publishing.

Merchant, Carolyn. 1989. *The Death of Nature: Women, Ecology, and the Scientific Revolution*. New York: Harper and Row.

——. 2008. *Introduction to Ecology—Key Concepts in Critical Theory*. Amherst, N.Y.: Humanity Books.

Mignolo, Walter. 2002. "Commentary." In *Natural and Moral History of the Indies, José de Acosta*, edited by Jane Mangan, 451–518. Durham, N.C.: Duke University Press.

——. 2011. *The Darker Side of Western Modernity: Global Futures, Decolonial Options*. Durham, N.C.: Duke University Press.

Miller, Shawn William. 2007. *An Environmental History of Latin America*. Cambridge: Cambridge University Press.

Mires, Fernando. 1990. *El discurso de la naturaleza*. Santiago, Chile: Espacio Editorial.

Moore, Donald S., Jake Kosek, and Anand Pandian. 2003. "Introduction: The Cultural Politics of Race and Nature; Terrains of Power and Practice." In *Race, Nature, and the Politics of Difference*, edited by Donald S. Moore, Jake Kosek, and Anand Pandian, 1–70. Durham, N.C.: Duke University Press.

Moreno, Mariano. 1965. "Free Trade versus Monopoly." In *The Origins of the Latin American Revolutions, 1808–1826*, edited by R. A. Humphreys and John Lynch, 184–89. New York: Knopf.

Moser, Benjamin. 2015. "The True Glamour of Clarice Lispector." *New Yorker*, July 10, 2015. https://www.newyorker.com/books/page-turner/the-true-glamour-of-clarice-lispector.

Navarro, Santiago Juan. 2009. "The Anarchist City of America: Libertarian Urban Utopias in the New World." *Atenea* 29, no. 1 (June): 91–112.

Nixon, Rob. 2017. "Environmental Martyrs: Defenders of the Forest." Lecture, Williams College, Williamstown, Mass., April 27, 2017.

Nouzeilles, Gabriela. 2002. "Introducción." In *La naturaleza en disputa: Retóricas del cuerpo y el paisaje en América Latina*, edited by Gabriela Nouzeilles, 11–38. Buenos Aires: Paidós.

——. 2007. "The Iconography of Desolation: Patagonia and the Ruins of Nature." *Review: Literature and Arts of the Americas* 40, no. 2 (October): 252–62.

O'Gorman, Edmundo. 2006. *La invención de América: Investigación acerca de la estructura histórica del nuevo mundo y del sentido de su devenir*. Mexico City: Fondo de Cultura Económica.

Olivera-Williams, María Rosa. 1998. "Sobre *An Ark for the Next Millennium*: Un bestiario de José Emilio Pacheco." *Literatura mexicana* 9, no. 1:139–54.

Oloff, Kerstin. 2016. "The 'Monstrous Head' and 'The Mouth of Hell': The Gothic Ecologies of the 'Mexican Miracle.'" In *Ecological Crisis and Cultural Representation in Latin America*, edited by Mark Anderson and Zélia M. Bora, 79–98. Lanham, Md.: Lexington Books.

Pagden, Anthony. 1987. *The Fall of Natural Man: The American Indian and the Origins of Comparative Ethnology*. Cambridge: Cambridge University Press.

Paravisini-Gebert, Lizabeth. 2010. "Caribbean Utopias and Dystopias." In *The Natural World in Latin American Literatures: Ecocritical Essays on Twentieth Century Writings*, edited by Adrian Taylor Kane, 113–35. Jefferson, N.C.: McFarland.

Pimentel, Juan. 2003. *Testigos del mundo: Ciencia, literatura y viajes en la Ilustración*. Madrid: Marcial Pons Historia.

Plumwood, Val. 1993. *Feminism and the Mastery of Nature*. London: Taylor and Francis.

Pratt, Mary Louise. 1992. *Imperial Eyes: Travel Writing and Transculturation*. London: Routledge.

———. 2002. "Why the Virgin of Zapopan Went to Los Angeles: Reflections on Mobility and Globality." Keynote address, Third Annual Encuentro, Lima, Peru, July 8, 2002. Accessed May 24, 2020. https://hemisphericinstitute.org/en/enc02-keynotes/item/1867-enc02-mary-pratt.html.

Prieto, José Manuel, Mayra Montero, and Marina Harss. 2000. "Mayra Montero." *BOMB* 70 (Winter): 86–90. http://www.jstor.org/stable/40426242.

Quijano, Aníbal. 2008. "Coloniality of Power, Eurocentrism, and Latin America." In *Coloniality at Large: The Postcolonial Debates in Latin America*, edited by Mabel Moraña, Enrique Dussel, and Carlos A. Jáuregui, 181–224. Durham, N.C.: Duke University Press.

Roberts, J. Timmons, and Nikki Demetria Thanos. 2003. *Trouble in Paradise: Globalization and Environmental Crises in Latin America*. London: Routledge.

Rodríguez, Ileana. 2004. *Transatlantic Topographies: Islands, Highlands, Jungles*. Minneapolis: University of Minnesota Press.

Rollenhagen, Luisa. 2019. "Samanta Schweblin's Deliberately Slow, Perfectly Timed Rise to American Fame." *Vulture*, May 7, 2019. https://www.vulture.com/2019/05/samanta-schweblins-perfectly-timed-rise-to-american-fame.html.

Romero, José Luis. 1976. *Latinoamérica: Las ciudades y las ideas*. Buenos Aires: Siglo Veintiuno.

Ruiza, M., T. Fernández, and E. Tamaro. 2004. "Biografía de César Uribe Piedrahita." *Biografías y vidas: La enciclopedia biográfica en línea*. Barcelona (España). https://www.biografiasyvidas.com/biografia/u/uribe_piedrahita.htm.

Salleh, Ariel Kay. 1984. "Deeper Than Deep Ecology: The Eco-Feminist Connection." *Environmental Ethics* 6, no. 4 (Winter): 339–45.

Santmire, Paul H. *The Travail of Nature: The Ambivalent Ecological Promise of Christian Theology*. Minneapolis: Fortress Press, 1985.

Scott, James C. 1998. *Thinking Like a State: How Certain Schemes to Improve the Human Condition Have Failed*. New Haven, Conn.: Yale University Press.

Smith, Neil. 2008. *Uneven Development: Nature, Capital, and the Production of Space*. Athens: University of Georgia Press.

Soper, Kate. 1995. *What Is Nature? Culture, Politics, and the Non-Human*. Malden, Mass.: Blackwell Publishers.

Stengers, Isabelle. 2015. *In Catastrophic Times: Resisting the Coming Barbarism*. Trans. Andre Goffey. Lüneburg, Germany: Open Humanities Press.

Sze, Julie. 2002. "From Environmental Justice Literature to the Literature of Environmental Justice." In *The Environmental Justice Reader: Politics, Poetics, and*

Pedagogy, edited by Joni Adamson, Mei Mei Evans, and Rachel Stein, 163–80. Tucson: University of Arizona Press.

Teles, Gilberto Mendonça. 2002. "Andrade, Oswald de (1890–1954)." In *Latin American Writers: Supplement 1*, edited by Carlos A. Solé, 31–53. New York: Scribner's.

Tolentino, Jia. 2017. "The Sick Thrill of *Fever Dream*." *New Yorker*, January 4, 2017. https://www.newyorker.com/books/page-turner/the-sick-thrill-of-fever-dream.

Truman, Harry S. 1949. *Inaugural Address*. January 20, 1949. https://avalon.law.yale.edu/20th_century/truman.asp.

Turner, Daymond. 1964. "Gonzalo Fernandez de Oviedo's Historia General y Natural—First American Encyclopedia." *Journal of Inter-American Studies* 6, no. 2 (April): 267–74.

Vitulli, Juan M., and David Solodkow. 2009. *Poéticas de lo criollo: La transformación del concepto 'criollo' en las letras hispanoamericanas (siglo XVI al XIX)*. Buenos Aires: Corregidor.

Viveiros de Castro, Eduardo. 1998. "Cosmological Deixis and Amerindian Perspectivism." *Journal of the Royal Anthropological Institute* 4, no. 3 (September): 469–88.

Ward, Henry George. 1829. *Mexico*. London: Henry Colburn.

Wallerstein, Immanuel. 1974. *The Modern World-System, I: Capitalist Agriculture and the Origins of the European World-Economy in the Sixteenth Century*. Cambridge, Mass.: Academic Press.

Watts, Jonathan. 2018. "Almost Four Environmental Defenders a Week Killed in 2017." *The Guardian*, February 2, 2018. https://www.theguardian.com/environment/2018/feb/02/almost-four-environmental-defenders-a-week-killed-in-2017.

Whigham, Thomas. 2009. *Lo que el río se llevó: Estado y comercio en Paraguay y Corrientes, 1776–1870*. Asunción: CEADUC.

White, Steven F. 2011. *Arando el aire: La ecología en la poesía y la música de Nicaragua*. Managua: 400 Elefantes.

White, Steven F. 2014. *El consumo de lo que somos: Muestra de poesía ecológica hispánica contemporánea*. Madrid: Amargord.

Wibel, John Frederick. 1975. "The Evolution of a Regional Community within the Spanish Empire and Peruvian Nation: Arequipa, 1780–1845." Ph.D. diss., Stanford University.

Williams, Raymond. 1980. "Ideas of Nature." In *Problems in Materialism and Culture*, 67–85. London: Verso.

Williams, Raymond L. 2009. *The Colombian Novel, 1844–1987*. Austin: University of Texas Press.

Worster, Donald. "Another Silent Spring." Environment & Society Portal, *Virtual Exhibitions* 2020, no. 1 (April 22, 2020). Rachel Carson Center for Environment and Society. doi.org/10.5282/rcc/9028.

Wynter, Sylvia. 1971. "Novel and History, Plot and Plantation." *Savacou* 5:95–102.

———. 1997. "Columbus, the Ocean Blue, and Fables That Stir the Mind." In *Poetics of the Americas: Race, Founding, and Textuality*, edited by Bainard Cowan and Jefferson Humphries, 141–64. Baton Rouge: Louisiana State University Press.

Zamora, Margarita. 1990–91. "Abreast of Columbus: Gender and Discovery." *Cultural Critique*, no. 17 (Winter): 127–249.

All possible care has been taken to trace ownership and secure permission for copyrighted material reproduced in this book. The editors wish to thank the following publishers and copyright holders. This page constitutes a continuation of the copyright page.

One. New World Natures

Christopher Columbus. "Letter to Various Persons Describing the Results of His First Voyage and Written on the Return Journey." From J. M. Cohen, *Four Voyages of Christopher Columbus* (Penguin Books, 1992). Copyright © J. M. Cohen 1969, 1992. Reprinted by permission of Penguin Books Ltd.

Gonzalo Fernández de Oviedo y Valdés. Selection from *General and Natural History of the Indies*, in *Fernández de Oviedo's Chronicle of America: A New History for a New World*, by Kathleen Ann Meyers, translations by Nina Scott. Copyright © 2007. Reprinted by permission of the University of Texas Press.

Fray Bartolomé de las Casas. "Plague of Ants," translated by Sandra Ferdman. From *The Oxford Book of Latin American Short Stories*, edited by Roberto González Echevarría, 34–37. Copyright © 1997 by Roberto González-Echevarría. Reprinted by permission of Oxford University Press, USA.

Gaspar de Carvajal. Selection from *The Discovery of the Amazon according to the Account of Friar Gaspar de Carvajal and Other Documents, as published by José Toribio Molina*. Edited by H. C. Heaton and translated by Bertram T. Lee (New York: American Geographical Society, 1934 [special publication No. 17]).

Jean de Léry. "Of the Trees, Herbs, Roots, and Exquisite Fruits Produced by the Land of Brazil." From Jean de Léry, *History of a Voyage to the Land of Brazil, Otherwise Called America*. Introduction and translation by Janet Whatley (Berkeley: University of California Press, 1990).

José de Acosta. "Of the three kinds of mixtures that will be dealt with in this history." From *Natural and Moral History of the Indies*, by José de Acosta, edited by Jane E. Mangan, 161–62. Copyright © 2002 by Duke University Press. All rights reserved.

Popul Vuh. From *Popol Vuh: The Sacred Book of the Ancient Quiché Maya*. English version by Delia Goetz and Sylvanus G. Morley, from the Spanish translation by Adrián Recinos (Norman: University of Oklahoma Press, 1950).

Garcilaso de la Vega, El Inca. Selection from *Royal Commentaries of the Incas and General History of Peru, Part I*, introduction and translation by Harold V. Livermore; foreword by Arnold J. Toynbee (Austin: University of Texas Press, 1966).

Two. Creole Landscapes

André João Antonil. Selection from *Brazil at the Dawn of the Eighteenth Century*, translated by Timothy Coates (Dartmouth, Mass.: Tagus, 2012). Reprinted by permission of Tagus Press.

Georges-Louis Leclerc, Count Buffon. Selection from *Buffon's Natural History, Abridged: Including the History of the Elements, the Earth, Mountains, Rivers, Seas, Winds, Whirlwinds, Waterspouts, Volcanoes, Earthquakes, Man, Quadrupeds, Birds, Fishes, Shell-fish, Lizards, Serpents, Insects, & Vegetables* (London: Published for C. & G. Kearsley, 1792). Reprinted by courtesy of Chapin Library, Williams College.

Three. Nature and the Foundation of the Nation-States

Simon Bolívar. "My Delirium on Chimborazo." From *El Libertador, Writings of Simón Bolívar*, translated by Frederick H. Fornoff, edited by David Bushnell (Oxford University Press, 2003), 135–36. Copyright © 2003 by Oxford University Press, Inc. Reprinted by permission of Oxford University Press, USA.

Andrés Bello. "Ode to Tropical Agriculture." From *Selected Writings of Andrés Bello*, translated by Frances M. López-Morillas, edited by Ivan Jaksič (Oxford University Press, 1997), 29–37. Copyright © 1997 by Oxford University Press, Inc. Reprinted by permission of Oxford University Press, USA.

Gertrudis Gómez de Avellaneda. Selection from *Sab and Autobiography*, by Gertrudis Gómez de Avellaneda y Arteaga, translated and edited by Nina M. Scott. Copyright © 1993. Reprinted by permission of the University of Texas Press.

Domingo F. Sarmiento. "Physical Aspect of the Argentine Republic, and the Ideas, Customs, and Characters It Engenders." From *Facundo: Civilization and Barbarism*, translated by Kathleen Ross (Berkeley and London: University of California Press, 2003).

Four. Regionalism and the Export Boom

José Martí. "Our America." From *Selected Writings*, by José Martí, edited and translated by Esther Allen, translation copyright © 2002 by Esther Allen. Used by permission of Viking Books, an imprint of Penguin Publishing Group, a division of Penguin Random House LLC. All rights reserved.

Horacio Quiroga. "The Log-Fishermen." From *The Exiles and Other Stories*, by Horacio Quiroga, translated by J. David Danielson. Copyright © 1987 by the University of Texas Press. Reprinted by permission of the University of Texas Press.

José Eustasio Rivera. Selection from *The Vortex*, by José Eustasio Rivera, translated by John Charles Chasteen, 147–218. Copyright © 2018 by Duke University Press. All rights reserved. Republished by permission of the copyright holder. www.dukeupress .edu.

César Uriba Piedrahita. "Mun Hospital." From *Oil Stain*. Reprinted courtesy of the Universidad Católica Cecilio Acosta.

Graciliano Ramos. "The Birds." From *Barren Lives*, by Graciliano Ramos, translated by Ralph Edward Dimmick. Copyright © 1965. Reprinted by permission of the University of Texas Press.

Ramón Amaya Amador. "Green Destiny." From *Green Prison*. Reprinted courtesy of the Editorial Ramón Amaya Amador.

Five. Modern Metropoles

Julián del Casal. "En el campo." ("In the Country.") Courtesy of Editorial Verbum.

Rafael Barrett. "Odio de los árboles." ("Tree Haters.") Courtesy of Ediciones Tantín.

Oswald de Andrade. "Cannibalist Manifesto." Copyright © Heirs of Oswald Andrade.

Rubén Darío. "Reincarnations," "Philosophy," "The Song of the Pines," and "Revelation," translated by Greg Simon and Steven F. White. From *Selected Writings*, by Rubén Darío, edited by Ilan Stavans. Translation copyright © 2005 by Andrew Hurley, Greg Simon, and Steven F. White. Used by permission of Penguin Books, an imprint of Penguin Publishing Group, a division of Penguin Random House LLC. All rights reserved.

María Luisa Bombal. "The Tree." Translated by Richard and Lucia Cunningham. From *New Islands and Other Stories*, by María Luisa Bombal. Translation copyright © 1982 by Farrar, Straus & Giroux, Inc. Reprinted by permission of Farrar, Straus & Giroux.

Six. Developmentalism

Pablo Neruda. "The Heights of Macchu Picchu" ("Alturas de Macchu Picchu"). From *Canto General*, by Pablo Neruda, translated by Jack Schmitt. Copyright © 2011 by the Regents of the University of California. Published by the University of California Press. Permission granted copyright © Pablo Neruda 1950, y Fundación Pablo Neruda.

Juan Rulfo. "Luvina." From *The Plain in Flames* by Juan Rulfo, translated from the Spanish by Ilan Stavans with Harold Augenbraum, copyright © 2012. Permission granted copyright © Juan Rulfo, 1953, and Heirs of Juan Rulfo. Reprinted by permission of the University of Texas Press.

Lydia Cabrera. "The Ceiba Tree." From *The Woods*. Reprinted by courtesy of the Cuban Heritage Collection at the University of Miami.

José María Arguedas. "Bridge over the World." From *Deep Rivers*, by José María Arguedas, translated by Frances Horning Barraclough (Long Grove, Ill.: Waveland Press, Inc.). Copyright © 1978, reissued 2002. All rights reserved. Reprinted by permission of Waveland Press, Inc.

Esteban Montejo. "Life in the Woods." From *Biography of a Runaway Slave* by Miguel Barnet. Translation copyright © 2016 by W. Nick Hill. First U.S. edition published by Pantheon Books, 1968. Revised edition published by Curbstone Press, 1994. Fiftieth anniversary edition published by Northwestern University Press, 2016. All rights reserved.

Clarice Lispector. Selection from *The Passion According to G.H.*, by Clarice Lispector, translated by Idra Novey. Copyright © 1960 by Paulo Gurgel Valente; translation copyright © 2012 by Idra Novey; introduction copyright © 2012 by Caetano Veloso. Reprinted by permission of New Directions Publishing Corp. and by permission of Penguin Books Ltd.

Rigoberta Menchú. Selection from *I, Rigoberta Menchú: An Indian Woman in Guatemala*, edited by Elisabeth Burgos-Debray and translated by Ann Wright (New York and London: Verso, 1984). Reprinted by permission of Verso Books UK.

Seven. Neoliberalism and Globalization

Chico Mendes. "The Landowners Strike Back." From Chico Mendes, Tony Gross, and Chris Whitehouse, *Fight for the Forest*, 2nd Edition: *Chico Mendes in His Own Words*. Ch. 4, pp. 59–69. Warwickshire: Practical Action Publishing, 1992.

Octavio Paz. "In Search of the Present." Copyright © 1990 by the Nobel Foundation. Source: http://nobelprize.org.

Fernando Contreras Castro. Selection from *Única Looking Out to Sea*. Reprinted by permission of the author.

Gioconda Belli. Selection from *Waslala*. Copyright © Gioconda Belli, c/o Schavelzon Graham Agencia Literaria.

"A Letter from Subcomandante Marcos to Saramago" ("Carta del Subcomandante Marcos a Saramago"). *Ecología Política* 18 (1999): 135–38. Reprinted by permission of *Revista Ecología Política*.

Esthela Calderón. "The Woman I Could Have Been," by Esthela Calderón, translated by Steven F. White, first published in *Review: Literature and Arts of the Americas*, no. 85 (45:2, Fall 2012). "Seed I Don't Know of What" and "Talking with My Worms," from *Los huesos de mi abuelo/ The Bones of My Grandfather*, translated by Steven F. White (Madrid: Amargord, 2018).

Juan Carlos Galeano. "Curupira," "Dark Shamans," "Cantagalo," and "Lupuna" From *Yakumama (and Other Mythical Beings)*, translated by James Kimbrall and Rebecca Morgan (Iquitos, Peru: Tierra Nueva, 2014). Reprinted courtesy of the author.

Eight. End Times: Climate Change and Mass Extinction

José Emilio Pacheco. "Ecuación de primer grado con un incógnita" ("Equation to the First Degree, with Unknown Quantity"), from *Los trabajos del mar*, copyright © Herederos de José Emilio Pacheco, 1983. "Ballenas" ("Whales"), from *La fábula del tiempo*, copyright © Herederos de José Emilio Pacheco, 2005. "Augury," from *Islas a la deriva*, copyright © Herederos de José Emilio Pacheco, 1976. "Monólogos del mono" ("Baboon Babble") from *Desde Entonces: Poemas, 1975–1978*, copyright © Herederos de José Emilio Pacheco, 1980.

Homero Aridjis. "La última noche del mundo," from *Tiempo de ángeles*, A *time of angels* by Homero Aridjis (pp. 26–28) D.R. copyright © 2012, Fondo de Cultura Económica, Ciudad de México. "Descreación," from *El consumo de lo que somos*, Steven F. White, editor, copyright © 1994 by Homero Aridjis. "Imágenes de mariposas," from *El Consumo de lo que somos*. Copyright © 2014 by Homero Aridjis. "The Hunt for the Red Jaguar," by Homero Aridjis. Copyright © 2010 by Homero Aridjis. Translation copyright © 2010 by George McWhirter.

Mayra Montero. "Indian Hut." Copyright © 1995 by Mayra Montero. Excerpted from *In the Palm of Darkness*, published by HarperCollins in English in 1997. By permission of Susan Bergholz Literary Services, New York, New York, and Lamy, New Mexico. All rights reserved. Translation copyright © Edith Grossman.

Jaime Huenún. "Ceremony of Love" and "Ceremony of Death," translated by John Bierhorst; from *Ül: Four Mapuche Poets* by Jaime Huenún, edited by Cecilia Vicuña (Pittsburgh: Latin American Literary Review, 1998). Reprinted by permission of the author and translator.

Samanta Schweblin. Excerpts from *Fever Dream*: A *Novel*, by Samanta Schweblin, translated by Megan McDowell, translation copyright © 2017 by Megan McDowell. Used by permission of Riverhead, an imprint of Penguin Publishing Group, a division of Penguin Random House LLC. All rights reserved. Reprinted by permission of Oneworld Publications 1786072386.

Berta Cáceres. Goldman Environmental Prize Acceptance Speech, 2015.

Pope Francis, the Holy See. Selection from *Laudato Si'* (2015). Copyright © Libreria Editrice Vaticana.

Eduardo Chirinos. "The K/T Boundary Chronicle," "The Toba Chronicle," and "The Chernobyl Chronicle." From *Thirty-Five Zoology Lessons (and Other Didactic Poems)*, by Eduardo Chirinos, translated by G. J. Racz (Diaz Grey Editores, 2015). Reprinted by permission of the publisher and the heirs.